# War
# and Christian Ethics

# War
# and Christian Ethics
*Classic Readings on the Morality of War*

*Edited by*
## Arthur F. Holmes

FAITH MENNONITE CHURCH
MINNEAPOLIS, MINN.

**BAKER BOOK HOUSE**
Grand Rapids, Michigan 49516

Permission to print portions of this anthology have been granted by the following publishers: Benziger Bruce & Glencoe—Thomas Aquinas's "Various Kinds of Law," "Hostility and Peace," "Laws of War," "Violence and Moral Intention," and "Rebellion"; The Bobbs-Merrill Company—Immanuel Kant, "Towards Perpetual Peace"; Walter J. Black—John Locke, "On Civil Government"; Carnegie Endowment for International Peace—Franciscus de Vitoria's "The Law of War" and "The Rights of the Indians," and Francisco Suarez's "The Law of Nations" and "On War"; The Clarendon Press, Oxford—Plato's "Moral Effects of War" and "War for the Sake of Peace"; Columbia University Press—Erasmus, "War and the Christian Prince"; Duke University Press— Paul Ramsey, "The Just War and Nuclear Deterrence"; Wm. B. Eerdmans Publishing—Athenagoras, "Non-violence," Tertullian, "Christians and Government," and "Christians and Military Service," Origen, "On Government Service," Lactantius, "The Natural Law of Love," Ambrose, "To the Emperor Theodosius," Augustine's "To Count Boniface," "Act, Agent, and Authority," "The Human Dilemma," and "Peace and Natural Law"; Fortress Press—Martin Luther, "The Soldier and His Conscience"; Harvard University Press—Cicero's "The Just War" and "Natural Law and Just War"; Herald Press—Menno Simons, "Two Kingdoms"; Henry Regnery Company—Bernard of Clairvaux, "A Holy War"; Charles Scribner's Sons—Reinhold Niebuhr, "Why the Christian Church Is Not Pacifist"; Sheed and Ward—Robert Drinan, "Is Pacifism the Only Option Left for Christians?"

# CONTENTS

Introduction /1

I. The Pagan Conscience/11
   1. *Plato:* Moral Effects of War/13
      War for the Sake of Peace/20
   2. *Cicero:* The Just War/24
      Natural Law and Just War/25

II. Conflict of Loyalties/33
   1. *Athenagoras:* Non-violence/37
   2. *Tertullian:* Christians and Government/39
      Christians and Military Service/43
   3. *Origen:* On Government Service/48
   4. *Lactantius:* The Natural Law of Love/51
   5. *Ambrose:* To the Emperor Theodosius/55
   6. *Augustine:* To Count Boniface/61
      Act, Agent, and Authority/63
      The Human Dilemma/68
      Peace and Natural Law/71

III. Christians and Infidels/85
   1. *Bernard of Clairvaux:* A Holy War/88
   2. *Thomas Aquinas:* Various Kinds of Law/92
      Hostility and Peace/102
      Laws of War/106
      Violence and Moral Intention/113
      Rebellion/114
   3. *Franciscus de Vitoria:* The Law of War/118
      The Rights of the Indians/119

IV. Church and State/137
   1. *Martin Luther:* The Soldier and His Conscience/140
   2. *John Calvin:* Civil Authority and the Use of Force/165
   3. *Erasmus:* War and the Christian Prince/177
   4. *Menno Simons:* Two Kingdoms/185

V. Human Rights and International Law/191
   1. *Francisco Suarez:*   The Law of Nations/195
                                On War/199
   2. *Hugo Grotius:*   Natural Laws and the Laws of War/226
   3. *John Locke:*   On Civil Government/239

VI. Idealism and Realism/271
   1. *Immanuel Kant:*   Towards Perpetual Peace/274
   2. *G. W. F. Hegel:*   War and National Destiny/284
   3. *Lyman Abbott:*   Pacifism and the Gospel/291
   4. *Reinhold Niebuhr:*   Why the Christian Church
                                  Is Not Pacifist/301

VII. Old Options and New Directions/315
   1. *Robert Drinan:*   Is Pacifism the Only Option Left for
                                  Christians?/318
   2. *Paul Ramsey:*   The Just War and Nuclear Deterrence/341

A Final Word/353

Index/355

# INTRODUCTION

# INTRODUCTION

## I.

Literature on the problems of war flows from the press with increasing rapidity in times of international conflict, and interest in the subject is likely to persist as long as there are wars and rumors of war. We have historical and sociological studies, moralistic diatribes, and religious writings of a pastoral sort. Since the Vietnam conflict, a growing body of ethical writing has appealed both to pacifist viewpoints and the just war tradition. But classic source materials that keep the issues in the context of political and ethical theory, as well as of the history of Christian thought, are not generally available.

The present volume attempts a limited remedy of this situation. It grew out of a course for undergraduates in which I introduced what from my own reading appeared to be the most influential patristic, medieval, and modern writers, and in which I tried to develop some understanding of the theoretical issues they faced while shaping a Christian criticism of war. The course also involved more accessible readings in ethical theory per se and in contemporary philosophical analysis on the subject of war. But to my knowledge no other historical anthology exists which treats war in the context of ethical and political theory.

These considerations have governed the process of selection. No attempt is made to argue one particular position, although I myself incline toward some form of the just war theory; rather, I have been concerned to provide the theoretical bases on which we must formulate our own conclusions. Pieces containing unsubstantiated moral judgments are avoided in favor of those which expose underlying theological and philosophical concerns. Wherever possible, material is omitted which simply reiterates an earlier position without either shedding more light on its bases or analyzing in more detail its essential concepts. The emphasis is on classic sources, those which have been profoundly influential either because they break new ground (Francisco de Vitoria), or because of their systematic qualities (Francisco Suarez), or because of the author (Aquinas, Calvin, and Luther). Such non-Christian writers as Plato and Cicero provide ethical contrast. In each historical period attention is focused on some major issue which was being clarified at that time and which retains its importance.

## II.

Much discussion in the early church focused on the legitimacy of military service and uncovered a potential conflict of loyalties. It is true that the Christian has responsibilities to government, for political authority is in the final analysis "ordained by God." But the Christian's overriding responsibility is to obey and serve God. He therefore has two vocations in life, political and spiritual; or, as Augustine put it, he is a citizen of two kingdoms, the earthly and the heavenly. Conflict arises when our earthly vocation requires pagan practices and symbols, or uses of violence which God forbids or moral law condemns, or political methods at variance with those of the spiritual life.

This conflict of loyalties within the church regarding military service was part of a much broader tension between Christianity and culture, and in general the same two options emerge today: either the spiritual vocation precludes military (and sometimes political) service, or the two vocations coexist, with the spiritual exercising moral judgment over all political and military activity.

During medieval times the two kingdoms merged, externally at least, in the Carolingian Empire and in church-state relations conceived by Aquinas and supposedly practised later in the Spanish Empire. The key issue was the conflict between Christians and infidels. Plato's double standard for the military treatment of Greeks and barbarians was reapplied to fit the concept of a holy war preached to the Crusaders. Yet a concept of universal human rights rooted in natural law gradually prevailed until in the sixteenth century Francisco de Vitoria condemned Spain's treatment of the North American Indians.

The Reformation reopened the question of church-state relations, and the return to biblical and patristic sources rekindled discussion of the moral justification of force. Luther and Calvin extended the right of magistrates to use force to include military action. Erasmus, however, advocated what is nowadays called "prudential pacifism," while Menno Simons' reaffirmation of non-violence initiated a long tradition of Christian pacifism grounded in a clear-cut two-kingdom theology.

The seventeenth and eighteenth centuries were torn by wars in which religious causes figured so large that religious appeals could hardly arrest violence, mediate disputes, or secure peace. The issue was one of justifying political power and establishing international justice. Natural law theories elaborated universal rights into a framework of international law that limited both the occasions and the effects of war. In Spain Suarez extended and systematized the work of Vitoria, while in the Netherlands Hugo Grotius produced a massive proposal on international law for war and peace; in England John Locke's political theory included provisions governing both conquest and rebellion. The rule of law became man's hope to replace the rule of violence.

The same hope extended to the ethical idealism of the nineteenth and early twentieth centuries, which under the influence of Immanuel Kant produced an optimistic theological liberalism that rooted pacifism in a concept of social evolution and in an ethic that subordinated justice to love. By contrast, Hegel's thesis that historical progress comes through dialectical conflict provided the stimulus for neo-orthodox Christian realism between the two world wars. Here the issue was neither one of two vocations nor of church and state nor of universal rights, for on these issues the lines had already been drawn from Tolstoi's Christian anarchism to Rauschenbusch's identification of Christianity with existing political programs. The issues were rather the nature of man, sin, and the Gospel, the meaning of history and the human predicament—profound theological and philosophical questions which challenged man's optimism both about a just rule of law and about an ethic of love.

The development of modern technology, with its opportunities for global warfare and its weapons of mass destruction, poses the issue of whether a just war ethic forged under less ominous conditions can still apply (as Paul Ramsey insists it must if we are to avoid the moral anarchy that brings nuclear destruction), or whether we are forced to a policy of prudential pacifism in which non-violent resistance is the only moral alternative.

### III.

Certain perennial questions run throughout the foregoing issues:

1. Is war ever morally justifiable? Two responses emerge in Christian ethics: the negative response of pacifism and the positive response of the just war theory. But both contain various levels and need qualification. At times the pacifist seems to say, not that all wars are unjustified, but that the Christian is never justified in participating in war. This is *selective* pacifism, for it does not deny the state the right of self-defense; it only denies to the Christian the right to participate. Likewise the just war theory gives no blanket endorsement of war but demands painstaking discrimination between just and unjust causes. Inevitably it produces *selective conscientious objection,* a position that is still not legally recognized in the United States but which has been explicitly taught by the just war theory since Francisco de Vitoria; it was implicit from the earliest days of the theory in both Christian and pagan contexts. I am convinced that the function of the just war theory, at least in the history of Christian ethics, is not to justify wars but to judge them, to criticize and thereby as far as possible to prevent the use of force and work for the abolition of war.

2. In addition to the justice of a cause (*jus ad bellum*), the just war theory addresses the problem of just means (*jus in bello*). While just war rules are variously enumerated, the following list is representative:

*Just cause:* the only morally legitimate reason for going to war is self-defense. If this rule were universally followed there would be no aggressors and no wars. War would never become an instrument of national policy or a means of ideological or religious conflict. In practice, of course, defense and aggression are hard to define and even harder to identify, and the question of preventive war is loaded with moral ambiguity.

*Just intent:* the only morally legitimate goal in war is the restoration of peace, with justice for both friend and foe. Vengeance, subjugation, and conquest are unjustifiable purposes. The Scholastics recognized the principle of double effect: unintentional effects (civilian casualties) may inevitably accompany the intended effect (restraint of violence).

*Last resort:* war should be entered upon only when negotiation, arbitration, compromise, and all other paths fail; for as a rational being man should, if at all possible, settle his disputes by reason and law, not by force.

*Lawful declaration:* only lawful government has the right to initiate war, for the use of force is limited to the state and its legally authorized agents; it is never the prerogative of individuals or parties within the state to use force on their own authority.

*Immunity of non-combatants:* those not officially serving as agents of the government in its use of force, including POW's and medical personnel and services, should not be permitted to fight and are not to be subjected to violence. This rule produced condemnations of allied obliteration bombings during World War II, but guerrilla warfare and modern weaponry present it with intense difficulties in determining who is or is not acting as a legitimate government agent in war.

*Limited objectives:* if the purpose of war is peace, then unconditional surrender is an unwarranted objective, as is the destruction of the enemy's economy or political institutions.

*Limited means:* only sufficient force should be used to resist violence or restore peace. The criterion for "sufficient" is not decisive victory but the restoration of a just peace. This suggests limits to the destructive power of weapons; it has resulted in the outlawing of poison gas and in continued criticism of both the use and the stockpiling of ABC weapons (atomic, bacteriological, chemical).

3. Are traditional pacifist and just war concepts applicable to rebellion? This raises further questions regarding the basis and the extent of political authority and the nature of what from early times was called "the tyrant." But once the consent of the governed is invoked, according to Locke, armed rebellion is countenanced on the same terms as a just war. This makes rebellion the "last resort" after less radical means have failed, including due process of law, non-

violent protest, and civil disobedience; it presupposes that a government has failed to uphold civil peace and justice. Then the people, says Locke, may establish a government and on its authority overthrow the tyrant who opposes that authority.

4. What is the basis of our moral judgments? What kind of reasoning supports a pacifist conclusion, and how are just war rules developed? If such positions are not to be arbitrary, then adequate theological and philosophical bases are essential.

## IV.

What the Bible says about war may be summarized in two statements: (1) the ideal we should strive for in national and international affairs is peace with justice; (2) war remains a tragic fact of human history.

The first statement finds expression in the Old Testament lament over war and violence (I Chron. 22:7-10; Ps. 46:8-11; Ps. 120; Lamentations), in the messianic hope (Isa. 2:1-5; 9:1-7; 11:1-9), in condemnations of unbridled warfare and excessive violence (Deut. 20:10-20; Amos 1), and in the summation of Old Testament ethics in the New Testament law of love (Matt. 5:9, 21-26, 38-48; Rom 13:8-10).

The truth of the second statement is abundantly evident in Old Testament history, in Christ's generalization about "wars and rumors of wars" (Matt. 24:6-8), and in eschatological passages such as Isaiah 11 and Revelation 19 and 20.

It should be noted that the sixth commandment (Exod. 20:13, "Thou shall not kill") does not in its context speak to the problem of war but rather to murder and manslaughter and personal vengeance (Exod. 21 and 22). The Old Testament explicitly allowed lawful government to use force, even capital punishment, when necessary; this rule is reiterated in the context of the New Testament law of love (Rom. 12:9-13:10).

These biblical materials present theologians with some of the most debated questions on the morality of war. Alternative theological formulations naturally result in alternative ethical positions:

1. The contrast between the ideal of peace and justice on the one hand and the present realities on the other produces the idealist and realist approaches to war, highlighted in chapter vi.

2. Those who assert continuity and agreement between Old

and New Testament moral teachings are likely to admit the tragic necessity and moral legitimacy of certain wars. Those who stress the discontinuity of the old and new covenants are more likely to interpret the New Testament as pacifistic. This disagreement is evident both in patristic and reformation times, and in the contrast between the liberal social gospel of Lyman Abbot and the prophetic realism of Reinhold Niebuhr.

3. The relation of the Christian to government gives rise both to the theology of two vocations, or kingdoms, and to the more positive appraisals of political responsibility by Aquinas, Calvin, Locke, and Niebuhr.

What one decides on these theological matters will largely determine the choice between pacifism and a just war theory (or some other ethic of military participation).[1]

## V.

Granted these biblical and theological considerations, what can philosophical ethics contribute? First, it analyzes the logical structure of moral reasoning, distinguishing three levels of ethical concern: (1) basic ethical principles, such as justice and love, that undergird all moral considerations; (2) general moral rules, such as those in the second half of the decalogue, that apply to various kinds of acts or

---

1. A further problem, less determinative in the above regards but nonetheless troublesome, concerns the seemingly excessive violence of wars in which Israel and Judah believed themselves to act justly. Three observations may be offered. (1) Some wars were cases of divine judgment in which Israel acted on divine authority. The problem has to do with divine retribution rather than with the moral decisions men and nations make in cases where no specific command of God is given. Such retribution is God's prerogative, not that of men and nations. (2) Some could have been concessions to the military practices of antiquity, so that Israel was allowed to follow current procedures more or less uncritically. An analogy might be found in the Mosaic concession regarding divorce "because of the hardness of your hearts" (Matt. 19:3-12), which is another case of conflict between biblical ideals and existing realities. (3) As Scripture records progress in the unfolding of divine revelation, so it records progress in the revelation and social application of moral law. For example, slavery in the Old Testament is circumscribed with laws to prevent needless abuse, while justice and love gradually erode the demand for slaves within a Christian community (Philemon). By the same token the social evils of violence are circumscribed by rules (Deut. 20, etc.), while the underlying principles of justice and love take effect on the social conscience through the believing community, and so restrain violence further.

situations; and (3) action decisions which require extensive empirical input, whether in situations that may be subsumed under general rules or in exceptional cases where the rules conflict or otherwise cannot be applied. In the latter cases decision procedures refer more directly to basic principles.

A second contribution, therefore, is the identification and elucidation of basic ethical principles. Understanding the meaning of justice, love, and political power is of paramount importance. A principle of benevolence alone ("seek the most good for most people") may well produce a utilitarian or pragmatic or other relativistic ethic. A deontological principle alone ("do your just duty regardless") may degenerate into an unfeeling legalism. Political power alone produces despotism. Differences in ethical and political theory have a profound effect on discussions of war. Much modern pacifism is based on utilitarian appeals, some on a pure agape principle. On the other hand, war is frequently defended on deontological grounds alone or in terms of political power alone, without reference to the other or to the agape principle. The reader to whom these theoretical matters are new should examine a primer in ethical theory such as William Frankena's *Ethics* (Prentice-Hall, 1973).

A third contribution is the theoretical justification of ethical principles—for instance, in the natural law theory. To my knowledge, Lactantius stands alone in deriving pacifist conclusions from natural law. In all other cases natural law provides a concept of justice and of just war. It creates a conceptual bridge between ethics on the one hand and political and legal theory on the other, a bridge that gives rise to rules of war and to international law.

The complexity of natural law theory is due to its varied roots. In essence it claims that this is a rational and moral universe; hence the moral order is rooted in the order of creation and in the essential nature of man and society. One traditional version of the theory goes back to Plato and Aristotle, who answered Sophist relativism by grounding justice in the universal nature of things, hence in the reality of unchanging forms. This tradition, converted to a theistic context, is evident in Thomas Aquinas, Vitoria, and Suarez. Another tradition, going back to the Stoic thought of Cicero, is criticized and converted to Christian uses by Lactantius and Augustine, is echoed by Calvin, and is later developed for the purpose of international law by Locke and Grotius.

Besides those Christian ethicists whose agape principle leads to a pacifist position, others like Niebuhr have criticized the natural law theory and its just war applications. They find it unduly optimistic about a rule of reason and law controlling sinful men and immoral society, questioning whether specific moral rules can be derived from natural law with sufficient certainty to gain universal acceptance. They find the appeal to justice as idealistic as the appeal to love in dealing with men as they are. They argue that force becomes an instrument of power rather than of justice or love, which must be exercised if we are to avoid anarchy, restrain demonic evil, and effect any semblance of justice on earth.

War is obviously no simple moral problem but involves us in considerations drawn from various branches of theological and philosophical inquiry. Some of these considerations, and their consequences, are represented in what follows. Each chapter includes suggestions for further reading. The following suggestions are of a general nature:

Bainton, Roland H. *Christian Attitudes toward War and Peace.* Abingdon, 1960.

Cairns, H. *Legal Philosophy from Plato to Hegel.* Johns Hopkins Press, 1969.

*The Challenge of Peace.* National Conference of Catholic Bishops, 1983.

Friedrich, C. J. *Philosophy of Law in Historical Perspective.* University of Chicago Press, 1953.

Johnson, James T. *Ideology, Reason, and the Limitations of War.* Princeton University Press, 1975.

_____. *Just War Tradition and the Restraint of War.* Princeton University Press, 1981.

_____. *The Quest for Peace: Three Moral Traditions in Western Cultural History.* Princeton University Press, 1987.

Laserre, Jean. *War and the Gospel.* Herald Press, 1962.

Mayer, Peter. *The Pacifist Conscience.* Holt, Rinehart and Winston, 1966.

Nuttal, G. F. *Christian Pacifism in History.* Blackwell, 1958.

Potter, Ralph B. *War and Moral Discourse.* John Knox, 1969.

Ramsey, Paul. *War and the Christian Conscience.* Duke University Press, 1961.

# I. THE PAGAN CONSCIENCE

## 1. PLATO (c. 427–c. 347 B.C.)

The Greeks valued courage, sometimes above and apart from the other classic virtues of temperance, wisdom, and justice. Some of them valued war as a means of teaching and testing courage. Plato reflects these values only in measure, for while he proposes that children learn courage from watching the courageous example of their soldier-parents in combat, he feels courage must be ruled by wisdom if justice is to prevail. These moral concerns dictate the limits he places on plunder and the enslavement of defeated peoples.

Even more far-reaching is his insistence, reiterated several times by Aristotle, that war is not an end in itself but only a means to a secure peace.

The following selection from Plato's *Republic* describes the communal life recommended for the soldier class that guards the state. In the *Laws* he comes back to the claim that war is a teacher of courage, arguing that other virtues require the state to work for peace, not war.

For further reading:

Wild, John. *Plato's Modern Enemies and the Theory of Natural Law.* University of Chicago Press, 1953.

### MORAL EFFECTS OF WAR

From *The Republic* 5, trans. Benjamin Jowett.

You agree then, I said, that men and women are to have a common way of life such as we have described—common education, common children; and they are to watch over the citizens in common whether abiding in the city or going out to war; they are to keep watch together, and to hunt together like dogs; and always and in all things, as far as they are able, women are to share with the men? And in so doing they will do what is best, and will not violate, but preserve the natural relation of the sexes.

I agree with you, he replied.

The enquiry, I said, has yet to be made, whether such a community will be found possible—as among other animals, so also among men—and if possible, in what way possible?

You have anticipated the question which I was about to suggest.

There is no difficulty, I said, in seeing how war will be carried on by them.

How?

Why, of course they will go on expeditions together; and will take with them any of their children who are strong enough, that, after the manner of the artisan's child, they may look on at the work which they will have to do when they are grown up; and besides looking on they will have to help and be of use in war, and to wait upon their fathers and mothers. Did you never observe in the arts how the potters' boys look on and help, long before they touch the wheel?

Yes, I have.

And shall potters be more careful in educating their children and in giving them the opportunity of seeing and practising their duties than our guardians will be?

The idea is ridiculous, he said.

There is also the effect on the parents, with whom, as with other animals, the presence of their young ones will be the greatest incentive to valour.

That is quite true, Socrates; and yet if they are defeated, which may often happen in war, how great the danger is! the children will be lost as well as their parents, and the state will never recover.

True, I said; but would you never allow them to run any risk?

I am far from saying that.

Well, but if they are ever to run a risk should they not do so on some occasion when, if they escape disaster, they will be the better for it?

Clearly.

Whether the future soldiers do or do not see war in the days of their youth is a very important matter, for the sake of which some risk may fairly be incurred.

Yes, very important.

This then must be our first step—to make our children spectators of war; but we must also contrive that they shall be secured against danger; then all will be well.

True.

Their parents may be supposed not to be blind to the risks of war, but to know, as far as human foresight can, what expeditions are safe and what dangerous?

That may be assumed.

And they will take them on the safe expeditions and be cautious about the dangerous ones?

True.

And they will place them under the command of experienced veterans who will be their leaders and teachers?

Very properly.

Still, the dangers of war cannot be always foreseen; there is a good deal of chance about them?

True.

Then against such chances the children must be at once furnished with wings, in order that in the hour of need they may fly away and escape.

What do you mean? he said.

I mean that we must mount them on horses in their earliest youth, and when they have learnt to ride, take them on horseback to see war; the horses must not be spirited and warlike, but the most tractable and yet the swiftest that can be had. In this way they will get an excellent view of what is hereafter to be their own business; and if there is danger they have only to follow their elder leaders and escape.

I believe that you are right, he said.

Next, as to war; what are to be the relations of your soldiers to one another and to their enemies? I should be inclined to propose that the soldier who leaves his rank or throws away his arms, or is guilty of any other act of cowardice, should be degraded into the rank of a husbandman or artisan. What do you think?

By all means, I should say.

And he who allows himself to be taken prisoner may as well be made a present of to his enemies; he is their lawful prey, and let them do what they like with him.

Certainly.

But the hero who has distinguished himself, what shall be done to him? In the first place, he shall receive honour in the army from his youthful comrades; every one of them in succession shall crown him. What do you say?

I approve.

And what do you say to his receiving the right hand of fellow-ship?

To that too, I agree.

But you will hardly agree to my next proposal.

What is your proposal?

That he should kiss and be kissed by them.

Most certainly, and I should be disposed to go further, and say: Let no one whom he has a mind to kiss refuse to be kissed by him while the expedition lasts. So that if there be a lover in the army, whether his love be youth or maiden, he may be more eager to win the prize of valour.

Capital, I said. That the brave man is to have more wives than others has been already determined: and he is to have first choices in such matters more than others, in order that he may have as many children as possible?

Agreed.

Again, there is another manner in which, according to Homer, brave youths should be honoured; for he tells how Ajax, after he had distinguished himself in battle, was rewarded with long chines, which seems to be a compliment appropriate to a hero in the flower of his age, being not only a tribute of honour but also a very strengthening thing.

Most true, he said.

Then in this, I said, Homer shall be our teacher; and we too, at sacrifices and on the like occasions, will honour the brave according to the measure of their valour, whether men or women, with hymns and those other distinctions which we were mentioning; also with

> seats of precedence, and meats and full cups;

and in honouring them, we shall be at the same time training them.

That, he replied, is excellent.

Yes, I said; and when a man dies gloriously in war shall we not say, in the first place, that he is of the golden race?

To be sure.

Nay, have we not the authority of Hesiod for affirming that when they are dead

> They are holy angels upon the earth, authors of
> good, averters of evil, the guardians of speech-
> gifted men?

Yes; and we accept his authority.

We must learn of the god how we are to order the sepulture of divine and heroic personages, and what is to be their special distinction; and we must do as he bids?

By all means.

And in ages to come we will reverence them and kneel before their sepulchres as at the graves of heroes. And not only they but any who are deemed pre-eminently good, whether they die from age, or in any other way, shall be admitted to the same honours.

That is very right, he said.

Next, how shall our soldiers treat their enemies? What about this?

In what respect do you mean?

First of all, in regard to slavery? Do you think it right that Hellenes should enslave Hellenic states, or allow others to enslave them, if they can help? Should not their custom be to spare them, considering the danger which there is that the whole race may one day fall under the yoke of the barbarians?

To spare them is infinitely better.

Then no Hellene should be owned by them as a slave; that is a rule which they will observe and advise the other Hellenes to observe.

Certainly, he said; they will in this way be united against the barbarians and will keep their hands off one another.

Next as to the slain; ought the conquerors, I said, to take anything but their armour? Does not the practice of despoiling an enemy afford an excuse for not facing the battle? Cowards skulk about the dead, pretending that they are fulfilling a duty, and many an army before now has been lost from this love of plunder.

Very true.

And is there not illiberality and avarice in robbing a corpse, and also a degree of meanness and womanishness in making an enemy of the dead body when the real enemy has flown away and left only his fighting gear behind him—is not this rather like a dog who cannot get at his assailant, quarrelling with the stones which strike him instead?

Very like a dog, he said.

Then we must abstain from spoiling the dead or hindering their burial?

Yes, he replied, we most certainly must.

Neither shall we offer up arms at the temples of the gods, least of all the arms of Hellenes, if we care to maintain good feeling with other Hellenes; and, indeed, we have reason to fear that the offering of spoils taken from kinsmen may be a pollution unless commanded by the god himself?

Very true.

Again, as to the devastation of Hellenic territory or the burning of houses, what is to be the practice?

May I have the pleasure, he said, of hearing your opinion?

Both should be forbidden, in my judgment; I would take the annual produce and no more. Shall I tell you why?

Pray do.

Why, you see, there is a difference in the names "discord" and "war," and I imagine that there is also a difference in their natures; the one is expressive of what is internal and domestic, the other of what is external and foreign; and the first of the two is termed discord, and only the second, war.

That is a very proper distinction, he replied.

And may I not observe with equal propriety that the Hellenic race is all united together by ties of blood and friendship, and alien and strange to the barbarians?

Very good, he said.

And therefore when Hellenes fight with barbarians and barbarians with Hellenes, they will be described by us as being at war when they fight, and by nature enemies, and this kind of antagonism should be called war; but when Hellenes fight with one another we shall say that Hellas is then in a state of disorder and discord, they being by nature friends; and such enmity is to be called discord.

I agree.

Consider then, I said, when that which we have acknowledged to be discord occurs, and a city is divided, if both parties destroy the lands and burn the houses of one another, how wicked does the strife appear! No true lover of his country would bring himself to tear in pieces his own nurse and mother: There might be reason in the conqueror depriving the conquered of their harvest, but still they would have the idea of peace in their hearts and would not mean to go on fighting for ever.

Yes, he said, that is a better temper than the other.

And will not the city, which you are founding, be an Hellenic city?

It ought to be, he replied.

Then will not the citizens be good and civilized?
Yes, very civilized.
And will they not be lovers of Hellas, and think of Hellas as their own land, and share in the common temples?
Most certainly.
And any difference which arises among them will be regarded by them as discord only—a quarrel among friends, which is not to be called a war?
Certainly not.
Then they will quarrel as those who intend some day to be reconciled?
Certainly.
They will use friendly correction, but will not enslave or destroy their opponents; they will be correctors, not enemies?
Just so.
And as they are Hellenes themselves they will not devastate Hellas, nor will they burn houses, nor even suppose that the whole population of a city—men, women, and children—are equally their enemies, for they know that the guilt of war is always confined to a few persons and that the many are their friends. And for all these reasons they will be unwilling to waste their lands and raze their houses; their enmity to them will only last until the many innocent sufferers have compelled the guilty few to give satisfaction?
I agree, he said, that our citizens should thus deal with their Hellenic enemies; and with barbarians as the Hellenes now deal with one another.
Then let us enact this law also for our guardians:—that they are neither to devastate the lands of Hellenes nor to burn their houses.
Agreed; and we may agree also in thinking that these, like all our previous enactments, are very good.
But still I must say, Socrates, that if you are allowed to go on in this way you will entirely forget the other question which at the commencement of this discussion you thrust aside:—Is such an order of things possible, and how, if at all? For I am quite ready to acknowledge that the plan which you propose, if only feasible, would do all sorts of good to the state. I will add, what you have omitted, that your citizens will be the bravest of warriors, and will never leave their ranks, for they will all know one another, and each will call the other father, brother, son; and if you suppose the women to join their armies, whether in the same rank or in the rear, either as a terror to the

enemy, or as auxiliaries in case of need, I know that they will then be absolutely invincible; and there are many domestic advantages which might also be mentioned and which I also fully acknowledge: but, as I admit all these advantages and as many more as you please, if only this state of yours were to come into existence, we need say no more about them; assuming then the existence of the state, let us now turn to the question of possibility and ways and means—the rest may be left. . . .

## WAR FOR THE SAKE OF PEACE

From *Laws* 1, trans. Benjamin Jowett.

*Cleinias.* . . . every city is in a natural state of war with every other, not indeed proclaimed by heralds, but everlasting. And if you look closely you will find that this was the intention of the Cretan legislator; all institutions, private as well as public, were arranged by him with a view to war; in giving them he was under the impression that no possessions or institutions are of any value to him who is defeated in battle; for all the good things of the conquered pass into the hands of the conquerors.

*Athenian Stranger.* You appear to me, Stranger, to have been thoroughly trained in the Cretan institutions, and to be well informed about them; will you tell me a little more explicitly what is the principle of government which you would lay down? You seem to imagine that a well-governed state ought to be so ordered as to conquer all other states in war: am I right in supposing this to be your meaning?

*Cle.* Certainly; and our Lacedaemonian friend, if I am not mistaken, will agree with me.

*Megillus.* Why, my good friend, how could any Lacedaemonian say anything else?

*Ath.* And is what you say applicable only to states, or also to villages?

*Cle.* To both alike.

*Ath.* The case is the same?

*Cle.* Yes.

*Ath.* And in the village will there be the same war of family against family, and of individual against individual?

*Cle.* The same.

*Ath.* And should each man conceive himself to be his own enemy:—what shall we say?

*Cle.* O Athenian Stranger—inhabitant of Attica I will not call you, for you seem to deserve rather to be named after the goddess herself, because you go back to first principles—you have thrown a light upon the argument, and will now be better able to understand what I was just saying—that all men are publicly one another's enemies, and each man privately his own.

*Ath.* My good sir, what do you mean?

*Cle.* . . . Moreover, there is a victory and defeat—the first and best of victories, the lowest and worst of defeats—which each man gains or sustains at the hands, not of another, but of himself; this shows that there is a war against ourselves going on within every one of us.

*Ath.* Let us now reverse the order of the argument: Seeing that every individual is either his own superior or his own inferior, may we say that there is the same principle in the house, the village, and the state?

*Cle.* You mean that in each of them there is a principle of superiority or inferiority to self?

*Ath.* Yes.

*Cle.* You are quite right in asking the question, for there certainly is such a principle, and above all in states; and the state in which the better citizens win a victory over the mob and over the inferior classes may be truly said to be better than itself, and may be justly praised, where such a victory is gained, or censured in the opposite case.

*Ath.* Whether the better is ever really conquered by the worse, is a question which requires more discussion, and may be therefore left for the present. But I now quite understand your meaning when you say that citizens who are of the same race and live in the same cities may unjustly conspire, and having the superiority in numbers may overcome and enslave the few just; and when they prevail, the state may be truly called its own inferior and therefore bad; and when they are defeated, its own superior and therefore good.

*Cle.* Your remark, Stranger, is a paradox, and yet we cannot possibly deny it.

*Ath.* Here is another case for consideration;—in a family there may be several brothers, who are the offspring of a single pair; very possibly the majority of them may be unjust, and the just may be in a minority.

*Cle.* Very possibly.

*Ath.* And you and I ought not to raise a question of words as to whether this family and household are rightly said to be superior when they conquer, and inferior when they are conquered; for we are not now considering what may or may not be the proper or customary way of speaking, but we are considering the natural principles of right and wrong in laws.

*Cle.* What you say, Stranger, is most true.

*Meg.* Quite excellent, in my opinion, as far as we have gone.

*Ath.* Again; might there not be a judge over these brethren, of whom we were speaking?

*Cle.* Certainly.

*Ath.* Now, which would be the better judge—one who destroyed the bad and appointed the good to govern themselves; or one who, while allowing the good to govern, let the bad live, and made them voluntarily submit? Or third, I suppose, in the scale of excellence might be placed a judge, who, finding the family distracted, not only did not destroy any one, but reconciled them to one another for ever after, and gave them laws which they mutually observed, and was able to keep them friends.

*Cle.* The last would be by far the best sort of judge and legislator.

*Ath.* And yet the aim of all the laws which he gave would be the reverse of war.

*Cle.* Very true.

*Ath.* And will he who constitutes the state and orders the life of man have in view external war, or that kind of intestine war called civil, which no one, if he could prevent, would like to have occurring in his own state; and when occurring, every one would wish to be quit of as soon as possible?

*Cle.* He would have the latter chiefly in view.

*Ath.* And would he prefer that this civil war should be terminated by the destruction of one of the parties, and by the victory of the other, or that peace and friendship should be reestablished, and that, being reconciled, they should give their attention to foreign enemies?

*Cle.* Every one would desire the latter in the case of his own state.

*Ath.* And would not that also be the desire of the legislator?

*Cle.* Certainly.

*Ath.* And would not every one always make laws for the sake of the best?

*Cle.* To be sure.

*Ath.* But war, whether external or civil, is not the best, and the need of either is to be deprecated; but peace with one another, and good will, are best. Nor is the victory of the state over itself to be regarded as a really good thing, but as a necessity; a man might as well say that the body was in the best state when sick and purged by medicine, forgetting that there is also a state of the body which needs no purge. And in like manner no one can be a true statesman, whether he aims at the happiness of the individual or state, who looks only, or first of all, to external warfare; nor will he ever be a sound legislator who orders peace for the sake of war, and not war for the sake of peace.

## 2. *CICERO* (106–43 B.C.)

The influence of this Roman jurist and philosopher on Western political philosophy cannot be overestimated. His ideas are evident in the writings of the Christian Lactantius, and Augustine brings Christian concepts of sin and of love to bear on Cicero's view of justice and of a just war. As a result, Cicero's views live on, not in their original pagan form, but through their influence on Christian thinkers from Augustine and Justinian to Aquinas and Grotius and Locke. From Cicero we gain the first clear statement on limiting war by means of criteria derived from natural law.

For further reading:

Rolfe, J. C. *Cicero and His Influence.* Cooper Square Press, 1963.

### THE JUST WAR

From *De Republica* 3, trans. C. W. Keyes, in *The Loeb Classical Library.*

XXII. . . . True law is right reason in agreement with nature; it is of universal application, unchanging and everlasting; it summons to duty by its commands, and averts from wrongdoing by its prohibitions. And it does not lay its commands or prohibitions upon good men in vain, though neither have any effect on the wicked. It is a sin to try to alter this law, nor is it allowable to attempt to repeal any part of it, and it is impossible to abolish it entirely. We cannot be freed from its obligations by senate or people, and we need not look outside ourselves for an expounder or interpreter of it. And there will not be different laws at Rome and at Athens, or different laws now and in the future, but one eternal and unchangeable law will be valid for all nations and all times, and there will be one master and ruler, that is, God, over us all, for he is the author of this law, its promulgator, and its enforcing judge. Whoever is disobedient is fleeing from himself and denying his human nature, and by reason of this very fact he will suffer the worst penalties, even if he escapes what is commonly considered punishment. . . .

XXIII. . . . a war is never undertaken by the ideal state, except in defence of its honour or its safety. . . .

But private citizens often escape those punishments which even the most stupid can feel—poverty, exile, imprisonment and stripes —by taking refuge in a swift death. But in the case of a state, death itself is a punishment, though it seems to offer individuals an escape from punishment; for a state ought to be so firmly founded that it will live forever. Hence death is not natural for a state as it is for a human being, for whom death is not only necessary, but frequently even desirable. On the other hand, there is some similarity, if we may compare small things with great, between the overthrow, destruction, and extinction of a state, and the decay and dissolution of the whole universe. . . .

Those wars are unjust which are undertaken without provocation. For only a war waged for revenge or defense can actually be just. . . .

No war is considered just unless it has been proclaimed and declared, or unless reparation has first been demanded. . . .

But our people by defending their allies have gained dominion over the whole world. . . .


## NATURAL LAW AND JUST WAR

From *De Officiis* 1, trans. W. Miller, in *The Loeb Classical Library.*

IV. First of all, Nature has endowed every species of living creature with the instinct of self-preservation, of avoiding what seems likely to cause injury to life or limb, and of procuring and providing everything needful for life—food, shelter, and the like. A common property of all creatures is also the reproductive instinct (the purpose of which is the propagation of the species) and also a certain amount of concern for their offspring. But the most marked difference between man and beast is this: the beast, just as far as it is moved by the senses and with very little perception of past or future, adapts itself to that alone which is present at the moment; while man—because he is endowed with reason, by which he comprehends the chain of consequences, perceives the causes of things, understands the relation of cause to effect and of effect to cause, draws analogies, and connects and associates the present and the future—easily surveys the course of his whole life and makes the necessary preparations for its conduct.

Nature likewise by the power of reason associates man with man in the common bonds of speech and life; she implants in him above all, I may say, a strangely tender love for his offspring. She also prompts men to meet in companies, to form public assemblies and to take part in them themselves; and she further dictates, as a consequence of this, the effort on man's part to provide a store of things that minister to his comforts and wants—and not for himself alone, but for his wife and children and the others whom he holds dear and for whom he ought to provide; and this responsibility also stimulates his courage and makes it stronger for the active duties of life.

Above all, the search after truth and its eager pursuit are peculiar to man. And so, when we have leisure from the demands of business cares, we are eager to see, to hear, to learn something new, and we esteem a desire to know the secrets or wonders of creation as indispensable to a happy life. Thus we come to understand that what is true, simple, and genuine appeals most strongly to a man's nature. To this passion for discovering truth there is added a hungering, as it were, for independence, so that a mind well-moulded by Nature is unwilling to be subject to anybody save one who gives rules of conduct or is a teacher of truth or who, for the general good, rules according to justice and law. From this attitude come greatness of soul and a sense of superiority to worldly conditions.

And it is no mean manifestation of Nature and Reason that man is the only animal that has a feeling for order, for propriety, for moderation in word and deed. And so no other animal has a sense of beauty, loveliness, harmony in the visible world; and Nature and Reason, extending the analogy of this from the world of sense to the world of spirit, find that beauty, consistency, order are far more to be maintained in thought and deed, and the same Nature and Reason are careful to do nothing in an improper or unmanly fashion, and in every thought and deed to do or think nothing capriciously.

It is from these elements that is forged and fashioned that moral goodness which is the subject of this inquiry—something that, even though it be not generally ennobled, is still worthy of all honour; and by its own nature, we correctly maintain, it merits praise, even though it be praised by none. . . .

The first office of justice is to keep one man from doing harm to another, unless provoked by wrong; and the next is to lead men to use common possessions for the common interests, private property for their own.

There is, however, no such thing as private ownership established by nature, but property becomes private either through long occupancy (as in the case of those who long ago settled in unoccupied territory) or through conquest (as in the case of those who took it in war) or by due process of law, bargain, or purchase, or by allotment. On this principle the lands of Arpinum are said to belong to the Arpinates, the Tusculan lands to the Tusculans; and similar is the assignment of private property. Therefore, inasmuch as in each case some of those things which by nature had been common property became the property of individuals, each one should retain possession of that which has fallen to his lot; and if anyone appropriates to himself anything beyond that, he will be violating the laws of human society.

But since, as Plato has admirably expressed it, we are not born for ourselves alone, but our country claims a share of our being, and our friends a share; and since, as the Stoics hold, everything that the earth produces is created for man's use; and as men, too, are born for the sake of men, that they may be able mutually to help one another; in this direction we ought to follow Nature as our guide, to contribute to the general good by an interchange of acts of kindness, by giving and receiving, and thus by our skill, our industry, and our talents to cement human society more closely together, man to man.

The foundation of justice, moreover, is good faith—that is, truth and fidelity to promises and agreements. And therefore we may follow the Stoics, who diligently investigate the etymology of words; and we may accept their statement that "good faith" is so called because what is promised is "made good," although some may find this derivation rather farfetched.

There are, on the other hand, two kinds of injustice—the one, on the part of those who inflict wrong, the other on the part of those who, when they can, do not shield from wrong those upon whom it is being inflicted. For he who, under the influence of anger or some other passion, wrongfully assaults another seems, as it were, to be laying violent hands upon a comrade; but he who does not prevent or oppose wrong, if he can, is just as guilty of wrong as if he deserted his parents or his friends or his country. Then, too, those very wrongs which people try to inflict on purpose to injure are often the result of fear: that is, he who premeditates injuring another is afraid that, if he does not do so, he may himself be made to suffer some hurt. But for the most part, people are led to wrongdoing in order to secure some personal end; in this vice, avarice is generally the controlling motive.

VIII. Again, men seek riches partly to supply the needs of life, partly to secure the enjoyment of pleasure. With those who cherish higher ambitions, the desire for wealth is entertained with a view to power and influence and the means of bestowing favours; Marcus Crassus, for example, not long since declared that no amount of wealth was enough for the man who aspired to be the foremost citizen of the state, unless with the income from it he could maintain an army. Fine establishments and the comforts of life in elegance and abundance also afford pleasure, and the desire to secure it gives rise to the insatiable thirst for wealth. Still, I do not mean to find fault with the accumulation of property, provided it hurts nobody, but unjust acquisition of it is always to be avoided.

The great majority of people, however, when they fall a prey to ambition for either military or civil authority are carried away by it so completely that they quite lose sight of the claims of justice. For Ennius says:

> There is no fellowship inviolate,
> No faith is kept, when kingship is concerned;

and the truth of his words has an uncommonly wide application. For whenever a situation is of such a nature that not more than one can hold preeminence in it, competition for it usually becomes so keen that it is an extremely difficult matter to maintain a "fellowship inviolate." . . . But the trouble about this matter is that it is in the greatest souls and in the most brilliant geniuses that we usually find ambitions for civil and military authority, for power, and for glory, springing up; and therefore we must be the more heedful not to go wrong in that direction. . . .

XI. Again, there are certain duties that we owe even to those who have wronged us. For there is a limit to retribution and to punishment; or rather, I am inclined to think, it is sufficient that the aggressor should be brought to repent of his wrongdoing, in order that he may not repeat the offence and that others may be deterred from doing wrong.

Then, too, in the case of a state in its external relations, the rights of war must be strictly observed. For since there are two ways of settling a dispute: first, by discussion; second, by physical force; and since the former is characteristic of man, the latter of the brute, we must resort to force only in case we may not avail ourselves of discussion. The only excuse, therefore, for going to war is that we may live in peace unharmed; and when the victory is won, we should spare those who have not been blood-thirsty and barbarous in their warfare. For instance, our forefathers actually admitted to full rights of citizenship the Tusculans, Aequians, Volscians, Sabines, and Hernicians, but they razed Carthage and Numantia to the ground. I wish they had not destroyed Corinth; but I believe they had some special reason for what they did—its convenient situation, probably—and feared that its very location might some day furnish a temptation to renew the war. In my opinion, at least, we should always strive to secure a peace that shall not admit of guile. And if my advice had been heeded on this point, we should still have at least some sort of constitutional government, if not the best in the world, whereas, as it is, we have none at all.

Not only must we show consideration for those whom we have conquered by force of arms but we must also ensure protection to those who lay down their arms and throw themselves upon the mercy of our generals, even though the battering ram has hammered at their walls. And among our countrymen justice has been observed so conscientiously in this direction, that those who have given promise of protection to states or nations subdued in war become, after the custom of our forefathers, the patrons of those states.

As for war, humane laws touching it are drawn up in the fetial code of the Roman people under all the guarantees of religion; and from this it may be gathered that no war is just, unless it is entered upon after an official demand for satisfaction has been submitted or warning has been given and a formal declaration made. Popilius was general in command of a province. In his army Cato's son was serving on his first campaign. When Popilius decided to disband one of his legions, he discharged also young Cato who was serving in that same legion. But when the young man out of love for the service stayed on in the field, his father wrote to Popilius to say that if he let him stay in the army, he should swear him into service with a new oath of allegiance, for in view of the voidance of his former oath he could not legally fight the foe. So extremely scrupulous was the observance of the laws in regard to the conduct of war. There is extant, too, a letter of the elder Marcus Cato to his son Marcus, in which he writes that he has heard that the youth has been discharged by the consul, when he was serving in Macedonia in the war with Perseus. He warns him, therefore, to be careful not to go into battle; for, he says, the man who is not legally a soldier has no right to be fighting the foe.

XII. This also I observe—that he who would properly have been called "a fighting enemy" (*perduellis*) was called "a guest" (*hostis*), thus relieving the ugliness of the fact by a softened expression; for "enemy" (*hostis*) meant to our ancestors what we now call "stranger" (*peregrinus*). This is proved by the usage in the Twelve Tables: "Or a day fixed for trial with a stranger" (*hostis*). And again: "Right of ownership is inalienable forever in dealings with a stranger" (*hostis*). What can exceed such charity, when he with whom one is at war is called by so gentle a name? And yet long lapse of time has given that word a harsher meaning: for it has lost its signification of "stranger" and has taken on the technical connotation of "an enemy under arms."

But when a war is fought out for supremacy and when glory is the object of war, it must still not fail to start from the same motives which I said a moment ago were the only righteous grounds for going to war. But those wars which have glory for their end must be carried on with less bitterness. For we contend, for example, with a fellow-citizen in one way, if he is a personal enemy, in another, if he is a rival: with the rival it is a struggle for office and position, with the enemy for life and honour. So with the Celtiberians and the Cimbrians we fought as with deadly enemies, not to determine which should be supreme, but which should survive; but with the Latins, Sabines, Samnites, Carthaginians, and Pyrrhus we fought for supremacy. The Carthaginians violated treaties; Hannibal was cruel; the others were more merciful. From Pyrrhus we have this famous speech on the exchange of prisoners:

> Gold will I none, nor price shall ye give; for I ask none;
> Come, let us not be chaff'rers of war, but warriors embattled.
> Nay; let us venture our lives, and the sword, not gold, weigh the
>     outcome.
> Make we the trial by valour in arms and see if Dame Fortune
> Wills it that ye shall prevail or I, or what be her judgment.
> Hear thou, too, this word, good Fabricius: whose valour soever

Spared hath been by the fortune of war—their freedom I grant them.
Such my resolve. I give and present them to you, my brave Romans;
Take them back to their homes; the great gods' blessings attend you.

A right kingly sentiment this and worthy a scion of the Aeacidae.
XIII. Again, if under stress of circumstances individuals have
made any promise to the enemy, they are bound to keep their word
even then. For instance, in the First Punic War, when Regulus was
taken prisoner by the Carthaginians, he was sent to Rome on parole
to negotiate an exchange of prisoners; he came and, in the first place,
it was he that made the motion in the senate that the prisoners should
not be restored; and in the second place, when his relatives and friends
would have kept him back, he chose to return to a death by torture
rather than prove false to his promise, though given to an enemy.

And again in the Second Punic War, after the Battle of Cannae,
Hannibal sent to Rome ten Roman captives bound by an oath to return to him, if they did not succeed in ransoming his prisoners; and
as long as any one of them lived, the censors kept them all degraded
and disfranchised, because they were guilty of perjury in not returning.
And they punished in like manner the one who had incurred guilt by
an evasion of his oath: with Hannibal's permission this man left the
camp and returned a little later on the pretext that he had forgotten
something or other; and then, when he left the camp the second
time, he claimed that he was released from the obligation of his oath;
and so he was, according to the letter of it, but not according to the
spirit. In the matter of a promise one must always consider the meaning and not the mere words.

Our forefathers have given us another striking example of justice
toward an enemy: when a deserter from Pyrrhus promised the senate
to administer poison to the king and thus work his death, the senate
and Gaius Fabricius delivered the deserter up to Pyrrhus. Thus they
stamped with their disapproval the treacherous murder even of an
enemy who was at once powerful, unprovoked, aggressive, and successful.

With this I will close my discussion of the duties connected with
war.

# II. CONFLICT OF LOYALTIES

The early church faced the problems of war and military service in a pagan world.[1] While courage is commendable, the highest virtue is neither courage nor honor nor even justice, but love; and love demands a compassion for one's enemies of which courage and honor and justice know little. Plato's and Cicero's reservations about excessive violence do not satisfy the demands of Christian love; this becomes evident in patristic writers such as Athenagoras, Tertullian, Lactantius, and Augustine. For some the outcome of such reservations is not just non-violence but non-resistance to violence as taught by Jesus. For others the result is a prophet-like criticism of military excesses and of misguided claims to justice.

These differences of opinion were complicated by the pagan symbols and rites associated with Roman army life. Some writers seemed to object more strenuously to these than to actually taking part in bloodshed. In times of danger, therefore, they resorted to prayer rather than accepting military service. A doctrine of two vocations developed, separating the political and military tasks of secular man from the directly religious duties of the Christian. But it is important to note that the pacifist church fathers neither denied to secular government the moral right of self-defense nor denied that Christians actually served in the military.

As Christianity spread among public officials the Christian's relation to government became more complex. Eventually the doctrine of two vocations became Augustine's doctrine of two kingdoms, and the Christian's involvement in government was therefore justified by his dual citizenship. Government, with its tragically necessary use of force in defense of peace and safety, is ordained by God. Augustine

1. Roland Bainton finds no documentation of Christian attitudes to soldiering until A.D. 170-180. From then on the greatest objection to it was in the Hellenistic East, while North African Christians were divided. The Roman church allowed military epitaphs, and Christians participated most in war on the Eastern frontier. See *Christian Attitudes Toward War and Peace*, chap. 5.

35

expresses this with the help of Cicero's natural law theory; yet Cicero's idea of a just society and his criteria for a just war are morally naïve. Not the reasoned assent of men of good will, but what people love most of all shapes both their justice and their attitudes to war.

For further reading:

Cadoux, C. J. *The Early Christian Attitude to War.* Headley, 1919.
————. *The Early Christian and the World.* T & T Clark, 1955.
Case, S. J. *The Social Triumph of the Ancient Church.* Harper, 1933.
Cochrane, C. N. *Christianity and Classical Culture.* Oxford University Press, 1944.
Deane, H. A. *The Political and Social Ideas of St. Augustine.* Columbia University Press, 1963.
Paolucci, H. *The Political Writings of St. Augustine.* Henry Regnery, 1962.

# 1. ATHENAGORAS (SECOND CENTURY A.D.)

Athenagoras was an Athenian philosopher who became one of the church's early apologists. In A.D. 177 he addressed to the emperors Marcus Aurelius and Commodius *A Plea for the Christians*, refuting charges of atheism, cannibalism, and incest. This selection indicates the aversion of Christians to killing in any form, not just to cannibalism, and reveals a love for their enemies that goes beyond the justice of meeting force with force.

## NON-VIOLENCE

From *A Plea for Christians* 34-35, trans. B. P. Pratten, in *The Ante-Nicene Fathers* 1.

These men, I say, revile us for the very things which they are conscious of themselves, and ascribe to their own gods, boasting of them as noble deeds, and worthy of the gods. These adulterers and paederasts defame the eunuchs and the once-married . . . so that not even the governors of the provinces sent by you suffice for the hearing of the complaints against those, to whom it even is not lawful, when they are struck, not to offer themselves for more blows, nor when defamed not to bless: for it is not enough to be just (and justice is to return like for like), but it is incumbent on us to be good and patient of evil.

What man of sound mind, therefore, will affirm, while such is our character, that we are murderers? For we cannot eat human flesh till we have killed some one. The former charge, therefore, being false, if any one should ask them in regard to the second, whether they have seen what they assert, not one of them would be so barefaced as to say that he had. And yet we have slaves, some more and some fewer, by whom we could not help being seen; but even of these, not one has been found to invent even such things against us. For when they know that we cannot endure even to see a man put to death, though justly, who of them can accuse us of murder or

37

cannibalism? Who does not reckon among the things of greatest interest the contests of gladiators and wild beasts, especially those which are given by you? But we, deeming that to see a man put to death is much the same as killing him, have abjured such spectacles. How, then, when we do not even look on, lest we should contract guilt and pollution, can we put people to death? And when we say that those women who use drugs to bring on abortion commit murder, and will have to give an account to God for the abortion, on what principle should we commit murder? For it does not belong to the same person to regard the very foetus in the womb as a created being, and therefore an object of God's care, and when it has passed into life, to kill it; and not to expose an infant, because those who expose them are chargeable with child-murder, and on the other hand, when it has been reared to destroy it. But we are in all things always alike and the same, submitting ourselves to reason, and not ruling over it.

## 2. TERTULLIAN (c. 155–c. 240)

Born of heathen parents, Tertullian became a Christian after years of education and practice as a jurist. Although he argues the case for Christianity with an evident disdain for pagan thought (which may reflect his Montanist asceticism), the Roman Stoics and his legal profession shape his view of natural law as a basis for ethics apart from the perversion of sin (*The Chaplet* 6).

The *Apology* sets forth a Christian view of government as ordained by God for the sake of peace and civil order. Tertullian consequently refuses the emperor divine honors and exempts Christians both from military oaths and celebrations that violate this rule and (in *The Chaplet*) from receiving the military crown with its idolatrous associations. But his objection to military service does not stop there. With this view of government he can pray for the emperor and "for brave armies," and also admit the widespread presence of Christians in the military; but he contends (*On Idolatry*) that Christians cannot carry the sword without violating the teaching of Jesus.

### CHRISTIANS AND GOVERNMENT

From *Apology* 30-38, trans. S. Thelwall, in *The Ante-Nicene Fathers* 3.

For we offer prayer for the safety of our princes to the eternal, the true, the living God, whose favour, beyond all others, they must themselves desire. They know from whom they have obtained their power; they know, as they are men, from whom they have received life itself; they are convinced that He is God alone, on whose power alone they are entirely dependent, to whom they are second, after whom they occupy the highest places, before and above all the gods. Why not, since they are above all living men, and the living, as living, are superior to the dead? They reflect upon the extent of their power, and so they come to understand the highest; they acknowledge that they have all their might from Him against whom their might is nought. Let the emperor make war on heaven; let him lead heaven captive in his triumph; let him put guards on heaven; let him impose taxes on heaven! He cannot. Just because he is less than heaven, he is great. For he himself is His to whom heaven and every creature appertains. He gets his sceptre where he first got his humanity; his power where he got the breath of life. Thither we lift our eyes, with hands outstretched, because free from sin; with head uncovered, for we have nothing whereof to be ashamed; finally, without a monitor, because it is from the heart we supplicate. Without ceasing, for all our emperors we offer prayer. We pray for life prolonged; for security to the empire; for protection to the imperial house; for brave armies, a faithful senate, a virtuous people, the world at rest, whatever, as man or Caesar, an emperor would wish. These things I cannot ask from any but the God from whom I know I shall obtain them, both because He alone bestows them and because I have claims upon Him for their gift, as being a servant of His, rendering homage to Him alone. . . .

But we merely, you say, flatter the emperor, and feign these prayers of ours to escape persecution. Thank you for your mistake, for you give us the opportunity of proving our allegations. Do you, then, who think that we care nothing for the welfare of Caesar, look into God's revelations, examine our sacred books, which we do not keep in hiding, and which many accidents put into the hands of those who are not of us. Learn from them that a large benevolence is enjoined upon us, even so far as to supplicate God for our enemies, and to beseech blessings on our persecutors. Who, then, are greater enemies and persecutors of Christians, than the very parties with treason against whom we are charged? Nay, even in terms, and most clearly, the Scripture says, "Pray for kings, and rulers, and powers, that all may be peace with you." For when there is disturbance in the empire, if the commotion is felt by its other members, surely we too, though we are not thought to be given to disorder, are to be found in some place or other which the calamity affects.

There is also another and a greater necessity for our offering prayer in behalf of the emperors, nay, for the complete stability of the empire, and for Roman interests in general. For we know that a mighty shock impending over the whole earth—in fact, the very end of all things threatening dreadful woes—is only retarded by the continued existence of the Roman empire. We have no desire, then, to be overtaken by these dire events; and in praying that their coming may be delayed, we are lending our aid to Rome's duration. More than this, though we decline to swear by the genii of the Caesars, we swear by their safety, which is worth far more than all your genii. Are you ignorant that these genii are called "Daemones," and thence the diminutive name "Daemonia" is applied to them? We respect in the emperors the ordinance of God, who has set them over the nations. We know that there is that in them which God has willed; and to what God has willed we desire all safety, and we count an oath by it a great oath. But as for daemons, that is, your genii, we have been in the habit of exorcising them, not of swearing by them, and thereby conferring on them divine honour.

But why dwell longer on the reverence and sacred respect of Christians to the emperor, whom we cannot but look up to as called by our Lord to his office? So that on valid grounds I might say Caesar is more ours than yours, for our God has appointed him. Therefore, as having this propriety in him, I do more than you for his welfare, not merely because I ask it of Him who can give it, or because I ask it as one who deserves to get it, but also because, in keeping the majesty of Caesar within due limits, and putting it under the Most High, and making it less than divine, I commend him the more to the favour of Deity, to whom I make him alone inferior. But I place him in subjection to one I regard as more glorious than himself. Never will I call the emperor God, and that either because it is not in me to be guilty of falsehood; or that I dare not turn him into ridicule; or that not even himself will desire to have that high name applied to him. If he is but a man, it is his interest as man to give God His higher place. Let him think it enough to bear the name of emperor. That, too, is a great name of God's giving. To call him God, is to rob him of his title. If he is not a man, emperor he cannot be. Even when, amid the honours of a triumph, he sits on that lofty chariot, he is reminded that he is only human. A voice at his back keeps whispering in his ear, "Look behind thee; remember thou art but a man." And it only adds to his exultation, that he shines with a glory so surpassing as to require an admonitory reference to his condition. It adds to his greatness that he needs such a reminiscence, lest he should think himself divine. . . .

This is the reason, then, why Christians are counted public enemies: that they pay no vain, nor false, nor foolish honours to the emperor; that, as men believing in the true religion, they prefer to celebrate their festal days with a good conscience, instead of with the common wantonness. It is, forsooth, a notable homage to bring fires and couches out before the public, to have feasting from street to street, to turn the city into one great tavern, to make mud with wine, to run in troops to acts of violence, to deeds of shamelessness, to lust allurements! What! is public joy manifested by public disgrace? Do things unseemly at other times beseem the festal days of princes? Do they who observe the rules of virtue out of reverence for Caesar, for his sake turn aside from them? Shall piety be a license to immoral deeds, and shall religion be regarded as affording the occasion for all riotous extravagance? Poor we, worthy of all condemnation! . . .

If we are enjoined, then, to love our enemies, as I have remarked above, whom have we to hate? If injured, we are forbidden to retaliate, lest we become as bad ourselves: who can suffer injury at our hands? In regard to this, recall your own experiences. How often you inflict gross cruelties on Christians, partly because it is your own inclination, and partly in obedience to the laws! How often, too, the hostile mob, paying no regard to you, takes the law into its own hand, and assails us with stones and flames! With the very frenzy of the Bacchanals, they do not even spare the Christian dead, but tear them, now sadly changed, no longer entire, from the rest of the tomb, from the asylum we might say of death, cutting them in pieces, rending them asunder. Yet, banded together as we are, ever so ready to sacrifice our lives, what single case of revenge for injury are you able to point to, though, if it were held right among us to repay evil by evil, a single night with a torch or two could achieve an ample vengeance? But away with the idea of a sect divine avenging itself by human fires, or shrinking from the sufferings in which it is tried. If we desired, indeed, to act the part of open enemies, not merely of secret avengers, would there be any lacking in strength, whether of numbers or resources? The Moors, the Marcomanni, the Parthians themselves, or any single people, however great, inhabiting a distinct territory, and confined within its own boundaries, surpasses, forsooth, in numbers, one spread over all the world! We are but of yesterday, and we have filled every place among you—cities, islands, fortresses, towns, market-places, the very camp, tribes, companies, palace, senate, forum—we have left nothing to you but the temples of your gods. For what wars should we not be fit, not eager, even with unequal forces, we who so willingly yield ourselves to the sword, if in our religion it were not counted better to be slain than to slay? Without arms even, and raising no insurrectionary banner, but simply in enmity to you, we could carry on the contest with you by an ill-willed severance alone. For if such multitudes of men were to break away from you, and betake themselves to some remote corner of the world, why, the very loss of so many citizens, whatever sort they were, would cover the empire with shame; nay, in the very forsaking, vengeance would be inflicted. Why, you would be horror-struck at the solitude in which you would find yourselves, at such an ill-prevailing silence, and that stupor as of a dead world. You would have to seek subjects to govern. You would have more enemies than citizens remaining. For now it is the immense number of Christians which makes your enemies so few— almost all the inhabitants of your various cities being followers of Christ. Yet you choose to call us enemies of the human race, rather than of human error. Nay, who would deliver you from those secret foes, ever busy both destroying your souls and ruining your health? Who would save you, I mean, from the attacks of those spirits of evil, which without reward or hire we exorcise? This alone would be revenge enough for us, that you were henceforth left free to the possession of unclean spirits. But instead of taking into account what is due to us for the important protection we afford you, and though we are not merely no trouble to you, but in fact necessary to your well-being, you prefer to hold us enemies, as indeed we are, yet not of man, but rather of his error.

Ought not Christians, therefore, to receive not merely a somewhat milder treatment, but to have a place among the law-tolerated societies, seeing they are not chargeable with any such crimes as are commonly dreaded from societies of the illicit class? . . .

## CHRISTIANS AND MILITARY SERVICE

From *On Idolatry* 19, trans. S. Thelwall, in *The Ante-Nicene Fathers* 3.

In that last section, decision may seem to have been given likewise concerning military service, which is between dignity and power. But now inquiry is made about this point, whether a believer may turn himself unto military service, and whether the military may be admitted unto the faith, even the rank and file, or each inferior grade, to whom there is no necessity for taking part in sacrifices or capital punishments. There is no agreement between the divine and the human sacrament, the standard of Christ and the standard of the devil, the camp of light and the camp of darkness. One soul cannot be due to two *masters*—God and Caesar. And yet Moses carried a rod, and Aaron wore a buckle, and John (Baptist) is girt with leather, and Joshua the son of Nun leads a line of march; and the People warred: if it pleases you to sport with the subject. But how will _a Christian man_ war, nay, how will he serve even in peace, without a sword, which the Lord has taken away? For albeit soldiers had come unto John, and had received the formula of their rule; albeit, likewise, a centurion had believed; *still* the Lord afterward, in disarming Peter, unbelted every soldier. No dress is lawful among us, if assigned to any unlawful action.

From *The Chaplet* 6, 11, 12, in *The Ante-Nicene Fathers* 3.

Demanding then a law of God, you have that common one prevailing all over the world, engraven on the natural tables to which the apostle too is wont to appeal, as when in respect of the woman's veil he says, "Does not even Nature teach you?"—as when to the Romans, affirming that the heathen do by nature those things which the law requires, he suggests both natural law and a law-revealing nature. Yes, and also in the first chapter of the epistle he authenticates nature, when he asserts that males and females changed among themselves the natural use of the creature into that which is unnatural, by way of penal retribution for their error. We first of all indeed know God Himself by the teaching of Nature, calling Him God of gods, taking for granted that He is good, and invoking Him as Judge. Is it a question with you whether for the enjoyment of His creatures, Nature should be our guide, that we may not be carried away in the direction in which the rival of God has corrupted, along with man himself, the entire creation which had been made over to our race for certain uses, whence the apostle says that it too unwillingly became subject to vanity, completely bereft of its original character, first by vain, then by base, unrighteous, and ungodly uses? It is thus, accordingly, in the pleasures of the shows, that the creature is dishonoured by those who by nature indeed perceive that all the materials of which shows are got up belong to God, but lack the knowledge to perceive as well that they have all been changed by the devil. . . .

To begin with the real ground of the military crown, I think we must first inquire whether warfare is proper at all for Christians. What sense is there in discussing the merely accidental, when that on which it rests is to be condemned? Do we believe it lawful for a human oath to be superadded to one divine, for a man to come under promise to another master after Christ, and to abjure father, mother, and all nearest kinsfolk, whom even the law has commanded us to honour and love next to God Himself, to whom the gospel, too, holding them only of less account than Christ, has in like manner rendered honour? Shall it be held lawful to make an occupation of the sword, when the Lord proclaims that he who uses the sword shall perish by the sword? And shall the son of peace take part in the battle when it does not become him even to sue at law? And shall he apply the chain, and the prison, and the torture, and the punishment, who is not the avenger even of his own wrongs? Shall he, forsooth, either keep watch-service for others more than for Christ, or shall he do it on the Lord's day, when he does not even do it for Christ Himself? And shall he keep guard before the temples which he has renounced? And shall he take a meal where the apostle has forbidden him? And shall he diligently protect by night those whom in the day-time he has put to flight by his exorcisms, leaning and resting on the spear the while with which Christ's side was pierced? Shall he carry a flag, too, hostile to Christ? And shall *he* ask a watchword from the emperor who has already received one from God? Shall *he* be disturbed in death by the trumpet of the trumpeter, who expects to be aroused by the angel's trump? And shall the Christian be burned according to camp rule, when he was not permitted to burn incense to an idol, when to him Christ remitted the punishment of fire? Then how many other offenses there are involved in the performances of camp offices, which we must hold to involve a transgression of God's law, you may see by a slight survey. The very carrying of the name over from the camp of light to the camp of darkness is a violation of it. Of course, if faith comes later, and finds any preoccupied with military service, their case is different, as in the instance of those whom John used to receive for baptism, and of those most faithful centurions, I mean the centurion whom Christ approves, and the centurion whom Peter instructs; yet, at the same time, when a man has become a believer, and faith has been sealed, there must be either an immediate abandonment of it, which has been the course with many; or all sorts of quibbling will have to be resorted to in order to avoid offending God, and that is not allowed even outside of military service; or, last of all, for God the fate must be endured which a citizen-faith has been no less ready to accept. Neither does military service hold out escape from punishment of sins, or exemption from martyrdom. Nowhere does the Christian change his character. There is one gospel, and the same Jesus, who will one day deny every one who denies, and acknowledge every one who acknowledges God—who will save, too, the life which has been lost for His sake; but, on the other hand, destroy that which for gain has been saved to His dishonour. With Him the faithful citizen is a soldier, just as the faithful soldier is a citizen. A state of faith admits no plea of necessity; they are under no necessity to sin, whose one necessity is, that they do not sin. For if one is pressed to the offering of sacrifice and the sheer denial of Christ by the necessity of torture or of punishment, yet discipline does not connive even at that necessity; because there is a higher necessity to dread denying and to undergo martyrdom, than to escape from suffering, and to render the homage required. In fact, an excuse of this sort overturns the entire essence of our sacrament, removing even the obstacle to voluntary sins; for it will be possible also to maintain that inclination is a necessity, as involving in it, forsooth, a sort of compulsion. I have, in fact, disposed of this very allegation of necessity with reference to the pleas by which crowns connected with official position are vindicated, in support of which it is in common use, since for this very reason offices must be either refused that we may not fall into acts of sin, or martyrdoms endured that we may get quit of offices. Touching this primary aspect of the question, as to the unlawfulness even of a military life itself, I shall not add more, that the secondary question may be restored to its place. Indeed, if, putting my strength to the question, I banish from us the military life, I should now to no purpose issue a challenge on the matter of the military crown. Suppose, then, that the military service is lawful, as far as the plea for the crown is concerned.

But I first say a word also about the crown itself. This laurel one is sacred to Apollo or Bacchus—to the former as the god of archery, to the latter as the god of triumphs. In like manner Claudius teaches, when he tells us that soldiers are wont too to be wreathed in myrtle. For the myrtle belongs to Venus, the mother of the Aeneadae, the mistress also of the god of war, who through Ilia and the Romuli is Roman. But I do not believe that Venus is Roman as well as Mars, because of the vexation the concubine gave her. When military service again is crowned with olive, the idolatry has respect to Minerva, who is equally the goddess of arms—but got a crown of the tree referred to, because of the peace she made with Neptune. In these respects, the superstition of the military garland will be everywhere defiled and all-defiling. And it is further defiled, I should think, also in the grounds of it. Lo! the yearly public pronouncing of vows, what does that bear on its face to be? It takes place first in the part of the camp where the general's tent is, and then in the temples. In addition to the places, observe the words also: "We vow that you, O Jupiter, will then have an ox with gold-decorated horns." What does the utterance mean? Without a doubt the denial [of Christ]. Albeit the Christian says nothing in these places with the mouth, he makes his response by having the crown on his head. The laurel is likewise commanded [to be used] at the distribution of the largess. So you see idolatry is not without its gain, selling, as it does, Christ for pieces of gold, as Judas did for pieces of silver. Will it be "Ye cannot serve God and mammon," to devote your energies to mammon, and to depart from God? Will it be "Render unto Caesar the things which are Caesar's, and unto God the things which are God's," not only not to render the human being to God, but even to take the denarius from Caesar? Is the laurel of the triumph made of leaves, or of corpses? Is it adorned with ribbons, or with tombs? Is it bedewed with ointments, or with the tears of wives and mothers? It may be of some Christians too; for Christ is also among the barbarians. Has not he who has carried [a crown for] this cause on his head, fought even against himself? Another sort of service belongs to the royal guards. And indeed crowns are called Castrenses, as belonging to the camp; *Munificae* likewise, from the Caesarean functions they perform. But even then you are still the soldier and the servant of another; and if of two masters, of God and Caesar; but assuredly then not of Caesar, when you owe yourself to God, as having higher claims, I should think, even in matters in which both have an interest.

## 3. ORIGEN (c. 185–c. 254)

The Alexandrian church father Origen was as appreciative of Greek culture as his older contemporary Tertullian was suspicious. In what is perhaps the greatest apologetic work of the early church, he responds at length to Celsus' charge that Christians are rebellious because they refuse both military service and government office.

Although he argues from silence that Jesus nowhere taught violence, his underlying position is clear. Christians have another vocation than political or military service, a spiritual one, in which they support the emperor and fight his enemies by prayer to God.

### ON GOVERNMENT SERVICE

From *Against Celsus* 3.7; 8.73-75, trans. F. Crombie, in *The Ante-Nicene Fathers* 4.

In like manner, as the statement is false "that the Hebrews, being [originally] Egyptians, dated the commencement [of their political existence] from the time of their rebellion," so also is this, "that in the days of Jesus others who were Jews rebelled against the Jewish state, and became His followers"; for neither Celsus nor they who think with him are able to point out any act on the part of Christians which savours of rebellion. And yet, if a revolt had led to the formation of the Christian commonwealth, so that it derived its existence in this way from that of the Jews, who were permitted to take up arms in defence of the members of their families, and to slay their enemies, the Christian Lawgiver would not have altogether forbidden the putting of men to death; and yet He nowhere teaches that it is right for His own disciples to offer violence to any one, however wicked. For He did not deem it in keeping with such laws as His, which were derived from a divine source, to allow the killing of any individual whatever. Nor would the Christians, had they owed their origin to a rebellion, have adopted laws of so exceedingly mild a character as not to allow them, when it was their fate to be slain as sheep, on any occasion to resist their persecutors. And truly, if we look a little deeper into things, we may say regarding the exodus from Egypt, that it is a miracle if a whole nation *at once* adopted the language called Hebrew, as if it had been a gift from heaven, when one of their own prophets said, "As they went forth from Egypt, they heard a language which they did not understand."

In the next place, Celsus urges us "to help the king with all our might, and to labour with him in the maintenance of justice, to fight for him: and if he requires it, to fight under him or lead an army along with him." To this our answer is, that we do, when occasion requires, give help to kings, and that, so to say, a divine help, "putting on the whole armour of God." And this we do in obedience to the injunction of the apostle, "I exhort, therefore, that first of all, supplications, prayers, intercessions, and giving of thanks, be made for all men; for kings, and for all that are in authority," and the more any one excels in piety, the more effective help does he render to kings, even more than is given by soldiers, who go forth to fight and slay as many of the enemy as they can. And to those enemies of our faith who require us to bear arms for the commonwealth, and to slay men, we can reply: "Do not those who are priests at certain shrines, and those who attend on certain gods, as you account them, keep their hands free from blood, that they may with hands unstained and free from human blood offer the appointed sacrifices to your gods; and even when war is upon you, you never enlist the priests in the army. If that, then, is a laudable custom, how much more so, that while others are engaged in battle, these too should engage as the priests and ministers of God, keeping their hands pure, and wrestling in prayers to God on behalf of those who are fighting in a righteous cause, and for the king who reigns righteously, that whatever is opposed to those who act righteously may be destroyed!" And as we by our prayers vanquish all demons who stir up war, and lead to the violation of oaths, and disturb the peace, we in this way are much more helpful to the kings than those who go into the field to fight for them. And we do take our part in public affairs, when along with righteous prayers we join self-denying exercises and meditations, which teach us to despise pleasures, and not to be led away by them. And none fight better for the king than we do. We do not indeed fight under him, although he require it; but we fight on his behalf, forming a special army—an army of piety—by offering our prayers to God.

And if Celsus would have us to lead armies in defence of our country, let him know that we do this too, and that not for the purpose of being seen by men, or of vainglory. For "in secret," and in our own hearts, there are prayers which ascend as from priests in behalf of our fellow citizens. And Christians are benefactors of their country more than others. For they train up citizens, and inculcate piety to the Supreme Being, and they promote those whose lives in the smallest cities have been good and worthy, to a divine and heavenly city, to whom it may be said, "Thou hast been faithful in the smallest city, come into a great one," where "God standeth in the assembly of the gods, and judgeth the gods in the midst"; and He reckons thee among them, if thou no more "die as a man, or fall as one of the princes."

Celsus also urges us to "take office in the government of the country, if that is required for the maintenance of the laws and the support of religion." But we recognize in each state the existence of another national organization, founded by the Word of God, and we exhort those who are mighty in word and of blameless life to rule over Churches. Those who are ambitious of ruling we reject; but we constrain those who, through excess of modesty, are not easily induced to take a public charge in the Church of God. And those who rule over us well are under the constraining influence of the great King, whom we believe to be the Son of God, God the Word. And if those who govern in the Church, and are called rulers of the divine nation—that is, the Church—rule well, they rule in accordance with the divine commands, and never suffer themselves to be led astray by worldly policy. And it is not for the purpose of escaping public duties that Christians decline public offices, but that they may reserve themselves for a diviner and more necessary service in the Church of God—for the salvation of men. And this service is at once necessary and right. They take charge of all—of those that are within, that they may day by day lead better lives, and of those that are without, that they may come to abound in holy words and in deeds of piety; and that, while thus worshipping God truly, and training up as many as they can in the same way, they may be filled with the word of God and the law of God, and thus be united with the Supreme God through His Son the Word, Wisdom, Truth, and Righteousness, who unites to God all who are resolved to conform their lives in all things to the law of God.

## 4. LACTANTIUS (c. 250–c. 330)

Called "The Christian Cicero," Lactantius was a distinguished rhetorician who became a Christian shortly after A.D. 300 and brought his learning and skills to the apologetic task. His *Divine Institutes,* written around A.D. 313, commends the faith to intellectuals and other leaders. A few years thereafter Constantine appointed him tutor to his son Crispus.

The Ciceronian element is evident in this selection: natural law, as well as the image of God in man, argues against violence and war. Even indifference about human life is a sin against nature and nature's God.

### THE NATURAL LAW OF LOVE

From *The Divine Institutes* 6.10-11, trans. W. Fletcher, in *The Ante-Nicene Fathers* 7.

I have said what is due to God, I will now say what is to be given to man; although this very thing which you shall give to man is given to God, for man is the image of God. But, however, the first office of justice is to be united with God, the second with man. But the former is called religion; the second is named mercy or kindness; which virtue is peculiar to the just, and to the worshippers of God, because this alone comprises the principle of common life. For God, who has not given wisdom to the other animals, has made them more safe from attack in danger by natural defences. But because He made him naked and defenceless that He might rather furnish him with wisdom, He gave him, besides other things, this feeling of kindness; so that man should protect, love, and cherish man, and both receive and afford assistance against all dangers. Therefore kindness is the greatest bond of human society; and he who has broken this is to be deemed impious, and a parricide. For if we all derive our origin from one man, whom God created, we are plainly of one blood; and therefore, it must be considered the greatest wickedness to hate a man,

51

even though guilty. On which account God has enjoined that enmities are never to be contracted by us, but that they are always to be removed, so that we soothe those who are our enemies, by reminding them of their relationship. Likewise, if we are all inspired and animated by one God, what else are we than brothers? And, indeed, the more closely united, because we are united in soul rather than in body. Accordingly Lucretius does not err when he says: "In short, we are all sprung from a heavenly seed; all have that same father." Therefore they are to be accounted as savage beasts who injure man; who, in opposition to every law and right of human nature, plunder, torture, slay, and banish.

On account of this relationship of brotherhood, God teaches us never to do evil, but always good. And He also prescribes in what this doing good consists: in affording aid to those who are oppressed and in difficulty, and in bestowing food on those who are destitute. For God, since He is kind, wished us to be a social animal. Therefore, in the case of other men, we ought to think of ourselves. We do not deserve to be set free in our own dangers, if we do not succour others; we do not deserve assistance, if we refuse to render it. There are no precepts of philosophers to this purport, inasmuch as they, being captivated by the appearance of false virtue, have taken away mercy from man, and while they wish to heal, have corrupted. And though they generally admit that the mutual participation of human society is to be retained, they entirely separate themselves from it by the harshness of their inhuman virtue. This error, therefore, is also to be refuted, of those who think that nothing is to be bestowed on any one. They have introduced not one origin only, and cause of building a city; but some relate that those men who were first born from the earth, when they passed a wandering life among the woods and plains, and were not united by any mutual bond of speech or justice, but had leaves and grass for their beds, and caves and grottos for their dwellings, were a prey to the beasts and stronger animals. Then, that those who had either escaped, having been torn, or had seen their neighbours torn, being admonished of their own danger, had recourse to other men, implored protection, and at first made their wishes known by nods; then that they tried the beginnings of conversation, and by attaching names to each object, by degrees completed the system of speech. But when they saw that numbers themselves were not safe against the beasts, they began also to build towns, either that they might make their nightly repose safe, or that they might ward off the incursions and attacks of beasts not by fighting, but by interposing barriers.

O minds unworthy of men, which produced these foolish trifles! O wretched and pitiable men, who committed to writing and handed down to memory the record of their own folly; who, when they saw that the plan of assembling themselves together, or of mutual intercourse, or of avoiding danger, or of guarding against evil, or of preparing for themselves sleeping places and lairs, was natural even to the dumb animals, thought, however, that men could not have been admonished and learned, except by examples, what they ought to fear, what to avoid, and what to do, or that they would never have assembled together, or have discovered the method of speech, had not the beasts devoured them! These things appeared to others senseless, as they really were; and they said that the cause of their coming together was not the tearing of wild beasts, but rather the very feeling of humanity itself; and that therefore they collected themselves together, because the nature of men avoided solitude, and was desirous of communion and society. The discrepancy between them is not great; since the causes are different, the fact is the same. Each might have been true, because there is no direct opposition. But, however, neither is by any means true, because men were not born from the ground throughout the world, as though sprung from the teeth of some dragon, as the poets relate; but one man was formed by God, and from that one man all the earth was filled with the human race, in the same way as again took place after the deluge, which they certainly cannot deny. Therefore no assembling together of this kind took place at the beginning; and that there were never men on the earth who could not speak except those who were infants, every one who is possessed of sense will understand. Let us suppose, however, that these things are true which idle and foolish old men vainly say, that we may refute them especially by their own feelings and arguments.

If men were collected together on this account, that they might protect their weakness by mutual help, therefore we must succour man, who needs help. For, since men entered into and contracted fellowship with men for the sake of protection, either to violate or not to preserve that compact which was entered into among men from the commencement of their origin, is to be considered as the greatest impiety. For he who withdraws himself from affording assistance must also of necessity withdraw himself from receiving it; for he who refuses his aid to another thinks that he stands in need of the aid of none.

But he who withdraws and separates himself from the body at large, must live not after the custom of men, but after the manner of wild beasts. But if this cannot be done, the bond of human society is by all means to be retained, because man can in no way live without man. But the preservation of society is a mutual sharing of kind offices; that is, the affording help, that we may be able to receive it. But if, as those others assert, the assembling together of men has been caused on account of humanity itself, man ought undoubtedly to recognize man. But if those ignorant and as yet uncivilized men did this, and that, when the practice of speaking was not yet established, what must we think ought to be done by men who are polished, and connected together by interchange of conversation and all business, who, being accustomed to the society of men, cannot endure solitude?

Therefore humanity is to be preserved, if we wish rightly to be called men. But what else is this preservation of humanity than the loving a man because he is a man, and the same as ourselves? Therefore discord and dissension are not in accordance with the nature of man; and that expression of Cicero is true, which says that man, while he is obedient to nature, cannot injure man. Therefore, if it is contrary to nature to injure a man, it must be in accordance with nature to benefit a man; and he who does not do this deprives himself of the title of a man, because it is the duty of humanity to succour the necessity and peril of a man. I ask, therefore, of those who do not think it the part of a wise man to be prevailed upon and to pity, if a man were seized by some beast, and were to implore the aid of an armed man, whether they think that he ought to be succoured or not? They are not so shameless as to deny that that ought to be done which humanity demands and requires. Also, if any one were surrounded by fire, crushed by the downfall of a building, plunged in the sea, or carried away by a river, would they think it the duty of a man not to assist him? They themselves are not men if they think so; for no one can fail to be liable to dangers of this kind. Yes, truly, they will say that it is the part of a human being, and of a brave man too, to preserve one who was on the point of perishing. . . .

## 5. AMBROSE (c. 339–397)

While Bishop Ambrose of Milan is perhaps best known for his role in Augustine's conversion, he also anticipates Augustine's attitude to war. Having previously served as the local Roman governor, Ambrose used his contacts with the imperial authorities as a preacher of righteousness. His letters recognize the necessity of war for the sake of a secure peace (just intent), but he unhesitatingly denounces the needless bloodshed at the siege of Thessalonica. His stand illustrates the church's growing role as social prophet and its insistence on justice and compassion in the conduct of war.

### TO THE EMPEROR THEODOSIUS

Letter 51, trans. H. De Romestin, in *The Nicene and Post-Nicene Fathers* (2nd series) 10.

1. The memory of your old friendship is pleasant to me, and I gratefully call to mind the kindnesses which, in reply to my frequent intercessions, you have most graciously conferred on others. Whence it may be inferred that I did not from any ungrateful feeling avoid meeting you on your arrival, which I had always before earnestly desired. And I will now briefly set forth the reason for my acting as I did.

2. I saw that from me alone in your court the natural right of hearing was withdrawn, so that I was deprived also of the office of speaking; for you were frequently troubled because certain matters which had been decided in your consistory had come to my knowledge. I, therefore, am without a part in the common privilege, since the Lord Jesus says: "That nothing is hidden, which shall not be made known." I, therefore, as reverently as I could, complied with the imperial will, and took heed that neither yourself should have any reason for displeasure, when I effected that nothing should be related to me of the imperial decrees; and that I, when present, either should not hear, through fear of all others, and so incur the reputation of

55

connivance, or should hear in such a fashion that my ears might be open, my utterance prevented, that I might not be able to utter what I had heard lest I should injure and bring in peril those who had incurred the suspicion of treachery.

3. What, then, could I do? Should I not hear? But I could not close my ears with the wax of the old fables. Should I utter what I heard? But I was bound to be on my guard in my words against that which I feared in your commands, namely, lest some deed of blood should be committed. Should I keep silence? But then my conscience would be bound, my utterance taken away, which would be the most wretched condition of all. And where would be that text? If the priest speak not to him that erreth, he who errs shall die in his sin, and the priest shall be liable to the penalty because he warned not the erring.

4. Listen, august Emperor. I cannot deny that you have a zeal for the faith; I do confess that you have the fear of God. But you have a natural vehemence, which, if any one endeavours to soothe, you quickly turn to mercy; if any one stirs up, you rouse it so much more that you can scarcely restrain it. Would that if no one soothe it, at least no one may inflame it! To yourself I willingly entrust it, you restrain yourself, and overcome your natural vehemence by the love of piety.

5. This vehemence of yours I preferred to commend privately to your own consideration, rather than possibly raise it by any action of mine in public. And so I have preferred to be somewhat wanting in duty rather than in humility, and that others should rather think me wanting in priestly authority than that you should find me lacking in most loving reverence, that having restrained your vehemence your power of deciding on your counsel should not be weakened. I excuse myself by bodily sickness, which was in truth severe, and scarcely to be lightened but by great care. Yet I would rather have died than not wait two or three days for your arrival. But it was not possible for me to do so.

6. There was that done in the city of the Thessalonians of which no similar record exists, which I was not able to prevent happening; which, indeed, I had before said would be most atrocious when I so often petitioned against it, and that which you yourself show by revoking it too late you consider to be grave, this I could not extenuate when done. When it was first heard of, a synod had met because of the arrival of the Gallican Bishops. There was not one who did

not lament it, not one who thought lightly of it; your being in fellowship with Ambrose was no excuse for your deed. Blame for what had been done would have been heaped more and more on me, had no one said that your reconciliation to our God was necessary.

7. Are you ashamed, O Emperor, to do that, which the royal prophet David, the forefather of Christ, according to the flesh, did? To him it was told how the rich man who had many flocks seized and killed the poor man's one lamb, because of the arrival of his guest, and recognizing that he himself was being condemned in the tale, for that he himself had done it, he said: "I have sinned against the Lord." Bear it, then, without impatience, O Emperor, if it be said to you: "You have done that which was spoken of to King David by the prophet. For if you listen obediently to this, and say: "I have sinned against the Lord," if you repeat those words of the royal prophet: "O come let us worship and fall down before Him, and mourn before the Lord our God, Who made us," it shall be said to you also: "Since thou repentest, the Lord putteth away thy sin, and thou shalt not die."

8. And again, David, after he had commanded the people to be numbered, was smitten in heart, and said to the Lord: "I have sinned exceedingly, because I have commanded this, and now, O Lord, take away the iniquity of Thy servant, for I have transgressed exceedingly." And the prophet Nathan was sent again to him, to offer him the choice of three things, that he should select the one he chose—famine in the land for three years, or that he should flee for three months before his enemies, or mortal pestilence in the land for three days. And David answered: "These three things are a great strait to me, but let me fall into the hand of the Lord, for very many are His mercies, and let me not fall into the hands of man." Now his fault was that he desired to know the number of the whole of the people which was with him, which knowledge he ought to have left to God alone.

9. And, we are told, when death came upon the people, on the very first day at dinner time, when David saw the angel smiting the people, he said: "I have sinned, and I, the shepherd, have done wickedly, and this flock, what hath it done? Let Thine hand be upon me, and upon my father's house." And so it repented the Lord, and He commanded the angel to spare the people, and David to offer a sacrifice, for sacrifices were then offered for sins; sacrifices are now those of penitence. And so by that humbling of himself he became

more acceptable to God, for it is no matter of wonder that man should sin, but this is reprehensible, if he does not recognize that he has erred, and humble himself before God.

10. Holy Job, himself also powerful in this world, says: "I hid not my sin, but declared it before all the people." His son Jonathan said to the fierce King Saul himself: "Do not sin against thy servant David"; and: "Why dost thou sin against innocent blood, to slay David without a cause?" For, although he was a king, yet he would have sinned if he slew the innocent. And again, David also, when he was in possession of the kingdom, and had heard that innocent Abner had been slain by Joab, the leader of his host, said: "I am guiltless and my kingdom is guiltless henceforth and forever of the blood of Abner, the son of Ner," and he fasted for sorrow.

11. I have written this, not in order to confound you, but that the examples of these kings may stir you up to put away this sin from your kingdom, for you will do it away by humbling your soul before God. You are a man, and it has come upon you, conquer it. Sin is not done away but by tears and penitence. Neither angel can do it, nor archangel. The Lord Himself, Who alone can say, "I am with you," if we have sinned, does not forgive any but those who repent.

12. I urge, I beg, I exhort, I warn, for it is a grief to me, that you who were an example of unusual piety, who were conspicuous for clemency, who would not suffer single offenders to be put in peril, should not mourn that so many have perished. Though you have waged battle most successfully, though in other matters, too, you are worthy of praise, yet piety was ever the crown of your actions. The devil envied that which was your most excellent possession. Conquer him whilst you still possess that wherewith you may conquer. Do not add another sin to your sin by a course of action which has injured many.

13. I, indeed, though a debtor to your kindness, for which I cannot be ungrateful, that kindness which has surpassed that of many emperors, and has been equalled by one only; I, I say, have no cause for a charge of contumacy against you, but have cause for fear; I dare not offer the sacrifice if you intend to be present. Is that which is not allowed after shedding the blood of one innocent person, allowed after shedding the blood of many? I do not think so.

14. Lastly, I am writing with my own hand that which you alone may read. As I hope that the Lord will deliver me from all troubles, I have been warned, not by man, nor through man, but

plainly by Himself that this is forbidden me. For when I was anxious, in the very night in which I was preparing to set out, you appeared to me in a dream to have come into the Church, and I was not permitted to offer the sacrifice. I pass over other things, which I could have avoided, but I bore them for love of you, as I believe. May the Lord cause all things to pass peaceably. Our God gives warnings in many ways, by heavenly signs, by the precepts of the prophets; by the visions even of sinners He wills that we should understand, that we should entreat Him to take away all disturbances, to preserve peace for you emperors, that the faith and peace of the Church, whose advantage it is that emperors should be Christians and devout, may continue.

15. You certainly desire to be approved by God. "To everything there is a time," as it is written: "It is time for Thee, Lord, to work." "It is an acceptable time, O Lord." You shall then make your offering when you have received permission to sacrifice, when your offering shall be acceptable to God. Would it not delight me to enjoy the favour of the Emperor, to act according to your wish, if the case allowed it? And prayer by itself is a sacrifice, it obtains pardon, when the oblation would bring offense, for the one is a sign of humility, the other of contempt. For the Word of God Himself tells us that He prefers the performance of His commandments to the offering of sacrifice. God proclaims this, Moses declares it to the people, Paul preaches it to the Gentiles. Do that which you understand is most profitable for the time. "I prefer mercy," it is said, "rather than sacrifice." Are they not, then, rather Christians in truth who condemn their own sin, than they who think to defend it? "The just is an accuser of himself in the beginning of his words." He who accuses himself when he has sinned is just, not he who praises himself.

16. I wish, O Emperor, that before this I had trusted rather to myself, than to your habits. When I consider that you quickly pardon, and quickly revoke your sentence, as you have often done; you have been anticipated, and I have not shunned that which I needed not to fear. But thanks be to the Lord, Who willeth to chastise His servants, that He may not lose them. This I have in common with the prophets, and you shall have it in common with the saints.

17. Shall I not value the father of Gratian more than my very eyes? Your other holy pledges also claim pardon. I conferred beforehand a dear name on those to whom I bore a common love. I follow you with my love, my affection, and my prayers. If you believe me, be

guided by me; if, I say, you believe me, acknowledge what I say; if you believe me not, pardon that which I do, in that I set God before you. May you, most august Emperor, with your holy offspring, enjoy perpetual peace with perfect happiness and prosperity.

## 6. *AUGUSTINE* (354-430)

Augustine, Bishop of Hippo, lived during the barbarian invasions of the empire and died in Carthage while that city was under siege by the Vandals. The city's defender was Boniface, to whom Augustine wrote in 418 that war is not a matter of choice but a matter of necessity, forced on us by the twisted dilemmas of a sinful world. *The City of God,* which contains the first explicit Christian philosophy of history, was written to answer those who blamed the sack of Rome by the Goths in 410 on Christianity's bad influence.

Augustine's *Reply to Faustus the Manichean* argues for the continuity of Old and New Testament ethics and points out the unavoidable dilemmas caused by human sin. In addition, his distinction between act, agent, and authority is of crucial importance in assigning moral responsibility for violence.

In the *City of God* selections (all from Book 19) he argues from both natural law and the love of God that the right end of society, even in war, is peace and justice, and that authority must be exercised to this end as loving service to both men and God. War that restores peace and justice to foe as well as friend can therefore be an act of love. Augustine objects to Cicero's definition of the just state as one that gives each his due, for if God is not honored such a state cannot exist. As Paul Ramsey has shown (*War and the Christian Conscience,* chap. 2), this definition also influences Cicero's idea of a just war. Rather, the state is "an assemblage of reasonable beings bound together by a common agreement as to the objects of their love."

### TO COUNT BONIFACE

Letter 189, trans. J. G. Cunningham, in *The Nicene and Post-Nicene Fathers* (1st series) 1.

4. Do not think that it is impossible for any one to please God while engaged in active military service. Among such persons was the holy David, to whom God gave so great a testimony; among them also were many righteous men of that time; among them was also that

61

centurion who said to the Lord: "I am not worthy that Thou shouldest come under my roof, but speak the word only, and my servant shall be healed: for I am a man under authority, having soldiers under me: and I say to this man, Go, and he goeth; and to another, Come, and he cometh; and to my servant, Do this, and he doeth it"; and concerning whom the Lord said: "Verily, I say unto you, I have not found so great faith, no, not in Israel." Among them was that Cornelius to whom an angel said: "Cornelius, thine alms are accepted, and thy prayers are heard," when he directed him to send to the blessed Apostle Peter, and to hear from him what he ought to do, to which apostle he sent a devout soldier, requesting him to come to him. Among them were also the soldiers who, when they had come to be baptized by John—the sacred forerunner of the Lord, and the friend of the Bridegroom, of whom the Lord says: "Among them that are born of women there hath not risen a greater than John the Baptist"—and had inquired of him what they should do, received the answer, "Do violence to no man, neither accuse any falsely; and be content with your wages." Certainly he did not prohibit them to serve as soldiers when he commanded them to be content with their pay for the service.

5. They occupy indeed a higher place before God who, abandoning all these secular employments, serve Him with the strictest chastity; but "every one," as the apostle says, "hath his proper gift of God, one after this manner, and another after that." Some, then, in praying for you, fight against your invisible enemies; you, in fighting for them, contend against the barbarians, their visible enemies. Would that one faith existed in all, for then there would be less weary struggling, and the devil with his angels would be more easily conquered; but since it is necessary in this life that the citizens of the kingdom of heaven should be subjected to temptations among erring and impious men, that they may be exercised, and "tried as gold in the furnace," we ought not before the appointed time to desire to live with those alone who are holy and righteous, so that, by patience, we may deserve to receive this blessedness in its proper time.

6. Think, then, of this first of all, when you are arming for the battle, that even your bodily strength is a gift of God; for, considering this, you will not employ the gift of God against God. For, when faith is pledged, it is to be kept even with the enemy against whom the war is waged, how much more with the friend for whom the battle is fought! Peace should be the object of your desire; war should be

waged only as a necessity, and waged only that God may by it deliver men from the necessity and preserve them in peace. For peace is not sought in order to the kindling of war, but war is waged in order that peace may be obtained. Therefore, even in waging war, cherish the spirit of a peacemaker, that, by conquering those whom you attack, you may lead them back to the advantages of peace; for our Lord says: "Blessed are the peacemakers; for they shall be called the children of God." If, however, peace among men be so sweet as procuring temporal safety, how much sweeter is that peace with God which procures for men the eternal felicity of the angels! Let necessity, therefore, and not your will, slay the enemy who fights against you. As violence is used towards him who rebels and resists, so mercy is due to the vanquished or the captive, especially in the case in which future troubling of the peace is not to be feared.

## ACT, AGENT, AND AUTHORITY

From *Reply to Faustus the Manichean* 22, trans. R. Stothert, in *The Nicene and Post-Nicene Fathers* (1st series) 4.

73. According to the eternal law, which requires the preservation of natural order, and forbids the transgression of it, some actions have an indifferent character, so that men are blamed for presumption if they do them without being called upon, while they are deservedly praised for doing them when required. The act, the agent, and the authority for the action are all of great importance in the order of nature. For Abraham to sacrifice his son of his own accord is shocking madness. His doing so at the command of God proves him faithful and submissive. This is so loudly proclaimed by the very voice of truth, that Faustus, eagerly rummaging for some fault, and reduced at last to slanderous charges, has not the boldness to attack this action. It is scarcely possible that he can have forgotten a deed so famous, that it recurs to the mind of itself without any study or reflection, and is in fact repeated by so many tongues, and portrayed in so many places, that no one can pretend to shut his eyes or his ears to it. If, therefore, while Abraham's killing his son of his own accord would have been unnatural, his doing it at the command of God shows not only guiltless but praiseworthy compliance, why does Faustus blame Moses for spoiling the Egyptians? Your feeling of disapproval for the mere human action should be restrained by a regard for the divine sanction. Will you venture to blame God Him-

self for desiring such actions? Then "Get thee behind me, Satan, for thou understandest not the things which be of God, but those which be of men." Would that this rebuke might accomplish in you what it did in Peter, and that you might hereafter preach the truth concerning God, which you now, judging by feeble sense, find fault with! as Peter became a zealous messenger to announce to the Gentiles what he objected to at first, when the Lord spoke of it as His intention.

74. Now, if this explanation suffices to satisfy human obstinacy and perverse misinterpretation of right actions of the vast difference between the indulgence of passion and presumption on the part of men, and obedience to the command of God, who knows what to permit or to order, and also the time and the persons, and the due action or suffering in each case, the account of the wars of Moses will not excite surprise or abhorrence, for in wars carried on by divine command, he showed not ferocity but obedience; and God, in giving the command, acted not in cruelty, but in righteous retribution, giving to all what they deserved, and warning those who needed warning. What is the evil in war? Is it the death of some who will soon die in any case, that others may live in peaceful subjection? This is mere cowardly dislike, not any religious feeling. The real evils in war are love of violence, revengeful cruelty, fierce and implacable enmity, wild resistance, and the lust of power, and such like; and it is generally to punish these things, when force is required to inflict the punishment, that, in obedience to God or some lawful authority, good men undertake wars, when they find themselves in such a position as regards the conduct of human affairs, that right conduct requires them to act, or to make others act in this way. Otherwise John, when the soldiers who came to be baptized asked, What shall we do? would have replied, Throw away your arms; give up the service; never strike, or wound, or disable any one. But knowing that such actions in battle were not murderous, but authorized by law, and that the soldiers did not thus avenge themselves, but defend the public safety, he replied, "Do violence to no man, accuse no man falsely, and be content with your wages." But as the Manichaeans are in the habit of speaking evil of John, let them hear the Lord Jesus Christ Himself ordering this money to be given to Caesar, which John tells the soldiers to be content with. "Give," He says, "to Caesar the things that are Caesar's." For tribute money is given on purpose to pay the soldiers for war. Again, in the case of the centurion who said, "I am a man under authority, and have soldiers under me: and I say to one, Go, and he

goeth; and to another, Come, and he cometh; and to my servant, Do this, and he doeth it," Christ gave due praise to his faith; He did not tell him to leave the service. But there is no need here to enter on the long discussion of just and unjust wars.

75. A great deal depends on the causes for which men undertake wars, and on the authority they have for doing so; for the natural order which seeks the peace of mankind, ordains that the monarch should have the power of undertaking war if he thinks it advisable, and that the soldiers should perform their military duties in behalf of the peace and safety of the community. When war is undertaken in obedience to God, who would rebuke, or humble, or crush the pride of man, it must be allowed to be a righteous war; for even the wars which arise from human passion cannot harm the eternal well-being of God, nor even hurt His saints; for in the trial of their patience, and the chastening of their spirit, and in bearing fatherly correction, they are rather benefited than injured. No one can have any power against them but what is given him from above. For there is no power but of God, who either orders or permits. Since, therefore, a righteous man, serving it may be under an ungodly king, may do the duty belonging to his position in the state in fighting by the order of his sovereign—for in some cases it is plainly the will of God that he should fight, and in others, where this is not so plain, it may be an unrighteous command on the part of the king, while the soldier is innocent, because his position makes obedience a duty—how much more must the man be blameless who carries on war on the authority of God, of whom every one who serves Him knows that He can never require what is wrong?

76. If it is supposed that God could not enjoin warfare, because in after times it was said by the Lord Jesus Christ, "I say unto you, That ye resist not evil: but if any one strike thee on the right cheek, turn to him the left also," the answer is, that what is here required is not a bodily action, but an inward disposition. The sacred seat of virtue is the heart, and such were the hearts of our fathers, the righteous men of old. But order required such a regulation of events, and such a distinction of times, as to show first of all that even earthly blessings (for so temporal kingdoms and victory over enemies are considered to be, and these are the things which the community of the ungodly all over the world are continually begging from idols and devils) are entirely under the control and at the disposal of the one true God. Thus, under the Old Testament, the secret of the kingdom of heaven,

which was to be disclosed in due time, was veiled, and so far obscured, in the disguise of earthly promises. But when the fullness of time came for the revelation of the New Testament, which was hidden under the types of the Old, clear testimony was to be borne to the truth, that there is another life for which this life ought to be disregarded, and another kingdom for which the opposition of all earthly kingdoms should be patiently borne. . . . So in fullness of time the Son of God, made of a woman, made under the law, that He might redeem them that were under the law, made of the seed of David according to the flesh, sends His disciples as sheep into the midst of wolves, and bids them not fear those that can kill the body, but cannot kill the soul, and promises that even the body will be entirely restored, so that not a hair shall be lost. Peter's sword He orders back into its sheath, restoring as it was before the ear of His enemy that had been cut off. He says that He could obtain legions of angels to destroy His enemies, but that He must drink the cup which His Father's will had given Him. He sets the example of drinking this cup, then hands it to His followers, manifesting thus, both in word and deed, the grace of patience. Therefore God raised Him from the dead, and has given Him a name which is above every name; that in the name of Jesus every knee should bow, of things in heaven and of things in earth, and of things under the earth; and that every tongue should confess that Jesus is Lord, to the glory of God the Father. The patriarchs and prophets, then, have a kingdom in this world, to show that these kingdoms, too, are given and taken away by God: the apostles and martyrs had no kingdom here, to show the superior desirableness of the kingdom of heaven. The prophets, however, could even in those times die for the truth, as the Lord Himself says, "From the blood of Abel to the blood of Zacharia; and in these days, since the commencement of the fulfillment of what is prophesied in the psalm of Christ, under the figure of Solomon, which means the peacemaker, as Christ is our peace, "All kings of the earth shall bow to Him, all nations shall serve Him," we have seen Christian emperors, who have put all their confidence in Christ, gaining splendid victories over ungodly enemies, whose hope was in the rites of idolatry and devil-worship. . . .

78. It is therefore mere groundless calumny to charge Moses with making war, for there would have been less harm in making war of his own accord, than in not doing it when God commanded him. And to dare to find fault with God Himself for giving such a com-

mand, or not to believe it possible that a just and good God did so, shows, to say the least, an inability to consider that in the view of divine providence, which pervades all things from the highest to the lowest, time can neither add anything nor take away; but all things go, or come, or remain according to the order of nature or desert in each separate case, while in men a right will is in union with the divine law, and ungoverned passion is restrained by the order of divine law; so that a good man wills only what is commanded, and a bad man can do only what he is permitted, at the same time that he is punished for what he wills to do unjustly. Thus, in all the things which appear shocking and terrible to human feebleness, the real evil is the injustice; the rest is only the result of natural properties or of moral demerit. This injustice is seen in every case where a man loves for their own sake things which are desirable only as means to an end, and seeks for the sake of something else things which ought to be loved for themselves. For thus, as far as he can, he disturbs in himself the natural order which the eternal law requires us to observe. Again, a man is just when he seeks to use things only for the end for which God appointed them, and to enjoy God as the end of all, while he enjoys himself and his friend in God and for God. For to love in a friend the love of God is to love the friend for God. Now both justice and injustice, to be acts at all, must be voluntary; otherwise, there can be no just rewards or punishments; which no man in his senses will assert. The ignorance and infirmity which prevent a man from knowing his duty, or from doing all he wishes to do, belong to God's secret penal arrangement, and to His unfathomable judgments, for with Him there is no iniquity. Thus we are informed by the sure word of God of Adam's sin; and Scripture truly declares that in him all die, and that by him sin entered into the world, and death by sin. And our experience gives abundant evidence, that in punishment for this sin our body is corrupted, and weighs down the soul, and the clay tabernacle clogs the mind in its manifold activity; and we know that we can be freed from this punishment only by gracious interposition. So the apostle cries out in distress, "O wretched man that I am! who shall deliver me from the body of this death? The grace of God through Jesus Christ our Lord." So much we know; but the reasons for the distribution of divine judgment and mercy, why one is in this condition, and another in that, though just, are unknown. Still, we are sure that all these things are due either to the mercy or the judgment of God, while the measures and numbers and weights by which the Creator of all natural productions arranges all things are concealed from our view. For God is not the author, but He is the controller of sin; so that sinful actions, which are sinful because they are against nature, are judged and controlled, and assigned to their proper place and condition, in order that they may not bring discord and disgrace on universal nature. This being the case, and as the judgments of God and the movements of man's will contain the hidden reason why the same prosperous circumstances which some make a right use of are the ruin of others, and the same afflictions under which some give way are profitable to others, and since the whole mortal life of man upon earth is a trial, who can tell whether it may be good or bad in any particular case—in time of peace, to reign or to serve, or to be at ease or to die—or in time of war, to command or to fight, or to conquer or to be killed? At the same time, it remains true, that whatever is good is so by the divine blessing, and whatever is bad is so by the divine judgment. . . .

## THE HUMAN DILEMMA

From *The City of God* 19.5-7, trans. M. Dods, in *The Nicene and Post-Nicene Fathers* (1st series) 2.

But who can enumerate all the great grievances with which human society abounds in the misery of this mortal state? Who can weigh them? Hear how one of their comic writers makes one of his characters express the common feelings of all men in this matter: "I am married; this is one misery. Children are born to me; they are additional cares." What shall I say of the miseries of love which Terence also recounts—"slights, suspicions, quarrels, war today, peace tomorrow?" Is not human life full of such things? Do they not often occur even in honorable friendships? On all hands we experience these slights, suspicions, quarrels, war, all of which are undoubted evils; while, on the other hand, peace is a doubtful good, because we do not know the heart of our friend, and though we did know it today, we should be as ignorant of what it might be tomorrow. Who ought to be, or who are more friendly than those who live in the same family? And yet who can rely even upon this friendship, seeing that secret treachery has often broken it up, and produced enmity as bitter as the amity was sweet, or seemed sweet by the most perfect dissimulation? It is on this account that the words of Cicero so move the heart of every one, and provoke a sigh: "There are no snares more dangerous than those which lurk under the guise of duty or the name of relationship. For the man who is your declared foe you can easily baffle by precaution; but this hidden, intestine, and domestic danger not merely exists, but overwhelms you before you can foresee and examine it." It is also to this that allusion is made by the divine saying, "A man's foes are those of his own household"—words which one cannot hear without pain; for though a man have sufficient fortitude to endure it with equanimity, and sufficient sagacity to baffle the malice of a pretended friend, yet if he himself is a good man, he cannot but be greatly pained at the discovery of the perfidy of wicked men, whether they have always been wicked and merely feigned goodness, or have fallen from a better to a malicious disposition. If, then, home, the natural refuge from the ills of life, is itself not safe, what shall we say of the city, which, as it is larger, is so much the more filled with lawsuits civil and criminal, and is never free from the fear, if sometimes from the actual outbreak, of disturbing and bloody insurrections and civil wars?

What shall I say of these judgments which men pronounce on men, and which are necessary in communities, whatever outward peace they enjoy? Melancholy and lamentable judgments they are, since the judges are men who cannot discern the consciences of those at their bar, and are therefore frequently compelled to put innocent witnesses to the torture to ascertain the truth regarding the crimes of other men. What shall I say of torture applied to the accused himself? He is tortured to discover whether he is guilty, so that, though innocent, he suffers most undoubted punishment for crime that is still doubtful, not because it is proved that he committed it, but because it is not ascertained that he did not commit it. Thus the ignorance of the judge frequently involves an innocent person in suffering. And what is still more unendurable—a thing, indeed, to be bewailed, and, if that were possible, watered with fountains of tears—is this, that when the judge puts the accused to the question, that he may not unwittingly put an innocent man to death, the result of this lamentable ignorance is that this very person, whom he tortured that he might not condemn him if innocent, is condemned to death both tortured and innocent. For if he has chosen, in obedience to the philosophical instructions to the wise man, to quit this life rather than endure any longer such tortures, he declares that he has committed the crime which in fact he has not committed. And when he has been condemned and put to death, the judge is still in ignorance whether he has put to death an innocent or a guilty person, though he put the accused to the torture for the very purpose of saving himself from condemning the innocent; and consequently he has both tortured an innocent man to discover his innocence, and has put him to death without discovering it. If such darkness shrouds social life, will a wise judge take his seat on the bench or no? Beyond question he will. For human society, which he thinks it a wickedness to abandon, constrains him and compels him to this duty. And he thinks it no wickedness that innocent witnesses are tortured regarding the crimes of which other men are accused; or that the accused are put to the torture, so that they are often overcome with anguish, and, though innocent, make false confessions regarding themselves, and are punished; or that, though they be not condemned to die, they often die during, or in consequence of, the torture; or that sometimes the accusers, who perhaps have been prompted by a desire to benefit society by bringing criminals to justice, are themselves condemned through the ignorance of the judge, because they are unable to prove the truth of their accusations though they are true, and because the witnesses lie, and the accused endures the torture without being moved to confession. These numerous and important evils he does not consider sins; for the wise judge does these things, not with any intention of doing harm, but because his ignorance compels him, and because human society claims him as a judge. But though we therefore acquit the judge of malice, we must none the less condemn human life as miserable. And if he is compelled to torture and punish the innocent because his office and his ignorance constrain him, is he a happy as well as a guiltless man? Surely it were proof of more profound considerateness and finer feeling were he to recognize the misery of these necessities, and shrink from his own implication in that misery; and had he any piety about him, he would cry to God "From my necessities deliver Thou me."

After the state or city comes the world, the third circle of human society—the first being the house, and the second the city. And the world, as it is larger, so it is fuller of dangers, as the greater sea is the more dangerous. And here, in the first place, man is separated from man by the difference of languages. For if two men, each ignorant of the other's language, meet, and are not compelled to pass, but, on the contrary, to remain in company, dumb animals, though of different species, would more easily hold intercourse than they, human beings though they be. For their common nature is no help to friendliness when they are prevented by diversity of language from conveying their sentiments to one another; so that a man would more readily hold intercourse with his dog than with a foreigner. But the imperial city has endeavored to impose on subject nations not only her yoke, but her language, as a bond of peace, so that interpreters, far from being scarce, are numberless. This is true; but how many great wars, how much slaughter and bloodshed, have provided this unity! And though these are past, the end of these miseries has not yet come. For though there have never been wanting, nor are yet wanting, hostile nations beyond the empire, against whom wars have been and are waged, yet, supposing there were no such nations, the very extent of the empire itself has produced wars of a more obnoxious description—social and civil wars—and with these the whole race has been agitated, either by the actual conflict or the fear of a renewed outbreak. If I attempted to give an adequate description of these manifold disasters, these stern and lasting necessities, though I am quite unequal to the task, what limit could I set? But, say they, the wise man will wage just wars. As if he would not all the rather lament the necessity of just wars, if he remembers that he is a man; for if they were not just he would not wage them, and would therefore be delivered from all wars. For it is the wrongdoing of the opposing party which compels the wise man to wage just wars; and this wrongdoing, even though it gave rise to no war, would still be matter of grief to man because it is man's wrongdoing. Let every one, then, who thinks with pain on all these great evils, so horrible, so ruthless, acknowledge that this is misery. And if any one either endures or thinks of them without mental pain, this is a more miserable plight still, for he thinks himself happy because he has lost human feeling.

## PEACE AND NATURAL LAW

From *The City of God* 19.12-27, trans. M. Dods, in *The Nicene and Post-Nicene Fathers* (1st series) 2.

Whoever gives even moderate attention to human affairs and to our common nature, will recognize that if there is no man who does not wish to be joyful, neither is there any one who does not wish to have peace. For even they who make war desire nothing but victory—desire, that is to say, to attain to peace with glory. For what else is victory than the conquest of those who resist us? and when this is done there is peace. It is therefore with the desire for peace that wars are waged, even by those who take pleasure in exercising their warlike nature in command and battle. And hence it is obvious that peace is the end sought for by war. For every man seeks peace by waging war, but no man seeks war by making peace. For even they who intentionally interrupt the peace in which they are living have no hatred of peace, but only wish it changed into a peace that suits them better. They do not, therefore, wish to have no peace, but only one more to their mind. And in the case of sedition, when men have separated themselves from the community, they yet do not effect what they wish, unless they maintain some kind of peace with their fellow conspirators. And therefore even robbers take care to maintain peace with their comrades, that they may with greater effect and greater safety invade the peace of other men. And if an individual happen to be of such unrivalled strength, and to be so jealous of partnership, that he trusts himself with no comrades, but makes his own plots, and commits depredations and murders on his own account, yet he maintains some shadow of peace with such persons as he is unable to kill, and from whom he wishes to conceal his deeds. In his own home, too, he makes it his aim to be at peace with his wife and children, and any other members of his household; for unquestionably their prompt obedience to his every look is a source of pleasure to him. And if this be not rendered, he is angry, he chides and punishes; and even by this storm he secures the calm peace of his own home, as occasion demands. For he sees that peace cannot be maintained unless all the members of the same domestic circle be subject to one head, such as he himself is in his own house. And therefore if a city or nation offered to submit itself to him, to serve him in the same style as he had made his household serve him, he would no longer lurk in a brigand's hiding places, but lift his head in open day as a king, though the same coveteousness and wickedness should remain in him. And thus all men desire to have peace with their own circle whom they wish to govern as suits themselves. For even those whom they make war against they wish to make their own, and impose on them the laws of their own peace.

But let us suppose a man such as poetry and mythology speak of—a man so insociable and savage as to be called rather a semi-man than a man. Although, then, his kingdom was the solitude of a dreary cave, and he himself was so singularly bad-hearted that he was named   κακός , which is the Greek word for *bad;* though he had no wife to soothe him with endearing talk, no children to play with, no sons to do his bidding, no friend to enliven him with intercourse, not even his father Vulcan (though in one respect he was happier than his father, not having begotten a monster like himself); although he gave to no man, but took as he wished whatever he could, from whomsoever he could, when he could; yet in that solitary den, the floor of which, as Virgil says, was always reeking with recent slaughter, there was nothing else than peace sought, a peace in which no one should molest him, or disquiet him with any assault or alarm. With his own body he desired to be at peace, and he was satisfied only in proportion as he had this peace. For he ruled his members, and they obeyed him; and for the sake of pacifying his mortal nature, which rebelled when it needed anything, and of allaying the sedition of hunger which threatened to banish the soul from the body, he made forays, slew, and devoured, but used the ferocity and savageness he displayed in these actions only for the preservation of his own life's peace. So that, had he been willing to make with other men the same peace which he made with himself in his own cave, he would neither have been called bad, nor a monster, nor a semi-man. Or if the appearance of his body and his vomiting smoky fires frightened men from having any dealings with him, perhaps his fierce ways arose not from a desire to do mischief, but from the necessity of finding a living. But he may have had no existence, or, at least, he was not such as the poets fancifully describe him, for they had to exalt Hercules, and did so at the expense of Cacus. It is better, then, to believe that such a man or semi-man never existed, and that this, in common with many other fancies of the poets, is mere fiction. For the most savage animals (and he is said to have been almost a wild beast) encompass their own species with a ring of protecting peace. They cohabit, beget, produce, suckle, and bring up their young, though very many of them are not gregarious, but solitary—not like sheep, deer, pigeons, starlings, bees, but such as lions, foxes, eagles, bats. For what tigress does not gently purr over her cubs, and lay aside her ferocity to fondle them? What kite, solitary as he is when circling over his prey, does not seek a mate, build a nest, hatch the eggs, bring up the young birds, and maintain with the mother of his family as peaceful a domestic alliance as he can? How much more powerfully do the laws of man's nature move him to hold fellowship and maintain peace with all men so far as in him lies, since even wicked men wage war to maintain the peace of their own circle, and wish that, if possible, all men belonged to them, that all men and things might serve but one head, and might, either through love or fear, yield themselves to peace with him! It is thus that pride in its perversity apes God. It abhors equality with other men under Him; but, instead of His rule, it seeks to impose a rule of its own upon its equals. It abhors, that is to say, the just peace of God, and loves its own unjust peace; but it cannot help loving peace of one kind or other. For there is no vice so clean contrary to nature that it obliterates even the faintest traces of nature.

He, then, who prefers what is right to what is wrong, and what is well-ordered to what is perverted, sees that the peace of unjust men is not worthy to be called peace in comparison with the peace of the just. And yet even what is perverted must of necessity be in harmony with, and in dependence on, and in some part of the order of things, for otherwise it would have no existence at all. Suppose a man hangs with his head downwards, this is certainly a perverted attitude of body and arrangement of its members; for that which nature requires to be above is beneath, and *vice versa*. This perversity disturbs the peace of the body, and is therefore painful. Nevertheless the spirit is at peace with its body, and labors for its preservation, and hence the suffering; but if it is banished from the body by its pains, then, so long as the bodily framework holds together, there is in the remains a kind of peace among the members, and hence the body remains suspended. And inasmuch as the earthly body tends towards the earth, and rests on the bond by which it is suspended, it tends thus to its natural peace, and the voice of its own weight demands a place for it to rest; and though now lifeless and without feeling, it does not fall from the peace that is natural to its place in creation, whether it already has it, or is tending towards it. For if you apply embalming preparations to prevent the bodily frame from mouldering and dissolving, a kind of peace still unites part to part, and keeps the whole body in a suitable place on the earth—in other words, in a place that is at peace with the body. If, on the other hand, the body receive no such care, but be left to the natural course, it is disturbed by exhalations that do not harmonize with one another, and that offend our senses; for it is this which is perceived in putrefaction until it is assimilated to the elements of the world, and particle by particle enters into peace with them. Yet throughout this process the laws of the most high Creator and Governor are strictly observed, for it is by Him the peace of the universe is administered. For although minute animals are produced from the carcass of a larger animal, all these little atoms, by the law of the same Creator, serve the animals they belong to in peace. And although the flesh of dead animals be eaten by others, no matter where it be carried, nor what it be brought into contact with, nor what it be converted and changed into, it still is ruled by the same laws which pervade all things for the conservation of every mortal race, and which bring things that fit one another into harmony.

The peace of the body then consists in the duly proportioned arrangement of its parts. The peace of the irrational soul is the harmonious repose of the appetites, and that of the rational soul the harmony of knowledge and action. The peace of body and soul is the well-ordered and harmonious life and health of the living creature. Peace between man and God is the well-ordered obedience of faith to eternal law. Peace between man and man is well-ordered concord. Domestic peace is the well-ordered concord between those of the family who rule and those who obey. Civil peace is a similar concord among the citizens. The peace of the celestial city is the perfectly ordered and harmonious enjoyment of God, and of one another in God. The peace of all things is the tranquillity of order. Order is the distribution which allots things equal and unequal, each to its own place. And hence, though the miserable, in so far as they are such, do certainly not enjoy peace, but are severed from that tranquillity of order in which there is no disturbance, nevertheless, inasmuch as they are deservedly and justly miserable, they are by their very misery connected with order. They are not, indeed, conjoined with the blessed, but they are disjoined from them by the law of order. And though they are disquieted, their circumstances are notwithstanding adjusted to them, and consequently they have some tranquillity of order, and therefore some peace. But they are wretched because, although not wholly miserable, they are not in that place where any mixture of misery is impossible. They would, however, be more wretched if they had not that peace which arises from being in harmony with the natural order of things. When they suffer, their peace is in so far disturbed; but their peace continues in so far as they do not suffer, and in so far as their nature continues to exist. As, then, there may be life without pain, while there cannot be pain without some kind of life, so there may be peace without war, but there cannot be war without some kind of peace, because war supposes the existence of some natures to wage it, and these natures cannot exist without peace of one kind or other.

And therefore there is a nature in which evil does not or even cannot exist; but there cannot be a nature in which there is no good. Hence not even the nature of the devil himself is evil, in so far as it is nature, but it was made evil by being perverted. Thus he did not abide in the truth, but could not escape the judgment of the Truth; he did not abide in the tranquillity of order, but did not therefore escape the power of the Ordainer. The good imparted by God to his nature did not screen him from the justice of God by which order was preserved in his punishment; neither did God punish the good which He had created, but the evil which the devil had committed. God did not take back all He had imparted to his nature, but something He took and something He left, that there might remain enough to be sensible of the loss of what was taken. And this very sensibility to pain is evidence of the good which has been taken away and the good which has been left. For, were nothing good left, there could be no pain on account of the good which had been lost. For he who sins is still worse if he rejoices in his loss of righteousness. But he who is in pain, if he derives no benefit from it, mourns at least the loss of health. And as righteousness and health are both good things, and as the loss of any good thing is a matter of grief, not of joy—if, at least, there is no compensation, as spiritual righteousness may compensate for the loss of bodily health—certainly it is more suitable for a wicked man to grieve in punishment than to rejoice in his fault. As, then, the joy of a sinner who has abandoned what is good is evidence of a bad will, so his grief for the good he has lost when he is punished is evidence of a good nature. For he who laments the peace his nature has lost is stirred to do so by some relics of peace which make his nature friendly to itself. And it is very just that in the final punishment the wicked and godless should in anguish bewail the loss of the natural advantages they enjoyed, and should perceive that they were most justly taken from them by that God whose benign liberality they had despised. God, then, the most wise Creator and most just Ordainer of all natures, who placed the human race upon earth as its greatest ornament, imparted to men some good things adapted to this life, to wit, temporal peace, such as we can enjoy in this life from health and safety and human fellowship, and all things needful for the preservation and recovery of this peace, such as the objects which are accommodated to our outward senses, light, night, the air, and waters suitable for us, and everything the body requires to sustain, shelter, heal, or beautify it: and all under this most equitable condition, that every man who made a good use of these advantages suited to the peace of this mortal condition, should receive ampler and better blessings, namely, the peace of immortality, accompanied by glory and honor in an endless life made fit for the enjoyment of God and of one another in God; but that he who used the present blessings badly should both lose them and should not receive the others.

The whole use, then, of things temporal has a reference to this result of earthly peace in the earthly community, while in the city of God it is connected with eternal peace. And therefore, if we were irrational animals, we should desire nothing beyond the proper arrangement of the parts of the body and the satisfaction of the appetites—nothing, therefore, but bodily comfort and abundance of pleasures, that the peace of the body might contribute to the peace of the soul. For if bodily peace be awanting, a bar is put to the peace even of the irrational soul, since it cannot obtain the gratification of its appetites. And these two together help out the mutual peace of soul and body, the peace of harmonious life and health. For as animals, by shunning pain, show that they love bodily peace, and, by pursuing pleasure to gratify their appetites, show that they love peace of soul, so their shrinking from death is a sufficient indication of their intense love of that peace which binds soul and body in close alliance. But, as man has a rational soul, he subordinates all this which he has in common with the beasts to the peace of his rational soul, that his intellect may have free play and may regulate his actions, and that he may thus enjoy the well-ordered harmony of knowledge and action which constitutes, as we have said, the peace of the rational soul. And for this purpose he must desire to be neither molested by pain, nor disturbed by desire, nor extinguished by death, that he may arrive at some useful knowledge by which he may regulate his life and manners. But, owing to the liability of the human mind to fall into mistakes, this very pursuit of knowledge may be a snare to him unless he has a divine Master, whom he may obey without misgiving, and who may at the same time give him such help as to preserve his own freedom. And because, so long as he is in this mortal body, he is a stranger to God, he walks by faith, not by sight, and he therefore refers all peace, bodily or spiritual or both, to that peace which mortal man has with the immortal God, so that he exhibits the well-ordered obedience of faith to eternal law. But as this divine Master inculcates two precepts—the love of God and the love of our neighbor—and as in these precepts a man finds three things he has to love—God, himself, and his neighbor—and that he who loves God loves himself thereby, it follows that he must endeavor to get his neighbors to love God, since he is ordered to love his neighbor as himself. He ought to make this endeavor in behalf of his wife, his children, his household, all within his reach, even as he would wish his neighbor to do the same for him if he needed it; and consequently he will be at peace, or in well-ordered concord, with all men, as far as in him lies. And this is the order of this concord, that a man, in the first place, injure no one, and, in the second, do good to every one he can reach. Primarily, his own household are his care, for the law of nature and of society gives him readier access to them and greater opportunity of serving them. And hence the apostle says, "Now, if any provide not for his own, and specially for those of his own house, he hath denied the faith, and is worse than an infidel." This is the origin of domestic peace, or the well-ordered concord of those in the family who rule and those who obey. For they who care for the rest rule—the husband the wife, the parents the children, the masters the servants; and they who are cared for obey— the women their husbands, the children their parents, the servants their masters. But in the family of the just man who lives by faith, and is as yet a pilgrim journeying on to the celestial city, even those who rule serve whom they seem to command; for they rule not from a love of power, but from a sense of the duty they owe to others —not because they are proud of authority, but because they love mercy. . . .

But the families which do not live by faith seek their peace in the earthly advantages of this life; while the families which live by faith look for those eternal blessings which are promised, and use as pilgrims such advantages of time and of earth as do not fascinate and divert them from God, but rather aid them to endure with greater ease, and to keep down the number of those burdens of the corruptible body which weigh upon the soul. Thus the things necessary for this mortal life are used by both kinds of men and families alike, but each has its own peculiar and widely different aim in using them. The earthly city, which does not live by faith, seeks an earthly peace, and the end it proposes, in the well-ordered concord of civic obedience and rule, is the combination of men's wills to attain the things which are helpful to this life. The heavenly city, or rather the part of it which sojourns on earth and lives by faith, makes use of this peace only because it must, until this mortal condition which necessitates it shall pass away. Consequently, so long as it lives like a captive and a stranger in the earthly city, though it has already received the promise of redemption, and the gift of the Spirit as the earnest of it, it makes no scruple to obey the laws of the earthly city, whereby the things necessary for the maintenance of this mortal life are administered; and thus, as this life is common to both cities, so there is a harmony between them in regard to what belongs to it. But, as the earthly city has had some philosophers whose doctrine is condemned by the divine teaching, and who, being deceived either by their own conjectures or by demons, supposed that many gods must be invited to take an interest in human affairs, and assigned to each a separate function and a separate department—to one the body, to another the soul; and in the body itself, to one the head, to another the neck, and each of the other members to one of the gods; and in like manner, in the soul, to one god the natural capacity was assigned, to another education, to another anger, to another lust; and so the various affairs of life were assigned—cattle to one, corn to another, wine to another, oil to another, the words to another, money to another, navigation to another, wars and victories to another, marriages to another, births and fecundity to another, and other things to other gods: and as the celestial city, on the other hand, knew that one God only was to be worshipped, and that to Him alone was due that service which the Greeks call λατρεία and which can be given only to a god, it has come to pass that the two cities could not have common laws of religion, and that the heavenly city has been compelled in this matter to dissent, and to become obnoxious to those who think differently, and to stand the brunt of their anger and hatred and persecutions, except in so far as the minds of their enemies have been alarmed by the multitude of the Christians and quelled by the manifest protection of God accorded to them. This heavenly city, then, while it sojourns on earth, calls citizens out of all nations, and gathers together a society of pilgrims of all languages, not scrupling about diversities in the manners, laws, and institutions whereby earthly peace is secured and maintained, but recognizing that, however various these are, they all tend to one and the same end of earthly peace. It therefore is so far from rescinding and abolishing these diversities, that it even preserves and adopts them, so long only as no hindrance to the worship of the one supreme and true God is thus introduced. Even the heavenly city, therefore, while in its state of pilgrimage, avails itself of the peace of earth, and, so far as it can without injuring faith and godliness, desires and maintains a common agreement among men regarding the acquisition of the necessaries of life, and makes this earthly peace bear upon the peace of heaven; for this alone can be truly called and esteemed the peace of the reasonable creatures, consisting as it does in the perfectly ordered and harmonious enjoyment of God and of one another in God. When we shall have reached that peace, this mortal life shall give place to one that is eternal, and our body shall be no more this animal body which by its corruption weighs down the soul, but a spiritual body feeling no want, and in all its members subjected to the will. In its pilgrim state the heavenly city possesses this peace by faith; and by this faith it lives righteously when it refers to the attainment of that peace every good action towards God and man; for the life of the city is a social life. . . .

This, then, is the place where I should fulfill the promise I gave in the second book of this work, and explain, as briefly and clearly as possible, that if we are to accept the definitions laid down by Scipio in Cicero's *De Republica,* there never was a Roman republic; for he briefly defines a republic as the weal of the people. And if this definition be true, there never was a Roman republic, for the people's weal was never attained among the Romans. For the people, according to his definition, is an assemblage associated by a common acknowledgement of right and by a community of interests. And what he means by a common acknowledgment of right he explains at large, showing that a republic cannot be administered without justice. Where, therefore, there is no true justice there can be no right. For that which is done by right is justly done, and what is unjustly done cannot be done by right. For the unjust inventions of men are neither to be considered nor spoken of as rights; for even they themselves say that right is that which flows from the fountain of justice, and deny the definition which is commonly given by those who misconceive the matter, that right is that which is useful to the stronger party. Thus, where there is not true justice there can be no assemblage of men associated by a common acknowledgment of right, and therefore there can be no people, as defined by Scipio or Cicero; and if no people, then no weal of the people, but only of some promiscuous multitude unworthy of the name of people. Consequently, if the republic is the weal of the people, and there is no people if it be not associated by a common acknowledgment of right, and if there is no right where there is no justice, then most certainly it follows that there is no republic where there is no justice. Further, justice is that virtue which gives every one his due. Where, then, is the justice of man, when he deserts the true God and yields himself to impure demons? Is this to give every one his due? Or is he who keeps back a piece of ground from the purchaser, and gives it to a man who has no right to it, unjust, while he who keeps back himself from the God who made him, and serves wicked spirits, is just?

This same book, *De Republica*, advocates the cause of justice against injustice with great force and keenness. The pleading for injustice against justice was first heard, and it was asserted that without injustice a republic could neither increase nor even subsist, for it was laid down as an absolutely unassailable position that it is unjust for some men to rule and some to serve; and yet the imperial city to which the republic belongs cannot rule her provinces without having recourse to this injustice. It was replied in behalf of justice, that this ruling of the provinces is just, because servitude may be advantageous to the provincials, and is so when rightly administered—that is to say, when lawless men are prevented from doing harm. And further, as they became worse and worse so long as they were free, they will improve by subjection. To confirm this reasoning, there is added an eminent example drawn from nature: for "why," it is asked, "does God rule man, the soul the body, the reason the passions and other vicious parts of the soul?" This example leaves no doubt that, to some, servitude is useful; and, indeed, to serve God is useful to all. And it is when the soul serves God that it exercises a right control over the body; and in the soul itself the reason must be subject to God if it is to govern as it ought the passions and other vices. Hence, when a man does not serve God, what justice can we ascribe to him, since in this case his soul cannot exercise a just control over the body, nor his reason over his vices? And if there is no justice in such an individual, certainly there can be none in a community composed of such persons. Here, therefore, there is not that common acknowledgment of right which makes an assemblage of men a people whose affairs we call a republic. . . .

But if we discard this definition of a people, and, assuming another, say that a people is an assemblage of reasonable beings bound together by a common agreement as to the objects of their love, then, in order to discover the character of any people, we have only to observe what they love. Yet whatever it loves, if only it is an assemblage of reasonable beings and not of beasts, and is bound together by an agreement as to the objects of love, it is reasonably called a people; and it will be a superior people in proportion as it is bound together by higher interests, inferior in proportion as it is bound together by lower. According to this definition of ours, the Roman people is a people, and its weal is without doubt a commonwealth or republic. But what its tastes were in its early and subsequent days, and how it declined into sanguinary seditions and then to social and civil wars, and so burst asunder or rotted off the bond of concord in which the health of a people consists, history shows, and in the preceding books I have related at large. And yet I would not on this account say either that it was not a people, or that its administration was not a republic, so long as there remains an assemblage of reasonable beings bound together by a common agreement as to the objects of love. But what I say of this people and of this republic I must be understood to think and say of the Athenians or any Greek state, of the Egyptians, of the early Assyrian Babylon, and of every other nation, great or small, which had a public government. For, in general, the city of the ungodly, which did not obey the command of God that it should offer no sacrifice save to Him alone, and, which, therefore, could not give to the soul its proper command over the body, nor to the reason its just authority over the vices, is void of true justice.

For though the soul may seem to rule the body admirably, and the reason the vices, if the soul and reason do not themselves obey God, as God has commanded them to serve Him, they have no proper authority over the body and the vices. For what kind of mistress of the body and the vices can that mind be which is ignorant of the true God, and which, instead of being subject to His authority, is prostituted to the corrupting influences of the most vicious demons? It is for this reason that the virtues which it seems to itself to possess, and by which it restrains the body and the vices that it may obtain and keep what it desires, are rather vices than virtues so long as there is no reference to God in the matter. For although some suppose that virtues which have a reference only to themselves, and are desired only on their own account, are yet true and genuine virtues, the fact is that even they are inflated with pride, and are therefore to be reckoned vices rather than virtues. For as that which gives life to the flesh is not derived from flesh, but is above it, so that which gives blessed life to man is not derived from man, but is something above him; and what I say of man is true of every celestial power and virtue whatsoever.

Wherefore, as the life of the flesh is the soul, so the blessed life of man is God, of whom the sacred writings of the Hebrews say, "Blessed is the people whose God is the Lord." Miserable, therefore, is the people which is alienated from God. Yet even this people has a peace of its own which is not to be lightly esteemed, though, indeed, it shall not in the end enjoy it, because it makes no good use of it before the end. But it is our interest that it enjoy this peace meanwhile in this life; for as long as the two cities are commingled, we also enjoy the peace of Babylon. For from Babylon the people of God is so freed that it meanwhile sojourns in its company. And therefore the apostle also admonished the Church to pray for kings and those in authority, assigning as the reason, "that we may live a quiet and tranquil life in all godliness and love." And the prophet Jeremiah, when predicting the captivity that was to befall the ancient people of God, and giving them the divine command to go obediently to Babylonia, and thus serve their God, counselled them also to pray for Babylonia, saying, "In the peace thereof shall ye have peace"—the temporal peace which the good and the wicked together enjoy.

But the peace which is peculiar to ourselves we enjoy now with God by faith, and shall hereafter enjoy eternally with Him by sight. But the peace which we enjoy in this life, whether common to all or peculiar to ourselves, is rather the solace of our misery than the positive enjoyment of felicity. . . . But, in that final peace to which all our righteousness has reference, and for the sake of which it is maintained, as our nature shall enjoy a sound immortality and incorruption, and shall have no more vices, and as we shall experience no resistance either from ourselves or from others, it will not be necessary that reason should rule vices which no longer exist, but God shall rule the man, and the soul shall rule the body, with a sweetness and facility suitable to the felicity of a life which is done with bondage. And this condition shall there be eternal, and we shall be assured of its eternity; and thus the peace of this blessedness and the blessedness of this peace shall be the supreme good.

# III. CHRISTIANS AND INFIDELS

With the breakdown of the Carolingian Empire in the tenth century, a movement originated among the churches of Aquitaine to arrest the fighting among feudal barons and their preying on the people. Means of restraint were introduced, such as public censures and negotiated pacts of peace that stressed the sacredness of Christian lives and the immunity of non-combatants. This "Peace of God" movement spread throughout Europe.

A parallel development was the "Truce of God," a suspension of hostilities on certain "days of rest." Moreover, the Lateran Council of 1139 established a weekly truce from Wednesday sunset to Monday sunrise and for the whole of Advent.

But these restrictions applied only to fighting between Christians, not to warfare against infidels. The Crusades were regarded as holy wars, acts of divine vengeance, and were marked by needless bloodshed. Thomas Aquinas brought the universal principles of natural law and of love to bear on war in general, and on this basis the sixteenth century theologian Francisco de Vitoria was able to elaborate laws of war that protected all men equally, whether infidels or Christians.

For further reading:

Allen, J. W. *Political Thought in the Sixteenth Century*. Barnes & Noble, 1957.
Gilby, T. *The Political Thought of Thomas Aquinas*. University of Chicago Press, 1958.
Hamilton, B. *Political Thought in Sixteenth Century Spain*. Clarendon Press, 1963.
O'Connor, D. J. *Aquinas and Natural Law*. Macmillan, 1967.
Scott, J. B. *The Spanish Origin of International Law*. Georgetown Unisity Press, 1928.
Tooke, J. D. *The Just War in Aquinas and Grotius*. S.P.C.K., 1965.

## 1. BERNARD OF CLAIRVAUX (1090–1153)

An ambivalent figure, the famous Cistercian abbott of Clairvaux played a key role in the Peace of God, arbitrating disputes and serving as peacemaker among Christians on a number of occasions. But he supported war against infidels with equal ardor. The following letter to the English people, also sent to the clergy and people of Eastern France and Bavaria, expresses the militancy with which he preached the Second Crusade.

### A HOLY WAR

Letter 391 in *The Letters of St. Bernard of Clairvaux,* trans. and ed. B. S. James (1953).

I address myself to you, the people of England, in the cause of Christ, in whom lies your salvation. I say this so that the warrant of the Lord and my zeal in his interests may excuse my hardihood in addressing you. I am a person of small account, but my desire for you in Christ is not small. This is my reason and motive for writing, this is why I make bold to address you all by letter. I would have preferred to do so by word of mouth had I but the strength to come to you as I desire.

2. Now is the acceptable time, now is the day of abundant salvation. The earth is shaken because the Lord of heaven is losing his land, the land in which he appeared to men, in which he lived amongst men for more than thirty years; the land made glorious by his miracles, holy by his blood; the land in which the flowers of his resurrection first blossomed. And now, for our sins, the enemy of the Cross has begun to lift his sacrilegious head there, and to devastate with the sword that blessed land, the land of promise. Alas, if there should be none to withstand him, he will soon invade the city of the living God, overturn the arsenal of our redemption, and defile the holy places which have been adorned by the blood of the immaculate lamb. They have cast their greedy eyes especially on the holy sanctuaries

of our Christian Religion, and they long particularly to violate that couch on which, for our sakes, the Lord of our life fell asleep in death.

3. What are you doing, you mighty men of valour? What are you doing, you servants of the Cross? Will you thus cast holy things to dogs, pearls before swine? How great a number of sinners have here confessed with tears and obtained pardon for their sins since the time when these holy precincts were cleansed of pagan filth by the swords of our fathers! The evil one sees this and is enraged, he gnashes his teeth and withers away in fury. He stirs up his vessels of wrath so that if they do but once lay hands upon these holy places there shall be no sign or trace of piety left. Such a catastrophe would be a source of appalling grief for all time, but it would also be a source of confusion and endless shame for our generation. What think you, my brethren? Is the hand of the Lord shortened and is he now powerless to work salvation, so that he must call upon us, petty worms of the earth, to save and restore to him his heritage? Could he not send more than twelve legions of angels, or even just say the word and save his land? Most certainly he has the power to do this whenever he wishes, but I tell you that God is trying you. "He looks down from heaven at the race of men, to find one soul that reflects, and makes God its aim," one soul that sorrows for him. For God has pity on his people and on those who have grievously fallen away and has prepared for them a means of salvation. Consider with what care he plans our salvation, and be amazed. Look, sinners, at the depths of his pity, and take courage. He does not want your death but rather that you should turn to him and live. So he seeks not to overthrow you but to help you. When Almighty God so treats murderers, thieves, adulterers, perjurers, and such like, as persons able to find righteousness in his service, what is it but an act of exquisite courtesy all God's own? Do not hesitate. God is good, and were he intent on your punishment he would not have asked of you this present service or indeed have accepted it even had you offered it. Again I say consider the Almighty's goodness and pay heed to his plans of mercy. He puts himself under obligation to you, or rather feigns to do so, so that he can help you to satisfy your obligations towards himself. He puts himself in your debt so that, in return for your taking up arms in his cause, he can reward you with pardon for your sins and everlasting glory. I call blessed the generation that can seize an opportunity of such rich indulgence as this, blessed to be alive in this year of jubilee,

this year of God's choice. The blessing is spread throughout the whole world, and all the world is flocking to receive this badge of immortality.

4. Your land is well known to be rich in young and vigorous men. The world is full of their praises, and the renown of their courage is on the lips of all. Gird yourselves therefore like men and take up arms with joy and with zeal for your Christian name, in order to "take vengeance on the heathen, and curb the nations." For how long will your men continue to shed Christian blood; for how long will they continue to fight amongst themselves? You attack each other, you slay each other and by each other you are slain. What is this savage craving of yours? Put a stop to it now, for it is not fighting but foolery. Thus to risk both soul and body is not brave but shocking, is not strength but folly. But now, O mighty soldiers, O men of war, you have a cause for which you can fight without danger to your souls; a cause in which to conquer is glorious and for which to die is gain.

5. But to those of you who are merchants, men quick to seek a bargain, let me point out the advantages of this great opportunity. Do not miss them. Take up the sign of the Cross and you will find indulgence for all the sins which you humbly confess. The cost is small, the reward is great. Venture with devotion and the gain will be God's kingdom. They do well therefore who have taken up this heavenly sign, and they also will do well, and profit themselves, who hasten to take up what will prove to be for them a sign of salvation.

6. For the rest, not I but the Apostle warns you, brethren, not to believe every spirit. I have heard with great joy of the zeal for God's glory which burns in your midst, but your zeal needs the timely restraint of knowledge. The Jews are not to be persecuted, killed or even put to flight. Ask anyone who knows the Sacred Scriptures what he finds foretold of the Jews in the psalm. "Not for their destruction do I pray," it says. The Jews are for us the living words of Scripture, for they remind us always of what our Lord suffered. They are dispersed all over the world so that by expiating their crime they may be everywhere the living witnesses of our redemption. Hence the same psalm adds, "only let thy power disperse them." And so it is: dispersed they are. Under Christian princes they endure a hard captivity, but "they only wait for the time of their deliverance." Finally we are told by the Apostle that when the time is ripe all Israel shall be saved. But those who die before will remain in death. I will

not mention those Christian money lenders, if they can be called Christian, who, where there are no Jews, act, I grieve to say, in a manner worse than any Jew. If the Jews are utterly wiped out, what will become of our hope for their promised salvation, their eventual conversion? If the pagans were similarly subjugated to us then, in my opinion, we should wait for them rather than seek them out with swords. But as they have now begun to attack us, it is necessary for those of us who do not carry a sword in vain to repel them with force. It is an act of Christian piety both "to vanquish the proud" and also "to spare the subjected," especially those for whom we have a law and a promise, and whose flesh was shared by Christ whose name be for ever blessed.

## 2. *THOMAS AQUINAS* (1225-1274)

On the subject of war, as on many other topics, Aquinas unites the natural law tradition with a biblical ethic. Significantly enough, the two principal contexts within which he discusses the subject are the judicial precepts of the Jewish law and the virtue of love (*charitas*). The former briefly treats hostile relations with foreigners on the analogy of Jewish relations with their pagan neighbors, while the latter lays down three "just war" principles (proper authority, just cause, and just intention) and raises the question of just means. His responses to pacifist objections should be read in conjunction with his exemption of clergy from combat, for he uses the "two vocations" argument of patristic pacifism to exempt those with sacred callings. Other germinal comments are made about self-defense, double intention in killing, and rebellion.

Aquinas' ethic, like much subsequent discussion of war, depends on the view that laws of war and all essential "laws of nations" are rooted in the eternal wisdom of God and in the order of creation. The selections accordingly begin with a discussion of law.

## VARIOUS KINDS OF LAW

From *Summa Theologica* 1-2, Q. 91, trans. Fathers of English Dominican Province.

### FIRST ARTICLE
#### WHETHER THERE IS AN ETERNAL LAW?

*We proceed thus to the First Article:—*

*Objection* 1. It would seem that there is no eternal law. Because every law is imposed on someone. But there was not someone from eternity on whom a law could be imposed: since God alone was from eternity. Therefore no law is eternal.

*Obj.* 2. Further, promulgation is essential to law. But promulgation could not be from eternity: because there was no one to whom it could be promulgated from eternity. Therefore no law can be eternal.

*Obj.* 3. Further, a law implies order to an end. But nothing ordained to an end is eternal: for the last end alone is eternal. Therefore no law is eternal.

*On the contrary,* Augustine says (*De Lib. Arb.* 1. 6): *That Law which is the Supreme Reason cannot be understood to be otherwise than unchangeable and eternal.*

*I answer that,* As stated above (Q. 90, A. 1 *ad* 2; AA. 3, 4), a law is nothing else but a dictate of practical reason emanating from the ruler who governs a perfect community. Now it is evident, granted that the world is ruled by Divine Providence, as was stated in the First Part (Q. 22, AA. 1, 2), that the whole community of the universe is governed by Divine Reason. Wherefore the very Idea of the government of things in God the Ruler of the universe, has the nature of a law. And since the Divine Reason's conception of things is not subject to time but is eternal, according to Prov. 8:23, therefore it is that this kind of law must be called eternal.

*Reply Obj.* 1. Those things that are not in themselves, exist with God, inasmuch as they are foreknown and preordained by Him, according to Rom. 4:17: *Who calls those things that are not, as those that are.* Accordingly the eternal concept of the Divine law bears the character of an eternal law, in so far as it is ordained by God to the government of things foreknown by Him.

*Reply Obj.* 2. Promulgation is made by word of mouth or in writing; and in both ways the eternal law is promulgated: because both the Divine Word and the writing of the Book of Life are eternal. But the promulgation cannot be from eternity on the part of the creature that hears or reads.

*Reply Obj.* 3. The law implies order to the end actively, in so far as it directs certain things to the end; but not passively—that is to say, the law itself is not ordained to the end—except accidentally, in a governor whose end is extrinsic to him, and to which end his law must needs be ordained. But the end of the Divine government is God Himself, and His law is not distinct from Himself. Wherefore the eternal law is not ordained to another end.

## SECOND ARTICLE

### WHETHER THERE IS IN US A NATURAL LAW?

*We proceed thus to the Second Article:—*
*Objection* 1. It would seem that there is no natural law in us. Because man is governed sufficiently by the eternal law: for Augustine says (*De Lib. Arb.* 1) that *the eternal law is that by which it is right that all things should be most orderly.* But nature does not abound in superfluities as neither does she fail in necessaries. Therefore no law is natural to man.

*Obj.* 2. Further, by the law man is directed, in his acts, to the end, as stated above (Q. 90, A. 2). But the directing of human acts to their end is not a function of nature, as is the case in irrational creatures, which act for an end solely by their natural appetite; whereas man acts for an end by his reason and will. Therefore no law is natural to man.

*Obj.* 3. Further, the more a man is free, the less is he under the law. But man is freer than all the animals, on account of his free will, with which he is endowed above all other animals. Since therefore other animals are not subject to a natural law, neither is man subject to a natural law.

*On the contrary,* A gloss on Rom. 2:14: *When the Gentiles, who have not the law, do by nature those things that are of the law,* comments as follows: *Although they have no written law, yet they have the natural law, whereby each one knows, and is conscious of, what is good and what is evil.*

*I answer that,* As stated above (Q. 90, A. 1 *ad* 1), law, being a rule and measure, can be in a person in two ways: in one way, as in him that rules and measures; in another way, as in that which is ruled and measured, since a thing is ruled and measured, in so far as it partakes of the rule or measure. Wherefore, since all things subject to Divine providence are ruled and measured by the eternal law, as was stated above (A. 1); it is evident that all things partake somewhat of the eternal law, in so far as, namely, from its being imprinted on them, they derive their respective inclinations to their proper acts and ends. Now among all others, the rational creature is subject to Divine providence in the most excellent way, in so far as it partakes of a share of providence, by being provident both for itself and for others.

Wherefore it has a share of the Eternal Reason, whereby it has a natural inclination to its proper act and end: and this participation of the eternal law in the rational creature is called the natural law. Hence the Psalmist after saying (Ps. 4:6): *Offer up the sacrifice of justice,* as though someone asked what the works of justice are, adds: *Many say, Who showeth us good things?* in answer to which question he says: *The light of Thy countenance, O Lord, is signed upon us:* thus implying that the light of natural reason, whereby we discern what is good and what is evil, which is the function of the natural law, is nothing else than an imprint on us of the Divine light. It is therefore evident that the natural law is nothing else than the rational creature's participation of the eternal law.

*Reply Obj.* 1. This argument would hold, if the natural law were something different from the eternal law: whereas it is nothing but a participation thereof, as stated above.

*Reply Obj.* 2. Every act of reason and will in us is based on that which is according to nature, as stated above (Q. 10, A. 1): for every act of reasoning is based on principles that are known naturally, and every act of appetite in respect of the means is derived from the natural appetite in respect of the last end. Accordingly the first direction of our acts to their end must needs be in virtue of the natural law.

*Reply Obj.* 3. Even irrational animals partake in their own way of the Eternal Reason, just as the rational creature does. But because the rational creature partakes thereof in an intellectual and rational manner, therefore the participation of the eternal law in the rational creature is properly called a law, since a law is something pertaining to reason, as stated above (Q. 90, A. 1). Irrational creatures, however, do not partake thereof in a rational manner, wherefore there is no participation of the eternal law in them, except by way of similitude.

### THIRD ARTICLE

#### WHETHER THERE IS A HUMAN LAW?

*We proceed thus to the Third Article:—*

*Objection* 1. It would seem that there is not a human law. For the natural law is a participation of the eternal law, as stated above (A. 2). Now through the eternal law *all things are most orderly,* as Augustine states (*De Lib. Arb.* 1. 6). Therefore the natural law suf-

fices for the ordering of all human affairs. Consequently there is no
need for a human law.

*Obj.* 2. Further, a law bears the character of a measure, as
stated above (Q. 90, A. 1). But human reason is not a measure of
things, but vice versa, as stated in *Metaph.* 10, text 5. Therefore no
law can emanate from human reason.

*Obj.* 3. Further, a measure should be most certain, as stated in
*Metaph.* 10, text 3. But the dictates of human reason in matters of
conduct are uncertain, according to Wis. 9:14: *The thoughts of mortal
men are fearful, and our counsels uncertain.* Therefore no law can
emanate from human reason.

*On the contrary,* Augustine (*De Lib. Arb.* 1. 6) distinguishes two
kinds of law, the one eternal, the other temporal, which he calls
human.

*I answer that,* As stated above (Q. 90, A. 1, *ad* 2), a law is a
dictate of the practical reason. Now it is to be observed that the same
procedure takes place in the practical and in the speculative reason:
for each proceeds from principles to conclusions, as stated above (*ibid.*).
Accordingly we conclude that just as, in the speculative reason, from
naturally known indemonstrable principles, we draw the conclusions
of the various sciences, the knowledge of which is not imparted to
us by nature, but acquired by the efforts of reason, so too it is from
the precepts of the natural law, as from general and indemonstrable
principles, that the human reason needs to proceed to the more particular determination of certain matters. These particular determinations, devised by human reason, are called human laws, provided the
other essential conditions of law be observed, as stated above (Q. 90,
AA. 2, 3, 4). Wherefore Tully says in his *Rhetoric* that *justice has
its source in nature; thence certain things came into custom by reason
of their utility; afterwards these things which emanated from nature
and were approved by custom, were sanctioned by fear and reverence
for the law.*

*Reply Obj.* 1. The human reason cannot have a full participation of the dictate of the Divine Reason, but according to its own
mode, and imperfectly. Consequently, as on the part of the speculative reason, by a natural participation of Divine Wisdom, there is in
us the knowledge of certain general principles, but not proper knowledge of each single truth, such as that contained in the Divine Wisdom; so too, on the part of the practical reason, man has a natural
participation of the eternal law, according to certain general prin-

ciples, but not as regards the particular determinations of individual cases, which are, however, contained in the eternal law. Hence the need for human reason to proceed further to sanction them by law.

*Reply Obj. 2.* Human reason is not, of itself, the rule of things: but the principles impressed on it by nature, are general rules and measures of all things relating to human conduct, whereof the natural reason is the rule and measure, although it is not the measure of things that are from nature.

*Reply Obj. 3.* The practical reason is concerned with practical matters, which are singular and contingent: but not with necessary things, with which the speculative reason is concerned. Wherefore human laws cannot have that inerrancy that belongs to the demonstrated conclusions of sciences. Nor is it necessary for every measure to be altogether unerring and certain, but according as it is possible in its own particular genus.

## FOURTH ARTICLE

### WHETHER THERE WAS ANY NEED FOR A DIVINE LAW?

*We proceed thus to the Fourth Article:—*

*Objection 1.* It would seem that there was no need for a Divine law. Because, as stated above (A. 2), the natural law is a participation in us of the eternal law. But the eternal law is a Divine law, as stated above (A. 1). Therefore there is no need for a Divine law in addition to the natural law, and human laws derived therefrom.

*Obj. 2.* Further, it is written (Ecclus. 15:14) that *God left man in the hand of his own counsel.* Now counsel is an act of reason, as stated above (Q. 14, A. 1). Therefore man was left to the direction of his reason. But a dictate of human reason is a human law as stated above (A. 3). Therefore there is no need for man to be governed also by a Divine law.

*Obj. 3.* Further, human nature is more self-sufficing than irrational creatures. But irrational creatures have no Divine Law besides the natural inclination impressed on them. Much less, therefore, should the rational creature have a Divine law in addition to the natural law.

*On the contrary,* David prayed God to set His law before him, saying (Ps. 118:33): *Set before me for a law the way of Thy justifications, O Lord.*

*I answer that,* Besides the natural and the human law it was necessary for the directing of human conduct to have a Divine law. And this for four reasons. First, because it is by law that man is directed how to perform his proper acts in view of his last end. And indeed if man were ordained to no other end than that which is proportionate to his natural faculty, there would be no need for man to have any further direction on the part of his reason, besides the natural law and human law which is derived from it. But since man is ordained to an end of eternal happiness which is inproportionate to man's natural faculty, as stated above (Q. 5, A. 5), therefore it was necessary that, besides the natural and the human law, man should be directed to his end by a law given by God.

Secondly, because, on account of the uncertainty of human judgment, especially on contingent and particular matters, different people form different judgments on human acts; whence also different and contrary laws result. In order, therefore, that man may know without any doubt what he ought to do and what he ought to avoid, it was necessary for man to be directed in his proper acts by a law given by God, for it is certain that such a law cannot err.

Thirdly, because man can make laws in those matters of which he is competent to judge. But man is not competent to judge of interior movements, that are hidden, but only of exterior acts which appear: and yet for the perfection of virtue it is necessary for man to conduct himself aright in both kinds of acts. Consequently human law could not sufficiently curb and direct interior acts; and it was necessary for this purpose that a Divine law should supervene.

Fourthly, because as Augustine says (De Lib. Arb. 1. 5, 6), human law cannot punish or forbid all evil deeds: since while aiming at doing away with all evils, it would do away with many good things, and would hinder the advance of the common good, which is necessary for human intercourse. In order, therefore, that no evil might remain unforbidden and unpunished, it was necessary for the Divine law to supervene, whereby all sins are forbidden.

And these four causes are touched upon in Ps. 118:8, where it is said: *The law of the Lord is unspotted,* i.e., allowing no foulness of sin; *converting souls,* because it directs not only exterior, but also interior acts; *the testimony of the Lord is faithful,* because of the certainty of what is true and right; *giving wisdom to little ones,* by directing man to an end supernatural and Divine.

*Reply Obj.* 1. By the natural law the eternal law is participated proportionately to the capacity of human nature. But to his supernatural end man needs to be directed in a yet higher way. Hence the additional law given by God, whereby man shares more perfectly in the eternal law.

*Reply Obj.* 2. Counsel is a kind of inquiry: hence it must proceed from some principles. Nor is it enough for it to proceed from principles imparted by nature, which are the precepts of the natural law, for the reasons given above: but there is need for certain additional principles, namely, the precepts of the Divine law.

*Reply Obj.* 3. Irrational creatures are not ordained to an end higher than that which is proportionate to their natural powers: consequently the comparison fails.

From *Summa Theologica* 1-2, Q. 94.

SECOND ARTICLE

WHETHER THE NATURAL LAW CONTAINS SEVERAL PRECEPTS,
OR ONE ONLY?

*We proceed thus to the Second Article:—*

*Objection* 1. It would seem that the natural law contains, not several precepts, but one only. For law is a kind of precept, as stated above (Q. 92, A. 2). If therefore there were many precepts of the natural law, it would follow that there are also many natural laws.

*Obj.* 2. Further, the natural law is consequent to human nature. But human nature, as a whole, is one; though, as to its parts, it is manifold. Therefore, either there is but one precept of the law of nature, on account of the unity of nature as a whole; or there are many, by reason of the number of parts of human nature. The result would be that even things relating to the inclination of the concupiscible faculty belong to the natural law.

*Obj.* 3. Further, law is something pertaining to reason, as stated above (Q. 90, A. 1). Now reason is but one in man. Therefore there is only one precept of the natural law.

*On the contrary,* The precepts of the natural law in man stand in relation to practical matters, as the first principles to matters of demonstration. But there are several first indemonstrable principles. Therefore there are also several precepts of the natural law.

*I answer that,* As stated above (Q. 91, A. 3), the precepts of the natural law are to the practical reason, what the first principles of demonstrations are to the speculative reason; because both are self-evident principles. Now a thing is said to be self-evident in two ways: first, in itself; secondly, in relation to us. Any proposition is said to be self-evident in itself, if its predicate is contained in the notion of the subject: although, to one who knows not the definition of the subject, it happens that such a proposition is not self-evident. For instance, this proposition, *Man is a rational being,* is, in its very nature, self-evident, since who says *man,* says *a rational being:* and yet to one who knows not what a man is, this proposition is not self-evident. Hence it is that, as Boethius says, certain axioms or propositions are universally self-evident to all; and such are those propositions whose terms are known to all, as *Every whole is greater than its part,* and, *Things equal to one and the same are equal to one another.* But some propositions are self-evident only to the wise, who understand the meaning of the terms of such propositions: thus to one who understands that an angel is not a body, it is self-evident that an angel is not circumscriptively in a place: but this is not evident to the unlearned, for they cannot grasp it.

Now a certain order is to be found in those things that are apprehended universally. For that which, before aught else, falls under apprehension, is *being,* the notion of which is included in all things whatsoever a man apprehends. Wherefore the first indemonstrable principle is that *the same thing cannot be affirmed and denied at the same time,* which is based on the notion of *being* and *not-being:* and on this principle all others are based, as is stated in *Metaph.* 4, text 9. Now as *being* is the first thing that falls under the apprehension simply, so *good* is the first thing that falls under the apprehension of the practical reason, which is directed to action: since every agent acts for an end under the aspect of good. Consequently the first principle in the practical reason is one founded on the notion of good, viz., that *good is that which all things seek after.* Hence this is the first precept of law, that *good is to be done and pursued, and evil is to be avoided.* All other precepts of the natural law are based upon this: so that whatever the practical reason naturally apprehends as man's good (or evil) belongs to the precepts of the natural law as something to be done or avoided.

Since, however, good has the nature of an end, and evil, the nature of a contrary, hence it is that all those things to which man has a natural inclination, are naturally apprehended by reason as being good, and consequently as objects of pursuit, and their contraries as evil, and objects of avoidance. Wherefore according to the order of natural inclinations, is the order of the precepts of the natural law. Because in man there is first of all an inclination to good in accordance with the nature which he has in common with all substances: inasmuch as every substance seeks the preservation of its own being, according to its nature: and by reason of this inclination, whatever is a means of preserving human life, and of warding off its obstacles, belongs to the natural law. Secondly, there is in man an inclination to things that pertain to him more specially, according to that nature which he has in common with other animals: and in virtue of this inclination, those things are said to belong to the natural law, *which nature has taught to all animals,* such as sexual intercourse, education of offspring and so forth. Thirdly, there is in man an inclination to good, according to the nature of his reason, which nature is proper to him: thus man has a natural inclination to know the truth about God, and to live in society: and in this respect, whatever pertains to this inclination belongs to the natural law; for instance, to shun ignorance, to avoid offending those among whom one has to live, and other such things regarding the above inclination.

*Reply Obj.* 1. All these precepts of the law of nature have the character of one natural law, inasmuch as they flow from one first precept.

*Reply Obj.* 2. All the inclinations of any parts whatsoever of human nature, *e.g.,* of the concupiscible and irascible parts, in so far as they are ruled by reason, belong to the natural law, and are reduced to one first precept, as stated above: so that the precepts of the natural law are many in themselves, but are based on one common foundation.

*Reply Obj.* 3. Although reason is one in itself, yet it directs all things regarding man; so that whatever can be ruled by reason, is contained under the law of reason.

## HOSTILITY AND PEACE

From *Summa Theologica* 1-2, Q. 105, trans. Fathers of English Dominican Province.

### THIRD ARTICLE

#### WHETHER THE JUDICIAL PRECEPTS REGARDING FOREIGNERS WERE FRAMED IN A SUITABLE MANNER?

*We proceed thus to the Third Article:—*

*Objection* 1.   It would seem that the judicial precepts regarding foreigners were not suitably framed. For Peter said (Acts 10:34, 35): *In very deed I perceive that God is not a respecter of persons, but in every nation, he that feareth Him and worketh justice is acceptable to Him.* But those who are acceptable to God should not be excluded from the Church of God. Therefore it is unsuitably commanded (Deut. 23:3) that *the Ammonite and the Moabite, even after the tenth generation, shall not enter into the church of the Lord for ever:* whereas, on the other hand, it is prescribed (ibid. 7) to be observed with regard to certain other nations: *Thou shalt not abhor the Edomite, because he is thy brother; nor the Egyptian because thou wast a stranger in his land.*

*Obj.* 2.   Further, we do not deserve to be punished for those things which are not in our power. But it is not in a man's power to be an eunuch, or born of a prostitute. Therefore it is unsuitably commanded (Deut. 23:1, 2) that *an eunuch and one born of a prostitute shall not enter into the church of the Lord.*

*Obj.* 3.   Further, the Old Law mercifully forbade strangers to be molested: for it is written (Exod. 22:21): *Thou shalt not molest a stranger, nor afflict him; for yourselves also were strangers in the land of Egypt:* and (23:9): *Thou shalt not molest a stranger, for you know the hearts of strangers, for you also were strangers in the land of Egypt.* But it is an affliction to be burdened with usury. Therefore the Law unsuitably permitted them (Deut. 23:19, 20) to lend money to the stranger for usury.

*Obj.* 4. Further, men are much more akin to us than trees. But we should show greater care and love for these things that are nearest to us, according to Ecclus. 13:19: *Every beast loveth its like: so also every man him that is nearest to himself.* Therefore the Lord unsuitably commanded (Deut. 20:13-19) that all the inhabitants of a captured hostile city were to be slain, but that the fruit trees should not be cut down.

*Obj.* 5. Further, every one should prefer the common good of virtue to the good of the individual. But the common good is sought in a war which men fight against their enemies. Therefore it is unsuitably commanded (Deut. 20:5-7) that certain men should be sent home, for instance a man that had built a new house, or who had planted a vineyard, or who had married a wife.

*Obj.* 6. Further, no man should profit by his own fault. But it is a man's fault if he be timid or faint-hearted: since this is contrary to the virtue of fortitude. Therefore the timid and faint-hearted are unfittingly excused from the toil of battle (Deut. 20:8).

*On the contrary,* Divine Wisdom declares (Prov 8:8): *All my words are just, there is nothing wicked nor perverse in them.*

*I answer that,* Man's relations with foreigners are two-fold: peaceful, and hostile: and in directing both kinds of relation the Law contained suitable precepts. For the Jews were offered three opportunities of peaceful relations with foreigners. First, when foreigners passed through their land as travelers.—Secondly, when they came to dwell in their land as newcomers. And in both these respects the Law made kind provision in its precepts: for it is written (Exod. 22: 21): *Thou shalt not molest a stranger* (*advenam*); and again (ibid. 23:9): *Thou shalt not molest a stranger* (*peregrino*).—Thirdly, when any foreigners wished to be admitted entirely to their fellowship and mode of worship. With regard to these a certain order was observed. For they were not at once admitted to citizenship: just as it was the law with some nations that no one was deemed a citizen except after two or three generations, as the Philosopher says (*Polit.* 3. 1). The reason for this was that if foreigners were allowed to meddle with the affairs of a nation as soon as they settled down in its midst, many dangers might occur, since the foreigners not yet having the common good firmly at heart might attempt something hurtful to the people. Hence it was that the Law prescribed in respect of certain nations that had close relations with the Jews (viz., the Egyptians among whom they were born and educated, and the Idumeans,

the children of Esau, Jacob's brother), that they should be admitted
to the fellowship of the people after the third generation; whereas
others (with whom their relations had been hostile, such as the Am-
monites and Moabites) were never to be admitted to citizenship; while
the Amalekites, who were yet more hostile to them, and had no fellowship of kindred with them, were to be held as foes in perpetuity: for
it is written (Exod. 17:16): *The war of the Lord shall be against
Amalec from generation to generation.*

In like manner with regard to hostile relations with foreigners,
the Law contained suitable precepts. For, in the first place, it commanded that war should be declared for a just cause: thus it is commanded (Deut. 20:10) that when they advanced to besiege a city,
they should at first make an offer of peace.—Secondly, it enjoined
that when once they had entered on a war they should undauntedly
persevere in it, putting their trust in God. And in order that they
might be the more heedful of this command, it ordered that on the
approach of battle the priest should hearten them by promising them
God's aid.—Thirdly, it prescribed the removal of whatever might
prove an obstacle to the fight, and that certain men, who might be in
the way, should be sent home.—Fourthly, it enjoined that they should
use moderation in pursuing the advantage of victory, by sparing
women and children, and by not cutting down the fruit trees of that
country.

*Reply Obj.* 1. The Law excluded the men of no nation from
the worship of God and from things pertaining to the welfare of the
soul: for it is written (Exod. 12:48): *If any stranger be willing to
dwell among you, and to keep the Phase of the Lord; all his males
shall first be circumcised, and then shall he celebrate it according to
the manner, and he shall be as that which is born in the land.* But
in temporal matters concerning the public life of the people, admission was not granted to everyone at once, for the reason given above:
but to some, i.e., the Egyptians and Idumeans, in the third generation; while others were excluded in perpetuity, in detestation of their
past offense, i.e., the peoples of Moab, Ammon, and Amalec. For just
as one man is punished for a sin committed by him, in order that
others seeing this may be deterred and refrain from sinning; so too
may one nation or city be punished for a crime, that others may refrain from similar crimes.

Nevertheless it was possible by dispensation for a man to be admitted to citizenship on account of some act of virtue: thus it is re-

lated (Judith 14:6) that Achior, the captain of the children of Ammon, *was joined to the people of Israel, with all the succession of his kindred.*—The same applies to Ruth the Moabite, who was a *virtuous woman* (Ruth 3:11): although it may be said that this prohibition regarded men and not women, who are not competent to be citizens absolutely speaking.

*Reply Obj. 2.* As the Philosopher says (*Polit.* 3. 3), a man is said to be a citizen in two ways: first, simply; secondly, in a restricted sense. A man is a citizen simply if he has all the rights of citizenship, for instance, the right of debating or voting in the popular assembly. On the other hand, any man may be called citizen, only in a restricted sense, if he dwells within the state, even common people or children or old men, who are not fit to enjoy power in matters pertaining to the common weal. For this reason bastards, by reason of their base origin, were excluded from the *ecclesia*, i.e., from the popular assembly, down to the tenth generation. The same applies to eunuchs, who were not competent to receive the honor due to a father, especially among the Jews, where the divine worship was continued through carnal generation: for even among the heathens, those who had many children were marked with special honor, as the Philosopher remarks (*Polit.* 2. 6).—Nevertheless, in matters pertaining to the grace of God, eunuchs were not discriminated from others, as neither were strangers, as already stated: for it is written (Isa. 56:3): *Let not the son of the stranger that adhereth to the Lord speak, saying: The Lord will divide and separate me from His people. And let not the eunuch say: Behold I am a dry tree.*

*Reply Obj. 3.* It was not the intention of the Law to sanction the acceptance of usury from strangers, but only to tolerate it on account of the proneness of the Jews to avarice; and in order to promote an amicable feeling towards those out of whom they made a profit.

*Reply Obj. 4.* A distinction was observed with regard to hostile cities. For some of them were far distant, and were not among those which had been promised to them. When they had taken these cities, they killed all the men who had fought against God's people; whereas the women and children were spared. But in the neighboring cities which had been promised to them, all were ordered to be slain, on account of their former crimes, to punish which God sent the Israelites as executor of Divine justice: for it is written (Deut. 9:5): *Because they have done wickedly, they are destroyed at the coming in.*— The fruit-trees were commanded to be left untouched, for the use of the people themselves, to whom the city with its territory was destined to be subjected.

*Reply Obj.* 5. The builder of a new house, the planter of a vineyard, the newly married husband, were excluded from fighting, for two reasons. First, because man is wont to give all his affection to those things which he has lately acquired, or is on the point of having, and consequently he is apt to dread the loss of these above other things. Wherefore it was likely enough that on account of this affection they would fear death all the more, and be so much the less brave in battle.—Secondly, because, as the Philosopher says (*Phys.* 2. 5), *it is a misfortune for a man if he is prevented from obtaining something good when it is within his grasp.* And so lest the surviving relations should be the more grieved at the death of these men who had not entered into the possession of the good things prepared for them; and also lest the people should be horror-stricken at the sight of their misfortune: these men were taken away from the danger of death by being removed from the battle.

*Reply Obj.* 6. The timid were sent back home, not that they might be the gainers thereby; but lest the people might be the losers by their presence, since their timidity and flight cause others to be afraid and run away.


## LAWS OF WAR

From *Summa Theologica* 2-2, Q. 40, trans. Fathers of English Dominican Province.

### FIRST ARTICLE

#### Whether It Is Always Sinful to Wage War?

*We proceed thus to the First Article:—*

*Objection* 1. It would seem that it is always sinful to wage war. Because punishment is not inflicted except for sin. Now those who wage war are threatened by Our Lord with punishment, according to Matt. 26:52: *All that take the sword shall perish with the sword.* Therefore all wars are unlawful.

*Obj.* 2. Further, whatever is contrary to a Divine precept is a sin. But war is contrary to a Divine precept, for it is written (Matt. 5:39): *But I say to you not to resist evil;* and (Rom. 12:19): *Not revenging yourselves, my dearly beloved, but give place unto wrath.* Therefore war is always sinful.

*Obj.* 3. Further, nothing, except sin, is contrary to an act of virtue. But war is contrary to peace. Therefore war is always a sin.

*Obj.* 4. Further, the exercise of a lawful thing is itself lawful, as is evident in scientific exercises. But warlike exercises which take place in tournaments are forbidden by the Church, since those who are slain in these trials are deprived of ecclesiastical burial. Therefore it seems that war is a sin in itself.

*On the contrary,* Augustine says in a sermon on the son of the centurion: *If the Christian Religion forbade war altogether, those who sought salutary advice in the Gospel would rather have been counselled to cast aside their arms, and to give up soldiering altogether. On the contrary, they were told: "Do violence to no man; . . . and be content with your pay." If he commanded them to be content with their pay, he did not forbid soldiering.*

*I answer that,* In order for a war to be just, three things are necessary. First, the authority of the sovereign by whose command the war is to be waged. For it is not the business of a private individual to declare war, because he can seek for redress of his rights from the tribunal of his superior. Moreover it is not the business of a private individual to summon together the people, which has to be done in wartime. And as the care of the common weal is committed to those who are in authority, it is their business to watch over the common weal of the city, kingdom or province subject to them. And just as it is lawful for them to have recourse to the sword in defending that common weal against internal disturbances, when they punish evildoers, according to the words of the Apostle (Rom. 13:4): *He beareth not the sword in vain: for he is God's minister, an avenger to execute wrath upon him that doth evil;* so too, it is their business to have recourse to the sword of war in defending the common weal against external enemies. Hence it is said to those who are in authority (Ps. 81:4): *Rescue the poor: and deliver the needy out of the hand of the sinner;* and for this reason Augustine says (*Contra Faust.* 22. 75): *The natural order conducive to peace among mortals demands that the power to declare and counsel war should be in the hands of those who hold the supreme authority.*

Secondly, a just cause is required, namely that those who are attacked, should be attacked because they deserve it on account of some fault. Wherefore Augustine says (*QQ. in Hept.,* qu. 10, *super Jos.*): *A just war is wont to be described as one that avenges wrongs, when a nation or state has to be punished, for refusing to make amends for the wrongs inflicted by its subjects, or to restore what it has seized unjustly.*

Thirdly, it is necessary that the belligerents should have a rightful intention, so that they intend the advancement of good, or the avoidance of evil. Hence Augustine says (*De Verb. Dom.*): *True religion looks upon as peaceful those wars that are waged not for motives of aggrandizement, or cruelty, but with the object of securing peace, of punishing evildoers, and of uplifting the good.* For it may happen that the war is declared by the legitimate authority, and for a just cause, and yet be rendered unlawful through a wicked intention. Hence Augustine says (*Contra Faust.* 22. 74): *The passion for inflicting harm, the cruel thirst for vengeance, an unpacific and relentless spirit, the fever of revolt, the lust of power, and such like things, all these are rightly condemned in war.*

*Reply Obj.* 1. As Augustine says ( *Contra Faust.* 22. 70): *To take the sword is to arm oneself in order to take the life of anyone, without the command or permission of superior or lawful authority.* On the other hand, to have recourse to the sword (as a private person) by the authority of the sovereign or judge, or (as a public person) through zeal for justice, and by the authority, so to speak, of God, is not to *take the sword,* but to use it as commissioned by another, wherefore it does not deserve punishment. And yet even those who make sinful use of the sword are not always slain with the sword, yet they always perish with their own sword, because, unless they repent, they are punished eternally for their sinful use of the sword.

*Reply Obj.* 2. Such like precepts, as Augustine observes (*De Serm. Dom. in Monte* 1. 19), should always be borne in readiness of mind, so that we be ready to obey them, and, if necessary, to refrain from resistance or self-defense. Nevertheless it is necessary sometimes for a man to act otherwise for the common good, or for the good of those with whom he is fighting. Hence Augustine says (*Ep. ad Marcellin.* 138): *Those whom we have to punish with a kindly severity, it is necessary to handle in many ways against their will. For when we are stripping a man of the lawlessness of sin, it is good for him to be vanquished, since nothing is more hopeless than the happiness of sinners, whence arises a guilty impunity, and an evil will, like an internal enemy.*

*Reply Obj.* 3. Those who wage war justly aim at peace, and so they are not opposed to peace, except to the evil peace, which Our Lord *came not to send upon earth* (Matt. 10:34). Hence Augustine says (*Ep. ad Bonif.* 189): *We do not seek peace in order to be at war, but we go to war that we may have peace. Be peaceful, therefore, in warring, so that you may vanquish those whom you war against, and bring them to the prosperity of peace.*

*Reply Obj.* 4. Manly exercises in warlike feats of arms are not all forbidden, but those which are inordinate and perilous, and end in slaying or plundering. In olden times warlike exercises presented no such danger, and hence they were called *exercises of arms* or *bloodless wars,* as Jerome states in an epistle.

## SECOND ARTICLE

### WHETHER IT IS LAWFUL FOR CLERICS AND BISHOPS TO FIGHT?

*We proceed thus to the Second Article:—*

*Objection* 1. It would seem lawful for clerics and bishops to fight. For, as stated above (A. 1), wars are lawful and just in so far as they protect the poor and the entire common weal from suffering at the hands of the foe. Now this seems to be above all the duty of prelates, for Gregory says (*Hom. in Ev.* 14): *The wolf comes upon the sheep, when any unjust and rapacious man oppresses those who are faithful and humble. But he who was thought to be the shepherd, and was not, leaveth the sheep, and flieth, for he fears lest the wolf hurt him, and dares not stand up against his injustice.* Therefore it is lawful for prelates and clerics to fight.

*Obj.* 2. Further, Pope Leo IV. writes: *As untoward tidings had frequently come from the Saracen side, some said that the Saracens would come to the port of Rome secretly and covertly; for which reason we commanded our people to gather together, and ordered them to go down to the seashore.* Therefore it is lawful for bishops to fight.

*Obj.* 3. Further, apparently, it comes to the same whether a man does a thing himself, or consents to its being done by another, according to Rom. 1:32: *They who do such things, are worthy of death, and not only they that do them, but they also that consent to them that do them.* Now those, above all, seem to consent to a thing, who induce others to do it. But it is lawful for bishops and clerics to induce others to fight: for it is written that Charles went to war with the Lombards at the instance and entreaty of Adrian, bishop of Rome. Therefore they also are allowed to fight.

*Obj.* 4. Further, whatever is right and meritorious in itself, is lawful for prelates and clerics. Now it is sometimes right and meritorious to make war, for it is written that if a *man die for the true faith, or to save his country, or in defense of Christians, God will give him a heavenly reward.* Therefore it is lawful for bishops and clerics to fight.

*On the contrary,* It was said to Peter as representing bishops and clerics (Matt. 26:52): *Put up again thy sword into the scabbard.* Therefore it is not lawful for them to fight.

*I answer that,* Several things are requisite for the good of a human society: and a number of things are done better and quicker by a number of persons than by one, as the Philosopher observes (*Polit.* 1. 1), while certain occupations are so inconsistent with one another, that they cannot be fittingly exercised at the same time; wherefore those who are deputed to important duties are forbidden to occupy themselves with things of small importance. Thus according to human laws, soldiers who are deputed to warlike pursuits are forbidden to engage in commerce.

Now warlike pursuits are altogether incompatible with the duties of a bishop and a cleric, for two reasons. The first reason is a general one, because, to wit, warlike pursuits are full of unrest, so that they hinder the mind very much from the contemplation of Divine things, the praise of God, and prayers for the people, which belong to the duties of a cleric. Wherefore just as commercial enterprises are forbidden to clerics, because they unsettle the mind too much, so too are warlike pursuits, according to II Tim. 2:4: *No man being a soldier to God, entangleth himself with secular business.* The second reason is a special one, because, to wit, all the clerical Orders are directed to the ministry of the altar, on which the Passion of Christ is represented sacramentally, according to I Cor. 11:26: *As often as you shall eat this bread, and drink the chalice, you shall show the death of the Lord, until He come.* Wherefore it is unbecoming for them to slay or shed blood, and it is more fitting that they should be ready to shed their own blood for Christ, so as to imitate in deed what they portray in their ministry. For this reason it has been decreed that those who shed blood, even without sin, become irregular. Now no man who has a certain duty to perform, can lawfully do that which renders him unfit for that duty. Wherefore it is altogether unlawful for clerics to fight, because war is directed to the shedding of blood.

*Reply Obj.* 1. Prelates ought to withstand not only the wolf who brings spiritual death upon the flock, but also the pillager and the oppressor who work bodily harm; not, however, by having recourse themselves to material arms, but by means of spiritual weapons, according to the saying of the Apostle (II Cor. 10:4): *The weapons of our warfare are not carnal, but mighty through God.* Such are salutary warnings, devout prayers, and, for those who are obstinate, the sentence of excommunication.

*Reply Obj.* 2. Prelates and clerics may, by the authority of their superiors, take part in wars, not indeed by taking up arms themselves, but by affording spiritual help to those who fight justly, by exhorting and absolving them, and by other like spiritual helps. Thus in the Old Testament (Jos. 6:4) the priests were commanded to sound the sacred trumpets in the battle. It was for this purpose that bishops or clerics were first allowed to go to the front: and it is an abuse of this permission, if any of them take up arms themselves.

*Reply Obj.* 3. As stated above (Q. 23, A. 4, *ad* 2) every power, art or virtue that regards the end, has to dispose that which is directed to the end. Now, among the faithful, carnal wars should be considered as having for their end the Divine spiritual good to which clerics are deputed. Wherefore it is the duty of clerics to dispose and counsel other men to engage in just wars. For they are forbidden to take up arms, not as though it were a sin, but because such an occupation is unbecoming their personality.

*Reply Obj.* 4. Although it is meritorious to wage a just war, nevertheless it is rendered unlawful for clerics, by reason of their being deputed to works more meritorious still. Thus the marriage act may be meritorious; and yet it becomes reprehensible in those who have vowed virginity, because they are bound to a yet greater good.

## THIRD ARTICLE

### Whether It Is Lawful to Lay Ambushes in War?

*We proceed thus to the Third Article:—*

*Objection* 1. It would seem that it is unlawful to lay ambushes in war. For it is written (Deut. 16:20): *Thou shalt follow justly after that which is just.* But ambushes, since they are a kind of deception, seem to pertain to injustice. Therefore it is unlawful to lay ambushes even in a just war.

*Obj.* 2. Further, ambushes and deception seem to be opposed to faithfulness even as lies are. But since we are bound to keep faith with all men, it is wrong to lie to anyone, as Augustine states (*Contra Mend.* 15). Therefore, as one is bound to keep faith with one's enemy, as Augustine states (*Ep. ad Bonifac.* 189), it seems that it is unlawful to lay ambushes for ones' enemies.

*Obj.* 3. Further, it is written (Matt. 7:12): *Whatsoever you would that men should do to you, do you also to them;* and we ought to observe this in all our dealings with our neighbor. Now our enemy is our neighbor. Therefore, since no man wishes ambushes or deceptions to be prepared for himself, it seems that no one ought to carry on war by laying ambushes.

*On the contrary,* Augustine says (*QQ. in Heptateuch.*, qu. x, *super Jos.*): *Provided the war be just, it is no concern of justice whether it be carried on openly or by ambushes:* and he proves this by the authority of the Lord, Who commanded Joshua to lay ambushes for the city of Hai (Jos. 8:2).

*I answer that,* The object of laying ambushes is in order to deceive the enemy. Now a man may be deceived by another's word or deed in two ways. First, through being told something false, or through the breaking of a promise, and this is always unlawful. No one ought to deceive the enemy in this way, for there are certain *rights of war and covenants, which ought to be observed even among enemies,* as Ambrose states (*De Offic.* 1).

Secondly, a man may be deceived by what we say or do, because we do not declare our purpose or meaning to him. Now we are not always bound to do this, since even in the Sacred Doctrine many things have to be concealed, especially from unbelievers, lest they deride it, according to Matt. 7:6: *Give not that which is holy, to dogs.* Wherefore much more ought the plan of campaign to be hidden from the enemy. For this reason among other things that a soldier has to learn is the art of concealing his purpose lest it come to the enemy's knowledge, as stated in the Book on *Strategy* by Frontinus. Such like concealment is what is meant by an ambush which may be lawfully employed in a just war.

Nor can these ambushes be properly called deceptions, nor are they contrary to justice or to a well-ordered will. For a man would have an inordinate will if he were unwilling that others should hide anything from him.

This suffices for the *Replies* to the *Objections.*

## VIOLENCE AND MORAL INTENTION

From *Summa Theologica* 2-2, Q. 41, trans. Fathers of English Dominican Province.

### FIRST ARTICLE

#### WHETHER STRIFE IS ALWAYS A SIN?

*We proceed thus to the First Article:—*

*Objection* 1. It would seem that strife is not always a sin. For strife seems a kind of contention: hence Isidore says (*Etym.* 10) that the word *rixosus* (*quarrelsome*) *is derived from the snarling (rictu) of a dog, because the quarrelsome man is ever ready to contradict; he delights in brawling, and provokes contention.* Now contention is not always a sin. Neither, therefore, is strife.

*Obj.* 2. Further, it is related (Gen. 26:21) that the servants of Isaac *digged* another well, *and for that they quarrelled likewise.* Now it is not credible that the household of Isaac quarrelled publicly, without being reproved by him, supposing it were a sin. Therefore strife is not a sin.

*Obj.* 3. Further, strife seems to be a war between individuals. But war is not always sinful. Therefore strife is not always a sin.

*On the contrary,* Strifes are reckoned among the works of the flesh (Gal. 5:20), and *they who do such things shall not obtain the kingdom of God.* Therefore strifes are not only sinful, but they are even mortal sins.

*I answer that,* While contention implies a contradiction of words, strife denotes a certain contradiction of deeds. Wherefore a gloss on Gal. 5:20 says that *strifes are when persons strike one another through anger.* Hence strife is a kind of private war, because it takes place between private persons, being declared not by public authority, but rather by an inordinate will. Therefore strife is always sinful. In fact it is a mortal sin in the man who attacks another unjustly, for it is not without mortal sin that one inflicts harm on another even if the deed be done by the hands. But in him who defends himself, it may be without sin, or it may sometimes involve a venial sin, or sometimes a mortal sin; and this depends on his intention and on his manner of defending himself. For if his sole intention be to withstand the injury done to him, and he defend himself with due moderation, it is no sin, and one cannot say properly that there is strife on his part. But if, on the other hand, his self-defense be inspired by vengeance and hatred, it is always a sin. It is a venial sin, if a slight movement of hatred or vengeance obtrude itself, or if he does not much exceed moderation in defending himself: but it is a mortal sin if he makes for his assailant with the fixed intention of killing him, or inflicting grievous harm on him.

*Reply Obj.* 1. Strife is not just the same as contention: and there are three things in the passage quoted from Isidore, which express the inordinate nature of strife. First, the quarrelsome man is always ready to fight, and this is conveyed by the words, *ever ready to contradict,* that is to say, whether the other man says or does well or ill. Secondly, he delights in quarrelling itself, and so the passage proceeds, *and delights in brawling.* Thirdly, *he* provokes others to quarrel, wherefore it goes on, *and provokes contention.*

*Reply Obj.* 2. The sense of the text is not that the servants of Isaac quarrelled, but that the inhabitants of that country quarrelled with them: wherefore these sinned, and not the servants of Isaac, who bore the calumny.

*Reply Obj.* 3. In order for a war to be just it must be declared by authority of the governing power, as stated above (Q. 40, A. 1); whereas strife proceeds from a private feeling of anger or hatred. For if the servants of a sovereign or judge, in virtue of their public authority, attack certain men and these defend themselves, it is not the former who are said to be guilty of strife, but those who resist the public authority. Hence it is not the assailants in this case who are guilty of strife and commit sin, but those who defend themselves inordinately.


## REBELLION

From *Summa Theologica* 2-2, Q. 42, trans. Fathers of English Dominican Province.

### FIRST ARTICLE

#### Whether Sedition Is a Special Sin Distinct from Other Sins?

*We proceed thus to the First Article:—*

*Objection* 1. It would seem that sedition is not a special sin distinct from other sins. For, according to Isidore, *a seditious man is one who sows dissent among minds, and begets discord.* Now, by provoking the commission of a sin, a man sins by no other kind of sin than that which he provoked. Therefore it seems that sedition is not a special sin distinct from discord.

*Obj*. 2. Further, sedition denotes a kind of division. Now schism takes its name from scission, as stated above (Q. 39, A. 1). Therefore, seemingly, the sin of sedition is not distinct from that of schism.

*Obj*. 3. Further, every special sin that is distinct from other sins, is either a capital vice, or arises from some capital vice. Now sedition is reckoned neither among the capital vices, nor among those vices which arise from them, as appears from *Moral*. 31. 45, where both kinds of vice are enumerated. Therefore sedition is not a special sin, distinct from other sins.

*On the contrary,* Seditions are mentioned as distinct from other sins (II Cor. 12:20).

*I answer that,* Sedition is a special sin, having something in common with war and strife, and differing somewhat from them. It has something in common with them, in so far as it implies a certain antagonism, and it differs from them in two points. First, because war and strife denote actual aggression on either side, whereas sedition may be said to denote either actual aggression, or the preparation for such aggression. Hence a gloss on II Cor. 12:20 says that *seditions are tumults tending to fight,* when, to wit, a number of people make preparations with the intention of fighting. Secondly, they differ in that war is, properly speaking, carried on against external foes, being as it were between one people and another, whereas strife is between one individual and another, or between few people on one side and few on the other, while sedition, in its proper sense, is between mutually dissentient parts of one people, as when one part of the state arises in tumult against another part. Wherefore, since sedition is opposed to a special kind of good, namely the unity and peace of a people, it is a special kind of sin.

*Reply Obj.* 1. A seditious man is one who incites others to sedition, and since sedition denotes a kind of discord, it follows that a seditious man is one who creates discord, not of any kind, but between the parts of a multitude. And the sin of sedition is not only in him who sows discord, but also in those who dissent from one another inordinately.

*Reply Obj.* 2. Sedition differs from schism in two respects. First, because schism is opposed to the spiritual unity of the multitude, viz., ecclesiastical unity, whereas sedition is contrary to the temporal or secular unity of the multitude, for instance of a city or kingdom. Secondly, schism does not imply any preparation for a material fight as sedition does, but only a spiritual dissent.

*Reply Obj.* 3. Sedition, like schism, is contained under discord, since each is a kind of discord, not between individuals, but between the parts of a multitude.

## SECOND ARTICLE

### WHETHER SEDITION IS ALWAYS A MORTAL SIN?

*We proceed thus to the Second Article:—*

*Objection* 1. It would seem that sedition is not always a mortal sin. For sedition denotes a *tumult tending to fight,* according to the gloss quoted above (A. 1). But fighting is not always a mortal sin, indeed it is sometimes just and lawful, as stated above (Q. 40, A. 1). Much more, therefore, can sedition be without a mortal sin.

*Obj.* 2. Further, sedition is a kind of discord, as stated above (A. 1, *ad* 3). Now discord can be without mortal sin, and sometimes without any sin at all. Therefore sedition can be also.

*Obj.* 3. Further, it is praiseworthy to deliver a multitude from a tyrannical rule. Yet this cannot easily be done without some dissension in the multitude, if one part of the multitude seeks to retain the tyrant, while the rest strive to dethrone him. Therefore there can be sedition without mortal sin.

*On the contrary,* The Apostle forbids seditions together with other things that are mortal sins (II Cor. 12:20).

*I answer that,* As stated above (A. 1, *ad* 2), sedition is contrary to the unity of the multitude, viz. the people of a city or kingdom. Now Augustine says (*De Civ. Dei* 2. 21) that *wise men understand the word people to designate not any crowd of persons, but the assembly of those who are united together in fellowship recognized by law and for the common good.* Wherefore it is evident that the unity to which sedition is opposed is the unity of law and common good: whence it follows manifestly that sedition is opposed to justice and the common good. Therefore by reason of its genus it is a mortal sin, and its gravity will be all the greater according as the common good which it assails surpasses the private good which is assailed by strife.

Accordingly the sin of sedition is first and chiefly in its authors, who sin most grievously; and secondly it is in those who are led by them to disturb the common good. Those, however, who defend the common good, and withstand the seditious party, are not themselves seditious, even as neither is a man to be called quarrelsome because he defends himself, as stated above (Q. 41, A. 1).

*Reply Obj.* 1. It is lawful to fight, provided it be for the common good, as stated above (Q. 40, A. 1). But sedition runs counter to the common good of the multitude, so that it is always a mortal sin.

*Reply Obj.* 2. Discord from what is not evidently good, may be without sin, but discord from what is evidently good, cannot be without sin: and sedition is discord of this kind, for it is contrary to the unity of the multitude, which is a manifest good.

*Reply Obj.* 3. A tyrannical government is not just, because it is directed, not to the common good, but to the private good of the ruler, as the Philosopher states (*Polit.* 3. 5; *Ethic.* 8. 10). Consequently there is no sedition in disturbing a government of this kind, unless indeed the tyrant's rule be disturbed so inordinately, that his subjects suffer greater harm from the consequent disturbance than from the tyrant's government. Indeed it is the tyrant rather that is guilty of sedition, since he encourages discord and sedition among his subjects, that he may lord over them more securely; for this is tyranny, being conducive to the private good of the ruler, and to the injury of the multitude.

## 3. FRANCISCO DE VITORIA (c. 1483-1546)

A Spanish theologian who lived during the Spanish conquests in the New World, Francisco de Vitoria took the king to task for his treatment of the American Indians and argued for the equal rights of both Indians and Spaniards regardless of their religious or cultural status.

He discussed four principal questions: (1) May Christians make war at all? (2) Who has the authority to declare and make war? (3) What may be the cause of a just war? (4) What degree of force is lawful in a just war?

In the process he affirmed the immunity of non-combatants, and by exempting from fighting those convinced of the injustice of a particular war he made room for selective conscientious objection.

### THE LAW OF WAR

From *De Indiis et de Iure Belli Relectiones* second reflection, trans. J. P. Bate, in *Classics of International Law*, ed. J. B. Scott (1944).

All this can be summarized in a few canons or rules of warfare. First canon: Assuming that a prince has authority to make war, he should first of all not go seeking occasions and causes of war, but should, if possible, live in peace with all men, as St. Paul enjoins on us (Rom. 12). Moreover, he should reflect that others are his neighbors, whom we are bound to love as ourselves, and that we all have one common Lord, before whose tribunal we shall have to render our account. For it is the extreme of savagery to seek for and rejoice in grounds for killing and destroying men whom God has created and for whom Christ died. But only under compulsion and reluctantly should he come to the necessity of war.

Second canon: When war for a just cause has broken out, it must not be waged so as to ruin the people against whom it is directed, but only so as to obtain one's rights and the defense of one's country and in order that from that war peace and security may in time result.

Third canon: When victory has been won and the war is over, the victory should be utilized with moderation and Christian humility, and the victor ought to deem that he is sitting as judge between two states, the one which has been wronged and the one which has done the wrong, so that it will be as judge, and not as accuser that he will deliver the judgment whereby the injured state can obtain satisfaction, and this, so far as possible should involve the offending state in the least degree of calamity and misfortune, the offending individuals being chastised within lawful limits; and an especial reason for this is that in general among Christians all the fault is to be laid at the door of their princes, for subjects when fighting for their princes act in good faith and it is thoroughly unjust, in the words of the poet, that—

For every folly their Kings commit the punishment should fall upon the Greeks.

## THE RIGHTS OF THE INDIANS

From *De Indiis et de Iure Belli Relectiones* first reflection, trans. J. P. Bate, in *Classics of International Law*, ed. J. B. Scott (1944).

### FIRST SECTION

The whole of this controversy and discussion was started on account of the aborigines of the New World, commonly called Indians, who came forty years ago into the power of the Spaniards, not having been previously known to our world. This present disputation about them will fall into three parts. In the first part we shall inquire by what right these Indian natives came under Spanish sway. In the second part, what rights the Spanish sovereigns obtained over them in temporal and civil matters. In the third part, what rights these sovereigns or the Church obtained over them in matters spiritual and touching religion, in the course of which an answer will be given to the question before us. . . .

When, then, we return to the question before us, namely, the matter of the barbarians, we see that it is not in itself so evidently unjust that no question about its justice can arise, nor again so evidently just that no doubt is possible about its injustice, but that it has a look of both according to the standpoint. For, at first sight, when we see that the whole of the business has been carried on by men who are alike well-informed and upright, we may believe that everything has been done properly and justly. But then, when we hear of so many massacres, so many plunderings of otherwise innocent men, so many princes evicted from their possessions and stripped of their rule, there is certainly ground for doubting whether this is rightly or wrongly done. And in this way the discussion in question does not seem at all superfluous and so we get a clear answer to the objection. . . .

But some one may come forward and say: Although there were at one time some elements of doubt in this business, yet they have now been discussed and settled by the wise and so everything is now being administered in accordance with their advice and we have no need of a fresh enquiry. To such a person I answer first, God be blessed if it is so; our discussion raises no obstacle thereto; nor would I raise any new complaints. Secondly, I assert that it is not for jurists to settle this question or at any rate not for jurists only, for since the barbarians in question, as I shall forthwith show, were not in subjection by human law, it is not by human, but by divine law that questions concerning them are to be determined. Now, jurists are not skilled enough in the divine law to be able by themselves to settle questions of this sort. Nor am I sure that in the discussion and determination of this question theologians have ever been called competent to pronounce on so grave a matter. And as the issue concerns the forum of conscience, its settlement belongs to the priests, that is, to the Church. Accordingly in Deut. 17, it is enjoined on the king that he take a copy of the law from the hand of the priest. Thirdly, in order that the whole of the matter be adequately examined and assured, is it not possible that so weighty a business may produce other special doubts deserving of discussion? Accordingly I think I shall be doing something which is not only not futile and useless, but well worth the trouble, if I am enabled to discuss this question in a manner befitting its importance.

Returning now to our main topic, in order that we may proceed in order, I ask first whether the aborigines in question were true owners in both private and public law before the arrival of the Spaniards; that is, whether they were true owners of private property and possessions and also whether there were among them any who were the true princes and overlords of others. The answer might seem to be No, the reason being that slaves own no property, "for a slave can have nothing of his own," and so all his acquisitions belong to his master. But the aborigines in question are slaves. Therefore the matter is proved; for as Aristotle (*Politics* 1) neatly and correctly says, "Some are by nature slaves, those, to wit, who are better fitted to serve than to rule." Now these are they who have not sufficient reason to govern even themselves, but only to do what they are bidden, and whose strength lies in their body rather than in their mind. But, of a surety, if there be any such, the aborigines in question are preeminently such, for they really seem little different from brute animals and are utterly incapable of governing, and it is unquestionably better for them to be ruled by others than to rule themselves. Aristotle says it is just and natural for such to be slaves. Therefore they and their like can not be owners. And it is immaterial that before the arrival of the Spaniards they had no other masters; for there is no inconsistency in a slave having no master. . . . a slave who has been abandoned by his master and not taken into possession by any one else can be taken into possession by any one. If, then, these were slaves they could be taken into possession by the Spaniards.

On the opposite side we have the fact that the people in question were in peaceable possession of their goods, both publicly and privately. Therefore, unless the contrary is shown, they must be treated as owners and not be disturbed in their possession unless cause be shown.

In aid of a solution I am loath to recall to notice the numerous utterances of the doctors on the nature of dominion. . . . And so let me pass them over in order to observe that, if the aborigines had not dominion, it would seem that no other cause is assignable therefor except that they were sinners or were unbelievers or were witless or irrational. . . .

Now, some have maintained that grace is the title to dominion and consequently that sinners, at any rate those in mortal sin, have no dominion over anything. That was the error of the poor folk of Lyons, or Waldenses, and afterwards of John Wycliffe. One error of his, namely, that "no one is a civil owner, while he is in mortal sin," was condemned by the Council of Constance. . . .

But against this doctrine I advance the proposition that mortal sin does not hinder civil dominion and true dominion. Although this proposition was established in the Council of Constance, yet Almain . . . bases an argument in favor of it, on the fact that a person already in mortal sin who finds himself in extreme need would be in a dilemma, inasmuch as he must eat bread, and if he can not own any himself he takes another's. Therefore he cannot escape mortal sin. This reasoning is, however, unsatisfactory, in the first place, because neither Armachanus nor Wycliffe seems to be speaking of natural dominion, but of civil; and, secondly, the consequence is denied, it being retorted that in case of necessity a man could take what is another's; and, thirdly, he is in no dilemma, because he can repent. The argument, therefore, must be differently framed.

First, if a sinner has not civil dominion (which is what they seem to be speaking of), he, therefore, has not natural dominion; but the consequent is untrue; therefore, etc. I prove the consequence; for natural dominion is a gift of God, just as civil dominion is, nay, more so, for civil dominion seems an institute of human law. Therefore, if for an offense against God a man loses civil dominion, he would for the same reason lose his natural dominion also. But the falsity of the consequent is demonstrated by the fact that the man in question does not lose dominion over his own acts and over his own limbs, for a sinner has a right to defend his own life.

Secondly, Holy Scripture often names as kings those who were wicked and sinners, as appears in the case of Solomon and Ahab and many others; but one cannot be a king without having dominion; therefore, etc.

Thirdly, I employ against the opposing party their own argument: Dominion is founded on the image of God; but man is God's image by nature, that is, by his reasoning powers; therefore, dominion is not lost by mortal sin. The minor is proved from St. Augustine (*De Trinitate* 9), and from the doctors.

Fourthly, David called Saul his lord and king even when he was persecuting him (I Sam. 16, and elsewhere). Nay, David himself sinned at times, yet did not lose his kingdom on that account.

Fifthly (Gen. 49), "The sceptre shall not depart from Judah, nor a leader from between his feet, until he that is to be sent shall come," etc.; yet there were many bad kings; therefore, etc.

Sixthly, spiritual power is not lost by mortal sin; therefore not civil, for it seems much less assuredly to be founded in grace than spiritual power is. Now, the antecedent is obvious, because a bad priest consecrates the Eucharist and a bad bishop consecrates a priest, beyond all doubt. Although Wycliffe denies this, Armachanus admits it.

Seventhly, it is not at all likely, seeing that we are bidden to obey princes (Rom. 13; and I Pet. 2: "Be subject to your masters, not only to the good but also to the froward"), and not to take what belongs to another, that God meant that there should be any uncertainty as to who were true princes and owners.

And, in sum, this is a manifest heresy. And in the same way that God makes His sun to rise on the good and on the bad and sends His rain on the just and on the unjust, so also He has given temporal goods alike to good and to bad. Nor is this subject discussed, because it is in doubt, but in order that from one crime, to wit, from this insensate heresy, we may learn the character of all heretics.

Now it remains to consider whether at any rate dominion may be lost by reason of unbelief. It might seem to be so, on the ground that heretics have no dominion, and therefore other unbelievers have not, inasmuch as their condition is not better than that of heretics. . . . My answer is in the following propositions: The first proposition is that unbelief does not prevent anyone from being a true owner. This is the conclusion of St. Thomas Aquinas (*Secunda Secundae,* qu. 10, art. 12). It is proved also, firstly, by the fact that Scripture gives the name of king to many unbelievers, such as Sennacherib and Pharaoh and many other kings. Also by the fact that hatred of God is a graver sin than unbelief; but through hatred, etc. Also, St. Paul (Rom. 13) and St. Peter (I Pet. 2) enjoin obedience to princes, all of whom at that time were unbelievers, and slaves are there bidden to obey their masters. . . . The proposition is also supported by the reasoning of St. Thomas, namely: Unbelief does not destroy either natural law or human law; but ownership and dominion are based either on natural law or human law; therefore they are not destroyed by want of faith. In fine, this is as obvious an error as the foregoing. Hence it is manifest that it is not justifiable to take anything that they possess from either Saracens or Jews or other unbelievers as such, that is, because they are unbelievers; but the act would be theft or robbery no less than if it were done to Christians.

But because heresy presents peculiar difficulties, let a second proposition be: From the standpoint of the divine law a heretic does not lose the ownership of his property. This is generally accepted and is notorious. For since loss of property is a penalty and no penalty is ordained by the divine law for that condition, it is clear that from the standpoint of the divine law property is not forfeited on the ground of heresy. Further, this proposition is evident from the first proposition. For if ownership be not forfeited on the ground of any other unbelief, it follows that it is not forfeited on the ground of heresy, seeing that no special rules upon this point are enacted about heresy in the divine law. . . .

It remains to ask whether the Indians lacked ownership because of want of reason or unsoundness of mind. This raises the question whether the use of reason is a precondition of capacity for ownership in general. Conrad, indeed, propounds the conclusion that ownership is competent to irrational creatures, alike sensible and insensible. The proof consists in the fact that ownership is nothing more than the right to put a thing to one's own use. But brutes have this right over the herbs and plants (Gen. 1): "Behold I have given you every herb bearing seed which is upon the face of all the earth and every tree in the which is the fruit of a tree yielding seed; to you it shall be for meat and to every beast of the earth." The stars, too, have the right to shine for light (Gen. 1), "And God set them in the firmament of the heaven to give light upon the earth and to rule over the day and over the night." And the lion has dominion over all animals that walk, whence he is called the king of beasts. And the eagle is lord among the birds whence in Psalm 103 the verse about his house being their leader. Sylvester (under the word *dominium*, at the beginning) is of the same opinion as Conrad, saying that the "elements exercise dominion one over the other."

I answer by the following propositions:

First: Irrational creatures cannot have dominion. This is clear, because dominion is a right, as even Conrad admits. But irrational creatures cannot have a right. Therefore they cannot have dominion. The proof of the minor is that they cannot suffer a wrong and therefore can have no right. The proof of this assumption is that he who kept off a wolf or a lion from its prey or an ox from its pasture would not do it a wrong, nor would he who shut a window to prevent the sun from shining in do the sun a wrong. And this is confirmed by the fact that, if the brutes have dominion, he who took away the grass from a stag would commit theft, for he would be taking what belongs to another against the owner's will.

Also, wild beasts have not dominion over themselves. Therefore much less over other things. The proof of the assumption is that they may be killed with impunity, even for pleasure; and so Aristotle (*Politics* 1) says that the chase of wild beasts is just and natural.

Also, wild beasts themselves and all irrational animals are more fully within the ownership of man than slaves are. Therefore, if slaves cannot have anything of their own, much less can irrational animals.

Our proposition is also confirmed by the authority of St. Thomas Aquinas (*Prima Secundae,* qu. 1, art. 1 and 2, and qu. 6, art. 2, and *Contra Gentiles,* bk. 3, c. 110), to the effect that only rational creatures have dominion over their acts, the test of man's being master of his acts being (as St. Thomas says, *Prima Pars,* qu. 82, art. 1, on obj. 3) that he has the power of choice. Hence (as he says in the same place) we are not masters of our appetite as regards its final end. If, then, the brutes have not dominion over their acts, they have it not over other things. And although this seems to be a dispute about a name, it is assuredly a highly improper and unusual mode of speech to attribute dominion to things irrational. For we do not ordinarily say that a man has dominion save over that which is placed within his control. For when we have not dominion, we speak thus: "It is not within my control." "It is not in my power." Now, as the brutes are rather moved than move themselves, as St. Thomas says (*Prima Secundae*, as above), they for that reason have no dominion. . . .

However this may be, let our fourth proposition be: The Indian aborigines are not barred on this ground from the exercise of true dominion. This is proved from the fact that the true state of the case is that they are not of unsound mind, but have, according to their kind, the use of reason. This is clear, because there is a certain method in their affairs, for they have polities which are orderly arranged and they have definite marriage and magistrates, overlords, laws, and workshops, and a system of exchange, all of which call for the use of reason; they also have a kind of religion. Further, they make no error in matters which are self-evident to others; this is witness to their use of reason. Also, God and nature are not wanting in the supply of what is necessary in great measure for the race. Now, the most conspicuous feature of man is reason, and power is useless which is not reducible to action. Also, it is through no fault of theirs that these aborigines have for many centuries been outside the pale of salvation, in that they have been born in sin and void of baptism and the use of reason whereby to seek out the things needful for salvation. Accordingly I for the most part attribute their seeming so unintelligent and stupid to a bad and barbarous upbringing, for even among ourselves we find many peasants who differ little from brutes. . . .

The upshot of all the preceding is, then, that the aborigines undoubtedly had true dominion in both public and private matters, just like Christians, and that neither their princes nor private persons could be despoiled of their property on the ground of their not being true owners. It would be harsh to deny to those, who have never done any wrong, what we grant to Saracens and Jews, who are the persistent enemies of Christianity. We do not deny that these latter peoples are true owners of their property, if they have not seized lands elsewhere belonging to Christians. . . .

## SECOND SECTION

It being premised, then, that the Indian aborigines are or were true owners, it remains to inquire by what title the Spaniards could have come into possession of them and their country.

And first, I shall advert to the titles which might be alleged, but which are not adequate or legitimate.

Secondly, I shall set out the legitimate titles under which the aborigines could have come under the sway of the Spaniards.

Now, there are seven titles, which might be alleged, but which are not adequate, and seven or eight others, which are just and legitimate.

The first title that might be alleged, then, is that the Emperor is the lord of the world, and in such a way that, even if it be granted that in time past there was a defect in his claim, it would by now be purged as regards our present, most Christian Emperor. For, even if we assume that the Indian aborigines may be true owners, yet they might have superior lords, just as inferior princes have a king and as some kings have the Emperor over them. There can in this way be many persons having dominion over the same thing; and this accounts for the well-worn distinction drawn by the jurists between dominion high and low, dominion direct and available, dominion pure and mixed. The question, therefore, is whether the aborigines had any superior lord. And, as this question can only arise with regard to either the Emperor or the Pope, let us speak of these.

The first allegation to consider is that the Emperor is lord of the whole world and therefore of these barbarians also. This is supported, firstly, by the appellation, "Lord of the world," commonly given to the late Emperor Maximilian or to the present Emperor Charles, ever August. Also (Luke 2), "There went out a decree from Caesar Augustus that a census should be taken of all the world"; but Christian Emperors ought not to be in any worse condition than he; therefore, etc. Also, our Lord seems to have pronounced Caesar to be the true lord of the Jews. "Render unto Caesar," said he, "the things that are Caesar's," etc. (Luke 20). But it does not seem that Caesar could have this right, save as Emperor. Therefore Bartolus . . . expressly holds that "the Emperor is the rightful lord of the whole world." . . .

The allegation might also be supported by the fact that Adam first and then Noah seem to have been lords of the world: "Let us make man in our image, after our likeness, and let them have dominion over the fish of the sea and over the fowl of the air and over all the earth," etc. (Gen. 1), and a little later on, "Be fruitful and multiply and replenish the earth and subdue it," etc.; and there is a similar pronouncement made to Noah (Gen. 8). But these two had successors. Therefore . . .

Now, this contention is baseless. Let our first conclusion, then, be: The Emperor is not the lord of the whole earth. This is proved from the fact that dominion must be founded either on natural or divine or human law; but there is no lord of the earth in any of these; therefore, etc. The minor is proved, first as regards natural law, by what St. Thomas well says (*Prima Pars*, qu. 92, art. 1, on obj. 2, and qu. 96, art. 4), namely, that by natural law mankind is free save from paternal and marital dominion—for the father has dominion over his children and the husband over the wife by natural law; therefore no one by natural law has dominion over the world. And, as St. Thomas also says (*Secunda Secundae,* qu. 10, art. 10), dominion and preeminence were introduced by human law; they, therefore, were not by natural law. Nor would there be any greater reason why this dominion should be more proper for Germans than for Gauls. And Aristotle (*Politics* 1) says, Power is of two kinds, the one originates in the family, like that of the father over his sons and that of the husband over the wife, and this is a natural power; the other is civil, for, although it may take its rise in nature and so may be said to be of natural law, as St. Thomas says (*De regimine principum*, bk. 1, ch. 2), yet, man being a political animal, it is founded not on nature, but on law. . . .

Second conclusion: Granted that the Emperor were the lord of the world, still that would not entitle him to seize the provinces of the Indian aborigines and erect new lords there and put down the former ones or take taxes. The proof is herein, namely, that even those who attribute lordship over the world to the Emperor do not claim that he is lord in ownership, but only in jurisdiction, and this latter right does not go so far as to warrant him in converting provinces to his own use or in giving towns or even estates away at his pleasure. This, then, shows that the Spaniards can not justify on this ground their seizure of the provinces in question.

A second alleged title to the lawful possession of these lands, and one which is vehemently asserted, is traced through the Supreme Pontiff. For it is claimed that the Pope is temporal monarch, too, over all the world and that he could consequently make the Kings of Spain sovereign over the aborigines in question, and that so it has been done. In this matter there are some jurists, who hold that the Pope has full jurisdiction in temporal matters over the whole earth, and they even add that the power of all secular princes comes to them from the Pope. . . . Sylvester holds the same doctrine, making a much more ample and liberal concession of this power to the Pope, under the word *infidelitas* and under the word *Papa* and under the word *legitimus*. He has some singular remarks on this topic in the passages mentioned, as, for example, that "the power of the Emperor and all other princes is sub-delegated as regards the Pope, being derived from God through the medium of the Pope," and that "all their power is dependent on the Pope," and that "Constantine gave lands to the Pope in recognition of his temporal power," and on the other hand that "the Pope gave the Empire to Constantine to his use and profit," nay, that "Constantine's act was really not a gift, but merely the return of what had previously been taken away," and that, "if the Pope does not exercise jurisdiction in temporal matters outside the patrimony of the Church, this is not for want of authority, but in order to avoid the scandal of the Jews and in order to promote peace"; and many other things even more empty and absurd than these. The sole proof that he gives herefor is in the passages "The earth is the Lord's and the fulness thereof," and "All power is given unto me, both in heaven and in earth," and the Pope is the vicar of God and of Christ, and (Phil. 2) Christ "for our sake became obedient even unto death," etc. Bartolus, too, seems to be of this opinion in his comment on the Extravagans, *Ad reprimendum*, and St. Thomas seems to favor it at the end of the second book of the *Sententiae*, the closing words of which are by way of solution of the fourth argument, which is the last of the whole book, namely, that the Pope holds the summit of both kinds of power, both secular and spiritual, and Herveus is of the same opinion in his *De potestate Ecclesiae*.

This, then, being laid as a basis, the authors of this opinion say as follows: In the first place, that the Pope has free power, on the footing of supreme temporal lord, to make the Kings of Spain rulers over the Indian aborigines. Secondly, they say that, even if it be assumed that he could not do this, at any rate if these aborigines refused to recognize the temporal power of the Pope over them, this would warrant him in making war on them and in putting rulers over them. Now, each of these things has been done. For, first, the Supreme

Pontiff granted the provinces in question to the Kings of Spain. Secondly, the aborigines were notified that the Pope is the vicar of God and His vicegerent on earth and it was claimed that they should, therefore, recognize him as their superior, and their refusal furnishes a good ground for making war on them and seizing their lands, etc. Hostiensis, *place cited,* expressly makes this point, so does Angelus in his *Summa.*

Now, inasmuch as I have fully discussed the temporal power of the Pope in my *Relectio de Potestate Ecclesiastica,* I will put my answer to the above into a few brief propositions:

First: The Pope is not civil or temporal lord of the whole world in the proper sense of the words "lordship" and "civil power." . . . The opposite opinion seems contrary to the precept of our Lord who, (Matt. 20, and Luke 22), says, "Ye know that the princes of the Gentiles exercise lordship over them," etc. "But it shall not be so among you." And contrary also to the precept of the Apostle Peter, "neither as being lords over [God's] heritage but being ensamples to the flock." And if Christ the Lord had not temporal power, as has been shown in the foregoing discussion to be more probable and as is also the opinion of St. Thomas, much less has the Pope it, he being Christ's vicar. The above-mentioned thinkers attribute to the Pope that which he has never claimed for himself; nay, he admits the contrary in many passages, as I have shown in the Relectio referred to. And the proof is sufficient, like that given above concerning the Emperor, for no lordship can come to him save either by natural law or by divine law or by human law. Now, it is certain that none comes to him by natural or by human law, and none is shown to come to him by divine law. Therefore the assertion is ungrounded and arbitrary.

Further, our Lord's injunction to Peter, "Feed my sheep," clearly shows that power in spiritual and not in temporal matters is meant. It is, moreover, demonstrable that the Pope has not the whole world for his sphere. For our Lord said (John 10) that there should be "one flock and one shepherd" at the end of the age. This is sufficient proof that at the present day all are not sheep of this flock. Again, assuming that Christ had this power, it is manifest that it has not been entrusted to the Pope. This appears from the fact that the Pope is no less vicar of Christ in spiritual than in temporal matters. But the Pope has no spiritual jurisdiction over unbelievers, as even our opponents admit, and, as seems (I Cor. 5) to have been the express teaching of the Apostle: "For what have I to do to judge them also that are without?" Therefore he has it not also in temporal matters. And of a truth there is nothing in the argument that, as Christ had temporal power over the world, therefore the Pope also has it. For Christ undoubtedly had spiritual power over the whole world, not less over believers than over unbelievers and could make laws which bound the whole world, as he did with regard to baptism and the articles of faith. And yet the Pope has not that power over unbelievers and may not excommunicate them or forbid their marriage within the degrees permitted by the divine law. Therefore. Also, the fact that, according to the doctors, Christ did not entrust supremacy in power even to the Apostles shows that there is no force in the consequence: Christ had temporal power over the world; therefore the Pope has it too.

Second proposition: Even assuming that the Supreme Pontiff had this secular power over the whole world, he could not give it to secular princes. This is obvious, because it would be annexed to the Papacy. Nor can any Pope sever it from the office of Supreme Pontiff or deprive his successor of that power, for the succeeding Supreme Pontiff can not be less than his predecessor; and, if some one Pontiff had made a gift of this power, either the grant would be null or the succeeding Pontiff could cancel it. . . .

### THIRD SECTION

I will now speak of the lawful and adequate titles whereby the Indians might have come under the sway of the Spaniards. (1) The first title to be named is that of natural society and fellowship. And hereon let my first conclusion be: (2) The Spaniards have a right to travel into the lands in question and to sojourn there, provided they do no harm to the natives, and the natives may not prevent them. Proof of this may in the first place be derived from the law of nations (*jus gentium*), which either is natural law or is derived from natural law (*Inst.*, 1, 2, 1): "What natural reason has established among all nations is called the *jus gentium*." For, congruently herewith, it is reckoned among all nations inhumane to treat visitors and foreigners badly without some special cause, while, on the other hand, it is humane and correct to treat visitors well; but the case would be different, if the foreigners were to misbehave when visiting other nations.

Secondly, it was permissible from the beginning of the world (when everything was in common) for any one to set forth and travel wheresoever he would. Now this was not taken away by the division of property, for it was never the intention of peoples to destroy by that division the reciprocity and common use which prevailed among men, and indeed in the days of Noah it would have been inhumane to do so.

Thirdly, everything is lawful which is not prohibited or which is not injurious or hurtful to others in some other way. But (so we suppose) the travel of the Spaniards does no injury or harm to the natives. Therefore it is lawful.

Fourthly, it would not be lawful for the French to prevent the Spanish from traveling or even from living in France, or vice versa, provided this in no way enured to their hurt and the visitors did no injury. Therefore it is not lawful for the Indians.

Further, fifthly, banishment is one of the capital forms of punishment. Therefore it is unlawful to banish strangers who have committed no fault.

Further, sixthly, to keep certain people out of the city or province as being enemies, or to expel them when already there, are acts of war. Inasmuch, then, as the Indians are not making a just war on the Spaniards (it being assumed that the Spaniards are doing no harm), it is not lawful for them to keep the Spaniards away from their territory.

Further, seventhly, there is the Poet's verse,

What race of men is this? or what country is barbarous enough to allow this usage? We are driven off from the hospitality of its shore.

Also, eighthly, "Every animal loveth its kind" (Ecclus. 15). Therefore, it appears that friendship among men exists by natural law and it is against nature to shun the society of harmless folk.

Also, ninthly, there is the passage (Matt. 25): "I was a stranger and ye took me not in." Hence, as the reception of strangers seems to be by natural law, that judgment of Christ will be pronounced with universal application.

Tenthly, "by natural law running water and the sea are common to all, so are rivers and harbors, and by the law of nations ships from all parts may be moored there" (*Inst.*, 2, 1); and on the same principle they are public things. Therefore it is not lawful to keep any one from them. Hence it follows that the aborigines would be doing a wrong to the Spaniards, if they were to keep them from their territories.

Also, eleventhly, these very persons admit all other barbarians from all parts. Therefore, they would be doing a wrong, if they were not to admit the Spaniards.

Also, twelfthly, if it were not lawful for the Spaniards to travel among them, this would be either by natural law or by divine law or by human law. Now, it is certainly lawful by natural and by divine law. And if there were any human law which without any cause took away rights conferred by natural and divine law, it would be inhumane and unreasonable and consequently would not have the force of law.

Thirteenthly, either the Spaniards are subjects of the Indians or they are not. If they are not, then the Indians cannot keep them away. If they are, then the Indians ought to treat them well.

Also, fourteenthly, the Spaniards are the neighbors of the barbarians, as appears from the Gospel parable of the Samaritan (Luke 10). But they are bound to love their neighbors as themselves (Matt. 22). Therefore they may not keep them away from their country without cause: "When it is said 'Love thy neighbour,' it is clear that every man is our neighbour" (St. Augustine's *De Doctrina Christiana*).

Second proposition: The Spaniards may lawfully carry on trade among the native Indians, so long as they do no harm to their country, as, for instance, by importing thither wares which the natives lack and by exporting thence either gold or silver or other wages of which the natives have abundance. Neither may the native princes hinder their subjects from carrying on trade with the Spanish; nor, on the other hand, may the princes of Spain prevent commerce with the natives. This is proved by means of my first proposition.

Firstly, because it is an apparent rule of the *jus gentium* that foreigners may carry on trade, provided they do no hurt to citizens.

Also, secondly, a similar proof lies in the fact that this is permitted by the divine law. Therefore a law prohibiting it would undoubtedly not be reasonable.

Also, thirdly, the sovereign of the Indians is bound by the law of nature to love the Spaniards. Therefore the Indians may not causelessly prevent the Spaniards from making their profit where this can be done without injury to themselves.

A fourth reason is that such conduct would be against the

proverb: "Thou shalt not do to another what thou wouldest not wish done to thyself."

And, in sum, it is certain that the aborigines can no more keep off the Spaniards from trade than Christians can keep off other Christians. Now, it is clear that if the Spaniards kept off the French from trade with the Spaniards, and this not for the good of Spain, but in order to prevent the French from sharing in some advantage, that practice would offend against righteousness and charity. If, then, there can be no just legal ordinance to this effect, it also cannot be accomplished in actual fact (for the injustice of a law consists solely in the execution of the law). And, as is said in *Dig.*, 1, 1, 3, "Nature has established a bond of relationship between all men," and so it is contrary to natural law for one man to dissociate himself from another without good reason. "Man," says Ovid, "is not a wolf to his fellow man, but a man."

Third proposition: If there are among the Indians any things which are treated as common both to citizens and to strangers, the Indians may not prevent the Spaniards from a communication and participation in them. If, for example, other foreigners are allowed to dig for gold in the land of the community or in rivers, or to fish for pearls in the sea or in a river, the natives cannot prevent the Spaniards from doing this, but they have the same right to do it as others have, so long as the citizens and indigenous population are not hurt thereby. This is proved by my first and second propositions. For if the Spaniards may travel and trade among them, they may consequently make use of the laws and advantages enjoyed by all foreigners.

Secondly, inasmuch as things that belong to nobody are acquired by the first occupant according to the law of nations, it follows that if there be in the earth gold or in the sea pearls or in a river anything else which is not appropriated by the law of nations those will vest in the first occupant, just as the fish in the sea do. And, indeed, there are many things in this connection which issue from the law of nations, which, because it has a sufficient derivation from natural law, is clearly capable of conferring rights and creating obligations. And even if we grant that it is not always derived from natural law, yet there exists clearly enough a consensus of the greater part of the whole world, especially in behalf of the common good of all. For if after the early days of the creation of the world or its recovery from the flood the majority of mankind decided that ambassadors should everywhere be reckoned inviolable and that the sea should be common and that prisoners of war should be made slaves, and if this, namely, that strangers should not be driven out, were deemed a desirable principle, it would certainly have the force of law, even though the rest of mankind objected thereto.

Fourth proposition: If children of any Spaniard be born there and they wish to acquire citizenship, it seems they cannot be barred either from citizenship or from the advantages enjoyed by other citizens—I refer to the case where the parents had their domicile there. The proof of this is furnished by the rule of the law of nations, that he is to be called and is a citizen who is born within the state (Cod., 7, 62, 11). And the confirmation lies in the fact that, as man is a civil animal, whoever is born in any one state is not a citizen of another state. Therefore, if he were not a citizen of the state referred to, he would not be a citizen of any state, to the prejudice of his rights under both natural law and the law of nations . Aye, and if there be any persons who wish to acquire a domicile in some state of the Indians, as by marriage or in virtue of any other fact whereby other foreigners are wont to become citizens, they cannot be impeded any more than others, and consequently they enjoy the privileges of citizens just as others do, provided they also submit to the burdens to which others submit. And the passages wherein hospitality is commended are to the same effect (I Pet. 4): "Use hospitality one to another"; and (I Tim. 3, about a bishop): "A bishop must be given to hospitality." Hence, on the other hand, refusal to receive strangers and foreigners is wrong in itself.

Fifth proposition: If the Indian natives wish to prevent the Spaniards from enjoying any of their above-named rights under the law of nations, for instance, trade or other above-named matters, the Spaniards ought in the first place to use reason and persuasion in order to remove scandal and ought to show in all possible methods that they do not come to the hurt of the natives, but wish to sojourn as peaceful guests and to travel without doing the natives any harm; and they ought to show this not only by word, but also by reason, according to the saying, "It behoveth the prudent to make trial of everything by words first." But if, after this recourse to reason, the barbarians decline to agree and propose to use force, the Spaniards can defend themselves and do all that consists with their own safety, it being lawful to repel force by force. And not only so, but, if safety cannot otherwise be had, they may build fortresses and defensive works, and, if they have sustained a wrong, they may follow it up with war on the authorization of their sovereign and may avail themselves of the other rights of war. The proof hereof lies in the fact that warding-off and avenging a wrong make a good cause of war, as said above, following St. Thomas (*Secunda Secundae,* qu. 40). But when the Indians deny the Spaniards their rights under the law of nations they do them a wrong. Therefore, if it be necessary, in order to preserve their right, that they should go to war, they may lawfully do so.

It is, however, to be noted that the natives being timid by nature and in other respects dull and stupid, however much the Spaniards may desire to remove their fears and reassure them with regard to peaceful dealings with each other, they may very excusably continue afraid at the sight of men strange in garb and armed and much more powerful than themselves. And therefore, if, under the influence of these fears, they unite their efforts to drive out the Spaniards or even to slay them, the Spaniards might, indeed, defend themselves but within the limits of permissible self-protection, and it would not be right for them to enforce against the natives any of the other rights of war (as, for instance, after winning the victory and obtaining safety, to slay them or despoil them of their goods or seize their cities), because on our hypothesis the natives are innocent and are justified in feeling afraid. Accordingly, the Spaniards ought to defend themselves, but so far as possible with the least damage to the natives, the war being a purely defensive one.

There is no inconsistency, indeed, in holding the war to be a just war on both sides, seeing that on one side there is right and on the other side there is invincible ignorance. For instance, just as the French hold the province of Burgundy with demonstrable ignorance, in the belief that it belongs to them, while our Emperor's right to it is certain, and he may make war to regain it, just as the French may defend it, so it may also befall in the case of the Indians—a point deserving careful attention. For the rights of war which may be invoked against men who are really guilty and lawless differ from those which may be invoked against the innocent and ignorant, just as the scandal of the Pharisees is to be avoided in a different way from that of the self-distrustful and weak.

Sixth proposition: If after recourse to all other measures, the Spaniards are unable to obtain safety as regards the native Indians, save by seizing their cities and reducing them to subjection, they may lawfully proceed to these extremities. The proof lies in the fact that "peace and safety are the end and aim of war," as St. Augustine says, writing to Boniface. And since it is now lawful for the Spaniards, as has been said, to wage defensive war or even if necessary offensive war, therefore, everything necessary to secure the end and aim of war, namely, the obtaining of safety and peace, is lawful. . . .

# IV.  CHURCH AND STATE

The Reformation period was marked by violence and religious wars that posed repeated questions about the relation of church and state. For whether or not the Christian should fight depended on whether the church could support the use of force at all. Differences at this point undergird Luther's and Calvin's emphasis on civil authority in justifying military action by the Christian; they also undergird Erasmus' appeal to the Christian prince and Menno Simon's pacifism.

For further reading:

Adams, R. P. *The Better Part of Valor.* University of Washington Press, 1962.

Hershberger, G. F. *War, Peace and Non-Resistance.* Herald Press, 1944.

Luther, Martin. *The Christian in Society*, vols. 44-47 of *Luther's Works.* Edited by F. Sherman. Fortress Press, 1971.

Mueller, W. A. *Church and State in Luther and Calvin.* Broadman Press, 1954.

Rutenber, C. G. *The Dagger and the Cross.* Fellowship Publication, 1950.

Williams, G. H. *The Radical Reformation.* Westminster Press, 1962.

## 1. *MARTIN LUTHER* (c. 1483–1546)

Although as a nominalist he appeals rather to the will of God than to natural law as the basis for his ethics, Luther nevertheless draws on natural law and the just war tradition. He even expounds Aristotle's classic discussion of justice (*Nicomachean Ethics* 5) and applies it to the motives and intentions of the heart. Augustine's act-agent-authority distinction is evident in the following selection, for Luther speaks not only to the act of killing but also to the moral status of the soldier and the authority of the ruler. War is only justified out of necessity, as a last resort, and even then with just intent and limited means. Of particular interest are his comments on conscription and selective conscientious objection.

### THE SOLDIER AND HIS CONSCIENCE

From "Whether Soldiers, Too, Can Be Saved," trans. C. M. Jacobs and rev. R. C. Schultz, in *Luther's Works* 46, ed. H. T. Lehman (1967).

To the worshipful and honorable Assa von Kram, knight, my gracious lord and friend, [from] Martin Luther.

Most honorable and dear sir and friend, grace and peace to you in Christ.

When you were in Wittenberg recently—at the time of the elector's entry into the city—we talked about men in military service. In the course of the conversation we discussed many matters involving questions of conscience. As a consequence, you and several others asked me to put my opinion into writing and publish it because many soldiers are offended by their occupation itself. Some soldiers have doubts. Others have so completely given themselves up for lost that they no longer even ask questions about God and throw both their souls and their consciences to the winds. I myself have heard some of them say that if they thought too much about these problems, they would never be able to go to war again. One would think that war was such an absorbing matter that they were unable to think about

God and their souls. Actually, however, we ought to think most about God and our souls when we are in danger of death.

I agreed to your request and promised to provide this book in order—to the best of my ability—to give the best advice to these weak, timid, and doubting consciences, and so that those who do not care may be better instructed. For whoever fights with a good and well-instructed conscience can also fight well. This is especially true since a good conscience fills a man's heart with courage and boldness. And if the heart is bold and courageous, the fist is more powerful, a man and even his horse are more energetic, everything turns out better, and every happening and deed contributes to the victory which God then gives. On the other hand, a timid and insecure conscience makes the heart fearful. It cannot possibly be otherwise: a bad conscience can only make men cowardly and fearful. This is what Moses says to his Jews, "If you are disobedient, God will make your heart fearful; You shall go out one way against your enemies and flee seven ways before them, and you will have no good fortune" [Deut. 28:20, 25]. Then both man and horse are lazy and clumsy; they lack vigor for the attack, and in the end they are defeated. There are indeed some rough and cynical people in service—they are called daredevils and roughnecks—for whom everything happens accidentally, whether they win or lose. The outcome of the battle is the same for them as for those who have good or bad consciences. They are simply part of the army. They are only the shells and not the true core of the army.

Accordingly, I now send you this opinion of mine, given according to the ability that God has granted me, so that you and others who would like to go to war in such a way that you will not lose God's favor and eternal life may know how to prepare and instruct yourselves. God's grace be with you. Amen.

In the first place, we must distinguish between an occupation and the man who holds it, between a work and the man who does it. An occupation or a work can be good and right in itself and yet be bad and wrong if the man who does the work is evil or wrong or does not do his work properly. The occupation of a judge is a valuable divine office. This is true both of the office of the trial judge who declares the verdict and the executioner who carries out the sentence. But when the office is assumed by one to whom it has not been committed or when one who holds it rightly uses it to gain riches or popularity, then it is no longer right or good. The married state is also precious and godly, but there are many rascals and scoundrels in it. It is the same way with the profession or work of the soldier; in itself it is right and godly, but we must see to it that the persons who are in this profession and who do the work are the right kind of persons, that is, godly and upright, as we shall hear.

In the second place, I want you to understand that here I am not speaking about the righteousness that makes men good in the sight of God. Only faith in Jesus Christ can do that; and it is granted and given us by the grace of God alone, without any works or merits of our own, as I have written and taught so often and so much in other places. Rather, I am speaking here about external righteousness which is to be sought in offices and works. In other words, to put it plainly, I am dealing here with such questions as these: whether the Christian faith, by which we are accounted righteous before God, is compatible with being a soldier, going to war, stabbing and killing, robbing and burning, as military law requires us to do to our enemies in wartime. Is this work sinful or unjust? Should it give us a bad conscience before God? Must a Christian only do good and love, and kill no one, nor do anyone harm? I say that this office or work, even though it is godly and right, can nevertheless become evil and unjust if the person engaged in it is evil and unjust.

In the third place, it is not my intention to explain here at length how the occupation and work of a soldier is in itself right and godly because I have written quite enough about that in my book *Temporal Authority: To What Extent It Should Be Obeyed.* Indeed, I might boast here that not since the time of the apostles have the temporal sword and temporal government been so clearly described or so highly praised as by me. Even my enemies must admit this, but the reward, honor, and thanks that I have earned by it are to have my doctrine called seditious and condemned as resistance to rulers.[1] God be praised for that! For the very fact that the sword has been instituted by God to punish the evil, protect the good, and preserve peace [Rom. 13:1-4; I Pet. 2:13-14] is powerful and sufficient proof that war and killing along with all the things that accompany wartime and martial law have been instituted by God. What else is war but the punishment of wrong and evil? Why does anyone go to war, except because he desires peace and obedience?

1. Luther alludes to the frequent charge that the Peasant's War was largely incited by his teaching.

Now slaying and robbing do not seem to be works of love. A simple man therefore does not think it is a Christian thing to do. In truth, however, even this is a work of love. For example, a good doctor sometimes finds so serious and terrible a sickness that he must amputate or destroy a hand, foot, ear, eye, to save the body. Looking at it from the point of view of the organ that he amputates, he appears to be a cruel and merciless man; but looking at it from the point of view of the body, which the doctor wants to save, he is a fine and true man and does a good and Christian work, as far as the work itself is concerned. In the same way, when I think of a soldier fulfilling his office by punishing the wicked, killing the wicked, and creating so much misery, it seems an un-Christian work completely contrary to Christian love. But when I think of how it protects the good and keeps and preserves wife and child, house and farm, property, and honor and peace, then I see how precious and godly this work is; and I observe that it amputates a leg or a hand, so that the whole body may not perish. For if the sword were not on guard to preserve peace, everything in the world would be ruined because of lack of peace. Therefore, such a war is only a very brief lack of peace that prevents an everlasting and immeasurable lack of peace, a small misfortune that prevents a great misfortune.

What men write about war, saying that it is a great plague, is all true. But they should also consider how great the plague is that war prevents. If people were good and wanted to keep peace, war would be the greatest plague on earth. But what are you going to do about the fact that people will not keep the peace, but rob, steal, kill, outrage women and children, and take away property and honor? The small lack of peace called war or the sword must set a limit to this universal, worldwide lack of peace which would destroy everyone.

This is why God honors the sword so highly that he says that he himself has instituted it [Rom. 13:1] and does not want men to say or think that they have invented it or instituted it. For the hand that wields this sword and kills with it is not man's hand, but God's; and it is not man, but God, who hangs, tortures, beheads, kills, and fights. All these are God's works and judgments.

To sum it up, we must, in thinking about a soldier's office, not concentrate on the killing, burning, striking, hitting, seizing, etc. This is what children with their limited and restricted vision see when they regard a doctor as a sawbones who amputates, but do not see that he does this only to save the whole body. So, too, we must look at the office of the soldier, or the sword, with the eyes of an adult and see why this office slays and acts so cruelly. Then it will prove itself to be an office which, in itself, is godly and as needful and useful to the world as eating and drinking or any other work.

There are some who abuse this office, and strike and kill people needlessly simply because they want to. But that is the fault of the persons, not of the office, for where is there an office or a work or anything else so good that self-willed, wicked people do not abuse it? They are like mad physicians who would needlessly amputate a healthy hand just because they wanted to. Indeed, they themselves are a part of that universal lack of peace which must be prevented by just wars and the sword and be forced into peace. It always happens and always has happened that those who begin war unnecessarily are beaten. Ultimately, they cannot escape God's judgment and sword. In the end God's justice finds them and strikes, as happened to the peasants in the revolt.

As proof, I quote John the Baptist, who, except for Christ, was the greatest teacher and preacher of all. When soldiers came to him and asked what they should do, he did not condemn their office or advise them to stop doing their work; rather, according to Luke 3 [:14], he approved it by saying, "Rob no one by violence or by false accusation, and be content with your wages." Thus he praised the military profession, but at the same time he forbade its abuse. Now the abuse does not affect the office. When Christ stood before Pilate he admitted that war was not wrong when he said, "If my kingship were of this world, then my servants would fight that I might not be handed over to the Jews" [John 18:36]. Here, too, belong all the stories of war in the Old Testament, the stories of Abraham, Moses, Joshua, the Judges, Samuel, David, and all the kings of Israel. If the waging of war and the military profession were in themselves wrong and displeasing to God, we should have to condemn Abraham, Moses, Joshua, David, and all the rest of the holy fathers, kings, and princes, who served God as soldiers and are highly praised in Scripture because of this service, as all of us who have read even a little in Holy Scripture know well, and there is no need to offer further proof of it here.

Perhaps someone will now say that the holy fathers[2] were in

2. I.e., the biblical patriarchs and rulers.

a different position because God had set them apart from the other nations by choosing them as his people, and had commanded them to fight, and that their example is therefore not relevant for a Christian under the New Testament because they had God's command and fought in obedience to God, while we have no command to fight, but rather to suffer, endure, and renounce everything. This objection is answered clearly enough by St. Peter and St. Paul, who both command obedience to wordly ordinances and to the commandments of worldly rulers even under the New Testament [Rom. 13:1-4; I Pet. 2:13-14]. And we have already pointed out that St. John the Baptist instructed soldiers as a Christian teacher and in a Christian manner and permitted them to remain soldiers, enjoining them only not to use their position to abuse people or to treat them unjustly, and to be satisfied with their wages. Therefore even under the New Testament the sword is established by God's word and commandment, and those who use it properly and fight obediently serve God and are obedient to his word.

Just think now! If we gave in on this point and admitted that war was wrong in itself, then we would have to give in on all other points and allow that the use of the sword was entirely wrong. For if it is wrong to use a sword in war, it is also wrong to use a sword to punish evildoers or to keep the peace. Briefly, every use of the sword would have to be wrong. For what is just war but the punishment of evildoers and the maintenance of peace? If one punishes a thief or a murderer or an adulterer, that is punishment inflicted on a single evildoer; but in a just war a whole crowd of evildoers, who are doing harm in proportion to the size of the crowd, are punished at once. If, therefore, one work of the sword is good and right, they are all good and right, for the sword is a sword and not a foxtail with which to tickle people. Romans 13 [:4] calls the sword "the wrath of God."

As for the objection that Christians have not been commanded to fight and that these examples are not enough, especially because Christ teaches us not to resist evil but rather suffer all things [Matt. 5:39-42], I have already said all that needs to be said on this matter in my book *Temporal Authority*. Indeed, Christians do not fight and have no worldly rulers among them. Their government is a spiritual government, and, according to the Spirit, they are subjects of no one but Christ. Nevertheless, as far as body and property are concerned, they are subject to worldly rulers and owe them obedience. If worldly rulers call upon them to fight, then they ought to and must fight and be obedient, not as Christians, but as members of the state and obedient subjects. Christians therefore do not fight as individuals or for their own benefit, but as obedient servants of the authorities under whom they live. This is what St. Paul wrote to Titus when he said that Christians should obey the authorities [Titus 3:1]. You may read more about this in my book *Temporal Authority*.

That is the sum and substance of it. The office of the sword is in itself right and is a divine and useful ordinance, which God does not want us to despise, but to fear, honor, and obey, under penalty of punishment, as St. Paul says in Romans 13 [:1-5]. For God has established two kinds of government among men. The one is spiritual; it has no sword, but it has the word, by means of which men are to become good and righteous, so that with this righteousness they may attain eternal life. He administers this righteousness through the word, which he has committed to the preachers. The other kind is worldly government, which works through the sword so that those who do not want to be good and righteous to eternal life may be forced to become good and righteous in the eyes of the world. He administers this righteousness through the sword. And although God will not reward this kind of righteousness with eternal life, nonetheless, he still wishes peace to be maintained among men and rewards them with temporal blessings. He gives rulers much more property, honor, and power than he gives to others so that they may serve him by administering this temporal righteousness. Thus God himself is the founder, lord, master, protector, and rewarder of both kinds of righteousness. There is no human ordinance or authority in either, but each is a divine thing entirely.

Since, then, there is no doubt that the military profession is in itself a legitimate and godly calling and occupation, we will now discuss the persons who are in it and the use they make of their position, for it is most important to know who is to use this office and how he is to use it. And here we have to face the fact that it is impossible to establish hard and fast rules and laws in this matter. There are so many cases and so many exceptions to any rule that it is very difficult or even impossible to decide everything accurately and equitably. This is true of all laws; they can never be formulated so certainly and so justly that cases do not arise which deserve to be made exceptions. If we do not make exceptions and strictly follow the law we do the greatest injustice of all, as the heathen author Terence has said, "The strictest law is the greatest injustice." And Solomon teaches in Ecclesiastes [7:16; 10:1] that we should not carry justice to an extreme and at times should not seek to be wise.

Let me give an example. In the recent rebellion of the peasants there were some who were involved against their will. These were especially people who were well-to-do, for the rebellion struck at the rich, as well as the rulers, and it may fairly be assumed that no rich man favored the rebellion. In any case, some were involved against their will. Some yielded under this pressure, thinking that they could restrain this mad mob and that their good advice would, to some extent, prevent the peasants from carrying out their evil purpose and doing so much evil. They thought that they would be doing both themselves and the authorities a service. Still others became involved with the prior consent and approval of their lords, whom they consulted in advance. There may have been other similar cases. For no one can imagine all of them, or take them all into account in the law.

Here is what the law says, "All rebels deserve death, and these three kinds of men were apprehended among the rebellious crowd, in the very act of rebellion." What shall we do to them? If we allow no exceptions and let the law take its strict course, they must die just like the others, who are guilty of deliberate and intentional rebellion, although some of the men of whom we speak were innocent in their hearts and honestly tried to serve the authorities. Some of our knightlets, however, refused to make such exceptions, especially if the man involved was rich. They thought they could take their property by saying, "You also were in the mob. You must die." In this way they have committed a great injustice to many people and shed innocent blood, made widows and orphans, and taken their property besides. And yet they call themselves "nobles." Nobles indeed! The excrement of the eagle can boast that it comes from the eagle's body even though it stinks and is useless; and so these men can also be of the nobility. We Germans are and remain Germans, that is, swine and senseless beasts.

Now I say that in cases like the three kinds mentioned above, the law ought to yield and justice take its place. For the law matter of factly says, "Rebellion is punishable with death; it is the *crimen lese maiestatis*, a sin against the rulers." [3] But justice says, "Yes, dear law, it is as you say; but it can happen that two men do similar acts with

3. Under the Roman and feudal law it was an offense against the person of the ruler.

differing motives in their hearts. Judas, for example, kissed Christ in the garden. Outwardly this was a good work; but his heart was evil and he used a good work, which Christ and his disciples at other times did for one another with good hearts, to betray his Lord [Matt. 26:49]. Here is another example: Peter sat down by the fire with the servants of Annas and warmed himself with the godless, and that was not good [Luke 22:55]. Now if we were to apply the law strictly, Judas would have to be a good man and Peter a rascal; but Judas' heart was evil and Peter's was good; therefore justice in this case must correct the law.

Therefore justice not only acquits those who were among the rebels with good intentions, but considers them worthy of double grace. They are just like the godly man, Hushai the Archite, who, acting under David's orders, joined and served the rebellious Absalom with the intention of helping David and restraining Absalom, as it is all finely written in II Samuel 15 [:32-37] and 16 [:16-19]. Outwardly considered, Hushai, too, was a rebel with Absalom against David; but he earned great praise and everlasting honor before God and all the world. If David had allowed Hushai to be condemned as a rebel, it would have been just as praiseworthy a deed as those which our princes and knightlets are now doing to equally innocent people, yes, even to people who have deserved good.

In Greek this virtue, or wisdom, which can and must guide and moderate the severity of law according to cases, and which judges the same deed to be good or evil according to the difference of the motives and intentions of the heart, is called *epieikeia*; in Latin it is *aequitas*, and *Billichkeit* in German. Now because law must be framed simply and briefly, it cannot possibly embrace all the cases and problems. This is why the judges and lords must be wise and pious in this matter and meet our reasonable justice, and let the law take its course, or set it aside, accordingly. The head of a household makes a law for his servants, telling them what they are to do on this day or that; that is the law, and the servant who does not keep it must take his punishment. But now one of them may be sick, or be otherwise hindered from keeping the law through no fault of his own; then the law is suspended, and anyone who would punish his servant for that kind of neglect of duty would have to be a mad lord of the house. Similarly, all laws that regulate men's actions must be subject to justice, their mistress, because of the innumerable and varied circumstances which no one can anticipate or set down.

So then, we have this to say about people who live under military law or who are involved in fighting a war. First, war may be made by three kinds of people. An equal may make war against his equal, that is, neither of the two persons is the vassal or subject of the other even though one may be less great or glorious or mighty than the other. Or an overlord may fight against his subject. Or a subject may fight against his overlord. Let us take the third case. Here is what the law says, "No one shall fight or make war against his overlord; for a man owes his overlord obedience, honor, and fear." (Romans 13 [:1-7]). If you chop over your head, the chips fall in your eyes. And Solomon says, "If you throw a stone into the air, it will land on your own head." That is the law in a nutshell. God himself has instituted it and men have accepted it, for it is not possible both to obey and resist, to be subject and not put up with their lords. . . .

Now we will move on to the second point and discuss the question whether equals may wage war against equals. I would have this understood as follows: It is not right to start a war just because some silly lord has gotten the idea into his head. At the very outset I want to say that whoever starts a war is in the wrong. And it is only right and proper that he who first draws his sword is defeated, or even punished, in the end. This is what has usually happened in history. Those who have started wars have lost them, and those who fought in self-defense have only seldom been defeated. Worldly government has not been instituted by God to break the peace and start war, but to maintain peace and to avoid war. Paul says in Romans 13 [:4] that it is the duty of the sword to protect and punish, to protect the good in peace and to punish the wicked with war. God tolerates no injustice and he has so ordered things that warmongers must be defeated in war. As the proverb says, "No one has ever been so evil that he does not meet someone more evil than he is." And in Psalm 68 [:30] God has the psalmist sing of him . . . "He scatters the peoples who delight in war."

Beware, therefore; God does not lie! Take my advice. Make the broadest possible distinction between what you want to do and what you ought to do, between desire and necessity, between lust for war and willingness to fight. Do not be tempted to think of yourself as though you were the Turkish sultan. Wait until the situation compels you to fight when you have no desire to do so. You will still have more than enough wars to fight and will be able to say with heartfelt sincerity, "How I would like to have peace. If only my neighbors wanted it too!" Then you can defend yourself with a good conscience,

for God's word says, "He scatters the peoples who delight in war."
Look at the real soldiers, those who have played the game of war.
They are not quick to draw their sword, they are not contentious;
they have no desire to fight. But when someone forces them to fight,
watch out! They are not playing games. Their sword is tight in the
sheath, but if they have to draw, it does not return bloodless to the
scabbard. Those fools who are the first to fight in their thoughts and
even make a good start by devouring the world with words and are
the first to flash their blades, are also the first to run away and sheathe
their swords. The mighty Roman Empire won most of its victories because the Romans were forced to fight; that is, everyone wanted a
chance at the Romans to win his spurs at their expense. When the
Romans were forced to defend themselves, they set about it vigorously
enough! Hannibal, the prince from Africa, hurt them so badly that
he almost destroyed them. But how shall I say it? He started it; he also
had to stop it. Courage (from God!) remained with the Romans even
when they were losing, and where courage stays, deeds surely follow.
For it is God who does the deeds; he desires peace and is the enemy
of those who start wars and break the peace.

I must mention here the example of Duke Frederick, elector of
Saxony, for it would be a shame if that wise prince's sayings were
to die with his body. He had to endure many wicked plots on the
part of his neighbors and many others. He had so many reasons to
start a war that if some mad prince who loved war had been in his
position, he would have started ten wars. But Frederick did not draw
his sword. He always responded with reasonable words and almost gave
the impression that he was afraid and was running away from a fight.
He let the others boast and threaten and yet he held his ground against
them. When he was asked why he let them threaten him so, he replied, "I shall not start anything; but if I have to fight, you will see
that I shall be the one who decides when it is time to stop." So although many dogs bared their fangs at him, he was never bitten. He
saw that the others were foolish and that he could be indulgent with
them. If the king of France had not started the war against Emperor
Charles, he would not have been so shamefully defeated and captured.
And now that the Venetians and Italians are setting themselves against
the Emperor and starting trouble, God grant that they must also
be the first to have to stop. (Although the emperor is my enemy, I
still do not like this kind of injustice.) Let the saying remain true,
"God scatters the peoples who delight in war" [Ps. 68:30].

God confirms all this with many excellent examples in the Scriptures. He had his people first offer peace to the kingdoms of the Amorites and Canaanites and would not permit his people to start a war with them. He thereby confirmed this as his principle. But when those kingdoms started the war and forced God's people to defend themselves, they were completely destroyed [Num. 21:21-30; Deut. 2:26-37]. Self-defense is a proper ground for fighting and therefore all laws agree that self-defense shall go unpunished; and he who kills another in self-defense is innocent in the eyes of all men. But when the people of Israel wanted to start an unnecessary war with the Canaanites, the Israelites were defeated, Numbers 14 [:40-45]. And when Joseph and Azariah wanted to fight to gain honor for themselves, they were beaten [I Mac. 5:55-60]. And Amaziah, king of Judah, wanted to start a war against the king of Israel; but read II Kings 14 [:8-14] and see what happened to him. King Ahab started a war against the Syrians at Ramoth, but lost both the war and his own life, I Kings 22 [:2-40]. And the men of Ephraim intended to devour Jephthah and lost forty-two thousand men [Judg. 12:1-6], and so on. You find that the losers were almost always those who started the war. Even good King Josiah had to be slain because he started a war against the king of Egypt [II Kings 23:29] so that the saying would hold true, "He scatters the peoples who delight in war." Therefore my countrymen in the Harz Mountains have a saying, "It is truly said that whoever strikes anyone else will be struck in return." Why? Because God rules the world powerfully and leaves no wrong unpunished. He who does wrong will be punished by God, as sure as he lives, unless he repents and makes amends to his neighbor. I believe that even Münzer and his peasants would have to admit this.[4]

Let this be, then, the first thing to be said in this matter: No war is just even if it is a war between equals, unless one has such a good reason for fighting and such a good conscience that he can say, "My neighbor compels and forces me to fight, though I would rather avoid it." In that case, it can be called not only war, but lawful self-defense, for we must distinguish between wars that somone begins because that is what he wants to do and does before anyone else attacks him, and those wars that are provoked when an attack is made by someone else. The first kind can be called wars of desire; the second, wars of necessity. The first kind are of the devil; God does not give

4. Münzer and many peasants were executed at the end of the Peasants' War.

good fortune to the man who wages that kind of war. The second kind are human disasters; God help in them!

Take my advice, dear lords. Stay out of war unless you have to defend and protect yourselves and your office compels you to fight. Then let war come. Be men, and test your armor. Then you will not have to think about war to fight. The situation itself will be serious enough, and the teeth of the wrathful, boasting, proud men who chew nails will be so blunt that they will scarcely be able to bite into fresh butter.

The reason is that every lord and prince is bound to protect his people and to preserve the peace for them. That is his office; that is why he has the sword, Romans 13 [:4]. This should be a matter of conscience for him. And he should on this basis be certain that this work is right in the eyes of God and is commanded by him. I am not now teaching what Christians are to do, for your government does not concern us Christians; but we are rendering you a service and telling you what you are to do before God, in your office of ruler. A Christian is a person to himself; he believes for himself and for no one else. But a lord and prince is not a person to himself, but on behalf of others. It is his duty to serve them, that is, to protect and defend them. It would indeed be good if he were also a Christian and believed in God, for then he would be saved. However, being a Christian is not princely, and therefore few princes can be Christians; as they say, "A prince is a rare bird in heaven." But even if princes are not Christians, they nevertheless ought to do what is right and good according to God's outward ordinance. God wants them to do this.

But if a lord or prince does not recognize this duty and God's commandment and allows himself to think that he is prince, not for his subjects' sake, but because of his handsome, blond hair as though God had made him a prince to rejoice in his power and wealth and honor, take pleasure in these things, and rely on them. If he is that kind of prince, he belongs among the heathen; indeed, he is a fool. That kind of prince would start a war over an empty nut and think of nothing but satisfying his own will. God restrains such princes by giving fists to other people, too. There are also people on the other side of the mountain. Thus one sword keeps the other in the scabbard. However, a sensible prince does not seek his own advantage. He is satisfied if his subjects are obedient. Though his enemies and neighbors boast and threaten and spew out many bad words, he thinks, "Fools always chatter more than wise men; an empty sack holds many words; silence is often the best answer." Therefore he does not concern himself much about them until he sees that his subjects are attacked or finds the sword actually drawn. Then he defends himself as well as he can, ought, and must. For anyone who is such a coward that he tries to catch every word and evaluate it is like a man who tries to trap the wind in his coat. And if you want to know what peace or profit he gets out of that, ask him and you will soon find out.

This is the first thing to be said in this matter. The second should be just as carefully observed. Even though you are absolutely certain that you are not starting a war but are being forced into one, you should still fear God and remember him. You should not march out to war saying, "Ah, now I have been forced to fight and have good cause for going to war." You ought not to think that that justifies anything you do and plunge headlong into battle. It is indeed true that you have a really good reason to go to war and to defend yourself, but that does not give you God's guarantee that you will win. Indeed, such confidence may result in your defeat—even though you have a just cause for fighting the war—for God cannot endure such pride and confidence except in a man who humbles himself before him and fears him. He is pleased with the man who fears neither man nor devil and is bold and confident, brave and firm against both, if they began the war and are in the wrong. But there is nothing to the idea that this will produce a victory, as though it were our deeds or power that did it. Rather, God wants to be feared and he wants to hear us sing from our hearts a song like this, "Dear Lord, you see that I have to go to war, though I would rather not. I do not trust, however, in the justice of my cause, but in your grace and mercy, for I know that if I were to rely on the justness of my cause and were confident because of it, you would rightly let me fall as one whose fall was just, because I relied upon my being right and not upon your sheer grace and kindness."

Just listen now to what the heathen say about this, the Greeks and Romans, who knew nothing of God and the fear of God. They thought that it was they who made war and won victories all by themselves. But by experience over a long period of time in which a great and well-armed people was often beaten by a small number of poorly armed people, they had to learn and freely admitted that nothing is more dangerous in war than to be secure and confident. So they concluded that one should never underestimate the enemy, no matter how small he may be; that one should surrender no advantage, no matter how small it may be; that one should neglect no precaution, vigilance, or concern, no matter how small it may be. One should be as careful with everything as one would if one were weighing gold. Foolish, confident, heedless people accomplish nothing in war, except to do harm. They regarded the words *"non putassem"*—"I did not think of it"—as the most shameful words a soldier could speak. These words indicate that he was one of those secure, confident, careless men, who in one moment, by one step, with one word, can do more damage than ten like him can repair, and then he will say, "Indeed, I did not think of it." Prince Hannibal badly defeated the Romans as long as they were confident and secure against him. And history is full of innumerable examples of this kind, just as we see them happening with our own eyes every day.

. The heathen learned this by experience and taught it, but they did not know how to account for it other than to blame it on Fortune. They felt that they had to be afraid of Fortune. However, as I have said, the actual cause of this is that God wants to demonstrate through such histories that he wants men to fear him, and that he will not tolerate confidence, contempt, temerity, or security in such things until we learn to receive from his hands all that we can and want to have, as a gift of pure grace and mercy. It is therefore remarkable for a soldier who has a good cause to be confident and discouraged at the same time. How can he fight if he is discouraged? But if he goes into battle with complete confidence, the danger is even greater. This, then, is what he should do: Before God he should be discouraged, fearful, and humble, and commit his cause to him that he may dispose things, not according to our understanding of what is right and just, but according to his kindness and grace. In this way he wins God to his side with a humble, fearful heart. Toward men he should be bold, free, and confident because they are in the wrong, and smite them with a confident and untroubled spirit. Why should we not do for our God what the Romans, the greatest fighters on earth, did for their false god, Fortune, whom they feared? Whenever they did not do this, they fought in great danger and even were badly beaten.

Our conclusion on this point, then, is that war against equals should be waged only when it is forced upon us and then it should be fought in the fear of God. Such a war is forced upon us when an enemy or neighbor attacks and starts the war, and refuses to cooperate in settling the matter according to law or through arbitration

and common agreement, or when one overlooks and puts up with the
enemy's evil words and tricks, but he still insists on having his own
way. I am assuming throughout that I am preaching to those who want
to do what is right in God's sight. Those who will neither offer nor
consent to do what is right do not concern me. Fearing God means
that we do not rely on the justness of our cause, but that we are
careful, diligent, and cautious, even in the very smallest details, in
so small a thing as a whistle. With all this, however, God's hands
are not bound so that he cannot bid us make war against those who
have not given us just cause, as he did when he commanded the children of Israel to go to war against the Canaanites. In such a case
God's command is necessity enough. However, even such a war
should not be fought without fear and care, as God shows in Joshua
3 [7:1-5] when the children of Israel marched confidently against
the men of Ai, and were beaten. The same kind of necessity arises if
subjects fight at the command of their rulers; for God commands us
to obey our rulers [Rom. 13:1], and his command requires that we
fight, though this too must be done with fear and humility. We shall
discuss this further below.

The third question is whether overlords have the right to go to
war with their subjects. We have, indeed, heard above that subjects
are to be obedient and are even to suffer wrong from their tyrants.
Thus, if things go well, the rulers have nothing to do with their subjects except to cultivate fairness, righteousness, and judgment. However, if the subjects rise up and rebel, as the peasants did recently,
then it is right and proper to fight against them. That, too, is what a
prince should do to his nobles and an emperor to his princes if they
are rebellious and start a war. Only it must be done in the fear of God,
and too much reliance must not be placed on being in the right, lest
God determine that the lords are to be punished by their subjects,
even though the subjects are in the wrong. This has often happened,
as we have heard above. For to be right and to do right do not always
go together. Indeed, they never go together unless God joins them.
Therefore, although it is right that subjects patiently suffer everything and do not revolt, nevertheless, it is not for men to decide
whether they shall do so. For God has appointed subjects to care for
themselves as individuals, has taken the sword from them, and has
put it into the hands of another. If they rebel against this, get others
to join them and break loose, and take the sword, then before God
they are worthy of condemnation and death.

Overlords, on the other hand, are appointed to be persons who exist for the sake of the community, and not for themselves alone. They are to have the support of their subjects and are to bear the sword. Compared to his overlord the emperor, a prince is not a prince, but an individual who owes obedience to the emperor, as do all others, each for himself. But when he is seen in relationship to his own subjects he is as many persons as he has people under him and attached to him. So the emperor, too, when compared with God, is not an emperor, but an individual person like all others; compared with his subjects, however, he is as many times emperor as he has people under him. The same thing can be said of all other rulers. When compared to their overlord, they are not rulers at all and are stripped of all authority. When compared with their subjects, they are adorned with all authority.

Thus, in the end, all authority comes from God, whose alone it is; for he is emperor, prince, count, noble, judge, and all else, and he assigns these offices to his subjects as he wills, and takes them back again for himself. Now no individual ought to set himself against the community or attract the support of the community to himself, for in so doing he is chopping over his head, and the chips will surely fall in his eyes. From this you see that those who resist their rulers resist the ordinance of God, as St. Paul teaches in Romans 13 [:2]. In I Corinthians 15 [:24] Paul also says that God will abolish all authority when he himself shall reign and return all things to himself.

So much on these three points; now come the questions. Now since no king can go to war alone (any more than he can administer the law courts alone—he must have people who serve him in war just as he must have counselors, judges, lawyers, jailers, executioners, and whatever else is necessary for the administration of justice), the question arises whether a man ought to hire himself out for wages . . . and commit himself to serve the prince as the occasion may demand, as is customary. To answer this question we must distinguish various types of soldiers.

In the first place, there are some subjects who, even without such an arrangement, are under obligation to aid their overlords with their body and property and to obey their lord's summons. This is especially true of the nobles and of those who hold property granted by charter from the authorities. For the properties held by counts, lords, and nobles were parceled out in ancient times by the Romans and the Roman emperors and were given in fief on the condition that those who possess them should always be armed and ready—the one with this many horses and men, the other with that many, according to the size of their holdings. These fiefs were the wages with which they were hired. This is why they are called fiefs and why these incumbrances still rest upon them. The emperor permits these holdings to be inherited; and this is right and fine in the Roman Empire. The Turk, it is said, does not allow such inheritances and tolerates no hereditary principality, county, or knights' fee or fief, but assigns and distributes them as, when, and to whom he will. This is why he has such immeasurable wealth and is absolute lord in the land, or rather a tyrant.

The nobles, therefore, should not think that they have their property for nothing, as though they had found it or won it by gambling. The encumbrance on it and the feudal rents show whence and why they have it, namely, as a loan from the emperor or the prince. Therefore they ought not use it to finance their own ostentatious display and riotous conduct, but be armed and prepared for war to defend the land and to maintain the peace. Now if they complain that they must keep horses and serve the princes and lords while others have peace and quiet, I reply: Dear sirs, let me tell you something. You have your pay and your fief, and you are appointed to this office and are well paid for it. But do not others also have to work hard enough to maintain their little properties? Or are you the only ones who have work to do? And your office[5] is seldom called for, but others must do their duty every day. If you are not willing to do this or think it burdensome or unjust, then give up your fief. It will be easy to find others who will be glad to accept it and do in return what it requires of them.

Therefore, wise men have divided the work of all men into two categories, *Agriculturam* and *Militiam,* that is, agricultural and military occupations. And this is the natural division. The farmers feed us and the soldiers defend us. Those who have the responsibility of defending are to receive their income and their food from those who have the responsibility of feeding, so that they will be able to defend. Those who have the responsibility of feeding are to be defended by those who have the responsibility of defending, so that they will be able to provide food. The emperor or prince in the land is to supervise both groups and see to it that those who have the responsibility of defending are armed and have mounts, and that those

5. I.e., the responsibility of military service.

who have the responsibility of feeding honestly try to increase the supply of food. However, he should not tolerate useless people, who neither feed nor defend, but only consume, are lazy, and live in idleness, and drive them out of the land, as do the bees, which sting the drones to death because they do not work and only eat up the honey of the other bees. This is why Solomon, in Ecclesiastes [5:8-9], calls the kings builders who build the land, for that should be their responsibility. But God preserve us Germans! We are not getting any wiser or doing this the right way, but are continuing for a while to be consumers, and we let those be feeders and defenders who have the desire for it or cannot evade it.

In Luke 2 [3:14] St. John the Baptist confirms the right of this first class to their pay and to hold fiefs, and says that they rightly do their duty when they help their lord make war and serve him. When the soldiers asked him what they were to do, he answered, "Be content with your wages." Now if it were wrong for them to take wages, or if their occupation were against God, he could not have let it continue, permitted it, and confirmed it, but, as a godly, Christian teacher, he would have had to condemn it and deter them from it. This is the answer to those who, because of tenderness of conscience—though this is now rare among these people—profess that it is dangerous to take up this occupation for the sake of temporal goods, since it is nothing but bloodshed, murder, and the inflicting of all kinds of suffering upon one's neighbor, as happens in wartime. These men should inform their consciences that they do not do this from choice, desire, or ill-will, but that this is God's work and that it is their duty to their prince and their God. Therefore, since it is a legitimate office, ordained by God, they should be paid and compensated for doing it, as Christ says in Matthew 10 [:10], "A laborer deserves his wage."

Of course, it is true that if a man serves as a soldier with a heart that neither seeks nor thinks of anything but acquiring wealth, and if temporal wealth is his only reason for doing it, he is not happy when there is peace and not war. Such a man strays from the path and belongs to the devil, even though he fights out of obedience to his lord and at his call. He takes a work that is good in itself and makes it bad for himself by not being very concerned about serving out of obedience and duty, but only about seeking his own profit. For this reason he does not have a good conscience which can say, "Well, for my part, I would like to stay at home, but because my lord calls me and needs me, I come in God's name and know that I am serving God by doing so, and that I will earn or accept the pay that is given me for it." A soldier ought to have the knowledge and confidence that he is doing and must do his duty to be certain that he is serving God and can say, "It is not I that smite, stab, and slay, but God and my prince, for my hand and my body are now their servants." That is the meaning of the watchwords and battle cries, "Emperor!" "France!" "Lüneburg!" "Braunschweig!" This is how the Jews cried against the Midianites, "The sword of God and Gideon!" Judges 7 [:20].

Such a greedy man spoils all other good works, too. For example, a man who preaches for the sake of temporal wealth is lost, though Christ says that a preacher shall live from the gospel. It is not wrong to do things for temporal wealth, for income, wages, and pay are also temporal wealth. If it were wrong, no one should work or do anything to support himself on the ground that it is done for temporal wealth. But to be greedy for temporal wealth and to make a Mammon of it is always wrong in every office, position, and occupation. Leave out greed and other evil thoughts, and it is not sin to fight in a war. Take your wages for it, and whatever is given you. This is why I said above that the work, in itself, is just and godly, but that it becomes wrong if the person is unjust or uses it unjustly.

A second question: "Suppose my lord were wrong in going to war." I reply: If you know for sure that he is wrong, then you should fear God rather than men, Acts 4 [5:29], and you should neither fight nor serve, for you cannot have a good conscience before God. "Oh, no," you say, "my lord would force me to do it; he would take away my fief and would not give me my money, pay, and wages. Besides, I would be despised and put to shame as a coward, even worse, as a man who did not keep his word and deserted his lord in need." I answer: You must take that risk and, with God's help, let whatever happens, happen. He can restore it to you a hundredfold, as he promises in the gospel, "Whoever leaves house, farm, wife, and property, will receive a hundredfold," etc. [Matt. 19:29].

In every other occupation we are also exposed to the danger that the rulers will compel us to act wrongly; but since God will have us leave even father and mother for his sake, we must certainly leave lords for his sake. But if you do not know, or cannot find out, whether your lord is wrong, you ought not to weaken certain obedience for the sake of an uncertain justice; rather you should think the best of your lord, as is the way of love, for "love believes all things" and

"does not think evil," I Corinthians 13 [:4-7]. So, then, you are secure
and walk well before God. If they put you to shame or call you dis-
loyal, it is better for God to call you loyal and honorable than for the
world to call you loyal and honorable. What good would it do you if
the world thought of you as a Solomon or a Moses, and in God's judgment you were considered as bad as Saul or Ahab?

The third question: "Can a soldier obligate himself to serve
more than one lord and take wages or salary from each?" Answer:
I said above that greed is wrong, whether in a good or an evil occupation. Agriculture is certainly one of the best occupations; nonetheless,
a greedy farmer is wrong and is condemned before God. So in this
case to take wages is just and right, and to serve for wages is also
right. But greed is not right, even though the wages for the whole
year were less than a gulden. Again, to take wages and serve for them
is right in itself; it does not matter whether the' wages come from one,
or two, or three, or however many lords, so long as your hereditary lord
or prince is not deprived of what is due him and your service to others
is rendered with his will and consent. A craftsman may sell his skill
to anyone who will have it, and thus serve the one to whom he sells
it, so long as this is not against his ruler and his community. In the
same way a soldier has his skill in fighting from God and can use it
in the service of whoever desires to have it, exactly as though his
skill were an art or trade, and he can take pay for it as he would for
his work. For the soldier's vocation also springs from the law of love.
If anyone needs me and calls for me, I am at his service, and for this
I take my wage or whatever is given me. This is what St. Paul says in
I Corinthians 9 [:7], "Who serves as a soldier at his own expense?"
Thereby Paul approves the soldier's right to his salary. If a prince
needs and requires another's subject for fighting, the subject, with
his own prince's consent and knowledge, may serve and take pay
for it.

"But suppose that one of the princes or lords were to make war
against the other, and I were obligated to both, but preferred to serve
the one who was in the wrong because he has showed me more grace
or kindness than the one who was in the right and from whom I get
less—what then?" Here is the quick, short answer: What is right, that
is, what pleases God, should be more important than wealth, body,
honor and friends, grace, and enjoyment; and in this case there is no
respecting of persons, but only of God. In this case, too, a man must
put up with it for God's sake if it is thought that he acts ungratefully

and is despised for doing it. He has an honorable excuse because God and right will not tolerate our serving the people we like and forsaking those whom we do not like. Although the old Adam does not listen willingly to this, nevertheless, this is what we must do if right is to be maintained. For there is no resisting God, and whoever resists what is right resists God, who gives, orders, and maintains all that is right.

The fourth question: "What is to be said about the man who goes to war not only for the sake of wealth, but also for the sake of temporal honor, to become a big man and be looked up to?" Answer: Greed for money and greed for honor are both greed; the one is as wrong as the other. Whoever goes to war because of this vice earns hell for himself. We should leave and give all honor to God alone and be satisfied with our wages and rations.

It is, therefore, a heathen and not a Christian custom to exhort soldiers before the battle with words like this, "Dear comrades, dear soldiers, be brave and confident; God willing, we shall this day win honor and become rich." On the contrary, they should be exhorted like this, "Dear comrades, we are gathered here to serve, obey, and do our duty to our prince, for according to God's will and ordinance we are bound to support our prince with our body and our possessions, even though in God's sight we are as poor sinners as our enemies are. Nevertheless, since we know that our prince is in the right in this case, or at least do not know otherwise, we are therefore sure and certain that in serving and obeying him we are serving God. Let everyone, then, be brave and courageous and let no one think otherwise than that his fist is God's fist, his spear God's spear, and cry with heart and voice, 'For God and the emperor!' If God gives us victory, the honor and praise shall be his, not ours, for he wins it through us poor sinners. But we will take the booty and the wages as presents and gifts of God's goodness and grace to us, though we are unworthy, and sincerely thank him for them. Now God grant the victory! Forward with joy!"

There can be no doubt but that if one seeks the honor of God and lets him have it—as is just and right, and as it ought to be— then more honor will come than anyone could want, for in I Samuel 2 [:30] God promises, "Those who honor me I will honor, and those who despise me shall be lightly esteemed." Since God cannot fail to keep his promise, he must honor those who honor him. Seeking one's own honor is one of the greatest sins. It is nothing less than *crimen lese maiestatis divine,* that is, robbery of the divine majesty. Let others, therefore, boast and seek honor; you be obedient and quiet, and your honor will find you. Many a battle has been lost that might have been won if honor alone could have done it. These honor-greedy warriors do not believe that God is in the war and gives the victory; therefore they do not fear God and are not joyful, but are foolhardy and mad, and in the end they are defeated.

But I think the "best comrades" [6] are those who encourage themselves and are encouraged before the battle by thinking about the women they love, and have this said to them, "Hey, now, let everyone think about the woman he loves best." I admit that if two credible men who are experienced in these matters had not told me this, I would never have believed that in a business of this kind, where the danger of death stares men in the face, the human heart could so forget itself and be so light. Of course, no one does this when he fights alone with death. But when the company is assembled one stirs up the other, and no one gives a thought to what affects him, because it affects many. But to a Chrstian heart it is terrible to think and hear that at a time when he is confronted by God's judgment and the peril of death, a man arouses and encourages himself with fleshly love; for those who are killed or die thus certainly send their souls straight to hell without delay.

"Indeed," they say, "if I were to think of hell, I could never again go to war." It is still worse to put God and his judgment wilfully out of mind and neither know nor think nor hear anything about them. For this reason a great many soldiers belong to the devil. And some of them are so full of the devil that they know no better way to prove their joy than by speaking contemptuously of God and his judgment, as if their boasting made them really tough; they also dare to swear shamefully by Christ's Passion, and curse and defy God in heaven. It is a lost crowd; it is chaff, and, as in other classes, there is much chaff and little wheat.

It follows that those mercenaries who wander about the country seeking war, although they might work and ply a trade till they were called for and thus from laziness or roughness and wildness of spirit waste their time, cannot be on good terms with God. They can neither give God any good explanation for this nor have a good conscience about their wandering. All they have is a foolhardy desire or eagerness

6. Luther is speaking ironically.

for war or to lead the free, wild life which is typical of such people. Ultimately some of them will become scoundrels and robbers. However, if they would labor or take up a trade and earn their bread, as God has commanded all men to do, until their prince summoned them for himself or permitted and asked them to serve someone else, then they could go to war with the good conscience of men who knew that they were serving at the pleasure of their overlord. Otherwise they could not have such a good conscience. Almighty God shows us a great grace when he appoints rulers for us as an outward sign of his will, so that we are sure we are pleasing his divine will and are doing right, whenever we do the will and pleasure of the ruler. For God has attached and bound his will to them when he says, "Render therefore to Caesar the things that are Caesar's" [Matt. 22:21], and in Romans 13 [:1], "Let every person be subject to the governing authorities." The whole world ought to think of this as a great joy and comfort and even as a compelling reason to love and honor those who rule over us.

Finally, soldiers have many superstitions in battle. One commends himself to St. George, another to St. Christopher; one to this saint, another to that. Some cast magical spells on iron and bullets; some bless horse and rider; some carry St. John's Gospel, or some other object on which they rely. All these soldiers are in a dangerous condition, for they do not believe in God. On the contrary, they sin through unbelief and false trust in God; and if they were to die, they could not avoid being lost.

This is what they ought to do. When the battle begins and the exhortation of which I spoke above has been given, they should simply commend themselves to God's grace and adopt a Christian attitude. For the above exhortation is only a form for doing the external work of war with a good conscience; but since good works save no man, everyone should also say this exhortation in his heart or with his lips, "Heavenly Father, here I am, according to your divine will, in the external work and service of my lord, which I owe first to you and then to my lord for your sake. I thank your grace and mercy that you have put me into a work which I am sure is not sin, but right and pleasing obedience to your will. But because I know and have learned from your gracious word that none of our good works can help us and that no one is saved as a soldier but only as a Christian, therefore, I will not in any way rely on my obedience and work, but place myself freely at the service of your will. I believe with all my heart that only the innocent blood of your dear Son, my Lord Jesus Christ, redeems and saves me, which he shed for me in obedience to your holy will. This is the basis on which I stand before you. In this faith I will live and die, fight, and do everything else. Dear Lord God the Father, preserve and strengthen this faith in me by your Spirit. Amen." If you then want to say the Creed and the Lord's Prayer, you may do so and let that be enough. In so doing commit body and soul into God's hands, draw your sword, and fight in God's name.

If there were many such soldiers in an army, do you think any one could do anything to them? They would devour the world without lifting a sword. Indeed, if there were nine or ten such men in a company, or even three or four, who could say these things with a true heart, I would prefer them to all the muskets, spears, horses, and armor. Then I would be willing to let the Turk come on, with all his power; for the Christian faith is not a joke, nor is it a little thing, but as Christ says in the gospel, "It can do all things" [Mark 9:23]. But, my dear friend, where are those who believe thus and who can do such things? Nevertheless, although the great majority does not do this, we must teach it and know it for the sake of those who will do it, however few they may be. As Isaiah 55 [:11] says God's word does not return empty, but accomplishes his purpose. The others who despise this wholesome teaching which is given for their salvation have their judge to whom they must answer. We are excused; we have done our part. . . .

## 2. JOHN CALVIN (1509-1564)

Schooled in Paris when the new Christian humanists were challenging the domination of scholasticism, himself schooled in law and the author of a commentary on Seneca, John Calvin understandably comes closer to the natural law tradition than does Luther. For him civil law both depends on and enforces the moral law of God summed up in the law of love; law requires equity, and equity is taught by both natural law and the law of love.

The same elements may be traced in Calvin as in other "just war" theorists. His views of civil authority and revolt bear strong resemblance to Luther's.

### CIVIL AUTHORITY AND THE USE OF FORCE

From *Institutes of the Christian Religion* 4.20, trans. J. Allen.

X. But here, it seems, arises an important and difficult question. If by the law of God all Christians are forbidden to kill, and the prophet predicts respecting the Church, that "they shall not hurt nor destroy in all my holy mountain, saith the Lord," how can it be compatible with piety for magistrates to shed blood? But if we understand, that in the infliction of punishment, the magistrate does not act at all from himself, but merely executes the judgments of God, we shall not be embarrassed with this scruple. The law of the Lord commands, "Thou shalt not kill"; but that homicide may not go unpunished, the legislator himself puts the sword into the hands of his ministers, to be used against all homicides. *To hurt* and *to destroy* are incompatible with the character of the godly; but to avenge the afflictions of the righteous at the command of God, is neither *to hurt* nor *to destroy*. Therefore it is easy to conclude that in this respect magistrates are not subject to the common law; by which, though the Lord binds the hands of men, he does not bind his own justice, which he exercises by the hands of magistrates. So, when a prince forbids all his

165

subjects to strike or wound any one, he does not prohibit his officers from executing that justice which is particularly committed to them. I sincerely wish that this consideration were constantly in our recollection, that nothing is done here by the temerity of men, but every thing by the authority of God, who commands it, and under whose guidance we never err from the right way. For we can find no valid objection to the infliction of public vengeance, unless the justice of God be restrained from the punishment of crimes. But if it be unlawful for us to impose restraints upon him, why do we calumniate his ministers? Paul says of the magistrate, that "He beareth not the sword in vain; for he is the minister of God, a revenger to execute wrath upon him that doeth evil." Therefore, if princes and other governors know that nothing will be more acceptable to God than their obedience, and if they desire to approve their piety, justice, and integrity before God, let them devote themselves to this duty. This motive influenced Moses, when, knowing himself to be destined to become the liberator of his people by the power of the Lord, "he slew the Egyptian"; and when he punished the idolatry of the people by the slaughter of three thousand men in one day. The same motive actuated David, when, at the close of his life, he commanded his son Solomon to put to death Joab and Shimei. Hence, also, it is enumerated among the virtues of a king, to "destroy all the wicked of the land, that he may cut off all wicked doers from the city of the Lord." The same topic furnishes the eulogium given to Solomon: "Thou lovest righteousness, and hatest wickedness." How did the meek and placid disposition of Moses burn with such cruelty, that, after having his hands imbrued in the blood of his brethren, he continued to go through the camp till three thousand were slain? How did David, who discovered such humanity all his lifetime, in his last moments bequeath such a cruel injunction to his son respecting Joab? "Let not his hoar head go down to the grave in peace"; and respecting Shimei: "His hoar head bring down to the grave with blood." Both Moses and David, in executing the vengeance committed to them by God, by this severity sanctified their hands, which would have been defiled by lenity. Solomon says, "It is an abomination to kings to commit wickedness; for the throne is established by righteousness." Again: "A king that sitteth in the throne of judgment, scattereth away all evil with his eyes." Again: "A wise king scattereth the wicked, and bringeth the wheel over them." Again: "Take away the dross from the silver, and there shall come forth a vessel for the finer. Take away the wicked from before the king, and his throne shall be established in righteousness." Again: "He that justifieth the wicked, and he that condemneth the just, even they both are an abomination to the Lord." Again: "An evil man seeketh only rebellion; therefore a cruel messenger shall be sent against him." Again: "He that saith unto the wicked, Thou art righteous; him shall the people curse, nations shall abhor him." Now, if it be true justice for them to pursue the wicked with a drawn sword, let them sheathe the sword, and keep their hands from shedding blood, while the swords of desperadoes are drenched in murders; and they will be so far from acquiring the praise of goodness and justice by this forbearance, that they will involve themselves in the deepest impiety. There ought not, however, to be any excessive or unreasonable severity, nor ought any cause to be given for considering the tribunal as a gibbet prepared for all who are accused. For I am not an advocate for unnecessary cruelty, nor can I conceive the possibility of an equitable sentence being pronounced without mercy of which Solomon affirms, that "mercy and truth preserve the king; and his throne is upholden by mercy." Yet it behoves the magistrate to be on his guard against both these errors; that he do not, by excessive severity, wound rather than heal; or, through a superstitious affectation of clemency, fall into a mistaken humanity, which is the worst kind of cruelty, by indulging a weak and ill-judged lenity, to the detriment of multitudes. For it is a remark not without foundation, that was anciently applied to the government of Nerva, that it is bad to live under a prince who permits nothing, but much worse to live under one who permits everything.

XI. Now, as it is sometimes necessary for kings and nations to take up arms for the infliction of such public vengeance, the same reason will lead us to infer the lawfulness of wars which are undertaken for this end. For if they have been intrusted with power to preserve the tranquillity of their own territories, to suppress the seditious tumults of disturbers, to succour the victims of oppression, and to punish crimes—can they exert this power for a better purpose, than to repel the violence of him who disturbs both the private repose of individuals and the general tranquillity of the nation; who excites insurrections, and perpetrates acts of oppression, cruelty, and every species of crime? If they ought to be the guardians and defenders of the laws, it is incumbent upon them to defeat the efforts of all by whose injustice the discipline of the laws is corrupted. And if they justly punish those robbers, whose injuries have only extended to a few persons, shall they suffer a whole district to be plundered and devastated with impunity? For there is no difference, whether he, who in a hostile manner invades, disturbs, and plunders the territory of another to which he has no right, be a king, or one of the meanest of mankind: all persons of this description are equally to be considered as robbers, and ought to be punished as such. It is the dictate both of natural equity, and of the nature of the office, therefore, that princes are armed, not only to restrain the crimes of private individuals by judicial punishments, but also to defend the territories committed to their charge by going to war against any hostile aggression; and the Holy Spirit, in many passages of Scripture, declares such wars to be lawful.

XII. If it be objected that the New Testament contains no precept or example, which proves war to be lawful to Christians, I answer, first, that the reason for waging war which existed in ancient times, is equally valid in the present age; and that, on the contrary, there is no cause to prevent princes from defending their subjects. Secondly, that no express declaration on this subject is to be expected in the writings of the apostles, whose design was, not to organize civil governments, but to describe the spiritual kingdom of Christ. Lastly, that in those very writings it is implied by the way, that no change has been made in this respect by the coming of Christ. "For," to use the words of Augustine, "if Christian discipline condemned all wars, the soldiers who inquired respecting their salvation ought rather to have been directed to cast away their arms, and entirely to renounce the military profession; whereas the advice given them was, 'Do violence to no man, neither accuse any falsely; and be content with your wages.' An injunction to be content with their wages was certainly not a prohibition of the military life." But here all magistrates ought to be very cautious, that they follow not in any respect the impulse of their passions. On the contrary, if punishments are to be inflicted, they ought not to be precipitated with anger, exasperated with hatred, or inflamed with implacable severity: they ought, as Augustine says, "to commiserate our common nature even in him whom they punish for his crime." Or, if arms are to be resorted to against an enemy, that is, an armed robber, they ought not to seize a trivial occasion, nor even to take it when presented, unless they are driven to it by extreme necessity. For, if it be our duty to exceed what was required by that heathen writer who maintained that the evident object of war ought to be the restoration of peace, certainly we ought to make every other attempt before we have recourse to the decision of arms. In short, in both cases they must not suffer themselves to be carried away by any private motive, but be wholly guided by public spirit; otherwise they grossly abuse their power, which is given them, not for their own particular advantage, but for the benefit and service of others. Moreover, on this right of war depends the lawfulness of garrisons, alliances, and other civil munitions. By *garrisons,* I mean soldiers who are stationed in towns to defend the boundaries of a country. By *alliances,* I mean confederations which are made between neighbouring princes, that, if any disturbance arise in their territories, they will render each other mutual assistance, and will unite their forces together for the common resistance of the common enemies of mankind. By *civil munitions,* I mean all the provisions which are employed in the art of war. . . .

XIV. From the magistracy, we next proceed to the laws, which are the strong nerves of civil polity, or, according to an appellation which Cicero has borrowed from Plato, the *souls of states,* without which magistracy cannot subsist, as, on the other hand, without magistrates laws are of no force. No observation, therefore, can be more correct than this, that the law is a silent magistrate, and a magistrate a speaking law. Though I have promised to show by what laws a Christian state ought to be regulated, it will not be reasonable for any person to expect a long discussion respecting the best kind of laws; which is a subject of immense extent, and foreign from our present object. I will briefly remark, however, by the way, what laws it may piously use before God, and be rightly governed by among men. And even this I would have preferred passing over in silence, if I did not know that it is a point on which many persons run into dangerous errors. For some deny that a state is well constituted, which neglects the polity of Moses, and is governed by the common laws of nations. The dangerous and seditious nature of this opinion I leave to the examination of others; it will be sufficient for me to have evinced it to be false and foolish. Now, it is necessary to observe that common distinction, which distributes all the laws of God promulgated by Moses into moral, ceremonial, and judicial, and these different kinds of laws are to be distinctly examined, that we may ascertain what belongs to us, and what does not. Nor let any one be embarrassed by this scruple, that even the ceremonial and judicial precepts are included in the moral. For the ancients, who first made this distinction, were not ignorant that these two kinds of precepts related to the conduct of moral agents; yet, as they might be changed and abrogated without affecting the morality of actions, therefore they did not call them moral precepts. They particularly applied this appellation to those precepts without which there can be no real purity of morals, nor any permanent rule of a holy life.

XV. The moral law, therefore, with which I shall begin, being comprised in two leading articles, of which one simply commands us to worship God with pure faith and piety, and the other enjoins us to embrace men with sincere love—this law, I say, is the true and eternal rule of righteousness, prescribed to men of all ages and nations, who wish to conform their lives to the will of God. For this is his eternal and immutable will, that he himself be worshipped by us all, and that we mutually love one another. The ceremonial law was the pupilage of the Jews, with which it pleased the Lord to exercise that people during a state resembling childhood, till that "fulness of the time" should come, when he would fully manifest his wisdom to the world, and would exhibit the reality of those things which were then adumbrated in figures. The judicial law, given to them as a political constitution, taught them certain rules of equity and justice, by which they might conduct themselves in a harmless and peaceable manner towards each other. And as that exercise of ceremonies properly related to the doctrine of piety, inasmuch as it kept the Jewish Church in the worship and service of God, which is the first article of the moral law, and yet was distinct from piety itself, so these judicial regulations, though they had no other end than the preservation of that love, which is enjoined in the eternal law of God, yet had something which distinguished them from that precept itself. As the ceremonies, therefore, might be abrogated without any violation or injury of piety, so the precepts and duties of love remain of perpetual obligation, notwithstanding the abolition of all these judicial ordinances. If this be true, certainly all nations are left at liberty to enact such laws as they shall find to be respectively expedient for them; provided they be framed according to that perpetual rule of love, so that, though they vary in form, they may have the same end. For those barbarous and savage laws which rewarded theft and permitted promiscuous concubinage, with others still more vile, execrable, and absurd, I am very far from thinking ought to be considered as laws; since they are not only violations of all righteousness, but outrages against humanity itself.

XVI. What I have said will be more clearly understood, if in all laws we properly consider these two things—the constitution of the law and its equity, on the reason of which the constitution itself is founded and rests. Equity, being natural, is the same to all mankind; and consequently all laws, on every subject, ought to have the same equity for their end. Particular enactments and regulations, being connected with circumstances, and partly dependent upon them, may be different in different cases without any impropriety, provided they are all equally directed to the same object of equity. Now, as it is certain that the law of God, which we call the moral law, is no other than a declaration of natural law, and of that conscience which has been engraven by God on the minds of men, the whole rule of this equity, of which we now speak, is prescribed in it. This equity, therefore, must alone be the scope, and rule, and end, of all laws. Whatever laws shall be framed according to that rule, directed to that object, and limited to that end, there is no reason why we should censure them, however they may differ from the Jewish law or from each other. The law of God forbids theft. What punishment was enacted for thieves, among the Jews, may be seen in the book of Exodus. The most ancient laws of other nations punished theft by requiring a compensation of double the value. Subsequent laws made a distinction between open and secret theft. Some proceeded to banishment, some to flagellation, and some to the punishment of death. False witness was punished, among the Jews, with the same punishment as such testimony would have caused to be inflicted on the person against whom it was given; in some countries it was punished with infamy, in others with hanging, in others with crucifixion. All laws agree in punishing murder with death, though in several different forms. The punishments of adulterers in different countries have been attended with different degrees of severity. Yet we see how, amidst this diversity, they are all directed to the same end. For they all agree in denouncing punishment against those crimes which are condemned by the eternal law of God; such as murders, thefts, adulteries, false testimonies, though there is not a uniformity in the mode of punishment; and, indeed, this is neither necessary, nor even expedient. One country, if it did not inflict the most exemplary vengeance upon murderers, would soon be ruined by murders and robberies. One age requires the severity of punishments to be increased. If a country be disturbed by any civil commotion, the evils which generally arise from it must be corrected by new edicts. In time of war all humanity would be forgotten amidst the din of arms, if men were not awed by more than a common dread of punishment. During famine and pestilence, unless greater severity be employed, every thing will fall into ruin. One nation is more prone than others to some particular vice, unless it be most rigidly restrained. What malignity and envy against the public good will be betrayed by him who shall take offence at such diversity, which is best adapted to secure the observance of the law of God? For the objection made by some, that it is an insult to the law of God given by Moses, when it is abrogated, and other laws are preferred to it, is without any foundation; for neither are other laws preferred to it, when they are more approved, not on a simple comparison, but on account of the circumstances of time, place, and nation; nor do we abrogate that which was never given to us. For the Lord gave not that law by the hand of Moses to be promulgated among all nations, and to be universally binding; but after having taken the Jewish nation into his special charge, patronage, and protection, he was pleased to become, in a peculiar manner, their legislator, and, as became a wise legislator, in all the laws which he gave them, he had a special regard to their peculiar circumstances. . . .

XXIV. Now, as we have hitherto described a magistrate who truly answers to his title; who is the father of his country, and, as the poet calls him, the pastor of his people, the guardian of peace, the protector of justice, the avenger of innocence; he would justly be deemed insane who disapproved of such a government. But, as it has happened, in almost all ages, that some princes, regardless of every thing to which they ought to have directed their attention and provision, give themselves up to their pleasures in indolent exemption from every care; others, absorbed in their own interest, expose to sale all laws, privileges, rights, and judgments; others plunder the public of wealth, which they afterwards lavish in mad prodigality; others commit flagrant outrages, pillaging houses, violating virgins and matrons, and murdering infants; many persons cannot be persuaded that such ought to be acknowledged as princes, whom, as far as possible, they ought to obey. For in such enormities, and actions so completely incompatible, not only with the office of a magistrate, but with the duty of every man, they discover no appearance of the image of God, which ought to be conspicuous in a magistrate; while they perceive no vestige of that minister of God who is "not a terror to good works, but to the evil," who is sent "for the punishment of evil-doers, and for the praise of them that do well"; nor recognize that governor, whose dignity and authority the Scripture recommends to us. And certainly the minds of men have always been naturally disposed to hate and execrate tyrants as much as to love and reverence legitimate kings.

XXV. But, if we direct our attention to the word of God, it will carry us much further; even to submit to the government, not only of those princes who discharge their duty to us with becoming integrity and fidelity, but of all who possess the sovereignty, even though they perform none of the duties of their function. For, though the Lord testifies that the magistrate is an eminent gift of his liberality to preserve the safety of men, and prescribes to magistrates themselves the extent of their duty, yet he at the same time declares, that whatever be their characters, they have their government only from him; that those who govern for the public good are true specimens and mirrors of his beneficence; and that those who rule in an unjust and tyrannical manner are raised up by him to punish the iniquity of the people; that all equally possess that sacred majesty with which he has invested legitimate authority. I will not proceed any further till I have subjoined a few testimonies in proof of this point. It is unnecessary, however, to labour much to evince an impious king to be a judgment of God's wrath upon the world, as I have no expectation that any one will deny it: and in this we say no more of a king than of any other robber who plunders our property; or adulterer who violates our bed; or assassin who attempts to murder us; since the Scripture enumerates all these calamities among the curses inflicted by God. But let us rather insist on the proof of that which the minds of men do not so easily admit; that a man of the worst character, and most undeserving of all honour, who holds the sovereign power, really possesses that eminent and Divine authority, which the Lord has given by his word to the ministers of his justice and judgment; and, therefore, that he ought to be regarded by his subjects, as far as pertains to public obedience, with the same reverence and esteem which they would show to the best of kings, if such a one were granted to them. . . .

XXX. And here is displayed his wonderful goodness, and power, and providence; for sometimes he raises up some of his servants as public avengers, and arms them with his commission to punish unrighteous domination, and to deliver from their distressing calamities a people who have been unjustly oppressed: sometimes he accomplishes this end by the fury of men who meditate and attempt something altogether different. Thus he liberated the people of Israel from the tyranny of Pharaoh by Moses; from the oppression of Chusan by

Othniel; and from other yokes by other kings and judges. Thus he subdued the pride of Tyre by the Egyptians; the insolence of the Egyptians by the Assyrians; the haughtiness of the Assyrians by the Chaldeans; the confidence of Babylon by the Medes and Persians, after Cyrus had subjugated the Medes. The ingratitude of the kings of Israel and Judah, and their impious rebellion, notwithstanding his numerous favours, he repressed and punished, sometimes by the Assyrians, sometimes by the Babylonians. These were all the executioners of his vengeance, but not all in the same manner. The former, when they were called forth to the performance of such acts by a legitimate commission from God, in taking arms against kings, were not chargeable with the least violation of that majesty with which kings are invested by the ordination of God; but, being armed with authority from Heaven, they punished an inferior power by a superior one, as it is lawful for kings to punish their inferior officers. The latter, though they were guided by the hand of God in such directions as he pleased, and performed his work without being conscious of it, nevertheless contemplated in their hearts nothing but evil.

XXXI. But whatever opinion be formed of the acts of men, yet the Lord equally executed his work by them, when he broke the sanguinary sceptres of insolent kings, and overturned tyrannical governments. Let princes hear and fear. But, in the meanwhile, it behoves us to use the greatest caution, that we do not despise or violate that authority of magistrates, which is entitled to the greatest veneration, which God has established by the most solemn commands, even though it reside in those who are most unworthy of it, and who, as far as in them lies, pollute it by their iniquity. For though the correction of tyrannical domination is the vengeance of God, we are not, therefore, to conclude that it is committed to us, who have received no other command than to obey and suffer. This observation I always apply to private persons. For if there be, in the present day, any magistrates appointed for the protection of the people and the moderation of the power of kings, such as were, in ancient times, the Ephori, who were a check upon the kings among the Lacedaemonians, or the popular tribunes upon the consuls among the Romans, or the Demarchi upon the senate among the Athenians; or with power such as perhaps is now possessed by the three estates in every kingdom when they are assembled; I am so far from prohibiting them, in the discharge of their duty, to oppose the violence or cruelty of kings, that I affirm, that if they connive at kings in their oppression of their people, such forbearance involves the most nefarious perfidy, because they fraudulently betray the liberty of the people, of which they know that they have been appointed protectors by the ordination of God.

XXXII. But in the obedience which we have shown to be due to the authority of governors, it is always necessary to make one exception, and that is entitled to our first attention—that it do not seduce us from obedience to him, to whose will the desires of all kings ought to be subject, to whose decrees all their commands ought to yield, to whose majesty all their sceptres ought to submit. And, indeed, how preposterous it would be for us, with a view to satisfy men, to incur the displeasure of him on whose account we yield obedience to men! The Lord, therefore, is the King of kings; who, when he has opened his sacred mouth, is to be heard alone, above all, for all, and before all; in the next place, we are subject to those men who preside over us; but no otherwise than in him. If they command any thing against him, it ought not to have the least attention; nor, in this case, ought we to pay any regard to all that dignity attached to magistrates; to which no injury is done when it is subjected to the unrivalled and supreme power of God. On this principle Daniel denied that he had committed any crime against the king in disobeying his impious decree; because the king had exceeded the limits of his office, and had not only done an injury to men, but, by raising his arm against God, had degraded his own authority. On the other hand, the Israelites are condemned for having been too submissive to the impious edict of their king. For when Jeroboam had made his golden calves, in compliance with his will, they deserted the temple of God and revolted to new superstitions. Their posterity conformed to the decrees of their idolatrous kings with the same facility. The prophet severely condemns them for having "willingly walked after the commandment": so far is any praise from being due to the pretext of humility, with which courtly flatterers excuse themselves and deceive the unwary, when they deny that it is lawful for them to refuse compliance with any command of their kings; as if God had resigned his right to mortal men when he made them rulers of mankind; or as if earthly power were diminished by being subordinated to its author, before whom even the principalities of heaven tremble with awe. I know what great and present danger awaits this constancy, for kings cannot bear to be disregarded without the greatest indignation; and "the wrath of a king," says Solomon, "is as messengers of death." But since this edict has been proclaimed by that celestial herald, Peter, "We ought to obey God rather than men," let us console ourselves with this thought, that we truly perform the obedience which God requires of us, when we suffer any thing rather than deviate from piety. And that our hearts may not fail us, Paul stimulates us with another consideration—that Christ has redeemed us at the immense price which our redemption cost him, that we may not be submissive to the corrupt desires of men, much less be slaves to their impiety.

## 3. *ERASMUS* (c. 1466–1536)

Erasmus' work as a Christian humanist, textual scholar, and translator of the New Testament contributed immeasurably to the Protestant Reformation. But believing that truth advances by persuasion rather than by force, he objected to the emerging divisions within Christendom and in his later life pleaded for peace between warring Christian states. He appeals less to authority than Luther and Calvin, and more to a humanitarian concern for the tragic consequences of war.

## WAR AND THE CHRISTIAN PRINCE

"On Beginning War," in *The Education of a Christian Prince,* trans. and ed. L. K. Born (1965).

Although a prince ought nowhere to be precipitate in his plans, there is no place for him to be more deliberate and circumspect than in the matter of going to war. Some evils come from one source and others from another, but from war comes the shipwreck of all that is good and from it the sea of all calamities pours out. Then, too, no other misfortune clings so steadfastly. War is sown from war; from the smallest comes the greatest; from one comes two; from a jesting one comes a fierce and bloody one, and the plague arising in one place, spreads to the nearest peoples and is even carried into the most distant places.

A good prince should never go to war at all unless, after trying every other means, he cannot possibly avoid it. If we were of this mind, there would hardly be a war. Finally, if so ruinous an occurrence cannot be avoided, then the prince's main care should be to wage the war with as little calamity to his own people and as little shedding of Christian blood as may be, and to conclude the struggle as soon as possible. The really Christian prince will first weigh the great difference between man, who is an animal born for peace and good will, and beasts and monsters, who are born to predatory war; [he will weigh also] the difference between men and Christian men. Then

177

let him think over how earnestly peace is to be sought and how honorable and wholesome it is; on the other hand [let him consider] how disastrous and criminal an affair war is and what a host of all evils it carries in its wake even if it is the most justifiable war—if there really is any war which can be called "just." Lastly, when the prince has put away all personal feelings, let him take a rational estimate long enough to reckon what the war will cost and whether the final end to be gained is worth that much—even if victory is certain, victory which does not always happen to favor the best causes. Weigh the worries, the expenditures, the trials, the long wearisome preparation. That barbaric flux of men in the last stages of depravity must be got together, and while you wish to appear more generous in favor than the other prince, in addition to paying out money you must coax and humor the mercenary soldiers, who are absolutely the most abject and execrable type of human being. Nothing is dearer to a good prince than to have the best possible subjects. But what greater or more ready ruin to moral character is there than war? There is nothing more to the wish of the prince than to see his people safe and prospering in every way. But while he is learning to campaign he is compelled to expose his young men to so many dangers, and often in a single hour to make many and many an orphan, widow, childless old man, beggar, and unhappy wretch.

The wisdom of princes will be too costly for the world if they persist in learning from experience how dreadful war is, so that when they are old men, they may say: "I did not believe that war was so utterly destructive!" But—and I call God to witness—with what countless afflictions on the whole world have you learned that idea! The prince will understand some day that it was useless to extend the territory of the kingdom and that what in the beginning seemed a gain was [in reality] tremendous loss, but in the meantime a great many thousands of men have been killed or impoverished. These things should better be learned from books, from the stories of old men, from the tribulations of neighbors: "For many years this or that prince has been fighting on for such and such a kingdom. How much more is his loss than his gain!" Let the good prince establish matters of the sort that will be of lasting worth. Those things which are begun out of a fancy are to our liking while the fancy lasts, but the things which are based on judgment and which delight the young man, will also afford pleasure to the old man. Nowhere is this truth more to be observed than in the beginning of war.

Plato calls it sedition, not war, when Greeks war with Greeks; and if this should happen, he bids them fight with every restraint. What term should we apply, then, when Christians engage in battle with Christians, since they are united by so many bonds to each other? What shall we say when on account of a mere title, on account of a personal grievance, on account of a stupid and youthful ambition, a war is waged with every cruelty and carried on during many years?

Some princes deceive themselves that any war is certainly a just one and that they have a just cause for going to war. We will not attempt to discuss whether war is ever just; but who does not think his own cause just? Among such great and changing vicissitudes of human events, among so many treaties and agreements which are now entered into, now rescinded, who can lack a pretext—if there is any real excuse —for going to war? But the pontifical laws do not disapprove all war. Augustine approves of it in some instances, and St. Bernard praises some soldiers. But Christ himself and Peter and Paul everywhere teach the opposite. Why is their authority less with us than that of Augustine or Bernard? Augustine in one or two places does not disapprove of war, but the whole philosophy of Christ teaches against it. There is no place in which the apostles do not condemn it; and in how many places do those very holy fathers, by whom, to the satisfaction of some, war has been approved in one or two places, condemn and abhor it? Why do we slur over all these matters and fasten upon that which helps our sins? Finally, if any one will investigate the matter more carefully, he will find that no one has approved the kind of wars in which we are now commonly involved.

Certain arts are not countenanced by the laws on the ground that they are too closely allied to imposture and are too frequently practiced by deceit; for example, astrology and the so-called "alchemy," even if someone happens to be employing them for an honorable purpose. This restriction will be made with far more justice in the case of wars, for even if there are some which might be called "just," yet as human affairs are now, I know not whether there could be found any of this sort—that is, the motive for which was not ambition, wrath, ferocity, lust, or greed. It too often happens that nobles, who are more lavish than their private means allow, when the opportunity is presented stir up war in order to replenish their resources at home even by the plunder of their peoples. It happens sometimes that princes enter into mutual agreements and carry on a war on trumped-up grounds so as to reduce still more the power of the people and secure their own positions through disaster to their subjects. Wherefore the good Christian prince should hold under suspicion every war, no matter how just.

People may lay down the doctrine that your rights must not be forsaken. In the first place those rights are connected to a large extent with the private affairs of the prince if he has acquired them through alliances. How unfair it would be to maintain them at the expense of such great suffering to the people; and while you are seeking some addition or other to your power, to plunder the whole kingdom and to plunge it into deadliest turmoil. If one prince offends another on some trivial matter (probably a personal one such as a marriage alliance or other like affair) what concern is this to the people as a whole? A good prince measures everything by the advantage of his people, otherwise he is not even a prince. He does not have the same right over men as over animals. A large part of the ruling authority is in the consent of the people, which is the factor that first created kings. If a disagreement arises between princes, why not go to arbiters? There are plenty of bishops, abbots, and learned men, or reliable magistrates, by whose judgments the matter could better be settled than by such slaughter, despoliation, and calamity to the world.

The Christian prince should first question his own right, and then if it is established without a doubt he should carefully consider whether it should be maintained by means of catastrophes to the whole world. Those who are wise sometimes prefer to lose a thing rather than to gain it, because they realize that it will be less costly. Caesar, I think, would prefer to give up his rights rather than seek to attain the old monarchy and that right which the letter of the jurisconsults conferred on him. But what will be safe, they say, if no one maintains his rights? Let the prince insist by all means, if there is any advantage to the state, only do not let the right of the prince bear too hard on his subjects. But what is safe anywhere while everyone is maintaining his rights to the last ditch? We see wars arise from wars, wars following wars, and no end or limit to the upheaval! It is certainly obvious that nothing is accomplished by these means. Therefore other remedies should be given a trial. Not even between the best of friends will relations remain permanently harmonious unless sometimes one gives in to the other. A husband often makes some concession to his wife so as not to break their harmony. What does war cause but war? Courtesy, on the other hand, calls forth cour-

tesy, and fairness, fairness. The fact that he can see, from the countless calamities which war always carries in its wake, that the greatest
hardship falls on those to whom the war means nothing and who are
in no way deserving of these catastrophes, will have an effect on the
devoted and merciful prince.

After the prince has reckoned and added up the total of all the
catastrophes [which would come] to the world (if that could ever
be done), then he should think over in his own mind: "Shall I, one
person, be the cause of so many calamities? Shall I alone be charged
with such an outpouring of human blood; with causing so many
widows; with filling so many homes with lamentation and mourning;
with robbing so many old men of their sons; with impoverishing so
many who do not deserve such a fate; and with such utter destruction
of morals, laws, and practical religion? Must I account for all these
things before Christ?" The prince cannot punish his enemy unless
he first brings hostile activities upon his own subjects. He must fleece
his people, and he must receive [into his realm] the soldier, who has
been called ruthless (and not without justification) by Vergil. He
must cut off his subjects from those districts which they formerly enjoyed for their own advantage; [or else the reverse], he must shut up
his subjects in order to hem in the enemy. And it frequently happens
that we inflict worse sufferings upon our own people than upon the
enemy. It is more difficult, as well as more desirable, to build a fine
city than to destroy it. But we see flourishing cities which are established by inexperienced and common people, demolished by the
wrath of princes. Very often we destroy a town with greater labor and
expense than that with which we could build a new one, and we
carry on war at such great expense, such loss, such zeal, and pains, that
peace could be maintained at one-tenth of these costs.

Let the good prince always lean toward that glory which is not
steeped in blood nor linked with the misfortune of another. In war,
however fortunately it turns out, the good fortune of one is always
the ruin of the other. Many a time, too, the victor weeps over a
victory bought too dearly.

If you are not moved by devotion, nor by the calamity of the
world, surely you will be stirred by the honor of the term "Christian."
What do we think the Turks and Saracens are saying about us when
they see that for century after century there has been no harmony
between Christian princes; that no treaties have secured peace; that
there has been no end to bloodshed; and that there has been less

disorder among the heathen than among those who profess the most complete accord in following the teachings of Christ?

How fleeting, short, and delicate is the life of man, and how exposed to calamities, with so many diseases and accidents which are continually happening such as the falling of buildings, shipwrecks, earthquakes, and lightning? There is no need, then, of wars to stir up misfortunes; and more calamities come from that source than from all else. It was the duty of the preachers to have uprooted completely the ideas of discord from the hearts of the common people. But now practically every Angle hates the Gaul, and every Gaul the Angle, for no other reason than that he is an Angle. The Irishman, just because he is an Irishman, hates the Briton; the Italian hates the German; the Swabian, the Swiss; and so on throughout the list. District hates district, and city . . . hates city. Why do these stupid names do more to divide us than the common name of Christ does to unite us?

Although we may grant some war to be just, yet, since we see that all men go mad over this scourge, it is the part of wise priests to deflect the minds of commoners and princes into different channels. Now we see them often as the very firebrands of war. The bishops are not ashamed to go about in the camp, and there is the cross, and there the body of Christ, and they mix His heavenly sacraments with things that are more than Tartarean and in such bloody discord produce the symbols of the greatest charity. What is more ridiculous, Christ is in both camps, as if he were fighting against himself. It was not enough that war was tolerated among Christians, it must also be given the place of highest honor.

If the whole teachings of Christ do not everywhere inveigh against war, if a single instance of specific commendation of war can be brought forth in its favor, let us Christians fight. The Hebrews were allowed to engage in war, but only by consent of God. Our oracle, which we hear steadily in the Gospels, restrains us from war, and yet we wage war more madly than they. David was most pleasing to God for various good qualities, and yet He forbade His temple to be built by him on the one ground that he was tainted with blood; that is, he was a warrior. He chose the peaceful Solomon for this task. If these things were done among the Jews, what should be done among us Christians? They had a shadow of Solomon, we have the real Solomon, the Prince of Peace, Christ, who conciliates all things in heaven and earth.

Not even against the Turks do I believe we should rashly go to war, first reflecting in my own mind that the kingdom of Christ was created, spread out, and firmly established by far different means. Perchance then it is not right that it should be maintained by means differing from those by which it was created and extended. We see how many times under pretexts of wars of this kind the Christian people have been plundered and nothing else has been accomplished. Now, if the matter has to do with faith, that has been increased and made famous by the suffering of martyrs and not by forces of soldiery; but if it is for ruling power, wealth, and possessions, we must continuously be on guard lest the cause have too little of Christianity in it. But on the contrary, to judge from some who are conducting wars of this kind, it may more readily happen that we degenerate into Turks than that they become Christians through our efforts. First let us see that we ourselves are genuine Christians, and then, if it seems best, let us attack the Turks.

We have written elsewhere more extensively on the evils of war and should not repeat here. I will only urge princes of Christian faith to put aside all feigned excuses and all false pretexts and with wholehearted seriousness to work for the ending of that madness for war which has persisted so long and disgracefully among Christians, that among those whom so many ties unite there may arise a peace and concord. Let them develop their genius to this end, and for this let them show their strength, combine their plans, and strain every nerve. Whoever desires to appear great, let him prove himself great in this way. If any one accomplishes this, he will have done a deed far more magnificent than if he had subdued the whole of Africa by arms. It would not be so difficult to do, if everyone would cease to favor his own cause, if we could set aside all personal feelings and carry out the common aim, if Christ, not the world, was in our plans. Now, while everyone is looking out for his own interests, while popes and bishops are deeply concerned over power and wealth, while princes are driven headlong by ambition or anger, while all follow after them for the sake of their own gain, it is not surprising that we run straight into a whirlwind of affairs under the guidance of folly. But if, after common counsel, we should carry out our common task, even those things which are purely personal to each one would be more prosperous. Now even that for which alone we are fighting is lost.

I have no doubt, most illustrious of princes, but that you are of this mind; for you were born in that atmosphere and have been trained by the best and most honorable men along those lines. For the rest, I pray that Christ, who is all good and supreme, may continue to bless your worthy efforts. He gave you a kingdom untainted by blood; He would have it always so. He rejoices to be called the Prince of Peace; may you do the same, that by your goodness and your wisdom, at last there may be a respite from the maddest of mad wars. The memory of the misfortunes we have passed through will also commend peace to us, and the calamities of earlier times will render twofold the favor of your kindness.

## 4. *MENNO SIMONS* (c. 1496–1561)

Enthused with the idea of a Christian state, Anabaptist leaders like Thomas Münzer called for an apocalyptic war against heretics and infidels. Executed in 1525 for his role in the Peasant War, Münzer had created an image of Anabaptists against which Menno Simons and others were forced to protest.

Under the influence of Zwingli, Menno taught the separation of church and state, rejecting the Theodosian ideal of a Christain empire in favor of the patristic separation of the heavenly and temporal kingdoms. Members of the Kingdom of God have a higher loyalty and calling than to this present world. They give themselves to spiritual activities and support civil government by their prayers, but they engage in no political activity, take no oaths, and use no force. Even under persecution and attack true Christians remain non-violent.

The Mennonite position differs from that of Erasmus and of some Quakers primarily by its dependence on a two-kingdom theology.

## TWO KINGDOMS

From "A Reply to False Accusations," in *The Complete Writings of Menno Simons,* trans. L. Verduin and ed. J. C. Wenger (1956).

The Scriptures teach that there are two opposing princes and two opposing kingdoms: the one is the Prince of peace; the other the prince of strife. Each of these princes has his particular kingdom and as the prince is so is also the kingdom. The Prince of peace is Christ Jesus; His kingdom is the kingdom of peace, which is His church; His messengers are the messengers of peace; His Word is the word of peace; His body is the body of peace; His children are the seed of peace; and His inheritance and reward are the inheritance and reward of peace. In short, with this King, and His Kingdom and reign, it is nothing but peace. Everything that is seen, heard, and done is peace.

We have heard the word of peace, namely, the consoling Gospel of peace from the mouth of His messengers of peace. We, by His grace, have believed and accepted it in peace and have committed ourselves to the only, eternal, and true Prince of peace, Christ Jesus, in His kingdom of peace and under His reign, and are thus by the gift of His Holy Spirit, by means of faith, incorporated into His body. And henceforth we look with all the children of His peace for the promised inheritance and reward of peace.

Such exceeding grace of God has appeared unto us poor, miserable sinners that we who were formerly no people at all and who knew of no peace are now called to be such a glorious people of God, a church, kingdom, inheritance, body, and possession of peace. Therefore we desire not to break this peace, but by His great power by which He has called us to this peace and portion, to walk in this grace and peace, unchangeably and unwaveringly unto death.

Peter was commanded to sheathe his sword. All Christians are commanded to love their enemies; to do good unto those who abuse and persecute them; to give the mantle when the cloak is taken, the other cheek when one is struck. Tell me, how can a Christian defend scripturally retaliation, rebellion, war, striking, slaying, torturing, stealing, robbing and plundering and burning cities, and conquering countries?

The great Lord who has created you and us, who has placed our hearts within us knows, and He only knows that our hearts and hands are clear of all sedition and murderous mutiny. By His grace we will ever remain clear. For we truly confess that all rebellion is of the flesh and of the devil.

O beloved reader, our weapons are not swords and spears, but patience, silence, and hope, and the Word of God. With these we must maintain our heavy warfare and fight our battle. Paul says, The weapons of our warfare are not carnal; but mighty through God. With these we intend and desire to storm the kingdom of the devil; and not with sword, spears, cannon, and coats of mail. For He esteemeth iron as straw, and brass as rotten wood. Thus may we with our Prince, Teacher, and Example Christ Jesus, raise the father against the son, and the son against the father, and may cast down imagination and every high thing that exalteth itself against the knowledge of God, and bring into captivity every thought in obedience to Christ.

True Christians do not know vengeance, no matter how they are mistreated. In patience they possess their souls (Luke 21:18). And they do not break their peace, even if they should be tempted by bondage, torture, poverty, and besides, by the sword and fire. They do not cry, Vengeance, vengeance, as does the world; but with Christ they supplicate and pray: Father, forgive them; for they know not what they do (Luke 23:34; Acts 7:60).

According to the declaration of the prophets they have beaten their swords into plowshares and their spears into pruning hooks. They shall sit every man under his vine and under his fig-tree, Christ; neither shall they learn war any more (Isa. 2:4; Mic. 4:3).

They do not seek your money, goods, injury, nor blood, but they seek the honor and praise of God and the salvation of your souls. They are the children of peace; their hearts overflow with peace; their mouths speak peace, and they walk in the way of peace; they are full of peace. They seek, desire, and know nothing but peace; and are prepared to forsake country, goods, life, and all for the sake of peace. For they are the kingdom, people, congregation, city, property, and body of peace, as has been heard.

Beloved reader, I poor, miserable man (pardon me for writing this), have in my weakness these seventeen years feared the Word of the Lord and served my neighbors. I have without faltering borne scorn and cross with much misery, anxiety, tribulation, and peril. I trust by His grace that I will do so to the end, to testify with a good conscience to His holy Word, will, and ordinance with mouth, pen, life, and death as much as in me is. Is it possible that at heart I am a stormy, rebellious, vengeful, and bloody murderer? The Most High will save His poor servant from that.

Again, in Brabant, Flanders, Friesland, and Gelderland the God-fearing pious hearts are led daily to the slaughter as innocent sheep, and are tyrannically and inhumanly martyred. Their hearts are full of spirit and strength; their mouths flow like rivulets; their conduct savors of holy oil; their doctrine is powerful; and their life is beyond reproach. Neither emperor nor king, fire nor sword, life nor death, can frighten or separate them from the Word of the Lord. And do you suppose that their hearts are even then still ensnared by bitterness, sedition, vengeance, plunder, hatred, and bloodshed? If that were the case, then there has been a lot of suffering for naught.

Oh, no, reader, no! Learn to know what a true Christian is, of whom he is born, how he is minded, what his real intention and ambition is, and you will find that they are not rebels, murderers, and robbers as the learned ones rave, but that they are a God-fearing, pious, peaceable people as the Scriptures teach.

The other prince is the prince of darkness, Antichrist, and Satan. This prince is a prince of all tumult and blood. Raging and murder is his proper nature and policy. His commandments and teachings and his kingdom, body, and church are of the same nature (I John 3). Here we need not much Scripture, for seeing, hearing, and daily experience prove the truth.

Our opponents invent that we are intent upon rebellion; something of which we have never thought! But we say, and that truthfully, that they and their ancestors for more than a thousand years have been that which they make us out to be. Read history and you will be convinced of this. All those who place themselves in opposition to their shamefulness, dishonor, and evil-doing have had to suffer for it. Even so it is today.

For what they have done these last few years by their writings, teachings, and cries, cities and countries prove. How neatly they have placed one ruler against the others saying, Since the sword is placed in your hands you may maintain the Word of the Lord thereby, until they prevailed on them and have shed human blood like water, torn the hearts from each other's bodies, and have made countless harlots, rogues, widows, and orphans. The innocent citizen they have devoured and plundered; cities and lands they have destroyed. In short, they have done as if neither prophet nor Christ nor apostle nor the Word of God had even been upon the earth. Notwithstanding, they wish to be called the holy, Christian church and body. O dear Lord, how lamentably is Thy holy, worthy Word mocked, and Thy glorious work derided, as if Thy divine and powerful activity in Thy church were nothing but reading, shouting, water, bread, wine, and name; and as if rebellion, warring, robbing, murder, and devilish works were permissible. Dear reader, behold and observe, and learn to know this kingdom and body. For if they with such actions and doings were the kingdom and body of Christ, as the learned ones assure them, then Christ's holy, glorious kingdom, church, and body would be an inhuman, cruel, rebellious, bloody, rapacious, noisy, unmerciful, and unrighteous people. This is incontrovertible. Oh, damnable error, dark blindness!

And it is not enough that they by their light-minded, licentious doctrine lead the whole world into destruction and sorrow and deprive their own members of property, people, prosperity, and possessions. But besides, in their madness they must lay hands upon the innocent, peaceable, and humble kingdom and body of Christ which does not harm the least upon the earth. Incessantly they lie, slander, revile, betray, and incite. Well may one say with the holy Peter that they are born to torture and corruption: for their hearts, mouths, and hands drip and reek with blood.

Oh, how accurately the Holy Spirit has depicted them, saying, I saw the woman drunken with the blood of the saints and with the martyrs of Jesus. And in her was found the blood of the prophets, and of the saints and all that were slain upon the earth (Rev. 17:6; 18:20).

Behold, kind reader, thus you will observe that they fall by their own sword which they drew against us, as the prophet says. For we may with clear consciences appear before the world (eternal praise be to the Lord) and truthfully maintain that we from the time of our confession until the present moment have harmed no one, have desired nobody's property, much less laid hands on it. We have not sought the destruction or blood of any, either by word or deed. By the grace of God we shall never do this. But what they have done by their tumultuous crying, lying, slander, railing, writing, and betraying, we will commend to the judgment of the Lord.

The merciful and gracious Lord grant and give you and them wisdom that you may learn to know of what spirit and kingdom you are the children, what you seek, what prince you serve, what doctrine you maintain, what sacraments you have, what fruits you produce, what life you lead, and in what kingdom, body, and church you are incorporated. This is our sincere wish.

Kind reader, earnestly reflect upon this our brief delineation of the two princes and their kingdoms, and by the grace of God, it will give you no mean insight into the Scriptures.

# V. HUMAN RIGHTS AND INTERNATIONAL LAW

A Christian ethic that is concerned about war with infidels as well as between Christians has to find a universally applicable basis for placing moral limitations on war. One can hardly plead the rights of pagans to those convinced that Christians should rule the world, or appeal to Protestants on Catholic grounds.

Spanish conquests in the Americas had aroused the moral criticism of Francisco de Vitoria (see chapter III). His work laid the foundation for more systematic treatment by another Spanish writer, Francisco Suarez, and thereby prepared the way for a body of international law based on natural law. In the face of religious wars, the Dutch jurist Hugo Grotius sought a basis, admittedly established by God, to set limits on war which would be binding on men regardless of their religious persuasion. He resorted to the pre-Christian natural law theory of Cicero. Similarly John Locke, faced with religious conflicts that produced one English civil war and threatened another (see his *Letters Concerning Toleration*), appealed to natural rights shared by all men regardless of nationality or creed.

For further reading:

Cox, Richard H. *Locke on War and Peace.* Oxford University Press, 1960.

Dumbauld, E. *The Life and Legal Writings of Hugo Grotius.* University of Oklahoma Press, 1969.

Dunn, J. M. *The Political Thought of John Locke.* Cambridge University Press, 1969.

Gough, J. W. *John Locke's Political Philosophy.* Oxford University Press, 1968.

Greenspan, M. *The Modern Law of Land Warfare.* University of California Press, 1959.

Grotius, H. *The Law of War and Peace.* Oxford University Press, 1960.

Hamilton, B. *Political Thought in Sixteenth Century Spain.* Clarendon Press, 1963.

Locke, John. *Essays on the Law of Nature.* Edited by W. Von Leyden. Clarendon Press, 1954.

Scott, J. B. *The Spanish Conception of International Law and Its Sanctions.* Carnegie Endowment for International Peace, 1934.

———. *The Spanish Origin of International Law.* Georgetown University Press, 1928.

Tooke, J. D. *The Just War in Aquinas and Grotius.* S.P.C.K., 1965.

# 1. FRANCISCO SUAREZ (1548-1617)

Perhaps the most influential of Spanish theologians and philosophers, Suarez achieved fame as a commentator on and systematizer of Thomistic thought. In 1612 he published *On Laws and God the Lawgiver*, enlarging on Aquinas' concept of the law of nations (*jus gentium*). The specifics of civil law vary from nation to nation and depend on the decisions of legislators. By contrast, the law of nations is often unwritten; it is a body of general laws, common to all nations, which has gained acceptance in the course of history because it serves the well-being of all men and because it conforms to the universal and primary principles of natural law.

Like Aquinas, Suarez treats war within the context of love in *The Three Theological Virtues* (published posthumously in 1621). Discussing essentially the same questions as Vitoria, he lays the foundation for regarding the laws of war as binding on all nations, for limiting war through international law, for selective conscientious objection, and for considering rebellion in the light of just war principles.

## THE LAW OF NATIONS

From *On Laws and God the Lawgiver* 2, trans. G. L. Williams, A. Brown, and J. Waldron, in *Classics of International Law* 2, ed. J. B. Scott (1944).

### CAN THE *JUS GENTIUM* BE DISTINGUISHED FROM NATURAL LAW AS SIMPLY AS POSITIVE HUMAN LAW?

1. From what has thus far been said, the conclusion seems to follow that the *jus gentium*, properly so called, is not contained within the bounds of natural law, but that on the contrary it differs essentially therefrom; for although it agrees with natural law in many respects, nevertheless, the two are distinct from each other owing to practical differences in their respective characters.

The *jus gentium* and natural law agree, first, in that both are in a sense common to all mankind. And on this ground each may be

195

called a law of nations (*gentium*), if we are to confine our attention to terms alone. The characteristic of being common to all nations is clearly evident in the case of natural law, and for that reason the law of nature itself is called . . . the law of nations (*jus gentium*); as may be noted in the wording of many laws. However, this name is more properly bestowed upon the kind introduced by the custom of nations. . . .

Secondly, these two kinds of law agree in the fact that, just as the subject matter of the *jus gentium* has application to men alone, so also the subject matter of the natural law is peculiar to mankind, either in its entirety, or in great part. . . . Consequently, many examples which the jurists classify under the head of the *jus gentium* because of this characteristic alone, fall only nominally under the *jus gentium*, strictly viewed. For in reality such examples pertain to the natural law; as in the case, for instance, of reverence towards God, the honouring of one's parents, and dutiful patriotism . . . the observance of treaties of peace, of truces, of the immunity of ambassadors, and similar matters. . . .

Thirdly, the *jus gentium* and natural law agree in that both systems include precepts, prohibitions, and also concessions or permissions. . . .

On the other hand, the *jus gentium* differs from the natural law, primarily and chiefly, because it does not, in so far as it contains affirmative precepts, derive the necessity for these precepts solely, from the nature of the case, by means of a manifest inference drawn from natural principles; for everything of this character is [strictly] natural, as we have already demonstrated, [and therefore pertains to natural law]. Hence, such necessity [as may characterize the precepts of the *jus gentium*] must be derived from some other source. Similarly, the negative precepts of the *jus gentium* forbid nothing on the ground that the thing forbidden is evil in itself; for such prohibitions are [properly within the province of] the natural law. From the standpoint of human reason, then, the *jus gentium* is not so much indicative of what is [inherently] evil, as it is constitutive of evil. Thus it does not forbid evil acts on the ground that they are evil, but renders [certain] acts evil by prohibiting them.

These differences are, indeed, real and (as it were) essential differences in law; and therefore, from this standpoint, a distinction exists between natural law and the *jus gentium*.

Secondly, and consequently, the two systems under discussion differ in that the *jus gentium* cannot be immutable to the same degree as the natural law. For immutability springs from necessity; and therefore, that which is not equally necessary cannot be equally immutable. This point will be expounded more fully in the following chapter.

Thirdly, it follows from the above that even in those respects in which they seem to agree, these two systems of law are not entirely alike. For, in its universality and its general acceptance by all peoples, the natural law is common to all, and only through error can it fail of observance in any place; whereas the *jus gentium* is not observed always, and by all nations, but [only] as a general rule, and by almost all, as Isidore states. Hence, that which is held among some peoples to be *jus gentium*, may elsewhere and without fault fail to be observed. . . .

Similarly, in my judgment, the law of war—in so far as that law rests upon the power possessed by a given state or a supreme monarchy, for the punishment, avenging, or reparation of any injury inflicted upon it by another state—would seem to pertain properly to the law of nations. For it was not indispensable by virtue of natural reason alone that the power in question should exist within an injured state, since men could have established some other mode of inflicting vengeance, or entrusted that power to some third prince and quasi-arbitrator with coercive power. Nevertheless, since the mode in question, which is at present in practice, is easier and more in conformity with nature, it has been adopted by custom and is just to the extent that it may not be rightfully resisted.

In the same class, I place slavery. For peoples and nations, in their relations with one another, put into practice the law regarding slavery, although that institution was not necessary from the standpoint of natural reason; for, as I have said, another mode of punishment could have been introduced. Under present conditions, however, the law in question exists in such form that the guilty are bound to submit to the punishment of slavery in accordance with the manner in which that custom has been introduced, while the victors, on their side, may not justly punish their conquered enemies more severely at the close of the war unless there exists some other special ground for punishment which would justify such a course of action.

Likewise, treaties of peace and truces may be placed under this head [that is, under the law of nations, or *jus gentium* in the strict sense of the term]; not in so far as relates to the obligation to observe such treaties after they are made, since this obligation pertains rather to the natural law, but in so far as [offers of] such treaties should be heeded and not refused, when presented in due manner and for a reasonable cause. For while such compliance is to a great degree in harmony with natural reason, it appears to be still more firmly established by usage itself and by the law of nations, [thus] falling under a more binding obligation.

There are other examples of the same sort which could be pointed out and expounded.

The rational basis, moreover, of this phase of law consists in the fact that the human race, into howsoever many different peoples and kingdoms it may be divided, always preserves a certain unity, not only as a species, but also a moral and political unity (as it were) enjoined by the natural precept of mutual love and mercy; a precept which applies to all, even to strangers of every nation.

Therefore, although a given sovereign state, commonwealth, or kingdom may constitute a perfect community in itself, consisting of its own members, nevertheless, each one of these states is also, in a certain sense, and viewed in relation to the human race, a member of that universal society; for these states when standing alone are never so self-sufficient that they do not require some mutual assistance, association, and intercourse, at times for their own greater welfare and advantage, but at other times because also of some moral necessity or need. This fact is made manifest by actual usage.

Consequently, such communities have need of some system of law whereby they may be directed and properly ordered with regard to this kind of intercourse and association; and although that guidance is in large measure provided by natural reason, it is not provided in sufficient measure and in a direct manner with respect to all matters; therefore, it was possible for certain special rules of law to be introduced through the practice of these same nations. For just as in one state or province law is introduced by custom, so among the human race as a whole it was possible for laws to be introduced by the habitual conduct of nations. This was the more feasible because the matters comprised within the law in question are few, very closely related to natural law and most easily deduced therefrom in a manner so advantageous and so in harmony with nature itself that, while this derivation [of the law of nations from the natural law] may not be self-evident—that is, not essentially and absolutely required for moral rectitude—it is nevertheless quite in accord with nature, and universally acceptable for its own sake.

# ON WAR

From *The Three Theological Virtues: On Charity* disputation 13, trans. G. L. Williams, A. Brown, and J. Waldron, in *Classics of International Law* 2, ed. J. B. Scott (1944).

## SECTION I

### IS WAR INTRINSICALLY EVIL?

2. Our first conclusion is that war, absolutely speaking, is not intrinsically evil, nor is it forbidden to Christians. This conclusion is a matter of faith and is laid down in the Scriptures, for in the Old Testament, wars waged by most holy men are praised: "Blessed be Abram [. . . .] And blessed be God by whose protection the enemies are in thy hands." We find similar passages concerning Moses, Josue, Samson, Gedeon, David, the Machabees, and others, whom God often ordered to wage war upon the enemies of the Hebrews. Moreover, the apostle Paul (Heb. 11) said that by faith the saints conquered kingdoms. The same principle is confirmed by further testimony, that of the Fathers quoted by Gratian, and also that of Ambrose.

However, one may object, in the first place, that the Lord said to David "Thou shalt not build my temple because thou art a man who has shed blood."

Secondly, it will be objected that Christ said to Peter (John 18): "Put up thy sword into the scabbard," &c.; and that Isaias also said (Isa. 2): "They shall turn their swords into ploughshares [. . .] neither shall they be exercised any more to war," and, in another chapter (chap. 11): "They shall not hurt nor shall they kill in all [my] holy mountain." The Prophet is speaking, indeed, of the time of the coming of the Messiah, at which time, especially, it will be made clear, what is permissible and what is not permissible.

Thirdly, at the Council of Nicaea a penalty was imposed upon Christians who, after having received the faith, enrolled themselves for military service. Furthermore, Pope Leo wrote that war was forbidden to Christians, after a solemn penance.

Fourthly, war morally brings with it innumerable sins; and a given course of action is considered in itself evil and forbidden, if it is practically always accompanied by unseemly circumstances and harm to one's neighbours. [Furthermore,] one may add that war is opposed to peace, to the love of one's enemies, and to the forgiveness of injuries.

3. We reply to the first objection that [the Scriptural passage in question] is based upon the unjust slaying of Uriah; and, also, upon the particularly great reverence owed to the Temple.

[As for the second objection, we may answer, first, that] Christ our Lord is speaking of one who on his own initiative wishes to use the sword, and in particular, of one who so desires, against the will of his prince. Moreover, the words of Isaias, especially in chap. 11, are usually understood as referring to the state of glory. Secondly, it is said that future peace was symbolized in the coming of the Messiah, as is explained by Jerome, . . . Eusebius, and other Fathers [of the Church]; or, at least, that Isaias is referring to the spiritual warfare of the Apostles and of the preachers of the Gospel, who have conquered the world not by a material but by a spiritual sword. . . .

The Council of Nicaea, indeed, dealt especially with those Christians who, for a second time, were assuming the uniform of pagan soldiers which they had once cast off. And Pope Leo . . . was speaking of those Christians who, after a public penance had been imposed upon them, were returning to war, before the penance had been completed. Furthermore, it may have been expedient for the early Church to forbid those who had recently been converted to the faith, to engage in military service immediately, in company with unbelievers, and under pagan officers.

To the argument drawn from reason, Augustine replies (*On the City of God* 19) that he deems it advisable to avoid war in so far as is possible, and to undertake it only in cases of extreme necessity, when no alternative remains; but he also holds that war is not entirely evil, since the fact that evils follow upon war is incidental, and since greater evils would result if war were never allowed.

Wherefore, in reply to the confirmation of the argument in question one may deny that war is opposed to an honourable peace; rather, it is opposed to an unjust peace, for it is more truly a means of attaining peace that is real and secure. Similarly, war is not opposed to the love of one's enemies; for whoever wages war honourably hates, not individuals, but the actions which he justly punishes. And the same reasoning is true of the forgiveness of injuries, especially since this forgiveness is not enjoined under every circumstance, for punishment may sometimes be exacted, by legitimate means, without injustice.

4. Secondly, I hold that defensive war not only is permitted, but sometimes is even commanded. The first part of this proposition follows from the first conclusion, which even the Doctors cited above ac-

cept; and it holds true not only for public officials, but also for private individuals, since all laws allow the repelling of force with force. The reason supporting it is that the right of self-defense is natural and necessary. Whence the second part of our second proposition is easily proved. For self-defence may sometimes be prescribed, at least in accordance with the order of charity. . . . The same is true of the defence of the state, especially if such defence is an official duty. . . . If any one objects that in the Epistle to the Romans (chap. 12) these words are found: "Revenge not yourselves, my dearly beloved," and that this saying is in harmony with the passage (Matt. 5): "If one strike thee on the right cheek, turn to him also the other," we shall reply with respect to the first passage, that the reference is to vengeance, so that another version reads [Rom. 12]: "Not avenging yourselves," and that the Greek word, ἐκδικοῦντες , has both significations; but the meaning is clear from what follows: "For it is written: Revenge is mine," &c. The meaning of the second passage cited is the same, if it is interpreted as a precept; although it may also be understood, in accordance with Augustine's explanation, as referring to the preparation of the soul, at least when such a process is necessary; for otherwise [the passage in question is] merely a counsel [of perfection, and not a commandment].

5. My third conclusion is, that even when war is aggressive, it is not an evil in itself, but may be right and necessary. This is clear from the passages of Scripture cited above, which make no distinction [between aggressive and defensive wars]. The same fact is evidenced by the custom of the Church, one that has quite frequently been approved by the Fathers and the Popes. . . .

The reason supporting our third conclusion is that such a war is often necessary to a state, in order to ward off acts of injustice and to hold enemies in check. Nor would it be possible, without these wars, for states to be maintained in peace. Hence, this kind of warfare is allowed by natural law; and even by the law of the Gospel, which derogates in no way from natural law, and contains no new divine commands save those regarding faith and the Sacraments. The statement of Luther that it is not lawful to resist the punishment of God is indeed ridiculous; for God does not will the evils [against which war is waged,] but merely permits them; and therefore He does not forbid that they should be justly repelled.

6. It remains for us to explain what constitutes an aggressive war, and what, on the other hand, constitutes a defensive war; for

sometimes that which is merely an act of defence may present the appearance of an aggressive act. Thus, for example, if enemies seize the houses or the property of others, but have themselves suffered invasion from the latter, that is no aggression but defence. To this extent, civil laws are justified in conscience also, when they provide that if any one tries to dispossess me of my property, it is lawful for me to repel force with force. For such an act is not aggression, but defence, and may be lawfully undertaken even on one's own authority. The laws in question are extended to apply to him who, while absent, has been ejected from a tenure which they call a natural one, and who, upon his return, is prevented from recovering that tenure. For [the same laws decree] that any one who has been despoiled may, even on his own authority, have recourse to arms, because such an act is not really aggression, but a defence of one's legal possession. . . .

Consequently, we have to consider whether the injustice is, practically speaking, simply about to take place; or whether it has already done so, and redress is sought through war. In this second case, the war is aggressive. In the former case, war has the character of self-defence, provided that it is waged with a moderation of defence which is blameless. Now the injury is considered as beginning, when the unjust act itself, even physically regarded, is beginning; as when a man has not been entirely deprived of his rightful possession; or even when he has been so deprived, but immediately—that is, without noteworthy delay—attempts to defend himself and to reinstate himself in possession. The reason for this is as follows: When any one is, to all intents and purposes, in the very act of resisting, and attempts—in so far as is possible—to protect his right, he is not considered as having, in an absolute sense, suffered wrong, nor as having been deprived of his possession. . . .

7. Our fourth proposition is this: in order that a war may be justly waged, a number of conditions must be observed, which may be grouped under three heads. First, the war must be waged by a legitimate power; secondly, the cause itself and the reason must be just; thirdly, the method of its conduct must be proper, and due proportion must be observed at its beginning, during its prosecution and after victory. All of this will be made clear in the following sections. The underlying principle of this general conclusion, indeed, is that, while a war is not in itself evil, nevertheless, on account of the many misfortunes which it brings in its train, it is one of those undertakings that are often carried on in evil fashion; and

that therefore, it requires many [justifying] circumstances to make it righteous.

## SECTION II

### WHO HAS THE LEGITIMATE POWER OF DECLARING WAR?

1. Our question relates to aggressive war; for the power of defending oneself against an unjust aggressor is conceded to all.

I hold first: that a sovereign prince who has no superior in temporal affairs, or a state which has retained for itself a like jurisdiction, has by natural law legitimate power to declare war. This is the opinion held by St. Thomas and he is supported by all. . . .

A reason in support of this conclusion is, first, that this sort of war is at times permitted by the natural law, as we have demonstrated; hence, the power of declaring such a war must rest with someone; and therefore it must rest, most of all, with the possessor of sovereign power, for it is particularly his function to protect the state, and to command the inferior princes [within the realm].

A second reason is that the power of declaring war is (so to speak) a power of jurisdiction, the exercise of which pertains to punitive justice, which is especially necessary to a state for the purpose of constraining wrongdoers; wherefore, just as the sovereign prince may punish his own subjects when they offend others, so may he avenge himself on another prince or state which by reason of some offence becomes subject to him; and this vengeance cannot be sought at the hands of another judge, because the prince of whom we are speaking has no superior in temporal affairs; therefore, if that offender is not prepared to give satisfaction, he may be compelled by war to do so.

In this first conclusion, I used the words, "or a state," in order that I might include every kind of polity; for the same reasoning holds true of all polities. Only it must be noted of a monarchical régime that, after a state has transferred its power to some one person, it cannot declare war without that person's consent, because it is no longer supreme; unless the prince should chance to be so negligent in avenging or defending the state as to cause public and very grave harm to that state, for, in such a case, the commonwealth as a whole could take vengeance and deprive the sovereign of the authority in question. For the state is always regarded as retaining this power within itself, if the prince fails in his duty.

2. I hold, secondly, that an inferior prince, or an imperfect state, or whosoever in temporal affairs is under a superior, cannot justly declare war without the authorization of that superior. A reason for the conclusion is, first, that a prince of this kind can claim his right from his superior, and therefore has not the right to declare war; since, in this respect, he has the character of a private person. For it is because of the reason stated that private persons cannot declare war. A second reason in support of this same conclusion is that such a declaration of war is opposed to the rights of the sovereign prince, to whom that power has been specially entrusted; for without such power he could not govern peacefully and suitably. . . .

6. Thirdly, I hold that a war which, according to the preceding conclusion, is declared without legitimate authority, is contrary not only to charity, but also to justice, even if a legitimate cause for it exists. The reason supporting this conclusion is that such an act is performed without legitimate jurisdiction, and is consequently an illegitimate act. Therefore, it follows that a war of this kind gives rise to an obligation of making restitution for all ensuing damages.

Therefore, it is indeed true that if any one merely recovers his own property in such a war, he will not be bound to restore that property; but he will be held liable for all injuries and losses inflicted upon others. The reason for such a distinction is that in the latter case he has done an injustice, since there was no just cause for all that damage; whereas, in recovering his own property, he has not, strictly speaking, committed an injustice—save possibly in the means used, from which, in a strict sense, there arises no obligation to make restitution.

Whence follows the conclusion . . . that he who makes war without the authorization in question, even if he has, in other respects, a just ground for so doing, nevertheless incurs the penalties imposed upon those who wage an unjust war; so that if, for example, he be an incendiary, he will incur the excommunication promulgated against incendiaries. . . .

## Section IV

### WHAT IS A JUST CAUSE OF WAR, ON THE BASIS OF NATURAL REASON?

There was an old error current among the Gentiles, who thought that the rights of nations were based on military strength, and that it was permissible to make war solely to acquire prestige and wealth; a belief which, even from the standpoint of natural reason, is most absurd.

1. Therefore I hold, first: that there can be no just war without an underlying cause of a legitimate and necessary nature. The truth of this conclusion is indubitable and clearly evident. Now, that just and sufficient reason for war is the infliction of a grave injustice which cannot be avenged or repaired in any other way. . . .

The first reason in support of such a conclusion is the fact that war is permissible [only] that a state may guard itself from molestation; for in other respects, war is opposed to the welfare of the human race on account of the slaughter, material losses, and other misfortunes which it involves; and therefore, if the cause in question should cease to exist, the justice of war would also cease to exist.

Secondly, in war, men are despoiled of their property, their liberty, and their lives; and to do such things without just cause is absolutely iniquitous, for if this were permissible, men could kill one another without cause.

Thirdly, the sort of war which we are chiefly discussing is aggressive war, and it is frequently waged against non-subjects. Consequently, it is necessary that the latter shall have committed some wrong on account of which they render themselves subjects. Otherwise, on what ground could they be deserving of punishment or subject to an alien jurisdiction?

Furthermore, if the grounds or purposes which the Gentiles had in view (for example, ambition, avarice, and even vainglory or a display of ferocity) were legitimate and sufficient, any state whatsoever could aspire to these ends; and hence, a war would be just on both sides, essentially and apart from any element of ignorance. This supposition is entirely absurd; for two mutually conflicting rights cannot both be just.

2. But in order that this matter may be explained more clearly, there are several points which should be noted.

First, it is not every cause that is sufficient to justify war, but only those causes which are serious and commensurate with the losses that the war would occasion. For it would be contrary to reason to inflict very grave harm because of a slight injustice. In like manner, a judge can punish, not all offenses whatsoever, but only those which are opposed to the common peace and to the welfare of the realm. In this connexion, however, we must remember that not infrequently a wrong which appears to be slight is in fact serious, if all the circumstances are weighed, or if other and similar wrongs are permitted [as a consequence], since thereby great harm may gradually ensue. Thus, for example, to seize even the smallest town, or to make raids, &c., may sometimes constitute a grave injustice, especially when the prince who has done the wrong treats with scorn the protest that is made.

3. Secondly, it must be noted that there are various kinds of injuries which are causes of a just war. These may be grouped under three heads. One of the heads would be the seizure by a prince of another's property, and his refusal to restore it. Another head would be his denial, without reasonable cause, of the common rights of nations, such as the right of transit over highways, trading in common &c. The third would be any grave injury to one's reputation or honour. It should be added that it is a sufficient cause for war if an injury of this kind be inflicted either upon a prince himself or upon his subjects; for the prince is guardian of his state and also of his subjects. Furthermore, the cause is sufficient if the wrong be inflicted upon any one who has placed himself under the protection of a prince, or even if it be inflicted upon allies or friends, as may be seen in the case of Abraham (Gen. 14), and in that of David (I Kings 28). "For a friend is a second self," says Aristotle (*Nicomachean Ethics* 9). But it must be understood that such a circumstance justifies war only on condition that the friend himself would be justified in waging war, and consents thereto, either expressly or by implication. The reason for this limitation is that a wrong done to another does not give me the right to avenge him, unless he would be justified in avenging himself and actually proposes to do so. Assuming, however, that these conditions exist, my aid to him is an act of cooperation in a good and just deed; but if [the injured party] does not entertain such a wish, no one else may intervene, since he who committed the wrong has made himself subject not to every one indiscriminately, but only to the person who has been wronged. Wherefore, the assertion made by some writers, that sovereign kings have the power of avenging injuries done

in any part of the world, is entirely false, and throws into confusion all the orderly distinctions of jurisdictions; for such power was not [expressly] granted by God and its existence is not to be inferred by any process of reasoning.

4. Thirdly, we must note that, in regard to an injury inflicted, two arguments may be alleged, [to justify a declaration of war]. The first is [that a declaration is justifiable], in order that reparation for the losses suffered should be made to the injured party. For this cause, indeed, it is not to be questioned that war may legitimately be declared; for if this declaration is to be permitted because of an injury [already done], then it is in the highest degree permissible when the object is that each one may secure himself against loss. Many examples illustrating this point are to be found in the Scriptures (Gen. 14, and similar passages). The other argument is [that war should be declared] in order that the offender may be duly punished; a contention which presents its own difficulty.

5. Secondly, then, I hold that a war may also be justified on the ground that he who has inflicted an injury should be justly punished, if he refuses to give just satisfaction for that injury, without resort to war. This conclusion is commonly accepted. In connexion with it, and with the preceding conclusion, we must assume that the opposing party is not ready to make restitution, or to give satisfaction; for if he were so disposed, the warlike aggression would become unjust, as we shall demonstrate in the following sections.

The conclusion is proved, first, by certain Scriptural passages (Num. 25; II Kings 10 and 11), according to which, unconditional punishment for offences was carried into execution, by the command of God.

The reason in support of this same conclusion is that, just as within a state some lawful power to punish crimes is necessary to the preservation of domestic peace; so in the world as a whole, there must exist, in order that the various states may dwell in concord, some power for the punishment of injuries inflicted by one state upon another; and this power is not to be found in any superior, for we assume that these states have no commonly acknowledged superior; therefore, the power in question must reside in the sovereign prince of the injured state, to whom, by reason of that injury, the opposing prince is made subject; and consequently, war of the kind in question has been instituted in place of a tribunal administering just punishment.

6. But, on the other hand, one may object, first: that to fight in this manner seems opposed to the admonitions in the Epistle to the Romans (chap. 12): "To no man rendering evil for evil," and [ibid., v. 19]: "Not avenging yourselves." The reply to the objection is that the passages quoted refer to acts performed by private authority and with the intention of doing evil for its own sake, to another. But if the acts in question be done under legitimate and public authority, with the intention of holding an enemy to his duty and of reducing to its due order that which was disorderly, then they are not only not prohibited but even necessary. Hence, in that same Epistle (Rom. 13), we find this additional passage: "For he beareth not the sword in vain. For he is God's minister: to work vengeance upon evildoers."

Secondly, it is objected that [if our second general conclusion be true,] then, as a consequence, the same party in one and the same case is both plaintiff and judge, a situation which is contrary to the natural law. The truth of the conclusion is evident, since the prince who has been wronged, assumes the role of judge by his act of aggression.

The objection is confirmed, in the first place, by the fact that the right to avenge themselves is denied to private individuals, for this reason, namely, that they would practically exceed the bounds of justice; and yet the same danger exists in the case of a prince who avenges himself.

A second confirmation of the same objection is that, by a like reasoning, any private person who might be unable to secure such punishment through a judge could take the law into his own hands, executing it on his own authority; since this privilege is granted to princes, on the sole ground that there is no other way of securing a just vengeance.

7. Our reply is, that it cannot be denied that in this matter [of public vengeance], one and the same person assumes, in a sense, the role of plaintiff and that of judge; even as we perceive that God, to Whom there is some analogy in the public authority, assumes this double role. But the cause [of such an assumption on the part of public authority] is simply that this act of punitive justice has been indispensable to mankind, and that no more fitting method for its performance could, in the order of nature and humanly speaking, be found. This is especially true, since we must presuppose, prior to the war, the contumacy of the offending party in not wishing to give satisfac-

tion; for then (contumacy being established) if he finds himself in subjection to the offended party, he may impute his own misfortune to himself.

Neither is this case analogous to that of a private individual. For in the first place, such an individual is guided by his own [unaided] judgment, and therefore he will easily exceed the limits of vengeance; whereas public authority is guided by public counsel, to which heed must be paid, and consequently authority of this sort may more easily avoid the disadvantages arising from personal inclination. In the second place, this power of punishment has for its essential purpose not private but public good, and hence it has been committed not to the private individual, but to the public body. Therefore, if the latter is unable or unwilling to punish [an injury], the private individual shall patiently endure his loss. From the foregoing remarks, then, our reply to the first confirmation of the objection is evident.

As to the second confirmation, it has been said by some persons that in the situation referred to, a private individual is allowed to avenge himself secretly. . . . But this must be understood as referring to restitution for losses suffered; for in so far as it refers to the punishment of an offence, it is an inadmissible error. An act of punitive justice, indeed, is an exercise of that jurisdiction which private individuals do not possess, and cannot obtain through an offence committed by another. For if they could possess it, there would be no need to employ the public power of jurisdiction; or at least, since this power of jurisdiction is derived from men themselves, each one would have had the power to refrain from transferring it to the state official, retaining it, on the contrary, for himself; a conclusion which would be opposed to the natural law, and to the good governance of the human race.

Therefore, we deny the consequent involved in the second confirmation. For laws regard those things which are true in an absolute sense, and private individuals, absolutely speaking, may obtain a ready revenge for offences because there is a public authority, while the fact that sometimes they are not able to do so, is an accidental occurrence which, for that reason, must necessarily be endured, as we have said. But the relationship between two sovereign powers is based on an absolute necessity. . . .

8. Thirdly, I hold that whoever begins a war without just cause, sins not only against charity, but also against justice; and hence he is bound to make reparation for all the harm that results. The truth of this conclusion is manifest.

The only question which arises in connexion with this point is whether or not there may sometimes exist a cause for war which absolves one from the charge of injustice, but not from the charge of sinning against charity. The reply must be that such a situation rarely occurs; and yet it is by no means inconceivable. For just as it happens among private individuals that one person may take what is due to him from another, an act which is not opposed to justice, but which is opposed to charity at times (namely, when the debtor incurs very serious losses in consequence, while the property in question is not in great degree necessary to the creditor); even so, a similar situation might arise between princes or states. In this connexion, however, it should be noted that in a war of the kind described, it is possible to consider, first, the loss to the state against which the war is waged; secondly, the loss to the state which commences the war; thirdly and finally, the possible loss to the entire Church.

With respect to this third contingency, we may easily find support for our assertion. For although a Christian king may declare war on some particular just ground, it will nevertheless be possible for him to sin against the charity due to the Church, in pursuing his rights. For example, he may foresee the consequent growth in power of the enemies of the faith, and so forth; so that, in that case, it may be a sin to wage war, and yet there arises no obligation to make restitution, since the particular just ground that he has extinguishes such an obligation.

When the harm is of the kind first mentioned, [a harm, that is, to the state against which war is waged,] then there is no great obligation to make restitution, since the malicious intent of the state inflicting the original injury was the cause of the loss in question. Nevertheless, if in a particular case the latter state should be unable to give satisfaction or make restitution without suffering great injury, and if such satisfaction should not be necessary to the prince of the other state, then the latter, by insisting that satisfaction be given, would clearly be acting against charity.

Finally, turning to the second case mentioned, if one prince begins a war upon another, even with just cause, while exposing his own realm to disproportionate loss and peril, then he will be sinning not only against charity, but also against the justice due to his own state. The reason for this assertion is as follows: a prince is bound in justice to have greater regard for the common good of his state than for his own good; otherwise, he will become a tyrant. So a judge who condemns to hanging a criminal deserving of execution but very necessary to the state, would act in a manner opposed to his official obligations, and, consequently, to justice. Similarly, a physician would sin against the justice required by his profession if he should give medicine which would heal a present disease but would cause more serious diseases to ensue.

9. However, with respect to this last point, we must take into consideration the fact that a single king who rules over several kingdoms, can often make war for the sake of one of these to the detriment of another. For though the various kingdoms may be distinct from one another, nevertheless, inasmuch as they are subject to one head, they can and should be of mutual aid, since the defence of one contributes to the benefit of another and in this way, the principle of equality is preserved. For in its own emergency, one kingdom might require the aid of another. In addition to all these considerations, the mere fact that their [common] prince is rendered more powerful, is in itself extremely advantageous to each of the kingdoms involved. In short, greater peace, and other advantages, may perhaps accrue to a state so supported; and many other [similar] points can easily be perceived upon reflection. There are, then, numerous considerations which may oblige a prince to abandon his right to make war lest his realm suffer loss.

10. Furthermore, we should call attention to the conclusion, drawn from these primary considerations by Cajetan, namely, that for a war to be just, the sovereign ought to be so sure of the degree of his power, that he is morally certain of victory. The first reason for this conclusion is the fact that otherwise the prince would incur the evident peril of inflicting upon his state losses greater than the advantages involved. In the same way, says Cajetan, a judge would do wrong in attempting the arrest of a criminal without a force that, to his certain knowledge, could not be overpowered. Secondly, whoever begins a war assumes an active role; and the one who assumes such a role must always be the stronger, in order to vanquish the one who plays a passive part.

But this condition [of certitude] does not appear to me to be absolutely essential. First, because, from a human standpoint, it is almost impossible of realization. Secondly, because it is often to the common interest of the state not to await such a degree of certitude, but rather to test its ability to conquer the enemy, even when that ability is somewhat doubtful. Thirdly, because if the conclusion were true, a weaker sovereign could never declare war upon a stronger, since he is unable to attain the certitude which Cajetan demands.

Therefore, the following rules should be laid down. A prince [who declares war] is, indeed, bound to attain the maximum certitude possible regarding victory. Furthermore, he ought to balance the expectation of victory against the risk of loss, and ascertain whether, all things being carefully considered, expectation is preponderant. If so great a degree of certitude is impossible of attainment, he ought at least to have either a more probable expectation of victory, or one equally balanced as to the chances of victory or defeat, and that, in proportion to the need of the state and the communal welfare. But if the expectation of victory is less apt to be realized than the chance of defeat, and if the war is offensive in character, then in almost every case that war should be avoided. If [,on the other hand,] the war is defensive, it should be attempted; for in that case it is a matter of necessity, whereas the offensive war is a matter of choice. All of these conclusions are sufficiently clear in the light of the principles of conscience and justice.

## Section V

### CAN CHRISTIAN PRINCES HAVE ANY JUST GROUND FOR WAR BEYOND THAT WHICH NATURAL REASON DICTATES?

1. The first opinion [which we shall discuss in this connexion] is affirmative. . . .

The first ground is that of simple unbelief [on the part of the enemy], that is, a refusal to accept the true religion. But this is a false ground, a point with which we deal in the treatise *De Fide*.

The second ground is that God may be avenged for injuries which are done to Him by sins against nature, and by idolatry. . . . But this opinion is also false, and it is so first of all, even if we speak of "vengeance," in the strict sense. For God did not give to all men the power to avenge the injuries they do to Him, since He can easily avenge Himself, if He so wills. Moreover, it would not have been well for the human race had men received this power from God, for the greatest disorder would have resulted therefrom. The same argument holds true with respect to the plea of defending [the majesty of God]; since the sins against Him would thus be multiplied rather than prevented. On this same ground, moreover, Christian princes could declare war even upon one another, for many of these princes also are offenders against God. Likewise, since such a ground of aggression could never be sufficiently established, those who were so attacked could justly defend themselves, and the war would thus become just for both sides. . . .

4. A third ground for war is advanced, namely, the supreme temporal dominion [of Christians]. That is to say, the authorities mentioned above maintain either that unbelievers are not true owners of their possessions; or else that the Christian Emperor, or—at least—the supreme Pontiff, has direct temporal dominion over the whole world.

But all such claims are vain inventions, a point which we discuss elsewhere, on the subject of dominion and laws. In the second place, even if we grant that such a title does indeed exist, still it would be impossible either to demonstrate its existence to the satisfaction of infidels, or to force them to believe in the existence of such dominion; and therefore, they could not be forced to obey. Finally, on that same ground, the Pope or the Emperor could make war [even] upon all Christian princes. Wherefore, it must be observed that although the Pope has indirectly supreme power in temporal affairs, nevertheless, the existence of such temporal power is always based, essentially, upon the assumption of direct power in spiritual matters; and therefore, this indirect power does not essentially extend to unbelievers, over whom no direct spiritual dominion exists even in the Pope himself. But I use the term, "essentially" (per se loquendo), because "incidentally" (per accidens) the case may be otherwise, as I shall presently show.

5. A fourth ground urged is that unbelievers are barbarians and incapable of governing themselves properly; and that the order of nature demands that men of this condition should be governed by those who are more prudent, as Aristotle has taught, saying that a war is by nature just, when it is waged against men born to be under obedience but unwilling to accept that condition. . . .

In the first place, however, such a contention cannot have a general application; for it is evident that there are many unbelievers more gifted by nature than are the faithful, and better adapted to political life. Secondly, in order that the ground in question may be valid, it is not enough to judge that a given people are of inferior natural talents; for they must also be so wretched as to live in general more like wild beasts than like men, as those persons are said to live who have no human polity, and who go about entirely naked, eat human flesh, &c. If there are any such, they may be brought into subjection by war, not with the purpose of destroying them, but rather that they may be organized in human fashion, and justly governed. However, this ground for war should rarely or never be approved, except in circumstances in which the slaughter of innocent people, and similar wrongs take place; and therefore, the ground in question is more properly included under defensive than under offensive wars.

Finally, Aristotle, in the passage cited above, declares that a war of this sort is permissible only when those men who are subdued in order that they may be governed, are as different from the rest of mankind as is the body from the soul; a proposition from which one must conclude, however, that the said ground for war, if it really exists, is valid not only for Christians, but also for every sovereign who wishes to defend the law of nature, which, when understood in an absolute sense, gives rise to that ground.

6. Therefore, the assertion must be made that there is no ground for war so exclusively reserved to Christian princes that it has not some basis in, or at least some due relation to, natural law, being therefore also applicable to princes who are unbelievers.

By way of explaining this assertion, I conclude, first, that a Christian prince may not declare war save either by reason of some injury inflicted or for the defence of the innocent. We have already given sufficient proof of this fact, by rejecting all the invalid grounds for war, [advanced above]. The arguments we have adduced are a proof of this same fact; for the law of grace has not destroyed, but on the contrary completes the natural law. . . .

## Section VI

### WHAT CERTITUDE AS TO THE JUST CAUSE OF WAR IS REQUIRED IN ORDER THAT WAR MAY BE JUST

Three kinds of persons must here be distinguished, to wit: the sovereign king and prince, the leading men and generals, and the common soldiers. It is to be assumed that practical certitude is required of all these persons, a certitude which may be expressed in the statement: "It is lawful for me to make war." The whole doubt is concerned with theoretical certitude, which is to be expressed as follows: "This cause of war is just in itself," or, "This thing which I seek through war is rightfully mine."

1. I hold, first, that the sovereign ruler is bound to make a dili-

gent examination of the cause and its justice, and that after making this examination, he ought to act in accordance with the knowledge thus obtained.

The basis of the first part of this conclusion is that war is a matter of the gravest character; and reason demands that in any matter whatsoever, deliberation and diligence should be applied, commensurate with its importance. Furthermore, a judge, in order to pass judgment in a private matter, ought to make diligent investigation; hence, the necessity for such diligence exists in due proportion in a public cause of war. Finally, if the ruler were not bound to make this investigation, the rashness of princes would easily result in universal disturbance. With regard to the first part of this assertion, then, there is no difficulty.

2. The explanation of the second part of the conclusion is as follows. Let us suppose that the ground for a war is the fact that a certain king claims a certain city as belonging to him, or as falling newly to him by hereditary right. Now if, when the matter has been carefully examined, the truth of that claim is clearly established, what I have asserted is obviously true. But when the case of each side contains [an element of] probability, then the king ought to act as a just judge.

Therefore, if he finds that the opinion favouring his own side is the more probably true, he may, even justly, prosecute his own right; because, so I believe, the more probable opinion should always be preferred in passing judgment. For that is an act of distributive justice, in which the more worthy party is to receive the preference; and he is the more worthy party who enjoys the more probable right, as we shall explain below at greater length. For the same reason, however, if the more probable opinion favours the opposing side, the prince in question may on no account proceed to war.

3. If, finally, after diligent investigation, the probabilities on both sides are found to be equal, or if, at least, equal uncertainty exists—whatever the ground of the uncertainty—then, if the opposing party is in possession, he ought to have the preference, because even in a judicial process, that party is favoured, inasmuch as he has the greater right. On this account, the party who is not in possession cannot proceed to war against the possessor; while the latter, on the other hand, is secure [in his conscience] and may justly defend himself. . . .

4. Another aspect of the question regards the situation in which

no one is in possession and the doubts and probabilities balance each other. The more common opinion seems to be that either party has the right to seize first the thing in dispute. In accordance with this opinion, the war would become just simultaneously, on both sides; but this point is of no importance, when ignorance intervenes. The reason, indeed, which is offered in support of this opinion is that in a similar case a judge could award the property by his own decision to either one of the parties to the litigation, as he might choose.

However, I am unable to persuade myself that a judge may act thus in the case supposed. For certainly, under those circumstances, the judge is merely a distributor of property over which he personally has no right; consequently, if the rights of the parties in question are at all times entirely equal, there is no reason which would allow him to allot the whole property to either party; and therefore, the judge is bound to divide the property. Or, if this cannot be advantageously done, it will be necessary to satisfy both sides, in some fashion. Hence, in a question involving war, the princes shall be bound to this same attitude. Accordingly, they must either divide between them the thing in dispute, or cast lots for it, or settle the matter in some other way. But if one party should attempt to seize the whole possession to the exclusion of the other party, by that very act he would be doing the other a wrong which the latter might justly repel, thus seizing, on this ground of war, the entire disputed possession. . . .

7. Secondly, I hold that generals and other chief men of the kingdom, whenever they are summoned for consultation to give their opinion on beginning a war, are bound to inquire diligently into the truth of the matter; but if they are not called, they are under no greater obligation to do so than others who are common soldiers. The first part of this conclusion is clearly true; because these generals, having been summoned, are bound in justice to give a just opinion, for if they did not do so, any injustice that there might be in the war will be laid to their charge. The proof of the second part of the conclusion is the fact that, when they are not summoned [to give advice], their part in the affair becomes simply that of private soldiers, since they are merely set in action by others, but do not control action; while it is only incidental (*per accidens*) that they are wealthy or of noble birth. Nevertheless, Victoria adds that such generals are bound in charity to inquire into the justice of the war, in order to give warning when it shall be necessary. But if this obligation is derived from charity alone, it will exist only in case of necessity; and therefore,

generally speaking, apart from these cases where there is such need, they will not be so bound.

8. I hold thirdly, that: common soldiers, as subjects of princes, are in no wise bound to make diligent investigation, but rather may go to war when summoned to do so, provided it is not clear to them that the war is unjust. This conclusion may be proved by the following arguments: first, when the injustice of the war is not evident to these soldiers, the united opinion of the prince and of the realm is sufficient to move them to this action; secondly, subjects when in doubt (i.e. doubt of a theoretical character) are bound to obey their superiors. This last statement is based upon the best of reasons, namely, the fact that in cases of doubt the safer course should be chosen; therefore, since the prince possesses rightful authority, the safer course is to obey him.

The assertion is confirmed by the fact that the official subordinate of a judge may execute a sentence without any previous examination, provided that sentence is not manifestly unjust. . . .

9. Nevertheless, Sylvester would seem to limit this conclusion. For he says that, if the common soldiers have doubts, they are bound to make inquiries in order to dispel those doubts; but, if they cannot do so, it will be permissible for them to fight. Adrian indeed, absolutely denies that it is permissible to go to war with such doubts; both because it is never permissible to act with a doubtful conscience; and because soldiers who did act thus would be choosing the [morally] more dangerous course, since they would be exposing themselves to the peril of unjust slaughter and plundering; whereas, if they abstained from going, they would sin only by disobedience, and justice imposes a more rigorous obligation than that of obedience.

The reply to this objection, however, is that the doubt in such a case is not practical but speculative, and therefore this does not render the conscience doubtful. Furthermore, it would not be safer to disobey; for as a natural result of such disobedience, it would become impossible for princes to defend their rights, and this would be a serious and general misfortune.

With regard to Sylvester's limitation, we should observe: first, that the doubt may be a purely negative one, namely, that the soldiers are entirely ignorant of the basis of the justice or injustice underlying the war; in which case they are in no wise bound to make inquiry, being sufficiently supported by the fact that they have relied upon the authority of their sovereign; secondly, that the doubt may be positive, having its source in conflicting arguments adduced in favour of one side and the other. Indeed, if the arguments showing the war to be unjust were such that the soldiers themselves were unable to give a satisfactory answer, then they would be bound to inquire into the truth in some way. Even this obligation, however, is to be imposed, not readily, but only in case those arguments render the justice of the war extremely doubtful, for in that case, it would seem that the soldiers have inclined towards a moral judgment that the war was unjust; otherwise, however, if they have probable reason for thinking that the war is just, they may legitimately conform their conduct to these reasons. . . .

12. However, since the question is one of moral conduct, and in order that we may proceed with less risk of error, I lay down this conclusion: if the doubt [as to the justice of a war] is purely negative, it is probable that the soldiers in question may [rightfully] take part in that war without having made any examination of the question, all responsibility being thrown upon the prince to whom they are subject. We assume, to be sure, that this prince enjoys a good reputation among all men.

If, however, the doubt is positive, and if both sides advance plausible arguments, then, in my opinion, [those who are about to enlist] should make an inquiry into the truth of the matter. If they are unable to ascertain the truth, they will be bound to follow the course of action which is more probably just, and to aid him who is more probably in the right. For when the case involves doubt with respect to a fact, such as loss affecting one's neighbour, or with respect to the defence of the innocent, that course which appears to be more probably just should be followed, in accordance with the rules on conscience above set forth. To this end, indeed, it will be sufficient if the soldiers consult prudent and conscientious men upon the question of whether or not they are in an absolute sense able to take part in such a war. And if the soldiers in question form a single political body, and have their own chiefs, the inferiors will certainly satisfy all requirements, if each person examines the question of the justice of the war, through his own chief or prince, and follows the judgment of that authority. Finally, if the arguments on both sides contain an equal [element of] probability, the soldiers may under such circumstances conduct themselves as if the doubt were purely negative; for the balance is then equal, and the authority of the prince turns the scale. . . .

## Section VII

### WHAT IS THE PROPER MODE OF CONDUCTING WAR?

1. Three periods must be distinguished [with respect to every war]: its inception; its prosecution, before victory is gained; and the period after victory. The three classes of persons already mentioned must also be distinguished, namely: the sovereign prince; the intermediate group of leaders; and the soldiers of the rank and file. . . .

3. I hold, first that before a war is begun the [attacking] prince is bound to call to the attention of the opposing state the existence of a just cause of war, and to seek adequate reparation therefor; and if the other state offers such adequate reparation, he is bound to accept it, and desist from war; for if he does not do so, the war will be unjust. If, on the other hand, the opposing prince refuses to give satisfaction, the first prince may begin to make war.

This conclusion is commonly accepted in its entirety, and the latter part is clearly true because, assuming the obstinacy of the opposing prince or state, and the other conditions specified, there is no [other] point that calls for consideration. . . .

For where a full and sufficient satisfaction is voluntarily offered, there is no ground for violence; especially not, since reason demands that punitive justice be exercised with the least possible harm to all, provided, however, that the principle of equality be observed. Moreover, one sovereign has no coercive power over another sovereign, unless the latter acts unjustly, as is the case when he is unwilling to give satisfaction. . . .

6. I hold, secondly, that after war has been begun, and during the whole period thereof up to the attainment of victory, it is just to visit upon the enemy all losses which may seem necessary either for obtaining satisfaction or for securing victory, provided that these losses do not involve an intrinsic injury to innocent persons, which would be in itself an evil. Of this injury, we shall treat below, in the sixth conclusion. The reason in support of this conclusion is as follows: if the end is permissible, the necessary means to that end are also permissible; and hence it follows that in the whole course, or duration, of the war hardly anything done against the enemy involves injustice, except the slaying of the innocent. For all other damages are usually held to be necessary for attaining the end to which the war is directed.

7. In the third place, I hold that after the winning of victory, a prince is allowed to inflict upon the conquered state such losses as are

sufficient for a just punishment and satisfaction, and reimbursement for all losses suffered. This conclusion is commonly accepted and undoubtedly true, both because the exaction of such penalties is the object of war, and also because in a righteous judgment at law this same course of conduct is permissible. But it should be observed that in computing the sum required for this satisfaction, one should include all the losses by the state in question throughout the war, i.e. the deaths of men, conflagrations, &c.

In the first place, however, the additional comment made by Sylvester and by Victoria is not unacceptable, namely, that movable goods captured by soldiers during the war are not to be reckoned by the prince as part of the restitution. For this rule has become a part of the *jus gentium*, through common custom. The reason underlying it is that, since the soldiers' lives are exposed to dangers so numerous and so grave, they should be allowed something; and the same is true of their prince.

Secondly, it is necessary to observe with regard both to this, and the previous conclusions, that soldiers are not allowed to seize anything on their own authority, whether after or even before the victory is won: because they have in themselves no power, but possess it solely through their prince, as his agents, so that they may not justly take anything without his express or implied authorization.

Thirdly, it follows from this conclusion that, if all the penalties just enumerated seem insufficient in view of the gravity of the wrong, then, after the war has been entirely ended, certain guilty individuals among the enemy may also, with justice, be put to death; and, although the slaying of a great multitude would be thus permissible only when there was most urgent cause, nevertheless, even such slaughter may sometimes be allowed, in order to terrify the rest, as is indicated in the following passage from Deut. (chap. 20): "When the Lord thy God shall deliver the city into thy hands, thou shalt slay all that are therein of the male sex, with the edge of the sword, excepting women and children," &c. And from this passage it follows that with much more reason the guilty who have been vanquished may be reduced to captivity and all their property seized.

Fourthly, it is to be noted that one should interpret in accord with this conclusion the civil laws which assert that, through the *jus gentium*, it has been established that all the property of the enemy, both movable and immovable, passes to the victors. . . . But all of these passages must be interpreted in conformity with the rule previously laid down, namely, that a just equality must be preserved, and regard must be had for the future peace; a matter of which we shall treat below. For it is necessary to preserve in war the same quality as in a just judgment; and in such a judgment, the offender cannot be visited with every sort of punishment nor deprived of all his property without any restriction, but may be punished only in proportion to his fault. . . .

10. But another doubt remains, namely: whether it is equally allowable to inflict damages of this kind upon all those who are numbered among the enemy. In answering this question we must note that some of these persons are said to be guilty, and others innocent. It is implicit in natural law that the innocent include children, women, and all unable to bear arms; by the *jus gentium*, ambassadors, and among Christians, by positive [canon] law, religious persons, priests, &c. . . . All other persons are considered guilty; for human judgment looks upon those able to take up arms as having actually done so. Now, the hostile state is composed of both classes of persons, and therefore, all these persons are held to be enemies. In this respect, strangers and foreigners, since they form no part of the state and therefore are not reckoned among the enemy unless they are allies in the war, differ from the persons above mentioned.

11. Assuming that the foregoing is true, I hold, fourthly, that if the damages inflicted upon the guilty are sufficient for restitution and satisfaction, those damages cannot just be extended to affect the innocent. This fact is self-evident as a result of what has already been said, for one may not demand greater satisfaction than that which is just. The only question that might arise is whether or not victorious soldiers are always bound to observe this order in their procedure, taking vengeance upon the guilty and their property rather than upon the innocent. The reply is briefly that, other things being equal, and within the limits of the same class of property, they are so bound. For the principle of equity clearly imposes this rule, a fact which will become more evident from what follows.

12. Fifthly, I hold that if such a course of action is essential to complete satisfaction, it is permissible to deprive the innocent of their goods, even of their liberty. The reason is that the innocent form a portion of one whole and unjust state; and on account of the crime of the whole, this part may be punished even though it does not of itself share in the fault. . . .

15. Sixthly, I hold that innocent persons as such may in nowise be slain, even if the punishment inflicted upon their state would,

otherwise, be deemed inadequate; but incidentally they may be slain, when such an act is necessary in order to secure victory.

The reason supporting this conclusion is that the slaying of innocent persons is intrinsically evil. However, one may object that this is true with respect to killing upon private authority and without just cause, but that the case in question involves both public authority and a just cause. Nevertheless, such a plea must be rejected when the slaughter is not necessary for victory (a condition which we have already assumed to exist), and when the innocent can be distinguished from the guilty.

The conclusion is confirmed by the difference existing between life and other possessions. For the latter fall under human dominion; and the state as a whole has a higher right to them than single individuals; hence, individuals may be deprived of such property because of the guilt of the whole realm. But life does not fall under human dominion, and therefore, no one may be deprived of his life save by reason of his own guilt. . . .

17. The latter part of the [sixth] conclusion is also commonly accepted, and is clearly true in the case of certain means essential to victory, which, however, necessarily involve the death of innocent persons, as in the burning of cities and the destruction of fortresses. For, absolutely speaking, whoever has the right to attain the end sought by a war, has the right to use these means to that end. Moreover, in such a case, the death of the innocent is not sought for its own sake, but is an incidental consequence; hence, it is considered not as voluntarily inflicted but simply as allowed by one who is making use of his right in a time of necessity. . . .

20. Seventhly, I hold that, in addition to all the losses which have previously been enumerated and which may be claimed as necessary to satisfaction, a prince who has obtained a just victory may do everything with the property of the enemy that is essential to the preservation of an undisturbed peace in the future, provided that he spare the lives of the enemy. Therefore, if it is necessary, he may on this ground seize cities, provinces, &c.

That is the doctrine supported by all, and the rational basis thereof is derived from the very purpose of an honourable war; since war is permissible especially for this reason, namely, as a way (so to speak) to an upright peace.

This reasoning is confirmed by the fact that within the state itself, wrongdoing is punished in accordance with what is necessary for the public peace with the result that, frequently, some person is ordered into exile, or visited with a similar punishment, &c. From this example, one infers that, if a [precautionary] measure of this sort is taken under circumstances such that it may at the same time come into the category of a penalty, this step should be taken on both of these grounds; nor is it permissible to multiply without cause the harm inflicted upon the enemy.

21. Finally, I hold that a war will not be unjust, if all the precautions which we have enumerated are observed in it, and if at the same time the other general conditions of justice are fulfilled; and yet, such a war may contain some evil element opposed to charity or to some other virtue. . . .

## SECTION VIII

### IS SEDITION INTRINSICALLY EVIL?

1. Sedition is the term used to designate general warfare carried on within a single state, and waged either between two parts thereof or between the prince and the state. I hold, first, that sedition involving two factions of the state is always an evil on the part of the aggressor, but just on the defensive side. The truth of the latter statement is self-evident. The truth of the former is proved by the fact that no legitimate authority to declare war is discernible in such a situation, for this authority, as we have seen (Section II), resides in the sovereign prince.

The objection will be made that, sometimes, a prince will be able to delegate this authority, if urgent public necessity demands that he do so. In such a case, however, the prince himself, and not a part of the state, is held to be the aggressor; so that no sedition will exist in the sense in which we are using the term. But what if one part of the state actually suffers injury from another part, and is unable to secure its right through the prince? My reply is that this injured part may do nothing beyond that which a private individual may do, as can easily be gathered from what we have said above.

2. I hold, secondly, that a war of the state against the prince, even if it be aggressive, is not intrinsically evil; but that the conditions necessary for a war that is in other respects just must nevertheless be present in order that this sort of war may be righteous. This conclusion holds true only when the prince is a tyrant, a situation which may occur in one of two ways. . . . In the first place, the prince may be

a tyrant in regard to his [assertion of tyrannical] dominion, and power; secondly, he may be so merely in regard to his acts of government.

When the first kind of tyranny occurs, the whole state, or any portion thereof, has the right [to revolt] against the prince. Hence, it follows that any person whatsoever may avenge himself and the state against [such] tyranny. The reason supporting these statements is that the tyrant in question is an aggressor, and is waging war unjustly against the state and its separate parts, so that, in consequence, all those parts have the right of defence. . . .

John Huss upheld the same doctrine with respect to the second kind of tyrant, and, indeed, with respect to every unjust superior. But this teaching was condemned at the Council of Constance. Consequently, it is most certain that no private person, nor any imperfect power, may justly begin an aggressive war against this kind of tyrant, and that such a war would be sedition in the true sense of the term.

The proof of these assertions is as follows: the prince in question is, we assume, the true sovereign; and inferiors have not the right of declaring war, but only that of defending themselves, a right which does not apply in connexion with this sort of tyrant; for the latter does not always do wrong to individuals, and in any attack which [these individuals] might make, they would be obliged to confine themselves to necessary self-defence. The state as a whole, however, may rise in revolt against such a tyrant; and this uprising would not be a case of sedition in the strict sense, since the word is commonly employed with a connotation of evil. The reason for this distinction is that under the circumstances described the state, as a whole, is superior to the king, for the state, when it granted him his power, is held to have granted it upon these conditions: that he should govern in accord with the public weal, and not tyrannically; and that, if he did not govern thus, he might be deposed from that position of power.

[In order that such rebellion may justly occur,] however, the situation must be one in which it is observed that the king does really and manifestly behave in a tyrannical manner; and the other conditions laid down for a just war must concurrently be present. . . .

3. I hold, thirdly, that a war of the state against a king who is tyrannical in neither of these two ways, is sedition in the truest sense and intrinsically evil. This is certainly true, as is evident from the fact that, in such a case, both a just cause and a [rightful] authority are lacking. From this, conversely, it is also evident that the war of a prince against a state subject to himself, may be just, from the stand-

point of rightful authority, if all the other required conditions be present, but that, in the absence of those conditions, that same war is entirely unjust.

## 2. *HUGO GROTIUS* (1583–1645)

Grotius' celebrated treatise *On the Law of War and Peace* was published in 1625, four years after Suarez' discussion of war appeared in *The Three Theological Virtues.* Grotius had not seen that work and was dependent rather on Suarez' work on law. Suarez, however, was a Thomist; Grotius seems rather to have favored the Stoic philosophy of Roman jurisprudence.

In the *Prolegomena* to his treatise, he poses the choice between the legal positivism of Carneades the Sceptic, who based laws on expediency alone, and Cicero's appeal to rationally self-evident natural law. In the absence of clearly enacted laws to govern relationships between nations, Carneades allows expediency to guide military action, but Grotius argues that war is not exempt from legal restraint. The law of nations is operative. In the main body of his work he spells out what the law of nations contributes to the questions Vitoria and Suarez discussed: whether war is ever justified, what constitutes a just cause (*jus ad bellum*), and the regulation of conduct in war (*jus in bello*). Grotius' rules provide the basis for modern international law.

## NATURAL LAWS AND THE LAWS OF WAR

From *Prolegomena to the Law of War and Peace,* trans. F. W. Kelsey.

1. The municipal law of Rome and of other states has been treated by many, who have undertaken to elucidate it by means of commentaries or to reduce it to a convenient digest. That body of law, however, which is concerned with the mutual relations among states or rulers of states, whether derived from nature, or established by divine ordinances, or having its origin in custom and tacit agreement, few have touched upon. Up to the present time no one has treated it in a comprehensive and systematic manner; yet the welfare of mankind demands that this task be accomplished.

2. Cicero justly characterized as of surpassing worth a knowledge of treaties of alliance, conventions, and understandings of peoples, kings and foreign nations—a knowledge, in short, of the whole law

of war and peace. And to this knowledge Euripides gives the preference over an understanding of things divine and human, for he represents Theoclymenus as being thus addressed:

> For you, who know the fate of men and gods,
> What is, what shall be, shameful would it be
> To know not what is just.

3. Such a work is all the more necessary because in our day, as in former times, there is no lack of men who view this branch of law with contempt as having no reality outside of an empty name. On the lips of men quite generally is the saying of Euphemus, which Thucydides quotes, that in the case of a king or imperial city nothing is unjust which is expedient. Of like implication is the statement that for those whom fortune favors might makes right, and that the administration of a state cannot be carried on without injustice.

Furthermore, the controversies which arise between peoples or kings generally have Mars as their arbiter. That war is irreconcilable with all law is a view held not alone by the ignorant populace; expressions are often let slip by well-informed and thoughtful men which lend countenance to such a view. Nothing is more common than the assertion of antagonism between law and arms. Thus Ennius says:

> Not on grounds of right is battle joined,
> But rather with the sword do men
> Seek to enforce their claims.

Horace, too, describes the savage temper of Achilles in this wise:

> Laws, he declares, were not for him ordained;
> By dint of arms he claims all for himself.

Another poet depicts another military leader as commencing war with the words:

> Here peace and violated laws I leave behind.

Antigonus when advanced in years ridiculed a man who brought to him a treatise on justice when he was engaged in besieging cities that did not belong to him. Marius declared that the din of arms made it impossible for him to hear the voice of the laws. Even Pompey, whose expression of countenance was so mild, dared to say: "When I am in arms, am I to think of laws?"

4. Among Christian writers a similar thought finds frequent expression. A single quotation from Tertullian may serve in place of

many: "Deception, harshness, and injustice are the regular business of battles." They who so think will no doubt wish to confront us with this passage in Comedy:

> These things uncertain should you, by reason's aid,
> Try to make certain, no more would you gain
> Than if you tried by reason to go mad.

5. Since our discussion concerning law will have been undertaken in vain if there is no law, in order to open the way for a favorable reception of our work and at the same time to fortify it against attacks, this very serious error must be briefly refused. In order that we may not be obliged to deal with a crowd of opponents, let us assign to them a pleader. And whom should we choose in preference to Carneades? For he had attained to so perfect a mastery of the peculiar tenet of his Academy that he was able to devote the power of his eloquence to the service of falsehood not less readily than to that of truth.

Carneades, then, having undertaken to hold a brief against justice, in particular against that phase of justice with which we are concerned, was able to muster no argument stronger than this, that, for reasons of expediency, men imposed upon themselves laws, which vary according to customs, and among the same peoples often undergo changes as times change; moreover, that there is no law of nature, because all creatures, men as well as animals, are impelled by nature toward ends advantageous to themselves; that, consequently, there is no justice, or, if such there be, it is supreme folly, since one does violence to his own interests if he consults the advantage of others.

6. What the philosopher here says, and the poet reaffirms in verse,

> And just from unjust Nature cannot know,

must not for one moment be admitted. Man is, to be sure, an animal, but an animal of a superior kind, much farther removed from all other animals than the different kinds of animals are from one another; evidence on this point may be found in the many traits peculiar to the human species. But among the traits characteristic of man is an impelling desire for society, that is, for the social life—not of any and every sort, but peaceful, and organized according to the measure of his intelligence, with those who are of his own kind; this social trend the Stoics called "sociableness." Stated as a universal truth, therefore, the assertion that every animal is impelled by nature to seek only its own good cannot be conceded.

7. Some of the other animals, in fact, do in a way restrain the appetency for that which is good for themselves alone, to the advantage now of their offspring, now of other animals of the same species. This aspect of their behavior has its origin, we believe, in some extrinsic intelligent principle, because with regard to other actions, which involve no more difficulty than those referred to, a like degree of intelligence is not manifest in them. The same thing must be said of children. In children, even before their training has begun, some disposition to do good to others appears, as Plutarch sagely observed; thus sympathy for others comes out spontaneously at that age. The mature man in fact has knowledge which prompts him to similar actions under similar conditions, together with an impelling desire for society, for the gratification of which he alone among animals possesses a special instrument, speech. He has also been endowed with the faculty of knowing and acting in accordance with general principles. Whatever accords with that faculty is not common to all animals, but peculiar to the nature of man.

8. This maintenance of the social order, which we have roughly sketched, and which is consonant with human intelligence, is the source of law properly so called. To this sphere of law belong the abstaining from that which is another's, the restoration to another of anything of his which we may have, together with any gain which we may have received from it; the obligation to fulfill promises, the making good of a loss incurred through our fault, and the inflicting of penalties upon men according to their deserts.

9. From this signification of the word "law" there has flowed another and more extended meaning. Since over other animals man has the advantage of possessing not only a strong bent toward social life, of which we have spoken, but also a power of discrimination which enables him to decide what things are agreeable or harmful (as to both things present and things to come), and what can lead to either alternative, in such things it is meet for the nature of man, within the limitations of human intelligence, to follow the direction of a well-tempered judgment, being neither led astray by fear or the allurement of immediate pleasure, nor carried away by rash impulse. Whatever is clearly at variance with such judgment is understood to be contrary also to the law of nature, that is, to the nature of man.

10. To this exercise of judgment belongs moreover the rational

allotment to each man, or to each social group, of those things which are properly theirs, in such a way as to give the preference now to him who is more wise over the less wise, now to a kinsman rather than to a stranger, now to a poor man rather than a man of means, as the conduct of each or the nature of the thing suggests. Long ago the view came to be held by many that this discriminating allotment is a part of law, properly and strictly so called; nevertheless law, properly defined, has a far different nature, because its essence lies in leaving to another that which belongs to him, or in fulfilling our obligations to him.

11. What we have been saying would have a degree of validity even if we should concede that which cannot be conceded without the utmost wickedness, that there is no God, or that the affairs of men are of no concern to him. The very opposite of this view has been implanted in us partly by reason, partly by unbroken tradition, and confirmed by many proofs as well as by miracles attested by all ages. Hence it follows that we must without exception render obedience to God as our Creator, to whom we owe all that we are and have, especially since in manifold ways he has shown himself supremely good and supremely powerful, so that to those who obey him he is able to give supremely great rewards, even rewards that are eternal, since he himself is eternal. We ought, moreover, to believe that he has willed to give rewards, and all the more should we cherish such a belief if he has so promised in plain words; that he has done this, we Christians believe, convinced by the indubitable assurance of testimonies.

12. Herein, then, is another source of law besides the source in nature, that is, the free will of God, to which beyond all cavil our reason tells us we must render obedience. But the law of nature of which we have spoken, comprising alike that which relates to the social life of man and that which is so called in a larger sense, proceeding as it does from the essential traits implanted in man, can nevertheless rightly be attributed to God because of his having willed that such traits exist in us. In this sense, too, Chrysippus and the Stoics used to say that the origin of law should be sought in no other source than Jupiter himself; and from the name Jupiter the Latin word for law (jus) was probably derived.

13. There is an additional consideration in that, by means of the laws which he has given, God has made those fundamental traits more manifest, even to those who possess feebler reasoning powers; and he has forbidden us to yield to impulses drawing us in opposite

directions—affecting now our own interest, now the interest of others—in an effort to control more effectively our more violent impulses and to restrain them within proper limits.

14. But sacred history, besides enjoining rules of conduct, in no slight degree reinforces man's inclination toward sociableness by teaching that all men are sprung from the same first parents. In this sense we can rightly affirm also that which Florentinus asserted from another point of view, that a blood relationship has been established among us by nature; consequently it is wrong for a man to set a snare for a fellow man. Among mankind generally one's parents are as it were divinities, and to them is owed an obedience which, if not unlimited, is nevertheless of an altogether special kind.

15. Again, since it is a rule of the law of nature to abide by pacts (for it was necessary that among men there be some method of obligating themselves one to another, and no other natural method can be imagined), out of this source the bodies of municipal law have arisen. For those who had associated themselves with some group, or had subjected themselves to a man or to men, had either expressly promised, or from the nature of the transaction must be understood impliedly to have promised, that they would conform to that which should have been determined, in the one case by the majority, in the other by those upon whom authority had been conferred.

16. What is said, therefore, in accordance with the view not only of Carneades but also of others, that

> Expediency is, as it were, the mother
> Of what is just and fair,

is not true, if we wish to speak accurately. For the very nature of man, which even if we had no lack of anything would lead us into the mutual relations of society, is the mother of the law of nature. But the mother of municipal law is that obligation which arises from mutual consent; and since this obligation derives its force from the law of nature, nature may be considered, so to say, the great-grandmother of municipal law.

The law of nature nevertheless has the reinforcement of expediency; for the author of nature willed that as individuals we should be weak, and should lack many things needed in order to live properly, to the end that we might be the more constrained to cultivate the social life. But expediency afforded an opportunity also for municipal law, since that kind of association of which we have spoken, and subjection to authority, have their roots in expediency. From this it follows that those who prescribe laws for others in so doing are accustomed to have or ought to have some advantage in view.

17. But just as the laws of each state have in view the advantage of that state, so by mutual consent it has become possible that certain laws should originate as between all states, or a great many states; and it is apparent that the laws thus originating had in view the advantage, not of particular states, but of the great society of states. And this is what we called the law of nations, whenever we distinguish that term from the law of nature.

This division of law Carneades passed over altogether. For he divided all law into the law of nature and the law of particular countries. Nevertheless if undertaking to treat of the body of law which is maintained between states—for he added a statement in regard to war and things acquired by means of war—he would surely have been obliged to make mention of this law.

18. Wrongly, moreover, does Carneades ridicule justice as folly. For since, by his own admission, the national who in his own country obeys its laws is not foolish, even though, out of regard for that law he may be obliged to forego certain things advantageous for himself, so that nation is not foolish which does not press its own advantage to the point of disregarding the laws common to nations. The reason in either case is the same. For just as the national who violates the law of his country in order to obtain an immediate advantage breaks down that by which the advantage of himself and his posterity are for all future time assured, so the state which transgresses the laws of nature and of nations cuts away also the bulwarks which safeguard its own future peace. Even if no advantage were to be contemplated from the keeping of the law, it would be a mark of wisdom, not of folly, to allow ourselves to be drawn toward that to which we feel that our nature leads.

19. Wherefore, in general, it is by no means true that

> You must confess that laws were framed
> From fear of the unjust,

a thought which in Plato someone explains thus, that laws were invented from fear of receiving injury, and that men are constrained by a kind of force to cultivate justice. For that relates only to the institutions and laws which have been devised to facilitate the enforcement of right, as when many persons in themselves weak, in order that they might not be overwhelmed by the more powerful, leagued themselves together to establish tribunals and by combined force to maintain these, that as a united whole they might prevail against those with whom as individuals they could not cope.

And in this sense we may readily admit also the truth of the saying that right is that which is acceptable to the stronger, so that we may understand that law fails of its outward effect unless it has a sanction behind it. In this way Solon accomplished very great results, as he himself used to declare,

> By joining force and law together,
> Under a like bond.

20. Nevertheless law, even though without a sanction, is not entirely void of effect. For justice brings peace of conscience, while injustice causes torment and anguish, such as Plato describes, in the breasts of tyrants. Justice is approved, and injustice condemned, by the common agreement of good men. But, most important of all, in God injustice finds an enemy, justice a protector. He reserves his judgments for the life after this, yet in such a way that he often causes their effects to become manifest even in this life, as history teaches by numerous examples.

21. Many hold, in fact, that the standard of justice which they insist upon in the case of individuals within the state is inapplicable to a nation or the ruler of a nation. The reason for the error lies in this, first of all, that in respect to law they have in view nothing except the advantage which accrues from it, such advantage being apparent in the case of citizens who, taken singly, are powerless to protect themselves. But great states, since they seem to contain in themselves all things required for the adequate protection of life, seem not to have need of that virtue which looks toward the outside, and is called justice.

22. But, not to repeat what I have said, that law is not founded on expediency alone, there is no state so powerful that it may not at some time need the help of others outside itself, either for purposes of trade, or even to ward off the forces of many foreign nations united against it. In consequence we see that even the most powerful peoples and sovereigns seek alliances, which are quite devoid of significance according to the point of view of those who confine law within the boundaries of states. Most true is the saying that all things are uncertain the moment men depart from law.

23. If no association of men can be maintained without law, as Aristotle showed by his remarkable illustration drawn from brigands, surely also that association which binds together the human race, or binds many nations together, has need of law; this was perceived by him who said that shameful deeds ought not to be committed even for the sake of one's country. Aristotle takes sharply to task those who, while unwilling to allow anyone to exercise authority over themselves except in accordance with law, yet are quite indifferent as to whether foreigners are treated according to law or not.

24. That same Pompey whom I just now quoted for the opposite view, corrected the statement which a king of Sparta had made, that that state is the most fortunate whose boundaries are fixed by spear and sword; he declared that that state is truly fortunate which has justice for its boundary line. On this point he might have invoked the authority of another king of Sparta who gave the preference to justice over bravery in war, using this argument, that bravery ought to be directed by a kind of justice, but if all men were just they would have no need for bravery in war.

Bravery itself the Stoics defined as virtue fighting on behalf of equity. Themistius in his address to Valens argues with eloquence that kings who measure up to the rule of wisdom make account not only of the nation which has been committed to them, but of the whole human race, and that they are, as he himself says, not "friends of the Macedonians" alone, or "friends of the Romans," but "friends of mankind." The name of Minos became odious to future ages for no other reason than this that he limited his fair dealing to the boundaries of his realm.

25. Least of all should that be admitted which some people imagine, that in war all laws are in abeyance. On the contrary war ought not to be undertaken except for the enforcement of rights; when once undertaken, it should be carried on only within the bounds of law and good faith. Demosthenes well said that war is directed against those who cannot be held in check by judicial processes. For judgments are efficacious against those who feel that they are too weak to resist; against those who are equally strong, or think that they are, wars are undertaken. But in order that wars may be justified, they must be carried on with no less scrupulousness than judicial processes are wont to be.

26. Let the laws be silent, then, in the midst of arms, but only the laws of the state, those that the courts are concerned with, that

are adapted only to a state of peace; not those other laws, which are of perpetual validity and suited to all times. It was exceedingly well said by Dio of Prusa, that between enemies written laws, that is, laws of particular states, are not in force, but that unwritten laws are in force, that is, those which nature prescribes, or the agreement of nations has established. This is set forth by that ancient formula of the Romans: "I think that those things ought to be sought by means of a war that is blameless and righteous."

The ancient Romans, as Varro noted, were slow in undertaking war, and permitted themselves no license in that matter, because they held the view that a war ought not to be waged except when free from reproach. Camillus said that wars should be carried on justly no less than bravely; Scipio Africanus, that the Roman people commenced and ended wars justly. In another passage you may read: "War has its laws no less than peace." Still another writer admires Fabricius as a great man who maintained his probity in war—a thing most difficult—and believed that even in relation to an enemy there is such a thing as wrongdoing.

27. The historians in many a passage reveal how great in war is the influence of the consciousness that one has justice on his side; they often attribute victory chiefly to this cause. Hence the proverbs that a soldier's strength is broken or increased by his cause; that he who has taken up arms unjustly rarely comes back in safety; that hope is the comrade of a good cause; and others of the same purport.

No one ought to be disturbed, furthermore, by the successful outcome of unjust enterprises. For it is enough that the fairness of the cause exerts a certain influence, even a strong influence upon actions, although the effect of that influence, as happens in human affairs, is often nullified by the interference of other causes. Even for winning friendships, of which for many reasons nations as well as individuals have need, a reputation for having undertaken war not rashly nor unjustly, and of having waged it in a manner above reproach, is exceedingly efficacious. No one readily allies himself with those in whom he believes that there is only a slight regard for law, for the right, and for good faith.

28. Fully convinced, by the considerations which I have advanced, that there is a common law among nations, which is valid alike for war and in war, I have had many and weighty reasons for undertaking to write upon this subject. Throughout the Christian world I observed a lack of restraint in relation to war, such as even barbarous

races should be ashamed of; I observed that men rush to arms for slight causes, or no cause at all, and that when arms have once been taken up there is no longer any respect for law, divine or human; it is as if, in accordance with a general decree, frenzy had openly been let loose for the committing of all crimes.

29. Confronted with such utter ruthlessness, many men who are the very furthest from being bad men, have come to the point of forbidding all use of arms to the Christian, whose rule of conduct above everything else comprises the duty of loving all men. To this opinion sometimes John Ferus and my fellow countryman Erasmus seem to incline, men who have the utmost devotion to peace in both Church and State; but their purpose, as I take it, is, when things have gone in one direction, to force them in the opposite direction, as we are accustomed to do, that they may come back to a true middle ground. But the very effort of pressing too hard in the opposite direction is often so far from being helpful that it does harm, because in such arguments the detection of what is extreme is easy, and results in weakening the influence of other statements which are well within the bounds of truth. For both extremes therefore a remedy must be found, that men may not believe either that nothing is allowable, or that everything is.

30. At the same time through devotion to study in private life I have wished—as the only course now open to me, undeservedly forced out from my native land, which had been graced by so many of my labors—to contribute somewhat to the philosophy of the law, which previously, in public service, I practiced with the utmost degree of probity of which I was capable. Many heretofore have purposed to give to this subject a well-ordered presentation; no one has succeeded. And in fact such a result cannot be accomplished unless—a point which until now has not been sufficiently kept in view—those elements which come from positive law are properly separated from those which arise from nature. For the principles of the law of nature, since they are always the same, can easily be brought into a systematic form; but the elements of positive law, since they often undergo change and are different in places, are outside the domain of systematic treatment, just as other notions of particular things are. . . .

32. What procedure we think should be followed we have shown by deed rather than by words in this work, which treats by far the noblest part of jurisprudence.

33. In the first book, having by way of introduction spoken of

the origin of law, we have examined the general question, whether there is any such thing as a just war; then, in order to determine the differences between public war and private war, we found it necessary to explain the nature of sovereignty—what nations, what kings possess complete sovereignty; who possesses sovereignty only in part, who with right of alienation, who otherwise; then it was necessary to speak also concerning the duty of subjects to their superiors.

34. The second book, having for its object to set forth all the causes from which war can arise, undertakes to explain fully what things are held in common, what may be owned in severalty; what rights persons have over persons, what obligation arises from ownership; what is the rule governing royal successions; what right is established by a pact or a contract; what is the force of treaties of alliance; what of an oath private or public, and how it is necessary to interpret these; what is due in reparation for damage done; in what the inviolability of ambassadors consists; what law controls the burial of the dead, and what is the nature of punishments.

35. The third book has for its subject, first, what is permissible in war. Having distinguished that which is done with impunity, or even that which among foreign peoples is defended as lawful, from that which actually is free from fault, it proceeds to the different kinds of peace, and all compacts relating to war. . . .

39. . . . I have made it my concern to refer the proofs of things touching the law of nature to certain fundamental conceptions which are beyond question, so that no one can deny them without doing violence to himself. For the principles of that law, if only you pay strict heed to them, are in themselves manifest and clear, almost as evident as are those things which we perceive by the external senses; and the senses do not err if the organs of perception are properly formed and if the other conditions requisite to perception are present. . . .

40. In order to prove the existence of this law of nature, I have, furthermore, availed myself of the testimony of philosophers, historians, poets; finally also of orators. Not that confidence is to be reposed in them without discrimination, for they were accustomed to serve the interests of their sect, their subject, or their cause. But when many at different times and in different places affirm the same thing as certain, that ought to be referred to a universal cause; and this cause, in the lines of inquiry which we are following, must be either a correct conclusion drawn from the principles of nature, or common

consent. The former points to the law of nature, the latter to the law of nations.

The distinction between these kinds of law is not to be drawn from the testimonies themselves (for writers everywhere confuse the terms law of nature and law of nations), but from the character of the matter. For whatever cannot be deduced from certain principles by a sure process of reasoning, and yet is clearly observed everywhere, must have its origin in the free will of man.

41. These two kinds of law, therefore, I have always particularly sought to distinguish from each other and from municipal law. Furthermore, in the law of nations I have distinguished between that which is truly and in all respects law, and that which produces merely a kind of outward effect simulating that primitive law, as, for example, the prohibition to resist by force, or even the duty of defense in any place by public force, in order to secure some advantage, or for the avoidance of serious disadvantages. How necessary it is, in many cases, to observe this distinction, will become apparent in the course of our work. . . .

## 3. JOHN LOCKE (1632–1704)

In 1689, shortly after his return to England from political exile in Holland, Locke presented *Two Treatises on Civil Government* as an apologetic for the 1688 revolution. The *Second Treatise*, with its emphasis on a free social contract, became one of the most influential writings in modern political thought. While Locke desires government for the preservation of natural rights and shares the optimism of Enlightenment rationalists, he attempts to relate these views to the belief in divine creation from which, as a Christian, his thinking stems.

The violation of individual rights to life or liberty or property precipitates a state of war. On this basis Locke discusses the justice of both war between nations and war against tyranny. The influence of the just war tradition is evident, but Locke develops far more fully what was still embryonic in Aquinas and Suarez, namely, the implications of government by popular consent for the legitimacy of revolution.

## ON CIVIL GOVERNMENT

From *Second Treatise on Civil Government,* chap. 2-5, 9, 16-19, in *John Locke on Politics and Education,* ed. H. R. Penniman (1947).

### CHAPTER 2

#### *Of the State of Nature*

4. To understand political power aright, and derive it from its original, we must consider what estate all men are naturally in, and that is, a state of perfect freedom to order their actions, and dispose of their possessions and persons as they think fit, within the bounds of the law of Nature, without asking leave or depending upon the will of any other man.

A state also of equality, wherein all the power and jurisdiction is reciprocal, no one having more than another, there being nothing more evident than that creatures of the same species and rank, promiscuously born to all the same advantages of Nature, and the use of the same faculties, should also be equal one amongst another, without subordination or subjection, unless the lord and master of them all should, by any manifest declaration of his will, set one above another, and confer on him, by an evident and clear appointment, an undoubted right to dominion and sovereignty.

5. This equality of men by Nature, the judicious Hooker looks upon as so evident in itself, and beyond all question, that he makes it the foundation of that obligation to mutual love amongst men on which he builds the duties they owe one another, and from whence he derives the great maxims of justice and charity. His words are:

"The like natural inducement hath brought men to know that it is no less their duty to love others than themselves, for seeing those things which are equal, must needs all have one measure; if I cannot but wish to receive good, even as much at every man's hands, as any man can wish unto his own soul, how should I look to have any part of my desire herein satisfied, unless myself be careful to satisfy the like desire, which is undoubtedly in other men weak, being of one and the same nature: to have anything offered them repugnant to this desire must needs, in all respects, grieve them as much as me; so that if I do harm, I must look to suffer, there being no reason that others should show greater measure of love to me than they have by me showed unto them; my desire, therefore, to be loved of my equals in Nature, as much as possible may be, imposeth upon me a natural duty of bearing to themward fully the like affection. From which relation of equality between ourselves and them that are as ourselves, what several rules and canons natural reason hath drawn for direction of life no man is ignorant." (*Eccl. Pol.* 1.)

6. But though this be a state of liberty, yet it is not a state of license; though man in that state have an uncontrollable liberty to dispose of his person or possessions, yet he has not liberty to destroy himself, or so much as any creature in his possession, but where some nobler use than its bare preservation calls for it. The state of Nature has a law of Nature to govern it, which obliges everyone, and reason, which is that law, teaches all mankind who will but consult it, that being all equal and independent, no one ought to harm another in his life, health, liberty or possessions; for men being all the workmanship of one omnipotent and infinitely wise Maker; all the servants of one sovereign Master, sent into the world by His order and about His business; they are His property, whose workmanship they are made

to last during His, not one another's pleasure. And, being furnished with like faculties, sharing all in one community of Nature, there cannot be supposed any such subordination among us that may authorize us to destroy one another, as if we were made for one another's uses, as the inferior ranks of creatures are for ours. Everyone as he is bound to preserve himself, and not to quit his station willfully, so by the like reason, when his own preservation comes not in competition, ought he as much as he can to preserve the rest of mankind, and not unless it be to do justice on an offender, take away or impair the life, or what tends to the preservation of the life, the liberty, health, limb, or goods of another.

7. And that all men may be restrained from invading others' rights, and from doing hurt to one another, and the law of Nature be observed, which willeth the peace and preservation of all mankind, the execution of the law of Nature is in that state put into every man's hands, whereby everyone has a right to punish the transgressors of that law to such a degree as may hinder its violation. For the law of Nature would, as all other laws that concern men in this world, be in vain if there were nobody that in the state of Nature had a power to execute that law, and thereby preserve the innocent and restrain offenders; and if anyone in the state of Nature may punish another for any evil he has done, everyone may do so. For in that state of perfect equality, where naturally there is no superiority or jurisdiction of one over another, what any may do in prosecution of that law, everyone must needs have a right to do.

8. And thus, in the state of Nature, one man comes by a power over another, but yet no absolute or abritrary power to use a criminal, when he has got him in his hands, according to the passionate heats or boundless extravagancy of his own will, but only to retribute to him so far as calm reason and conscience dictate, what is proportionate to his transgression, which is so much as may serve for reparation and restraint. For these two are the only reasons why one man may lawfully do harm to another, which is that we call punishment. In transgressing the law of Nature, the offender declares himself to live by another rule than that of reason and common equity, which is that measure God has set to the actions of men for their mutual security, and so he becomes dangerous to mankind; the tie which is to secure them from injury and violence being slighted and broken by him, which being a trespass against the whole species, and the peace and safety of it, provided for by the law of Nature, every man upon this

score, by the right he hath to preserve mankind in general, may restrain, or where it is necessary, destroy things noxious to them, and so may bring such evil on anyone who hath transgressed that law, as may make him repent the doing of it, and thereby deter him, and, by his example, others from doing the like mischief. And in this case, and upon this ground, every man hath a right to punish the offender, and be executioner of the law of Nature.

9. I doubt not but this will seem a very strange doctrine to some men; but before they condemn it, I desire them to resolve me by what right any prince or state can put to death or punish an alien for any crime he commits in their country? It is certain their laws, by virtue of any sanction they receive from the promulgated will of the legislature, reach not a stranger. They speak not to him, nor, if they did, is he bound to hearken to them. The legislative authority by which they are in force over the subjects of that commonwealth hath no power over him. Those who have the supreme power of making laws in England, France, or Holland are, to an Indian, but like the rest of the world—men without authority. And therefore, if by the law of Nature every man hath not a power to punish offenses against it, as he soberly judges the case to require, I see not how the magistrates of any community can punish an alien of another country, since, in reference to him, they can have no more power than what every man naturally may have over another.

10. Besides the crime which consists in violating the laws, and varying from the right rule of reason, whereby a man so far becomes degenerate, and declares himself to quit the principles of human nature and to be a noxious creature, there is commonly injury done, and some person or other, some other man, receives damage by his transgression; in which case, he who hath received any damage has (besides the right of punishment common to him, with other men) a particular right to seek reparation from him that hath done it. And any other person who finds it just may also join with him that is injured, and assist him in recovering from the offender so much as may make satisfaction for the harm he hath suffered.

11. From these two distinct rights (the one of punishing the crime, for restraint and preventing the like offense, which right of punishing is in everybody, the other of taking reparation, which belongs only to the injured party) comes it to pass that the magistrate, who by being magistrate hath the common right of punishing put into his hands, can often, where the public good demands not the execution

of the law, remit the punishment of criminal offenses by his own authority, but yet cannot remit the satisfaction due to any private man for the damage he has received. That he who hath suffered the damage has a right to demand in his own name, and he alone can remit. The damnified person has this power of appropriating to himself the goods or service of the offender by right of self-preservation, as every man has a power to punish the crime to prevent its being committed again, by the right he has of preserving all mankind, and doing all reasonable things he can in order to that end.

And thus it is that every man in the state of Nature has a power to kill a murderer, both to deter others from doing the like injury (which no reparation can compensate) by the example of the punishment that attends it from everybody, and also to secure men from the attempts of a criminal who, having renounced reason, the common rule and measure God hath given to mankind, hath, by the unjust violence and slaughter he hath committed upon one, declared war against all mankind, and therefore may be destroyed as a lion or a tiger, one of those wild savage beasts with whom men can have no society nor security. And upon this is grounded that great law of Nature, "Whoso sheddeth man's blood, by man shall his blood be shed." And Cain was so fully convinced that everyone had a right to destroy such a criminal, that, after the murder of his brother, he cries out, "Everyone that findeth me shall slay me," so plain was it writ in the hearts of all mankind.

12. By the same reason may a man in the state of Nature punish the lesser breaches of that law, it will, perhaps, be demanded, with death? I answer: Each transgression may be punished to that degree, and with so much severity, as will suffice to make it an ill bargain to the offender, give him cause to repent, and terrify others from doing the like. Every offense that can be committed in the state of Nature may, in the state of Nature, be also punished equally, and as far forth, as it may, in a commonwealth. For though it would be beside my present purpose to enter here into the particulars of the law of Nature, or its measures of punishment, yet it is certain there is such a law, and that too as intelligible and plain to a rational creature and a studier of that law as the positive laws of commonwealths, nay, possibly plainer; as much as reason is easier to be understood than the fancies and intricate contrivances of men, following contrary and hidden interests put into words; for truly so are a great part of the municipal laws of countries, which are only so far right as they are

founded on the law of Nature, by which they are to be regulated and interpreted.

13. To this strange doctrine—viz., That in the state of Nature everyone has the executive power of the law of Nature—I doubt not but it will be objected that it is unreasonable for men to be judges in their own cases, that self-love will make men partial to themselves and their friends; and, on the other side, ill-nature, passion, and revenge will carry them too far in punishing others, and hence nothing but confusion and disorders will follow, and that therefore God hath certainly appointed government to restrain the partiality and violence of men. I easily grant that civil government is the proper remedy for the inconveniences of the state of Nature, which must certainly be great where men may be judges in their own case, since it is easy to be imagined that he who was so unjust as to do his brother an injury will scarce be so just as to condemn himself for it. But I shall desire those who make this objection to remember that absolute monarchs are but men; and if government is to be the remedy of those evils which necessarily follow from men being judges in their own cases, and the state of Nature is therefore not to be endured, I desire to know what kind of government that is, and how much better it is than the state of Nature, where one man commanding a multitude has the liberty to be judge in his own case, and may do to all his subjects whatever he pleases without the least question or control of those who execute his pleasure? and in whatsoever he doth, whether led by reason, mistake, or passion, must be submitted to? which men in the state of Nature are not bound to do one to another. And if he that judges, judges amiss in his own or any other case, he is answerable for it to the rest of mankind.

14. It is often asked as a mighty objection, where are, or ever were, there any men in such a state of Nature? To which it may suffice as an answer at present, that since all princes and rulers of "independent" governments all through the world are in a state of Nature, it is plain the world never was, nor never will be, without numbers of men in that state. I have named all governors of "independent" communities, whether they are, or are not, in league with others; for it is not every compact that puts an end to the state of Nature between men, but only this one of agreeing together mutually to enter into one community, and make one body politic; other promises and compacts men may make one with another, and yet still be in the state of Nature. The promises and bargains for truck, etc.,

between the two men in Soldania, in or between a Swiss and an Indian, in the woods of America, are binding to them, though they are perfectly in a state of Nature in reference to one another for truth, and keeping of faith belongs to men as men, and not as members of society.

15. To those that say there were never any men in the state of Nature, I will not only oppose the authority of the judicious Hooker (*Eccl. Pol.* 1. 10), where he says, "the laws which have been hitherto mentioned"—i.e., the laws of Nature—"do bind men absolutely, even as they are men, although they have never any settled fellowship, never any solemn agreement amongst themselves what to do or not to do; but for as much as we are not by ourselves sufficient to furnish ourselves with competent store of things needful for such a life as our Nature doth desire, a life fit for the dignity of man, therefore to supply those defects and imperfections which are in us, as living single and solely by ourselves, we are naturally induced to seek communion and fellowship with others; this was the cause of men uniting themselves as first in politic societies." But I, moreover, affirm that all men are naturally in that state, and remain so till, by their own consents, they make themselves members of some politic society, and I doubt not, in the sequel of this discourse, to make it very clear.

CHAPTER 3
*Of the State of War*

16. The state of war is a state of enmity and destruction; and therefore declaring by word or action, not a passionate and hasty, but sedate, settled design upon another man's life puts him in a state of war with him against whom he has declared such an intention, and so has exposed his life to the other's power to be taken away by him, or anyone that joins with him in his defense, and espouses his quarrel; it being reasonable and just I should have a right to destroy that which threatens me with destruction; for by the fundamental law of Nature, man being to be preserved as much as possible, when all cannot be preserved, the safety of the innocent is to be preferred, and one may destroy a man who makes war upon him, or has discovered an enmity to his being, for the same reason that he may kill a wolf or a lion, because they are not under the ties of the common law of reason, have no other rule but that of force and violence, and so may be treated as a beast of prey, those dangerous and noxious creatures that will be sure to destroy him whenever he falls into their power.

17. And hence it is that he who attempts to get another man into his absolute power does thereby put himself into a state of war with him; it being to be understood as a declaration of a design upon his life. For I have reason to conclude that he who would get me into his power without my consent would use me as he pleased when he had got me there, and destroy me too when he had a fancy to it; for nobody can desire to have me in his absolute power unless it be to compel me by force to that which is against the right of my freedom—i.e., make me a slave. To be free from such force is the only security of my preservation, and reason bids me look on him as an enemy to my preservation who would take away that freedom which is the fence to it; so that he who makes an attempt to enslave me thereby puts himself into a state of war with me. He that in the state of Nature would take away the freedom that belongs to anyone in that state must necessarily be supposed to have a design to take away everything else, that freedom being the foundation of all the rest; as he that in the state of society would take away the freedom belonging to those of that society or commonwealth must be supposed to design to take away from them everything else, and so be looked on as in a state of war.

18. This makes it lawful for a man to kill a thief who has not in the least hurt him, or declared any design upon his life, any farther than by the use of force, so to get him in his power as to take away his money, or what he pleases, from him; because using force, where he has no right to get me into his power, let his pretense be what it will, I have no reason to suppose that he who would take away my liberty would not, when he had me in his power, take away everything else. And, therefore, it is lawful for me to treat him as one who has put himself into a state of war with me—i.e., kill him if I can; for to that hazard does he justly expose himself whoever introduces a state of war, and is aggressor in it.

19. And here we have the plain difference between the state of Nature and the state of war, which however some men have confounded, are as far distant as a state of peace, goodwill, mutual assistance, and preservation; and a state of enmity, malice, violence and mutual destruction are one from another. Men living together according to reason without a common superior on earth, with authority to judge between them, is properly the state of Nature. But force, or a declared design of force upon the person of another, where there is no common superior on earth to appeal to for relief, is the state of

war; and it is the want of such an appeal gives a man the right of war even against an aggressor, though he be in society and a fellow-subject. Thus, a thief whom I cannot harm, but by appeal to the law, for having stolen all that I am worth, I may kill when he sets on me to rob me but of my horse or coat, because the law, which was made for my preservation, where it cannot interpose to secure my life from present force, which if lost is capable of no reparation, permits me my own defense and the right of war, a liberty to kill the aggressor, because the aggressor allows not time to appeal to our common judge, nor the decision of the law, for remedy in a case where the mischief may be irreparable. Want of a common judge with authority puts all men in a state of Nature; force without right upon a man's person makes a state of war both where there is, and is not, a common judge.

20. But when the actual force is over, the state of war ceases between those that are in society and are equally on both sides subject to the judge; and, therefore, in such controversies, where the question is put, "Who shall be judge?" it cannot be meant who shall decide the controversy; everyone knows what Jephtha here tells us, that "the Lord the Judge" shall judge. Where there is no judge on earth the appeal lies to God in Heaven. That question then cannot mean who shall judge, whether another hath put himself in a state of war with me, and whether I may, as Jephtha did, appeal to Heaven in it? Of that I myself can only judge in my own conscience, as I will answer it at the great day to the Supreme Judge of all men.

CHAPTER 4

*Of Slavery*

21. The natural liberty of man is to be free from any superior power on earth, and not to be under the will or legislative authority of man, but to have only the law of Nature for his rule. The liberty of man in society is to be under no other legislative power but that established by consent in the commonwealth, not under the dominion of any will, or restraint of any law, but what that legislative shall enact according to the trust put in it. Freedom, then, is not what Sir Robert Filmer tells us: "A liberty for everyone to do what he lists, to live as he pleases, and not to be tied by any laws"; but freedom of men under government is to have a standing rule to live by, common to everyone of that society, and made by the legislative power erected it in. A liberty to follow my own will in all things where that

rule prescribes not, not to be subject to the inconstant, uncertain, unknown, arbitrary will of another man, as freedom of nature is to be under no other restraint but the law of Nature.

22. This feedom from absolute, arbitrary power is so necessary to, and closely joined with, a man's preservation, that he cannot part with it but by what forfeits his preservation and life together. For a man, not having the power of his own life, cannot by compact or his own consent enslave himself to anyone, nor put himself under the absolute, arbitrary power of another to take away his life when he pleases. Nobody can give more power than he has himself, and he that cannot take away his own life cannot give another power over it. Indeed, having by his fault forfeited his own life by some act that deserves death, he to whom he has forfeited it may, when he has him in his power, delay to take it, and make use of him to his own service; and he does him no injury by it. For, whenever he finds the hardship of his slavery outweigh the value of his life, it is in his power, by resisting the will of his master, to draw on himself the death he desires.

23. This is the perfect condition of slavery, which is nothing else but the state of war continued between a lawful conqueror and a captive, for if once compact enter between them, and make an agreement for a limited power on the one side, and obedience on the other, the state of war and slavery ceases as long as the compact endures; for, as has been said, no man can by agreement pass over to another that which he hath not in himself—a power over his own life.

I confess, we find among the Jews, as well as other nations, that men did sell themselves; but it is plain this was only to drudgery, not to slavery; for it is evident the person sold was not under an absolute, arbitrary, despotical power, for the master could not have power to kill him at any time, whom at a certain time he was obliged to let go free out of his service; and the master of such a servant was so far from having an arbitrary power over his life that he could not at pleasure so much as maim him, but the loss of an eye or tooth set him free (Exod. 21).

## CHAPTER 5
### Of Property

24. Whether we consider natural reason, which tells us that men, being once born, have a right to their preservation, and consequently to meat and drink and such other things as Nature affords for their subsistence, or "revelation," which gives us an account of those grants

God made of the world to Adam, and to Noah and his sons, it is very clear that God, as King David says (Psalm 115:16), "has given the earth to the children of men," given it to mankind in common. But, this being supposed, it seems to some a very great difficulty how any-one should ever come to have a property in anything, I will not con-tent myself to answer, that, if it be difficult to make out "property" upon a supposition that God gave the world to Adam and his posterity in common, it is impossible that any man but one universal monarch should have any "property" upon a supposition that God gave the world to Adam and his heirs in succession, exclusive of all the rest of his posterity; but I shall endeavor to show how men might come to have a property in several parts of that which God gave to mankind in common, and that without any express compact of all the com-moners.

25. God, who hath given the world to men in common, hath also given them reason to make use of it to the best advantage of life and convenience. The earth and all that is therein is given to men for the support and comfort of their being. And though all the fruits it naturally produces, and beasts it feeds, belong to mankind in common, as they are produced by the spontaneous hand of Nature, and nobody has originally a private dominion exclusive of the rest of mankind in any of them, as they are thus in their natural state, yet being given for the use of men, there must of necessity be a means to appropriate them some way or other before they can be of any use, or at all beneficial, to any particular men. The fruit or venison which nourishes the wild Indian, who knows no enclosure, and is still a tenant in common, must be his, and so his—i.e., a part of him, that another can no longer have any right to it before it can do him any good for the support of his life.

26. Though the earth and all inferior creatures be common to all men, yet every man has a "property" in his own "person." This nobody has any right to but himself. The "labor" of his body and the "work" of his hands, we may say, are properly his. Whatsoever, then, he removes out of the state that Nature hath provided and left it in, he hath mixed his labor with it, and joined to it something that is his own, and thereby makes it his property. It being by him removed from the common state Nature placed it in, it hath by this labor something annexed to it that excludes the common right of other men. For this "labor" being the unquestionable property of the laborer, no man but he can have a right to what that is once joined

to, at least where there is enough, and as good left in common for others. . . .

CHAPTER 9

*Of the Ends of Political Society and Government*

123.  If man in the state of Nature be so free as has been said, if he be absolute lord of his own person and possessions, equal to the greatest and subject to nobody, why will he part with his freedom, this empire, and subject himself to the dominion and control of any other power? To which it is obvious to answer, that though in the state of Nature he has such a right, yet the enjoyment of it is very uncertain and constantly exposed to the invasion of others; for all being kings as much as he, every man his equal, and the greater part no strict observers of equity and justice, the enjoyment of the property he has in this state is very unsafe, very insecure. This makes him willing to quit this condition which, however free, is full of fears and continual dangers; and it is not without reason that he seeks out and is willing to join in society with others who are already united, or have a mind to unite for the mutual preservation of their lives, liberties and estates, which I call by the general name—property.

124.  The great and chief end, therefore, of men uniting into commonwealths, and putting themselves under government, is the preservation of their property; to which in the state of Nature there are many things wanting.

Firstly, there wants an established, settled, known law, received and allowed by common consent to be the standard of right and wrong, and the common measure to decide all controversies between them. For though the law of Nature be plain and intelligible to all rational creatures, yet men, being biased by their interest, as well as ignorant for want of study of it, are not apt to allow of it as a law binding to them in the application of it to their particular cases.

125.  Secondly, in the state of Nature there wants a known and indifferent judge, with authority to determine all differences according to the established law. For everyone in that state being both judge and executioner of the law of Nature, men being partial to themselves, passion and revenge is very apt to carry them too far, and with too much heat in their own cases, as well as negligence and unconcernedness, make them too remiss in other men's.

126.  Thirdly, in the state of Nature there often wants power to back and support the sentence when right, and to give it due exe-

cution. They who by any injustice offended will seldom fail where they are able by force to make good their injustice. Such resistance many times makes the punishment dangerous, and frequently destructive to those who attempt it.

127. Thus mankind, notwithstanding all the privileges of the state of Nature, being but in an ill condition while they remain in it are quickly driven into society. Hence it comes to pass, that we seldom find any number of men live any time together in this state. The inconveniences that they are therein exposed to by the irregular and uncertain exercise of the power every man has of punishing the transgressions of others, make them take sanctuary under the established laws of government, and therein seek the preservation of their property. It is this makes them so willingly give up everyone his single power of punishing to be exercised by such alone as shall be appointed to it amongst them, and by such rules as the community, or those authorized by them to that purpose, shall agree on. And in this we have the original right and rise of both the legislative and executive power as well as of the governments and societies themselves.

128. For in the state of Nature to omit the liberty he has of innocent delights, a man has two powers. The first is to do whatsoever he thinks fit for the preservation of himself and others within the permission of the law of Nature; by which law, common to them all, he and all the rest of mankind are one community, make up one society distinct from all other creatures, and were it not for the corruption and viciousness of degenerate men, there would be no need of any other, no necessity that men should separate from this great and natural community, and associate into lesser combinations. The other power a man has in the state of Nature is the power to punish the crimes committed against that law. Both these he gives up when he joins in a private, if I may so call it, or particular political society, and incorporates into any commonwealth separate from the rest of mankind.

129. The first power—viz., of doing whatsoever he thought fit for the preservation of himself and the rest of mankind, he gives up to be regulated by laws made by the society, so far forth as the preservation of himself and the rest of that society shall require; which laws of the society in many things confine the liberty he had by the law of Nature.

130. Secondly, the power of punishing he wholly gives up,

and engages his natural force, which he might before employ in the execution of the law of Nature, by his own single authority, as he thought fit, to assist the executive power of the society as the law thereof shall require. For being now in a new state, wherein he is to enjoy many conveniences from the labor, assistance, and society of others in the same community, as well as protection from its whole strength, he is to part also with as much of his natural liberty, in providing for himself, as the good, prosperity, and safety of the society shall require, which is not only necessary but just, since the other members of the society do the like.

131. But though men when they enter into society give up the equality, liberty, and executive power they had in the state of Nature into the hands of the society, to be so far disposed of by the legislative as the good of the society shall require, yet it being only with an intention in everyone the better to preserve himself, his liberty and property (for no rational creature can be supposed to change his condition with an intention to be worse), the power of the society or legislative constituted by them can never be supposed to extend farther than the common good, but is obliged to secure everyone's property by providing against those three defects above mentioned that made the state of Nature so unsafe and uneasy. And so, whoever has the legislative or supreme power of any commonwealth, is bound to govern by established standing laws, promulgated and known to the people, and not by extemporary decrees, by indifferent and upright judges, who are to decide controversies by those laws; and to employ the force of the community at home only in the execution of such laws, or abroad to prevent or redress foreign injuries and secure the community from inroads and invasion. And all this to be directed to no other end but the peace, safety, and public good of the people.

## CHAPTER 16
### Of Conquest

175. Though governments can originally have no other rise than that before mentioned, nor polities be founded on anything but the consent of the people, yet such have been the disorders ambition has filled the world with, that in the noise of war, which makes so great a part of the history of mankind, this consent is little taken notice of; and, therefore, many have mistaken the force of arms for the consent of the people, and reckon conquest as one of the originals

of government. But conquest is as far from setting up any government as demolishing a house is from building a new one in the place. Indeed, it often makes way for a new frame of a commonwealth by destroying the former; but, without the consent of the people, can never erect a new one.

176. That the aggressor, who puts himself into the state of war with another, and unjustly invades another man's right, can, by such an unjust war, never come to have a right over the conquered, will be easily agreed by all men, who will not think that robbers and pirates have right of empire over whomsoever they have force enough to master, or that men are bound by promises which unlawful force extorts from them. Should a robber break into my house, and, with a dagger at my throat, make me seal deeds to convey my estate to him, would this give him any title? Just such a title by his sword has an unjust conqueror who forces me into submission. The injury and the crime is equal, whether committed by the wearer of a crown or some petty villain. The title of the offender and the number of his followers make no difference in the offense, unless it be to aggravate it. The only difference is, great robbers punish little ones to keep them in their obedience; but the great ones are rewarded with laurels and triumphs, because they are too big for the weak hands of justice in this world, and have the power in their own possession which should punish offenders. What is my remedy against a robber that so broke into my house? Appeal to the law for justice. But perhaps justice is denied, or I am crippled and cannot stir; robbed, and have not the means to do it. If God has taken away all means of seeking remedy, there is nothing left but patience. But my son, when able, may seek the relief of the law, which I am denied; he or his son may renew his appeal till he recover his right. But the conquered, or their children, have no court—no arbitrator on earth to appeal to. Then they may appeal, as Jephtha did, to Heaven, and repeat their appeal till they have recovered the native right of their ancestors, which was to have such a legislative over them as the majority should approve and freely acquiesce in. If it be objected this would cause endless trouble, I answer, no more than justice does, where she lies open to all that appeal to her. He that troubles his neighbor without a cause is punished for it by the justice of the court he appeals to. And he that appeals to Heaven must be sure he has right on his side, and a right, too, that is worth the trouble and cost of the appeal, as he will answer at a tribunal that cannot be

deceived, and will be sure to retribute to everyone according to the mischiefs he hath created to his fellow-subjects—that is, any part of mankind. From whence it is plain that he that conquers in an unjust war can thereby have no title to the subjection and obedience of the conquered.

177. But supposing victory favors the right side, let us consider a conqueror in a lawful war, and see what power he gets, and over whom.

First, it is plain he gets no power by his conquest over those that conquered with him. They that fought on his side cannot suffer by the conquest, but must, at least, be as much free men as they were before. And most commonly they serve upon terms, and on condition to share with their leader, and enjoy a part of the spoil and other advantages that attend the conquering sword, or, at least, have a part of the subdued country bestowed upon them. And the conquering people are not, I hope, to be slaves by conquest, and wear their laurels only to show they are sacrifices to their leader's triumph. They that found absolute monarchy upon the title of the sword make their heroes, who are the founders of such monarchies, arrant "draw-can-sirs," and forget they had any officers and soldiers that fought on their side in the battles they won, or assisted them in the subduing, or shared in possessing the countries they mastered. We are told by some that the English monarchy is founded in the Norman Conquest, and that our princes have thereby a title to absolute dominion, which, if it were true (as by the history it appears otherwise), and that William had a right to make war on this island, yet his dominion by conquest could reach no farther than to the Saxons and Britons that were then inhabitants of this country. The Normans that came with him and helped to conquer, and all descended from them, are free men and no subjects by conquest, let that give what dominion it will. And if I or anybody else shall claim freedom as derived from them, it will be very hard to prove the contrary; and it is plain, the law that has made no distinction between the one and the other intends not there should be any difference in their freedom or privileges.

178. But supposing, which seldom happens, that the conquerors and conquered never incorporate into one people under the same laws and freedom; let us see next what power a lawful conqueror has over the subdued, and that I say is purely despotical. He has an absolute power over the lives of those who, by an unjust war, have forfeited them, but not over the lives or fortunes of those who engaged

not in the war, nor over the possessions even of those who were actually engaged in it.

179. Secondly, I say, then, the conqueror gets no power but only over those who have actually assisted, concurred, or consented to that unjust force that is used against him. For the people having given to their governors no power to do an unjust thing, such as is to make an unjust war (for they never had such a power in themselves), they ought not to be charged as guilty of the violence and injustice that is committed in an unjust war any farther than they actually abet it, no more than they are to be thought guilty of any violence or oppression their governors should use upon the people themselves or any part of their fellow-subjects, they having empowered them no more to the one than to the other. Conquerors, it is true, seldom trouble themselves to make the distinction, but they willingly permit the confusion of war to sweep all together; but yet this alters not the right; for the conqueror's power over the lives of the conquered being only because they have used force to do or maintain an injustice, he can have that power only over those who have concurred in that force; all the rest are innocent, and he has no more title over the people of that country who have done him no injury, and so have made no forfeiture of their lives, than he has over any other who, without any injuries or provocations, have lived upon fair terms with him.

180. Thirdly, the power a conqueror gets over those he overcomes in a just war is perfectly despotical; he has an absolute power over the lives of those who, by putting themselves in a state of war, have forfeited them, but he has not thereby a right and title to their possessions. This I doubt not but at first sight will seem a strange doctrine, it being so quite contrary to the practice of the world; there being nothing more familiar in speaking of the dominion of countries than to say such a one conquered it, as if conquest, without any more ado, conveyed a right of possession. But when we consider that the practice of the strong and powerful, how universal soever it may be, is seldom the rule of right, however it be one part of the subjection of the conquered not to argue against the conditions cut out to them by the conquering swords.

181. Though in all war there be usually a complication of force and damage, and the aggressor seldom fails to harm the estate when he uses force against the persons of those he makes war upon, yet it is the use of force only that puts a man into the state of war. For

whether by force he begins the injury, or else having quietly and by fraud done the injury, he refuses to make reparation, and by force maintains it, which is the same thing as at first to have done it by force; it is the unjust use of force that makes the war. For he that breaks open my house and violently turns me out of doors, or having peaceably got in, by force keeps me out, does, in effect, the same thing; supposing we are in such a state that we have no common judge on earth whom I may appeal to, and to whom we are both obliged to submit, for of such I am now speaking. It is the unjust use of force, then, that puts a man into the state of war with another, and thereby he that is guilty of it makes a forfeiture of his life. For quitting reason, which is the rule given between man and man, and using force, the way of beasts, he becomes liable to be destroyed by him he uses force against, as any savage ravenous beast that is dangerous to his being.

182. But because the miscarriages of the father are no faults of the children, who may be rational and peaceable, notwithstanding the brutishness and injustice of the father, the father, by his miscarriages and violence, can forfeit but his own life, and involves not his children in his guilt or destruction. His goods which Nature, that willeth the preservation of all mankind as much as is possible, hath made to belong to the children to keep them from perishing, do still continue to belong to his children. For supposing them not to have joined in the war either through infancy or choice, they have done nothing to forfeit them, nor has the conqueror any right to take them away by the bare right of having subdued him that by force attempted his destruction, though perhaps he may have some right to them to repair the damages he has sustained by the war, and the defense of his own right, which how far it reaches to the possessions of the conquered we shall see by and by; so that he that by conquest has a right over a man's person, to destroy him if he pleases, has not thereby a right over his estate to possess and enjoy it. For it is the brutal force the aggressor has used that gives his adversary a right to take away his life and destroy him, if he pleases, as a noxious creature; but it is damage sustained that alone gives him title to another man's goods; for though I may kill a thief that sets on me in the highway, yet I may not (which seems less) take away his money and let him go; this would be robbery on my side. His force, and the state of war he put himself in, made him forfeit his life, but gave me no title to his goods. The right, then, of conquest extends only to the lives of those who joined in the

war, but not to their estates, but only in order to make reparation for the damages received and the charges of the war, and that, too, with reservation of the right of the innocent wife and children.

183. Let the conqueror have as much justice on his side as could be supposed, he has no right to seize more than the vanquished could forfeit; his life is at the victor's mercy, and his service and goods he may appropriate to make himself reparation; but he cannot take the goods of his wife and children, they too had a title to the goods he enjoyed, and their shares in the estate he possessed. For example, I in the state of Nature (and all commonwealths are in the state of Nature one with another) have injured another man, and refusing to give satisfaction, it is come to a state of war wherein my defending by force what I had gotten unjustly makes me the aggressor. I am conquered; my life, it is true, as forfeit, is at mercy, but not my wife's and children's. They made not the war, nor assisted in it. I could not forfeit their lives, they were not mine to forfeit. My wife had a share in my estate, that neither could I forfeit. And my children also, being born of me, had a right to be maintained out of my labor or substance. Here then is the case: The conqueror has a title to reparation for damages received, and the children have a title to their father's estate for their subsistence. For as to the wife's share, whether her own labor or compact gave her a title to it, it is plain her husband could not forfeit what was hers. What must be done in the case? I answer: the fundamental law of Nature being that all, as much as may be, should be preserved, it follows that if there be not enough full; to satisfy both—viz., for the conqueror's losses and children's maintenance, he that hath and to spare must remit something of his full satisfaction, and give way to the pressing and preferable title of those who are in danger to perish without it.

184. But supposing the charge and damages of the war are to be made up to the conqueror to the utmost farthing, and that the children of the vanquished, spoiled of all their father's goods, are to be left to starve and perish, yet the satisfying of what shall, on this score, be due to the conqueror will scarce give him a title to any country he shall conquer. For the damages of war can scarce amount to the value of any considerable tract of land in any part of the world, where all the land is possessed, and none lies waste. And if I have not taken away the conqueror's land which, being vanquished, it is impossible I should, scarce any other spoil I have done him can amount to the value of mine, supposing it of an extent any way com-

ing near what I had overrun of his, and equally cultivated too. The destruction of a year's product or two (for it seldom reaches four or five) is the utmost spoil that usually can be done. For as to money, and such riches and treasure taken away, these are none of Nature's goods, they have but a phantastical imaginary value; Nature has put no such upon them. They are of no more account by her standard than the Wampompeke of the Americans to an European prince, or the silver money of Europe would have been formerly to an American. And five years' product is not worth the perpetual inheritance of land, where all is possessed and none remains waste, to be taken up by him that is disseized, which will be easily granted, if one do but take away the imaginary value of money, the disproportion being more than between five and five thousand; though, at the same time, half a year's product is more worth than the inheritance where, there being more land than the inhabitants possess and make use of, anyone has liberty to make use of the waste. But their conquerors take little care to possess themselves of the lands of the vanquished. No damage therefore that men in the state of Nature (as all princes and governments are in reference to one another) suffer from one another can give a conqueror power to dispossess the posterity of the vanquished, and turn them out of that inheritance which ought to be the possession of them and their descendants to all generations. The conqueror indeed will be apt to think himself master; and it is the very condition of the subdued not to be able to dispute their right. But, if that be all, it gives no other title than what bare force gives to the stronger over the weaker; and, by this reason, he that is strongest will have a right to whatever he pleases to seize on.

185. Over those, then, that joined with him in the war, and over those of the subdued country that opposed him not, and the posterity even of those that did, the conqueror, even in a just war, hath, by his conquest, no right of dominion. They are free from any subjection to him, and if their former government be dissolved, they are at liberty to begin and erect another to themselves.

186. The conqueror, it is true, usually by the force he has over them, compels them, with a sword at their breasts, to stoop to his conditions, and submit to such a government as he pleases to afford them; but the inquiry is, what right he has to do so? If it be said they submit by their own consent, then this allows their own consent to be necessary to give the conqueror a title to rule over them. It remains only to be considered whether promises, extorted by force, without right, can

be thought consent, and how far they bind. To which I shall say, they bind not at all; because whatsoever another gets from me by force, I still retain the right of, and he is obliged presently to restore. He that forces my horse from me ought presently to restore him, and I have still a right to retake him. By the same reason, he that forced a promise from me ought presently to restore it—i.e., quit me of the obligation of it; or I may resume it myself—i.e., choose whether I will perform it. For the law of Nature laying an obligation on me, only by the rules she prescribes, cannot oblige me by the violation of her rules; such is the extorting anything from me by force. Nor does it at all alter the case, to say I gave my promise, no more than it excuses the force, and passes the right, when I put my hand in my pocket and deliver my purse myself to a thief who demands it with a pistol at my breast.

187. From all which, it follows that the government of a conqueror, imposed by force on the subdued, against whom he had no right of war, or who joined not in the war against him, where he had right, has no obligation upon them.

188. But let us suppose that all the men of that community being all members of the same body politic, may be taken to have joined in that unjust war, wherein they are subdued, and so their lives are at the mercy of the conqueror.

189. I say this concerns not their children who are in their minority. For since a father hath not, in himself, a power over the life or liberty of his child, no act of his can possibly forfeit it; so that the children, whatever may have happened to the fathers, are free men, and the absolute power of the conqueror reaches no farther than the persons of the men that were subdued by him, and dies with them; and should he govern them as slaves, subjected to his absolute, arbitrary power, he has no such right of dominion over their children. He can have no power over them but by their own consent, whatever he may drive them to say or do, and he has no lawful authority, whilst force, and not choice, compels them to submission.

190. Every man is born with a double right. First, a right of freedom to his person, which no other man has a power over, but the free disposal of it lies in himself. Secondly, a right before any other man, to inherit, with his brethren, his father's goods.

191. By the first of these, a man is naturally free from subjection to any government, though he be born in a place under its jurisdiction. But if he disclaim the lawful government of the country he

was born in, he must also quit the right that belonged to him, by the laws of it, and the possessions there descending to him from his ancestors, if it were a government made by their consent.

192. By the second, the inhabitants of any country, who are descended and derive a title to their estates from those who are subdued, and had a government forced upon them, against their free consents, retain a right to the possession of their ancestors, though they consent not freely to the government, whose hard conditions were, by force, imposed on the possessors of that country. For the first conqueror never having had a title to the land of that country, the people, who are the descendants of, or claim under those who were forced to submit to the yoke of a government by constraint, have always a right to shake it off, and free themselves from the usurpation or tyranny the sword hath brought in upon them, till their rulers put them under such a frame of government as they willingly and of choice consent to (which they can never be supposed to do, till either they are put in a full state of liberty to choose their government and governors, or at least till they have such standing laws to which they have, by themselves or their representatives, given their free consent, and also till they are allowed their due property, which is so to be proprietors of what they have that nobody can take away any part of it without their own consent, without which, men under any government are not in the state of free men, but are direct slaves under the force of war). And who doubts but the Grecian Christians, descendants of the ancient possessors of that country, may justly cast off the Turkish yoke they have so long groaned under, whenever they have a power to do it?

193. But granting that the conqueror, in a just war, has a right to the estates, as well as power over the persons of the conquered, which, it is plain, he hath not, nothing of absolute power will follow from hence in the continuance of the government. Because the descendants of these being all free men, if he grants them estate and possessions to inhabit his country, without which it would be worth nothing, whatsoever he grants them they have so far as it is granted property in; the nature whereof is, that, without a man's own consent, it cannot be taken from him.

194. Their persons are free by a native right, and their properties, be they more or less, are their own, and at their own dispose, and not at his; or else it is no property. Supposing the conqueror gives to one man a thousand acres, to him and his heirs for ever; to another he

lets a thousand acres, for his life, under the rent of £50 or £500 per annum. Has not the one of these a right to his thousand acres for ever, and the other during his life, paying the said rent? And hath not the tenant for life a property in all that he gets over and above his rent, by his labor and industry, during the said term, supposing it be double the rent? Can anyone say, the king, or conqueror, after his grant, may, by his power of conqueror, take away all, or part of the land, from the heirs of one, or from the other during his life, he paying the rent? Or, can he take away from either the goods or money they have got upon the said land at his pleasure? If he can, then all free and voluntary contracts cease, and are void in the world; there needs nothing but power enough to dissolve them at any time, and all the grants and promises of men in power are but mockery and collusion. For can there be anything more ridiculous than to say, I give you and yours this forever, and that in the surest and most solemn way of conveyance can be devised, and yet it is to be understood that I have right, if I please, to take it away from you again tomorrow?

195. I will not dispute now whether princes are exempt from the laws of their country, but this I am sure, they owe subjection to the laws of God and Nature. Nobody, no power can exempt them from the obligations of that eternal law. Those are so great and so strong in the case of promises, that Omnipotency itself can be tied by them. Grants, promises, and oaths are bonds that hold the Almighty, whatever some flatterers say to princes of the world, who, all together, with all their people joined to them, are, in comparison of the great God, but as a drop of the bucket, or a dust on the balance—inconsiderable, nothing!

196. The short of the case in conquest, is this: The conqueror, if he have a just cause, has a despotical right over the persons of all that actually aided and concurred in the war against him, and a right to make up his damage and cost out of their labor and estates, so he injure not the right of any other. Over the rest of the people, if there were any that consented not to the war, and over the children of the captives themselves or the possessions of either he has no power, and so can have, by virtue of conquest, no lawful title himself to dominion over them, or derive it to his posterity; but is an aggressor, and puts himself in a state of war against them, and has no better a right of principality, he, nor any of his successors, than Hingar, or Hubba, the Danes, had here in England, or Spartacus, had he conquered Italy,

which is to have their yoke cast off as soon as God shall give those under their subjection courage and opportunity to do it. Thus, notwithstanding whatever title the kings of Assyria had over Judah, by the
sword, God assisted Hezekiah to throw off the dominion of that conquering empire. "And the Lord was with Hezekiah, and he prospered;
wherefore he went forth, and he rebelled against the king of Assyria,
and served him not" (II Kings 18:7). Whence it is plain that
shaking off a power which force, and not right, hath set over anyone,
though it hath the name of rebellion, yet is no offense before God, but
that which He allows and countenances, though even promises and covenants, when obtained by force, have intervened. For it is very
probable, to anyone that reads the story of Ahaz and Hezekiah at-
tentively, that the Assyrians subdued Ahaz, and deposed him, and
made Hezekiah king in his father's lifetime, and that Hezekiah, by
agreement, had done him homage, and paid him tribute till this time.

### CHAPTER 17
#### Of Usurpation

197. As conquest may be called a foreign usurpation, so usurpation is a kind of domestic conquest, with this difference—that an usurper
can never have right on his side, it being no usurpation but where
one is got into the possession of what another has right to. This, so
far as it is usurpation, is a change only of persons, but not of the
forms and rules of the government; for if the usurper extend his
power beyond what, of right, belonged to the lawful princes or governors of the commonwealth, it is tyranny added to usurpation.

198. In all lawful governments the designation of the persons
who are to bear rule being as natural and necessary a part as the
form of the government itself, and that which had its establishment
originally from the people—the anarchy being much alike, to have
no form of government at all, or to agree that it shall be monarchical,
yet appoint no way to design the person that shall have the power
and be the monarch—all commonwealths, therefore, with the form
of government established, have rules also of appointing and conveying the right to those who are to have any share in the public
authority; and whoever gets into the exercise of any part of the power
by other ways than what the laws of the community have prescribed
hath no right to be obeyed, though the form of the commonwealth
be still preserved, since he is not the person the laws have appointed,
and, consequently, not the person the people have consented to. Nor

can such an usurper, or any deriving from him, ever have a title till the people are both at liberty to consent, and have actually consented, to allow and confirm in him the power he hath till then usurped.

## CHAPTER 18
### Of Tyranny

199. As usurpation is the exercise of power which another hath a right to, so tyranny is the exercise of power beyond right, which nobody can have a right to; and this is making use of the power anyone has in his hands, not for the good of those who are under it, but for his own private, separate advantage. When the governor, however entitled, makes not the law, but his will, the rule, and his commands and actions are not directed to the preservation of the properties of his people, but the satisfaction of his own ambition, revenge, covetousness, or any other irregular passion.

200. If one can doubt this to be truth or reason because it comes from the obscure hand of a subject, I hope the authority of a king will make it pass with him. King James, in his speech to the Parliament, 1603, tells them thus: "I will ever prefer the weal of the public and of the whole commonwealth, in making of good laws and constitutions, to any particular and private ends of mine, thinking ever the wealth and weal of the commonwealth to be my greatest weal and worldly felicity—a point wherein a lawful king doth directly differ from a tyrant; for I do acknowledge that the special and greatest point of difference that is between a rightful king and an usurping tyrant is this—that whereas the proud and ambitious tyrant doth think his kingdom and people are only ordained for satisfaction of his desires and unreasonable appetites, the righteous and just king doth, by the contrary, acknowledge himself to be ordained for the procuring of the wealth and property of his people." And again, in his speech to the Parliament, 1609, he hath these words: "The king binds himself, by a double oath, to the observation of the fundamental laws of his kingdom—tacitly, as by being a king, and so bound to protect, as well the people as the laws of his kingdom; and expressly by his oath at his coronation; so as every just king, in a settled kingdom, is bound to observe that paction made to his people, by his laws, in framing his government agreeable thereunto, according to that paction which God made with Noah after the deluge: 'Hereafter, seed-time, and harvest, and cold, and heat, and summer, and winter, and day, and night, shall not cease while the earth remaineth.' And therefore a king,

governing in a settled kingdom, leaves to be a king, and degenerates into a tyrant, as soon as he leaves off to rule according to his laws." And a little after: "Therefore, all kings that are not tyrants, or perjured, will be glad to bound themselves within the limits of their laws, and they that persuade them the contrary are vipers, pests, both against them and the commonwealth." Thus, that learned king, who well understood the notions of things, makes the difference betwixt a king and a tyrant to consist only in this: that one makes the laws the bounds of his power and the good of the public the end of his government; the other makes all give way to his own will and appetite.

201. It is a mistake to think this fault is proper only to monarchies. Other forms of government are liable to it as well as that; for wherever the power that is put in any hands for the government of the people and the preservation of their properties is applied to other ends, and made use of to impoverish, harass, or subdue them to the arbitrary and irregular commands of those that have it, there it presently becomes tyranny, whether those that thus use it are one or many. Thus we read of the thirty tyrants at Athens, as well as one at Syracuse; and the intolerable dominion of the Decemviri at Rome was nothing better.

202. Wherever law ends, tyranny begins, if the law be transgressed to another's harm; and whosoever in authority exceeds the power given him by the law, and makes use of the force he has under his command to compass that upon the subject which the law allows not, ceases in that to be a magistrate, and acting without authority may be opposed, as any other man who by force invades the right of another. This is acknowledged in subordinate magistrates. He that hath authority to seize my person in the street may be opposed as a thief and a robber if he endeavors to break into my house to execute a writ, notwithstanding that I know he has such a warrant and such a legal authority as will empower him to arrest me abroad. And why this should not hold in the highest, as well as in the most inferior magistrate, I would gladly be informed. Is it reasonable that the eldest brother, because he has the greatest part of his father's estate, should thereby have a right to take away any of his younger brothers' portions? Or that a rich man, who possessed a whole country, should from thence have a right to seize, when he pleased, the cottage and garden of his poor neighbor? The being rightfully possessed of great power and riches, exceedingly beyond the greatest part of the sons of Adam, is so far from being an excuse, much less a reason

for rapine and oppression, which the endamaging another without authority is, that it is a great aggravation of it. For exceeding the bounds of authority is no more a right in a great than a petty officer, no more justifiable in a king than a constable. But so much the worse in him as that he has more trust put in him, is supposed, from the advantage of education and counsellors, to have better knowledge and less reason to do it, having already a greater share than the rest of his brethren.

203. May the commands, then, of a prince be opposed? May he be resisted, as often as anyone shall find himself aggrieved, and but imagine he has not right done him? This will unhinge and overturn all polities, and instead of government and order, leave nothing but anarchy and confusion.

204. To this I answer: That force is to be opposed to nothing but to unjust and unlawful force. Whoever makes any opposition in any other case draws on himself a just condemnation, both from God and man; and so no such danger or confusion will follow, as is often suggested. . . .

CHAPTER 19

*Of the Dissolution of Government*

219. There is one way more whereby such a government may be dissolved, and that is: When he who has the supreme executive power neglects and abandons that charge, so that the laws already made can no longer be put in execution; this is demonstratively to reduce all to anarchy, and so effectively to dissolve the government. For laws not being made for themselves, but to be, by their execution, the bonds of the society to keep every part of the body politic in its due place and function. When that totally ceases, the government visibly ceases, and the people become a confused multitude without order or connection. Where there is no longer the administration of justice for the securing of men's rights, nor any remaining power within the community to direct the force, or provide for the necessities of the public, there certainly is no government left. Where the laws cannot be executed it is all one as if there were no laws, and a government without laws is, I suppose, a mystery in politics inconceivable to human capacity, and inconsistent with human society.

220. In these, and the like cases, when the government is dissolved, the people are at liberty to provide for themselves by erecting a new legislative differing from the other by the change of persons, or

form, or both, as they shall find it most for their safety and good. For the society can never, by the fault of another, lose the native and original right it has to preserve itself, which can only be done by a settled legislative and a fair and impartial execution of the laws made by it. But the state of mankind is not so miserable that they are not capable of using this remedy till it be too late to look for any. To tell people they may provide for themselves by erecting a new legislative, when, by oppression, artifice, or being delivered over to a foreign power, their old one is gone, is only to tell them they may expect relief when it is too late, and the evil is past cure. This is, in effect, no more than to bid them first be slaves, and then to take care of their liberty, and, when their chains are on, tell them they may act like free men. This, if barely so, is rather mockery than relief, and men can never be secure from tyranny if there be no means to escape it till they are perfectly under it; and, therefore, it is that they have not only a right to get out of it, but to prevent it.

221. There is, therefore, secondly, another way whereby governments are dissolved, and that is, when the legislative, or the prince, either of them act contrary to their trust.

For the legislative acts against the trust reposed in them when they endeavor to invade the property of the subject, and to make themselves, or any part of the community, masters or arbitrary disposers of the lives, liberties, or fortunes of the people.

222. The reason why men enter into society is the preservation of their property; and the end while they choose and authorize a legislative is that there may be laws made, and rules set, as guards and fences to the properties of all the society, to limit the power and moderate the dominion of every part and member of the society. For since it can never be supposed to be the will of the society that the legislative should have a power to destroy that which everyone designs to secure by entering into society, and for which the people submitted themselves to legislators of their own making: whenever the legislators endeavor to take away and destroy the property of the people, or to reduce them to slavery under arbitrary power, they put themselves into a state of war with the people, who are thereupon absolved from any farther obedience, and are left to the common refuge which God hath provided for all men against force and violence. Whensoever, therefore, the legislative shall transgress this fundamental rule of society, and either by ambition, fear, folly, or corruption, endeavor to grasp themselves, or put into the hands of any other, an absolute

power over the lives, liberties, and estates of the people, by this breach of trust they forfeit the power the people had put into their hands for quite contrary ends, and it devolves to the people, who have a right to resume their original liberty, and by the establishment of a new legislative (such as they shall think fit), provide for their own safety and security, which is the end for which they are in society.

What I have said here concerning the legislative in general holds true also concerning the supreme executor, who having a double trust put in him, both to have a part in the legislative and the supreme execution of the law, acts against both, when he goes about to set up his own arbitrary will as the law of the society. . . .

227. In both the forementioned cases, when either the legislative is changed, or the legislators act contrary to the end for which they were constituted, those who are guilty are guilty of rebellion. For if anyone by force takes away the established legislative of any society, and the laws by them made, pursuant to their trust, he thereby takes away the umpirage which everyone had consented to for a peaceable decision of all their controversies, and a bar to the state of war amongst them. They who remove or change the legislative take away this decisive power, which nobody can have but by the appointment and consent of the people, and so destroying the authority which the people did, and nobody else can set up, and introducing a power which the people hath not authorized, actually introduce a state of war, which is that of force without authority; and thus by removing the legislative established by the society, in whose decisions the people acquiesced and united as to that of their own will, they untie the knot, and expose the people anew to the state of war. And if those, who by force take away the legislative, are rebels, the legislators themselves, as has been shown, can be no less esteemed so, when they who were set up for the protection and preservation of the people, their liberties and properties shall by force invade and endeavor to take them away; and so they putting themselves into a state of war with those who made them the protectors and guardians of their peace, are properly, and with the greatest aggravation, *rebellantes*, rebels.

228. But if they who say it lays a foundation for rebellion mean that it may occasion civil wars or intestine broils to tell the people they are absolved from obedience when illegal attempts are made upon their liberties or properties, and may oppose the unlawful violence of those who were their magistrates when they invade their properties, contrary to the trust put in them, and that, therefore, this doctrine is not

to be allowed, being so destructive to the peace of the world; they may as well say, upon the same ground, that honest men may not oppose robbers or pirates, because this may occasion disorder or bloodshed. If any mischief come in such cases, it is not to be charged upon him who defends his own right, but on him that invades his neighbor's. If the innocent honest man must quietly quit all he has for peace sake to him who will lay violent hands upon it, I desire it may be considered what a kind of peace there will be in the world which consists only in violence and rapine, and which is to be maintained only for the benefit of robbers and oppressors. Who would not think it an admirable peace betwixt the mighty and the mean, when the lamb, without resistance, yielded his throat to be torn by the imperious wolf? Polyphemus' den gives us a perfect pattern of such a peace. Such a government wherein Ulysses and his companions had nothing to do but quietly to suffer themselves to be devoured. And no doubt Ulysses, who was a prudent man, preached up passive obedience, and exhorted them to a quiet submission by representing to them of what concernment peace was to mankind, and by showing the inconveniencies that might happen if they should offer to resist Polyphemus, who had now the power over them.

229. The end of government is the good of mankind; and which is best for mankind, that the people should be always exposed to the boundless will of tyranny, or that the rulers should be sometimes liable to be opposed when they grow exorbitant in the use of their power, and employ it for the destruction, and not the preservation, of the properties of their people?

230. Nor let anyone say that mischief can arise from hence as often as it shall please a busy head or turbulent spirit to desire the alteration of the government. It is true such men may stir whenever they please, but it will be only to their own just ruin and perdition. For till the mischief be grown general, and the ill designs of the rulers become visible, or their attempts sensible to the greater part, the people, who are more disposed to suffer than right themselves by resistance, are not apt to stir. The examples of particular injustice or oppression of here and there an unfortunate man moves them not. But if they universally have a persuasion grounded upon manifest evidence that designs are carrying on against their liberties, and the general course and tendency of things cannot but give them strong suspicions of the evil intention of their governors, who is to be blamed for it? Who can help it if they, who might avoid it, bring themselves into this

suspicion? Are the people to be blamed if they have the sense of rational creatures, and can think of things no otherwise than as they find and feel them? And is it not rather their fault who put things in such a posture that they would not have them thought as they are? I grant that the pride, ambition, and turbulency of private men have sometimes caused great disorders in commonwealths, and factions have been fatal to states and kingdoms. But whether the mischief hath oftener begun in the people's wantonness, and a desire to cast off the lawful authority of their rulers, or in the rulers' insolence and endeavors to get and exercise an arbitrary power over their people, whether oppression or disobedience gave the first rise to the disorder, I leave it to impartial history to determine.

This I am sure, whoever, either ruler or subject, by force goes about to invade the rights of either prince or people, and lays the foundation for overturning the constitution and frame of any just government, he is guilty of the greatest crime I think a man is capable of, being to answer for all those mischiefs of blood, rapine, and desolation, which the breaking to pieces of governments bring on a country; and he who does it is justly to be esteemed the common enemy and pest of mankind, and is to be treated accordingly.

231. That subjects or foreigners attempting by force on the properties of any people may be resisted with force is agreed on all hands; but that magistrates doing the same thing may be resisted, hath of late been denied; as if those who had the greatest privileges and advantages by the law had thereby a power to break those laws by which alone they were set in a better place than their brethren; whereas their offense is thereby the greater, both as being ungrateful for the greater share they have by the law, and breaking also that trust which is put into their hands by their brethren.

232. Whosoever uses force without right—as everyone does in society who does it without law—puts himself into a state of war with those against whom he so uses it, and in that state all former ties are canceled, all other rights cease, and everyone has a right to defend himself, and to resist the aggressor. . . .

# VI. IDEALISM AND REALISM

With the added impetus of nineteenth century evolutionary views of history, the idea of a rule of reason through international law produced utopian dreams of perpetual peace. These dreams did not go undisturbed. Just twenty-five years after Kant published his essay on peace, Hegel repudiated the underlying conception of a law of nations and asserted the historical necessity of war.

In the selections that follow, Kant's influence is seen in the optimism of Lyman Abbott's liberal social gospel, while Hegel finds echoes in Reinhold Niebuhr's concept of history.

For further reading:

Brown, I. V. *Lyman Abbott, Christian Evolutionist.* Harvard University Press, 1953.

Brunner, Emil. *Justice and the Social Order.* Harper, 1945.

Cadoux, C. J. *Christian Pacifism Reexamined.* Blackwell, 1940.

Friedrich, C. J. *Inevitable Peace.* Harvard University Press, 1948.

Hentoff, Nat, ed. *The Essays of A. J. Muste.* Bobbs-Merrill, 1967.

Kegley, C. W., ed. *Reinhold Niebuhr.* Macmillan, 1956.

MacGregor, G. C. *The New Testament Basis of Pacifism.* Fellowship of Reconciliation, 1954.

Niebuhr, Reinhold. *Christian Realism and Political Problems.* Scribner, 1953.

————. *Love and Justice.* Edited by D. B. Robertson. Westminster Press, 1957.

————. *Moral Man and Immoral Society.* Scribner, 1932.

Rauschenbusch, W. *A Theology of the Social Gospel.* Macmillan, 1918.

Raven, C. E. *The Theological Basis of Christian Pacifism.* Fellowship Publications, 1951.

————. *War and the Christian.* SCM Press, 1918.

Yoder, John. *Karl Barth and the Problem of War.* Abingdon, 1970.

## 1. *IMMANUEL KANT* (1724–1804)

When Kant wrote on war in 1795, he was impressed by the idea that social contract, equal rights, and international law would lead men to peace; he therefore echoed earlier objections to government by right of conquest, purchase, or inheritance. But he complained that Grotius and others placed their confidence in law without enforcement, something which manifestly does not work within a nation and, human nature being what it is, cannot work between nations. Since law is based on right reason and reason condemns war, Kant proposed that a league of nations be established by social contract in order to guarantee peace.

Underlying his recommendation is the belief, characteristic of nineteenth-century idealism, that history is guided by an immanent natural teleology. Our rational duty is to obey the right.

## TOWARDS PERPETUAL PEACE

*Perpetual Peace* in *On History*, trans. L. W. Beck, R. E. Anchor, and E. L. Fackenheim (1968).

### *"The Law of Nations Shall be Founded on a Federation of Free States"*

Peoples, as states, like individuals, may be judged to injure one another merely by their coexistence in the state of nature (i.e., while independent of external laws). Each of them may and should for the sake of its own security demand that the others enter with it into a constitution similar to the civil constitution, for under such a constitution each can be secure in his right. This would be a league of nations, but it would not have to be a state consisting of nations. That would be contradictory, since a state implies the relation of a superior (legislating) to an inferior (obeying), i.e., the people, and many nations in one state would then constitute only one nation. This contradicts the presupposition, for here we have to weigh the rights of nations against each other so far as they are distinct states and not amalgamated into one.

When we see the attachment of savages to their lawless freedom, preferring ceaseless combat to subjection to a lawful constraint which they might establish, and thus preferring senseless freedom to rational freedom, we regard it with deep contempt as barbarity, rudeness, and a brutish degradation of humanity. Accordingly, one would think that civilized people (each united in a state) would hasten all the more to escape, the sooner the better, from such a depraved condition. But, instead, each state places its majesty (for it is absurd to speak of the majesty of the people) in being subject to no external juridical restraint, and the splendor of its sovereign consists in the fact that many thousands stand at his command to sacrifice themselves for something that does not concern them and without his needing to place himself in the least danger. The chief difference between European and American savages lies in the fact that many tribes of the latter have been eaten by their enemies, while the former know how to make better use of their conquered enemies than to dine off them; they know better how to use them to increase the number of their subjects and thus the quantity of instruments for even more extensive wars.

When we consider the perverseness of human nature which is nakedly revealed in the uncontrolled relations between nations (this perverseness being veiled in the state of civil law by the constraint exercised by government), we may well be astonished that the word "law" has not yet been banished from war politics as pedantic, and that no state has yet been bold enough to advocate this point of view. Up to the present, Hugo Grotius, Pufendorf, Vattel, and many other irritating comforters have been cited in justification of war, though their code, philosophically or diplomatically formulated, has not and cannot have the least legal force, because states as such do not stand under a common external power. There is no instance on record that a state has ever been moved to desist from its purpose because of arguments backed up by the testimony of such great men. But the homage which each state pays (at least in words) to the concept of law proves that there is slumbering in man an even greater moral disposition to become master of the evil principle in himself (which he cannot disclaim) and to hope for the same from others. Otherwise the word "law" would never be pronounced by states which wish to war upon one another; it would be used only ironically, as a Gallic prince interpreted it when he said, "It is the prerogative which nature has given the stronger that the weaker should obey him."

States do not plead their cause before a tribunal; war alone is their way of bringing suit. But by war and its favorable issue in victory, right is not decided, and though by a treaty of peace this particular war is brought to an end, the state of war, of always finding a new pretext to hostilities, is not terminated. Nor can this be declared wrong, considering the fact that in this state each is the judge of his own case. Notwithstanding, the obligation which men in a lawless condition have under the natural law, and which requires them to abandon the state of nature, does not quite apply to states under the law of nations, for as states they already have an internal juridical constitution and have thus outgrown compulsion from others according to their ideas of right. This is true in spite of the fact that reason, from its throne of supreme moral legislating authority, absolutely condemns war as a legal recourse and makes a state of peace a direct duty, even though peace cannot be established or secured except by a compact among nations.

For these reasons there must be a league of a particular kind, which can be called a league of peace (*foedus pacificum*), and which would be distinguished from a treaty of peace (*pactum pacis*) by the fact that the latter terminates only one war, while the former seeks to make an end of all wars forever. This league does not tend to any dominion over the power of the state but only to the maintenance and security of the freedom of the state itself and of other states in league with it, without there being any need for them to submit to civil laws and their compulsion, as men in a state of nature must submit.

The practicability (objective reality) of this idea of federation, which should gradually spread to all states and thus lead to perpetual peace, can be proved. For if fortune directs that a powerful and enlightened people can make itself a republic, which by its nature must be inclined to perpetual peace, this gives a fulcrum to the federation with other states so that they may adhere to it and thus secure freedom under the idea of the law of nations. By more and more such associations, the federation may be gradually extended.

We may readily conceive that a people should say, "There ought to be no war among us, for we want to make ourselves into a state; that is, we want to establish a supreme legislative, executive, and judiciary power which will reconcile our differences peaceably." But when this state says, "There ought to be no war between myself and other states, even though I acknowledge no supreme legislative power by which our rights are mutually guaranteed," it is not at all clear on what I can base my confidence in my own rights unless it is the free federation, the surrogate of the civil social order, which reason necessarily associates with the concept of the law of nations—assuming that something is really meant by the latter.

The concept of a law of nations as a right to make war does not really mean anything, because it is then a law of deciding what is right by unilateral maxims through force and not by universally valid public laws which restrict the freedom of each one. The only conceivable meaning of such a law of nations might be that it serves men right who are so inclined that they should destroy each other and thus find perpetual peace in the vast grave that swallows both the atrocities and their perpetrators. For states in their relation to each other, there cannot be any reasonable way out of the lawless condition which entails only war except that they, like individual men, should give up their savage (lawless) freedom, adjust themselves to the constraints of public law, and thus establish a continuously growing state consisting of various nations (*civitas gentium*), which will ultimately include all the nations of the world. But under the idea of the law of nations they do not wish this, and reject in practice what is correct in theory. If all is not to be lost, there can be, then, in place of the positive idea of a world republic, only the negative surrogate of an alliance which averts war, endures, spreads, and holds back the stream of those hostile passions which fear the law, though such an alliance is in constant peril of their breaking loose again....

The guarantee of perpetual peace is nothing less than that great artist, nature (*natura daedala rerum*). In her mechanical course we see that her aim is to produce a harmony among men, against their will and indeed through their discord. As a necessity working according to laws we do not know, we call it destiny. But, considering its design in world history, we call it "providence," inasmuch as we discern in it the profound wisdom of a higher cause which predetermines the course of nature and directs it to the objective final end of the human race.[1] We do not observe or infer this providence in the cunning

---

1. In the mechanism of nature, to which man belongs as a sensuous being, a form is exhibited which is basic to its existence; we can conceive of this form only as dependent upon the end to which the Author of the world has previously destined it. This predetermination we call "divine providence" generally, and so far as it is exercised at the beginning of the world we call it "founding providence." As maintaining nature in its course by universal laws of design, it is called "ruling providence" (*providentia gubernatrix*); as directing nature

contrivances of nature, but, as in questions of the relation of the form of things to ends in general, we can and must supply it from our own minds in order to conceive of its possibility by analogy to actions of human art. The Idea of the relationship and harmony between these actions and the end which reason directly assigns to us is transcendent from a theoretical point of view; from a practical standpoint, with respect, for example, to the ideal of perpetual peace, the concept is dogmatic and its reality is well established, and thus

to ends not foreseen by man and only conjectured from the actual result, it is called "guiding providence" (*providentia directrix*). With respect to single events as divine ends, it is no longer called "providence" but "dispensation" (*directio extraordinaria*). But since "divine dispensation" indicates miracles, even if the events themselves are not called such, it is a foolish pretension of man to wish to interpret them as such, since it is absurd to infer from a single event to a particular principle of the efficient cause, namely, that this event is an end and not merely a mechanical corollary of another end wholly unknown to us. However pious and humble such talk may be, it is full of self-conceit. The division of providence, considered not formally but materially, i.e., with respect to objects in the world to which it is directed, into either general or particular providence, is false and self-contradictory. (This division appears, for instance, in the statement that providence cares for the preservation of the species but leaves individuals to chance.) It is contradictory because it is called universal in its purpose, and therefore no single thing can be excluded from it. Presumably, therefore, a formal distinction is intended, according to the way in which providence seeks its ends. This is the distinction between the ordinary and the special ways of providence. (Under the former we may cite the annual dying-out and rebirth of nature with the changes of the season; under the latter, the transport of wood by ocean currents to arctic lands where it cannot grow, yet where it is needed by the inhabitants who could not live without it.) Although we can very well explain the physico-mechanical cause of these extraordinary cases (e.g., by reference to the wooded banks of rivers in temperate lands, the falling of trees into the rivers, and then their being carried along by the Gulf Stream), we must not overlook the teleological cause, which intimates the foresight of a wisdom commanding over nature.

The concept of intervention or concurrence (*concursus*) in producing an effect in the world of sense must be given up, though it is quite usual in the schools. For to try to pair the disparate (*gryphes iungere equis*), and to let that which is itself the perfect cause of events in the world supplement its own predetermining providence in the course of the world (which would therefore have to have been inadequate), is self-contradictory. We fall into this self-contradiction, for example, when we say that next to God it was the physician who cured the ill, as if God had been his helper. For *causa solitaria non iuvat;* God is the author of the physician and all his medicines, and if we insist on ascending to the highest but theoretically inconceivable first cause, the effect must be ascribed entirely to Him. Or we can ascribe it entirely to the physician, so far as we consider the occurrence as explicable in a chain of causes under the order of nature.

But, besides being self-contradictory, such a mode of thought brings an end the mechanism of nature may be employed to that end. The use of the word "nature" is more fitting to the limits of human reason and more modest than an expression indicating a providence unknown to us. This is especially true when we are dealing with questions of theory and not of religion, as at present, for human reason in questions of the relation of effects to their causes must remain within the limits of possible experience. On the other hand, the use of the word "providence" here intimates the possession of wings like those of Icarus, conducting us toward the secret of its unfathomable purpose.

Before we more narrowly define the guarantee which nature gives, it is necessary to examine the situation in which she has placed her actors on her vast stage, a situation which finally assures peace among them. Then we shall see how she accomplishes the latter. Her preparatory arrangements are:

1. In every region of the world she has made it possible for men to live.

2. By war she has driven them even into the most inhospitable regions in order to populate them.

3. By the same means, she has forced them into more or less lawful relations with each other.

That in the cold wastes by the Arctic Ocean the moss grows which the reindeer digs from the snow in order to make itself the prey or the conveyance of the Ostyak or Samoyed; or that the saline sandy deserts are inhabited by the camel which appears created as it were in order that they might not go unused—that is already wonderful. Still clearer is the end when we see how besides the furry animals of the Arctic there are also the seal, the walrus, and the whale which afford the inhabitants food from their flesh and warmth from their blubber. But the care of nature excites the greatest wonder when we see how she brings wood (though the inhabitants do not know whence it comes) to these barren climates, without which they would have neither canoes, weapons, nor huts, and when we see how these na-

to all definite principles in judging an effect. In a morally practical point of view, however, which is directed exclusively to the supersensuous, the concept of the divine *concursus* is quite suitable and even necessary. We find this, for instance, in the belief that God will compensate for our own lack of justice, provided our intention was genuine; that He will do so by means that are inconceivable to us, and that therefore we should not relent in our endeavor after the good. But it is self-evident that no one should try to explain a good action (as an event in the world) as a result of this *concursus*, for this would be a vain theoretical knowledge of the supersensuous and therefore absurd.

tives are so occupied with their war against the animals that they live in peace with each other—but what drove them there was presumably nothing else than war.

The first instrument of war among the animals which man learned to tame and to domesticate was the horse (for the elephant belongs to later times, to the luxury of already established states). The art of cultivating certain types of plants (grain) whose original characteristics we do not know, and the increase and improvement of fruits by transplanting and grafting (in Europe perhaps only the crab apple and the wild pear), could arise only under conditions prevailing in already established states where property was secure. Before this could take place, it was necessary that men who had first subsisted in anarchic freedom by hunting, fishing, and sheepherding should have been forced into an agricultural life. Then salt and iron were discovered. These were perhaps the first articles of commerce for the various peoples and were sought far and wide; in this way a peaceful traffic among nations was established, and thus understanding, conventions, and peaceable relations were established among the most distant peoples.

As nature saw to it that men *could* live everywhere in the world, she also despotically willed that they *should* do so, even against their inclination and without this *ought* being based on a concept of duty to which they were bound by a moral law. She chose war as the means to this end. So we see peoples whose common language shows that they have a common origin. For instance, the Samoyeds on the Arctic Ocean and a people with a similar language a thousand miles away in the Altaian Mountains are separated by a Mongolian people adept at horsemanship and hence at war; the latter drove the former into the most inhospitable arctic regions where they certainly would not have spread of their own accord. Again, it is the same with the Finns who in the most northerly part of Europe are called Lapps; Goths and Sarmatians have separated them from the Hungarians to whom they are related in language. What can have driven the Eskimos, a race entirely distinct from all others in America and perhaps descended from primeval European adventurers, so far into the North, or the Pescherais as far south as Tierra del Fuego, if it were not war which nature uses to populate the whole earth? War itself requires no special motive but appears to be engrafted on human nature; it passes even for something noble, to which the love of glory impels men quite apart from any selfish urges. Thus among the American savages, just as much as among those of Europe during the age of chivalry, military valor is held to be of great worth in itself, not only during war (which is natural) but in order that there should be war. Often war is waged only in order to show valor; thus an inner dignity is ascribed to war itself, and even some philosophers have praised it as an ennoblement of humanity, forgetting the pronouncement of the Greek who said, "War is an evil inasmuch as it produces more wicked men than it takes away." So much for the measures nature takes to lead the human race, considered as a class of animals, to her own end.

Now we come to the question concerning that which is most essential in the design of perpetual peace: What has nature done with regard to this end which man's own reason makes his duty? That is, what has nature done to favor man's moral purpose, and how has she guaranteed (by compulsion but without prejudice to his freedom) that he shall do that which he ought to but does not do under the laws of freedom? This question refers to all three phases of public law, namely, civil law, the law of nations, and the law of world citizenship. If I say of nature that she wills that this or that occur, I do not mean that she imposes a duty on us to do it, for this can be done only by free practical reason; rather I mean that she herself does it, whether we will or not. . . .

1. Even if a people were not forced by internal discord to submit to public laws, war would compel them to do so, for we have already seen that nature has placed each people near another which presses upon it, and against this it must form itself into a state in order to defend itself. Now the republican constitution is the only one entirely fitting to the rights of man. But it is the most difficult to establish and even harder to preserve, so that many say a republic would have to be a nation of angels, because men with their selfish inclinations are not capable of a constitution of such sublime form. But precisely with these inclinations nature comes to the aid of the general will established on reason, which is revered even though impotent in practice. Thus it is only a question of a good organization of the state (which does lie in man's power), whereby the powers of each selfish inclination are so arranged in opposition that one moderates or destroys the ruinous effect of the other. The consequence for reason is the same as if none of them existed, and man is forced to be a good citizen even if not a morally good person.

The problem of organizing a state, however hard it may seem, can be solved even for a race of devils, if only they are intelligent.

The problem is: "Given a multitude of rational beings requiring universal laws for their preservation, but each of whom is secretly inclined to exempt himself from them, to establish a constitution in such a way that, athough their private intentions conflict, they check each other, with the result that their public conduct is the same as if they had no such intentions."

A problem like this must be capable of solution; it does not require that we know how to attain the moral improvement of men but only that we should know the mechanism of nature in order to use it on men, organizing the conflict of the hostile intentions present in a people in such a way that they must compel themselves to submit to coercive laws. Thus a state of peace is established in which laws have force. We can see, even in actual states, which are far from perfectly organized, that in their foreign relations they approach that which the idea of right prescribes. This is so in spite of the fact that the intrinsic element of morality is certainly not the cause of it. (A good constitution is not to be expected from morality, but, conversely, a good moral condition of a people is to be expected only under a good constitution.) Instead of genuine morality, the mechanism of nature brings it to pass through selfish inclinations, which naturally conflict outwardly but which can be used by reason as a means for its own end, the sovereignty of law, and, as concerns the state, for promoting and securing internal and external peace.

This, then, is the truth of the matter: Nature inexorably wills that the right should finally triumph. What we neglect to do comes about by itself, though with great inconveniences to us. "If you bend the reed too much, you break it; and he who attempts too much attempts nothing" (Bouterwek).

2. The idea of international law presupposes the separate existence of many independent but neighboring states. Although this condition is itself a state of war (unless a federative union prevents the outbreak of hostilities), this is rationally preferable to the amalgamation of states under one superior power, as this would end in one universal monarchy, and laws always lose in vigor what government gains in extent; hence a soulless despotism falls into anarchy after stifling the seeds of the good. Nevertheless, every state, or its ruler, desires to establish lasting peace in this way, aspiring if possible to rule the whole world. But nature wills otherwise. She employs two means to separate peoples and to prevent them from mixing: dif-

ferences of language and of religion.[2] These differences involve a tendency to mutual hatred and pretexts for war, but the progress of civilization and men's gradual approach to greater harmony in their principles finally leads to peaceful agreement. This is not like that peace which despotism (in the burial ground of freedom) produces through a weakening of all powers; it is, on the contrary, produced and maintained by their equilibrium in liveliest competition.

3. Just as nature wisely separates nations, which the will of every state, sanctioned by the principles of international law, would gladly unite by artifice or force, nations which could not have secured themselves against violence and war by means of the law of world citizenship unite because of mutual interest. The spirit of commerce, which is incompatible with war, sooner or later gains the upper hand in every state. As the power of money is perhaps the most dependable of all the powers (means) included under the state power, states see themselves forced, without any moral urge, to promote honorable peace and by mediation to prevent war wherever it threatens to break out. They do so exactly as if they stood in perpetual alliances, for great offensive alliances are in the nature of the case rare and even less often successful.

In this manner nature guarantees perpetual peace by the mechanism of human passions. Certainly she does not do so with sufficient certainty for us to predict the future in any theoretical sense, but adequately from a practical point of view, making it our duty to work toward this end, which is not just a chimerical one.

2. Difference of religion — a singular expression! It is precisely as if one spoke of different moralities. There may very well be different kinds of historical faiths attached to different means employed in the promotion of religion, and they belong merely in the field of learned investigation. Similarly there may be different religious texts (Zendavesta, the Veda, the Koran, etc.), but such differences do not exist in religion, there being only one religion valid for all men and in all ages. These can, therefore, be nothing else than accidental vehicles of religion, thus changing with times and places.

## 2. G. W. F. HEGEL (1770–1831)

Hegel's well-known view of the Absolute moving through history, embodied successively in one sovereign state after another, stands in radical contrast to the Enlightenment emphasis on universal rights and popular consent. According to Hegel, if reason rules, it does so through sovereign states gaining conscious identity in opposition to each other. In the dialectic of history nation confronts nation and war ensues.

War, then, is ethically justified for the welfare of the state. In company with the Greeks, and captivated by the Romantic image of Napoleon, Hegel values the courage war demands. His scheme contrasts with Kant's idealism in that the laws of war are purely customary and neither reason nor nature nor history offer hope of perpetual peace.

### WAR AND NATIONAL DESTINY

From *The Philosophy of Right*, trans. T. M. Knox (1967), pp. 208-15.

322. Individuality is awareness of one's existence as a unit in sharp distinction from others. It manifests itself here in the state as a relation to other states, each of which is autonomous *vis-à-vis* the others. This autonomy embodies mind's actual awareness of itself as a unit and hence it is the most fundamental freedom which a people possesses as well as its highest dignity.

Those who talk of the "wishes" of a collection of people constituting a more or less autonomous state with its own centre, of its "wishes" to renounce this centre and its autonomy in order to unite with others to form a new whole, have very little knowledge of the nature of a collection or of the feeling of selfhood which a nation possesses in its independence. . . .

324. This destiny whereby the rights and interests of individuals are established as a passing phase, is at the same time the positive

moment, i.e. the positing of their absolute, not their contingent and unstable, individuality. This relation and the recognition of it is therefore the individual's substantive duty, the duty to maintain this substantive individuality, i.e. the independence and sovereignty of the state, at the risk and the sacrifice of property and life, as well as of opinion and everything else naturally comprised in the compass of life.

An entirely distorted account of the demand for this sacrifice results from regarding the state as a mere civil society and from regarding its final end as only the security of individual life and property. This security cannot possibly be obtained by the sacrifice of what is to be secured—on the contrary.

The ethical moment in war is implied in what has been said in this paragraph. War is not to be regarded as an absolute evil and as a purely external accident, which itself therefore has some accidental cause, be it injustices, the passions of nations or the holders of power, &c., or in short, something or other which ought not to be. It is to what is by nature accidental that accidents happen, and the fate whereby they happen is thus a necessity. Here as elsewhere, the point of view from which things seem pure accidents vanishes if we look at them in the light of the concept and philosophy, because philosophy knows accident for a show and sees in it its essence, necessity. It is necessary that the finite—property and life—should be definitely established as accidental, because accidentality is the concept of the finite. From one point of view this necessity appears in the form of the power of nature, and everything is mortal and transient. But in the ethical substance, the state, nature is robbed of this power, and the necessity is exalted to be the work of freedom, to be something ethical. The transience of the finite becomes a willed passing away, and the negativity lying at the roots of the finite becomes the substantive individuality proper to the ethical substance.

War is the state of affairs which deals in earnest with the vanity of temporal goods and concerns—a vanity at other times a common theme of edifying sermonizing. This is what makes it the moment in which the ideality of the particular attains its right and is actualized. War has the higher significance that by its agency, as I have remarked elsewhere, "the ethical health of peoples is preserved in their indifference to the stabilization of finite institutions; just as the blowing of the winds preserves the sea from the foulness which would be the result of a prolonged calm, so also corruption in nations would be the product of prolonged, let alone 'perpetual,' peace." This, however, is said to be only a philosophic idea, or, to use another common expression, a "justification of Providence," and it is maintained that actual wars require some other justification. On this point, see below.

The ideality which is in evidence in war, i.e., in an accidental relation of a state to a foreign state, is the same as the ideality in accordance with which the domestic powers of the state are organic moments in a whole. This fact appears in history in various forms, e.g. successful wars have checked domestic unrest and consolidated the power of the state at home. Other phenomena illustrate the same point: e.g. peoples unwilling or afraid to tolerate sovereignty at home have been subjugated from abroad, and they have struggled for their independence with the less glory and success the less they have been able previously to organize the powers of the state in home affairs— their freedom has died from the fear of dying; states whose autonomy has been guaranteed not by their armed forces but in other ways (e.g. by their disproportionate smallness in comparison with their neighbours) have been able to subsist with a constitution of their own which by itself would not have assured peace in either home or foreign affairs.

325. Sacrifice on behalf of the individuality of the state is the substantial tie between the state and all its members and so is a universal duty. . . .

326. The matter at issue in disputes between states may be only one particular aspect of their relation to each other, and it is for such disputes that the particular class devoted to the state's defence is principally appointed. But if the state as such, if its autonomy, is in jeopardy, all its citizens are in duty bound to answer the summons to its defence. If in such circumstances the entire state is under arms and is torn from its domestic life at home to fight abroad, the war of defence turns into a war of conquest. . . .

327. In itself, courage is a *formal* virtue, because (i) it is a display of freedom by radical abstraction from all particular ends, possessions, pleasure, and life; but (ii) this negation is a negation of externalities, and their alienation, the culmination of courage, is not intrinsically of a spiritual (*geistiger*) character; (iii) the courageous man's inner motive need only be some particular reason or other, and even the actual result of what he does need be present solely to the minds of others and not to his own.

328. The intrinsic worth of courage as a disposition of mind is

to be found in the genuine, absolute, final end, the sovereignty of the state. The work of courage is to actualize this final end, and the means to this end is the sacrifice of personal actuality. This form of experience thus contains the harshness of extreme contradictions: a self-sacrifice which yet is the real existence of one's freedom; the maximum self-subsistence of individuality, yet only as a cog playing its part in the mechanism of an external organization; absolute obedience, renunciation of personal opinions and reasonings, in fact complete *absence* of mind, coupled with the most intense and comprehensive *presence* of mind and decision in the moment of acting; the most hostile and so most personal action against individuals, coupled with an attitude of complete indifference or even liking towards them as individuals.

To risk one's life is better than merely fearing death, but is still purely negative and so indeterminate and without value in itself. It is the positive aspect, the end and content, which first gives significance to this spiritedness. Robbers and murderers bent on crime as their end, adventurers pursuing ends planned to suit their own whims, &c., these too have spirit enough to risk their lives.

The principle of the modern world—thought and the universal— has given courage a higher form, because its display now seems to be more mechanical, the act not of this particular person, but of a member of a whole. Moreover, it seems to be turned not against single persons, but against a hostile group, and hence personal bravery appears impersonal. It is for this reason that thought has invented the gun, and the invention of this weapon, which has changed the purely personal form of bravery into a more abstract one, is no accident.

329. The state's tendency to look abroad lies in the fact that it is an individual subject. Its relation to other states therefore falls to the power of the crown. Hence it directly devolves on the monarch, and on him alone, to command the armed forces, to conduct foreign affairs through ambassadors &c., to make war and peace, and to conclude treaties of all kinds.

### International Law

330. International law springs from the relations between autonomous states. It is for this reason that what is absolute in it retains the form of an ought-to-be, since its actuality depends on different wills each of which is sovereign. . . .

333. The fundamental proposition of international law (i.e. the universal law which ought to be absolutely valid between states, as distinguished from the particular content of positive treaties) is that treaties, as the ground of obligations between states, ought to be kept. But since the sovereignty of a state is the principle of its relations to others, states are to that extent in a state of nature in relation to each other. Their rights are actualized only in their particular wills and not in a universal will with constitutional powers over them. This universal proviso of international law therefore does not go beyond an ought-to-be, and what really happens is that international relations in accordance with treaty alternate with the severance of these relations.

There is no Praetor to judge between states; at best there may be an arbitrator or a mediator, and even he exercises his functions contingently only, i.e. in dependence on the particular wills of the disputants. Kant had an idea for securing "perpetual peace" by a League of Nations to adjust every dispute. It was to be a power recognized by each individual state, and was to arbitrate in all cases of dissension in order to make it impossible for disputants to resort to war in order to settle them. This idea presupposes an accord between states; this would rest on moral or religious or other grounds and considerations, but in any case would always depend ultimately on a particular sovereign will and for that reason would remain infected with contingency.

334. It follows that if states disagree and their particular wills cannot be harmonized, the matter can only be settled by war. A state through its subjects has widespread connexions and many-sided interests, and these may be readily and considerably injured; but it remains inherently indeterminable which of these injuries is to be regarded as a specific breach of treaty or as an injury to the honour and autonomy of the state. The reason for this is that a state may regard its infinity and honour as at stake in each of its concerns, however minute, and it is all the more inclined to susceptibility to injury the more its strong individuality is impelled as a result of long domestic peace to seek and create a sphere of activity abroad. . . .

336. Since states are related to one another as autonomous entities and so as particular wills on which the very validity of treaties depends, and since the particular will of the whole is in content a will for its own welfare pure and simple, it follows that welfare is the highest law governing the relation of one state to another. This is all the more

the case since the Idea of the state is precisely the supersession of the clash between right (i.e. empty abstract freedom) and welfare (i.e. the particular content which fills that void), and it is when states become *concrete* wholes that they first attain recognition.

337. The substantial welfare of the state is its welfare as a particular state in its specific interest and situation and its no less special foreign affairs, including its particular treaty relations. Its government therefore is a matter of particular wisdom, not of universal Providence. . . . Similarly, its aim in relation to other states and its principle for justifying wars and treaties is not a universal thought (the thought of philanthropy) but only its actually injured or threatened welfare as something specific and peculiar to itself.

At one time the opposition between morals and politics, and the demand that the latter should conform to the former, were much canvassed. On this point only a general remark is required here. The welfare of a state has claims to recognition totally different from those of the welfare of the individual. The ethical substance, the state, has its determinate being, i.e. its right, directly embodied in something existent, something not abstract but concrete, and the principle of its conduct and behaviour can only be this concrete existent and not one of the many universal thoughts supposed to be moral commands. When politics is alleged to clash with morals and so to be always wrong, the doctrine propounded rests on superficial ideas about morality, the nature of the state, and the state's relation to the moral point of view.

338. The fact that states reciprocally recognize each other as states remains, even in war—the state of affairs when rights disappear and force and chance hold sway—a bond wherein each counts to the rest as something absolute. Hence in war, war itself is characterized as something which ought to pass away. It implies therefore the proviso of the *jus gentium* that the possibility of peace be retained (and so, for example, that envoys must be respected), and, in general, that war be not waged against domestic institutions, against the peace of family and private life, or against persons in their private capacity.

339. Apart from this, relations between states (e.g. in wartime, reciprocal agreements about taking prisoners; in peacetime, concessions of rights to subjects of other states for the purpose of private trade and intercourse, &c.) depend principally upon the customs of nations, custom being the inner universality of behaviour maintained in all circumstances.

340. It is as particular entities that states enter into relations with one another. Hence their relations are on the largest scale a maelstrom of external contingency and the inner particularity of passions, private interests and selfish ends, abilities and virtues, vices, force, and wrong. All these whirl together, and in their vortex the ethical whole itself, the autonomy of the state, is exposed to contingency. . . .

## 3. *LYMAN ABBOTT* (1835-1922)

An influential peacher who started his career as a theological conservative, Abbott moved steadily towards theological liberalism as he applied the evolutionary hypothesis to the history of religion and its influence in the world. *Christianity and Social Problems* represents his opposition to American chauvinism with its Hegelian adulation of heroes and patriots. Finding the law of love to be the essence of Christian ethics, he urges arbitration and the rule of law as the Christian means towards perpetual peace.

Although Abbott later supported both the Spanish-American War and American participation in World War I, the point of view presented here is characteristic of the evolutionary pacifism of the social gospel preached by Abbott, Walter Rauschenbusch, and Shailer Matthews.

### PACIFISM AND THE GOSPEL

From *Christianity and Social Problems* (1896), chap. 9.

In the preceding chapter I have endeavored to deduce from Christ's personal directions to his disciples certain general principles to be recognized by his followers in the settlement of personal controversies. It is my object in this and a succeeding chapter to show that these principles are equally applicable to the settlement of controversies between nations and between classes. Indeed, the history of civilization is to no inconsiderable extent the history of the very gradual adoption of these principles by Christendom, and their incorporation, first into custom and then into law. In order to trace the history of this adoption, it is first necessary to state a little more in detail the principles especially applicable to controversies between bodies of men—whether between different nations or between different organizations in the same nation. These principles are two, a negative

291

and a positive one—first, the abandonment of force as a method of settling controversies; second, the substitution therefor of arbitrament by an impartial tribunal.

The first principle finds its clearest statement in the following passage: "But I say unto you, that ye resist not evil; but whosoever shall smite thee on thy right cheek, turn to him the other also. And if any man will sue thee at the law and take away thy coat, let him have thy cloak also. And whosoever shall compel thee to go a mile, go with him twain." A careful scrutiny of this direction makes it clear that it covers the three forms of wrong under which men suffer— personal violence, legal injustice, governmental oppression. To smite on the right cheek is an act of personal violence; to attempt by law to take away one's coat is an act of legal injustice; to impress one to go a mile in public service without compensation is an act of govern- mental oppression. Such impressment, permitted by modern society only in times of war, was formerly allowed to the government in time of peace. Christ, referring to these forms of wrong—personal violence, legal injustice, governmental oppression—bids his followers oppose to them only a passive non-resistance. He sets in operation a new force in the world, what Milton has well called "the irresistible might of meekness." This might was before Christ's time almost absolutely unknown.

If these instructions were not in themselves perfectly clear, they are made so by the interpretation which he has put upon them by his life. The despotic government under which he lives sends out its officers to arrest him. He surrenders himself and is led away. And when one of his own disciples would resist the band, though he says, "I could have twelve legions of angels to rescue me," he will not. He condemns resistance. "They that take the sword shall perish with the sword." He is brought into the court. It was a well-settled principle in the Hebrew law, as it is with us, that a man accused could not be called upon to criminate himself. Those who accused Christ were unable to find any two witnesses who would agree in their testimony against him, and finally the High Priest calls Jesus to the stand and admin- isters the oath to him: "I adjure thee by the living God that thou tell us whether thou be the Son of God or no." He protests: "If I tell you, you will not believe me." Yet he submits, testifies under oath that he is the Son of God, and is led away to his death. In this trial, and fol- lowing it, he is beaten, spit upon, scourged. He protests, but does not resist. To each of these three forms of wrong he submits—the wrong of a despotic government, the wrong of a court of law, the wrong of personal violence.

Is there, then, to be no resistance to wrongdoing? Many have adduced this principle from these words. And yet Christ sometimes did resist wrongdoing. When he went up to the Temple, a corrupt and wicked government had put cattle in the one court where the Gentiles might go. He did not merely utter a verbal protest against it; he wove a whip of small cords of the straw that was at his feet and drove the frightened traders from the Temple, and with them the cattle, and overturned the money-changers' tables, and left the money to roll about the floor. When the Temple band came to arrest him, and his disciples were asleep before the gate, he went forward and put himself between the band and the disciples. They fell backward to the ground, it is said. For the moment he confronted the guard and held it at bay, that his disciples might escape, and then, and not till then, surrendered himself. Christ used force to defend others, but never to defend himself. The fundamental principle in Christ's teaching is this: Love may use force; selfishness may not. There is, says the Book of Revelation, a wrath of the Lamb. There is a combativeness of love which is legitimate. If a highwayman demands my purse, I may give it to him rather than take his life. But if he assaults my wife, or my children, whom God hath put in my keeping, that is another matter; then, if I do not defend those whom God has intrusted to my defense, I shall be recreant and a coward. Our lives are so intertwined that it is often impossible to tell whether one is defending himself or another. It is spirit, not rule or regulation, which Christ prescribes, and this is the spirit: Love may fight; selfishness may not.

To a considerable extent, modern civilization accepts this principle. In a barbaric community every man carries a pistol in his hip pocket. In civilized communities he does not. We trust other men to be our defenders and protectors. Disinterestedness defends the unarmed from wrongdoers. Even pride, passion, and selfishness go unarmed.

This is the negative principle. But this is only a preparation for the affirmative principle. Christ does not leave any to go without a remedy, nor controversies to remain without a settlement. He tells his disciples to substitute for force peaceful arbitrament by an impartial tribunal. "If thy brother shall trespass against thee, go and tell him his fault between thee and him alone"—that is conciliation; "if he will not hear thee, then take with thee one or two more, that in the mouth of two or three witnesses every word may be established"—

that is arbitration; "if he shall neglect to hear thee, tell it unto the church"—that is law; "but if he neglect to hear the church, let him be unto thee as a heathen man and a publican"—that is non-intercourse. This is Christ's method of settling controversies. The principle of non-resistance does not stand alone. It is coupled with the principle of impartial arbitration. The surrender of personal force as a means of self-protection is accompanied by the principle of appeal to the sense of justice—first in the wrongdoer, then in an amicably chosen tribunal, last of all, in the community. In the settlement of personal controversies this means, first, personal negotiation; second, friendly mediation; third, a legal tribunal. In the settlement of industrial controversies it means, first, conciliation; then arbitration; third, appeal to the community. In the settlement of international controversies it means, first, diplomacy; second, international mediation; third, an international tribunal. And in all these it means the abolition of the pagan system which makes the individual judge and jury in his own case; the abolition of the pistol and the bowie knife, and the substitution of the court; the abolition of the strike and the boycott, and the substitution of arbitration; the abolition of war, and the substitution of international law, and a tribunal to interpret and apply it.

Christianity, then, and war are absolutely inconsistent. Christianity proposes, as the method of settling all contests, an appeal to reason: first, in the contestants; then, if that fails, in an impartial tribunal. War prefers appeal to force. For war is not mere chance quarreling. It is the publicly recognized method of settling quarrels between nations. It is provided for and brought under the regulation of international law. "War," says Charles Sumner, "is a public armed contest between nations, under the sanction of international law, to establish justice between them." That it is a public armed contest between nations will be at once recognized by the reader. Every such contest is not, however, war. Legitimate war is carried on under the sanction of international law. This law determines measurably what is a proper occasion for war; what notice of war should be given before the first offensive act; how that notice should be given; who are combatants and who are non-combatants; what are the rights of non-combatants, and under what rules and regulations the war may be prosecuted. It is, for example, no longer legitimate to make war on a neighbor for the ostensible purpose of robbing him of his territory. It is no longer legitimate to pillage and destroy the property of inoffensive inhabitants who are not contributing to the enemy's strength. It is not legitimate to sell prisoners taken in war into slavery, nor to kill them in cold blood. International law determines, in other words, the conditions under which war may be declared and carried on; and the avowed object of this war between nations is to establish justice between them. "Though war," says Mr. Whewell, cited by Mr. Sumner in support of his definition, "is appealed to because there is no other ultimate tribunal to which states can have recourse, it is appealed to for justice. The object of international law is not to prevent but to regulate warfare; not to contrive some other method of securing justice between nations, certainly not to leave nations to suffer injustice without a remedy, but to make such regulations respecting war as a means of securing justice as will alleviate somewhat its terrors, and redeem it somewhat from its essential barbarism."

War thus resembles in its essential characteristics the now obsolete wager of battle. The difference between the two consists in this: war is a public armed contest between nations; wager of battle was a public armed contest between individuals. But the latter was, as the former still is, conducted under the sanction of law, and for the avowed purpose of establishing justice between the combatants. The rules for the regulation of personal battle were definite, explicit, and carefully enforced. If an individual were accused of crime, he could demand battle with his accuser as a means of determining his guilt or innocence. Each party was required to swear to the justice of his cause; his defeat involved him under the stigma of perjury. He might, under certain circumstances, employ a champion to fight for him, much as the king employs an army. The accused could challenge not only his accuser but the witnesses against him, and, in some cases, even the court itself. He must prove his innocence by his victory; in England he was acquitted if he fought successfully until the stars appeared. The whole system rested on the belief that God was present with men in battle, and would defend the innocent and give victory to virtue. Condemned by St. Louis in France in the thirteenth century, it gradually disappeared, but was not finally and authoritatively declared illegal in Great Britain until the year 1819. Abraham Thornton, accused of murder, demanded the right to vindicate his innocence by wager of battle. The court sustained his right to do so. The accuser abandoned the proceedings, and at the next session of Parliament trial by battle was, by legislative act, abolished forever.

It is the object of Christianity to abolish trial by battle between nations, as it has already abolished trial by battle between individuals—not merely to mitigate the horrors of war, not merely to reduce the occasions of war, not merely to lessen the preparations for war, but to put an end to public war absolutely, as it has put an end to private war absolutely. Fights there still are between individuals, but the right to fight is not recognized by law. Fights there may still continue to be between nations, but the right to fight will not be recognized by international law when Christianity has wrought among the nations what it has wrought within the nations. Christianity has taken the bowie knife from the belt and the pistol from the hip pocket. The individual citizen goes unarmed. He submits his controversies to an impartial tribunal. He trusts for his protection to a disinterested police. When Christianity has achieved its mission, nations also will be unarmed. They will also submit their controversies to an impartial tribunal, and trust for their protection to the cooperation of the nations of Christendom. We shall have no navy, except such as is necessary to patrol the sea and protect commerce from the brigands of the ocean. We shall as little think it necessary to put fortifications and torpedo boats at our harbors as now to put a moat and the drawbridge at the front door of our houses. In brief, Christianity has already substituted the appeal to law for the appeal to force in individual controversies. Its work will not be consummated until it has substituted law for war in controversies between nations. Law gives might to right; war gives might for right; law establishes justice, war simply demonstrates power; law evokes the judgment, war organizes the passions; law is civilization, war is barbarism. . . .

There are in our time two arguments suggested in favor of the perpetuation of war. It is said that war is glorious, and that a nation without war is without heroism. It is true that war affords opportunities for heroism, and thus opportunity for deeds truly glorious. It is true that something resplendent would be lacking in American history if there were no Bunker Hill, no Valley Forge, no Paul Jones or General Jackson, no Antietam or Gettysburg. Shall we, then, maintain a restless, burdensome, demoralizing, and inefficient method of securing justice, because under such a method men exhibit heroic qualities? Shall we retain burdens of which we might be relieved, because men proved themselves patient in bearing them? Shall we retain sin because if there were no sin there could be no redeeming love? Pestilence in a city brings glory with it, the glory of nurse and physician sacrificing themselves in self-denying service to save the lives of others. Shall we introduce pestilence into our cities? A great conflagration gives opportunity for glory in the firemen who fight the flames and rescue the imperiled. Shall we touch the torch to our homes, and wrap the city in a great conflagration, for the sake of giving opportunity for such glorious heroism? But neither pestilence nor conflagration brings with it a tithe of the perils, the suffering, the moral distress, which war inevitably entails.

The other argument for war is that it is necessary to promote patriotism. It is true that patriotism is often deepened by war, but it is not true that patriotism depends upon war. A strange inversion of the natural order is this doctrine which teaches us, not that we fight for our country because we love it, but that we love it only because we fight for it. A strange reversal of the Sermon on the Mount is this doctrine which says to us, It hath been said to them of olden time, Thou shalt love thy neighbor and hate thine enemy, but I say unto you that you cannot love your neighbor unless you hate your enemy. A strange contradiction of the very axiom of Christianity is this doctrine that love can be nourished only at the breast of hate.

Christianity has done much to mitigate the horrors of war, and something to lessen the incentives to it. It has itself created some of those regulations of international law to which I have briefly adverted. It has forbidden the torturing and the killing of captives; it has discouraged and finally abolished the practice of reducing them to slavery. It has made war, when undertaken for the avowed purpose of plunder, illegal, and in Christendom well-nigh impossible. It has created a spirit of humanity and justice which has provided on the one hand some protection for non-combatants, on the other some alleviation for the wounded and the captive; and it has inspired a spirit of chivalry which, surviving the Crusades, has given to civilized warfare a character in important respects different from that of ancient paganism. And it has taught continuously, through its great prophets, though certainly not always consistently by the voice of all its representatives, that war is righteous only when it is inevitable, that Jesus Christ is the Prince of Peace, and that Christ's disciples should constantly seek to hasten the time prophesied in Isaiah when "men shall beat their swords into ploughshares and their spears into pruning-hooks; when nation shall not lift up sword against nation, neither shall they learn war any more."

The movement gathering force in England and in the United States for the settlement of international controversies by Christ's method of reason, in lieu of the pagan method of brute force, has eighteen centuries of progress behind it. Though the world moves slowly, still it moves. The impatient reader must remember that once revenge was both a sacred right and a sacred duty. He who had been wronged was regarded under an obligation to revenge the wrong. Such vengeance was wreaked not only on the offender personally, but on the family to which he belonged. The first restraint in history upon this perpetual warfare was that imposed in the Mosaic law, which, in case of murder, limited the right of vengeance to the nearest relatives of the murdered man. Out of the right of personal vengeance grew what is known in history as "private war." From the ninth to the fifteenth century Europe was desolated with this species of war, waged between nobles and private citizens, rival cities and hostile communities, often arising from the most insignificant causes. A merchant imprisoned for debt demanded indemnity, and made war upon the city in which he had been imprisoned; a nobleman, counting himself insulted because a lady had broken her promise to dance with his cousin, made war upon the city in which she resided. In France the relatives of the one making war could be called on to render him assistance up to the seventh degree. The suffering and desolation resulting from this private war surpass the powers of description. One warrior, the Margrave of Brandenburg, boasted that he had burned one hundred and seventy villages.

At length the Church set itself against such war. Pilgrims preached through Europe the duty of peace. Missionaries from country to country acted as peacemakers. Associations formed to collect a fund to compensate sufferers from violence. Peace was imposed as a sacred duty during Lent, and then at other specified times; finally, four days in the week were declared days of holy truce. Finally, courts of arbitration were organized by the barons and the bishops, founded on the teachings of Christ and of the Apostle Paul.

This right of personal vengeance, this obligation of enforcing it, continued to be recognized far down into the Middle Ages. The wager of battle which I have already described grew out of an endeavor by a humane and partially Christian spirit to surround this right and duty with certain legal restrictions and safeguards. The time came when open attack was not permitted within the immediate demesne of the king, and the peace which there prevailed was known as the "king's peace." Little by little this king's peace extended over the highways, and finally over the whole country, and every act of personal violence was deemed a wrong, because it was a violation of the king's peace and an insult to him.

Thus Christianity, first ameliorating and restraining and finally abolishing private controversy, and substituting therefor courts of law, then ameliorating and abolishing private war, and substituting therefor laws of war recognized by all civilized nations, prepared the way for what is known as the "Great Design" of Henry of Navarre. This was nothing less than the establishment of a United States of Europe, composed of all its great powers excepting Russia, who were to combine in maintaining one standing army to keep peace between the states and to repel invasions of barbarians. The tragic death of Henry the Fourth by the assassin's knife, in 1610, prevented the consummation of the Great Design, though we may well doubt whether Christian influences had at that time sufficiently dominated the mind and heart of Europe to make this design practicable, nor was it wholly free from a ruthless character intermingled with its Christian purpose. A little less than a century later, William Penn reproduced in a different form a similar scheme for the settlement of international difficulties by a great court of arbitration. But not until a century after that was Christ's method of settling controversies introduced practically and on a large scale as a means of securing justice between nations. At the close of the last century, by treaty between the United States and Great Britain, negotiated by the Chief Justice of the Supreme Court, John Jay, it was declared that certain disputes between the United States and Great Britain should be adjusted by arbitration. Inspired by this precedent, and "under the beneficent working of this principle, nearly one international case a year has been settled during the past eighty years." Only four or five are known to most people, for one war makes more noise than a hundred arbitrations, and costs more than a thousand times as much. In accordance with its own spirit, in peace and quietness, international arbitration has been displacing war. . . .

Two causes provoke war—one, human passion, too hot and hasty to pause for consideration; law restrains such passion, and calls on the reason to act; the other, the absence of any other remedy for real or fancied injustice; law provides such other remedy, and the passion dies for want of fuel to feed it.

The issue between war and law has been decided by civilization in favor of law for the settlement of all personal controversies. War has been brought under law in international controversies, but the consummation of Christian progress will not be attained until law is substituted for war, reason for force, the spiritual for the animal, Christianity for barbarism.

## 4. REINHOLD NIEBUHR (1892–1971)

Niebuhr was disillusioned early by the idealism of liberal theologians. The human dilemma is far too intense to allow for optimism about the course of history; the fact is not that spirit is triumphing over nature and reason over barbarism, but that a great gulf separates rational and spiritual ideals from the realities of human existence. Along with such men as John C. Bennett, Emil Brunner, and William Temple, Niebuhr developed a "Christian realism" that sees both the natural law theory's rule of reason and the idealist's rule of love as presently unattainable ideals; it views pacifism as a kind of Renaissance optimism. The Christian hope is in neither natural law nor human love, but in the grace of God amid man's sin. Realistically, then, Christian love must leaven the evils of this life by means of just laws and, when necessary, by the use of force.

## WHY THE CHRISTIAN CHURCH IS NOT PACIFIST

From *Christianity and Power Politics* (1948), chap. 1.

Whenever the actual historical situation sharpens the issue, the debate whether the Christian Church is, or ought to be, pacifist is carried on with fresh vigor both inside and outside the Christian community. Those who are not pacifists seek to prove that pacifism is a heresy; while the pacifists contend, or at least imply, that the Church's failure to espouse pacifism unanimously can only be interpreted as apostasy, and must be attributed to its lack of courage or to its want of faith.

There may be an advantage in stating the thesis, with which we enter this debate, immediately. The thesis is, that the failure of the Church to espouse pacifism is not apostasy, but is derived from an understanding of the Christian Gospel which refuses simply to equate the Gospel with the "law of love." Christianity is not simply a new law, namely, the law of love. The finality of Christianity cannot be proved by analyses which seek to reveal that the law of love is stated more unambiguously and perfectly in the life and teachings of Christ than anywhere else. Christianity is a religion which measures the total dimension of human existence not only in terms of the final norm of human conduct, which is expressed in the law of love, but also in terms of the fact of sin. It recognizes that the same man who can become his true self only by striving infinitely for self-realization beyond himself is also inevitably involved in the sin of infinitely making his partial and narrow self the true end of existence. It believes, in other words, that though Christ is the true norm (the "second Adam") for every man, every man is also in some sense a crucifier of Christ.

The good news of the gospel is not the law that we ought to love one another. The good news of the gospel is that there is a resource of divine mercy which is able to overcome a contradiction within our own souls, which we cannot ourselves overcome. This contradiction is that, though we know we ought to love our neighbor as ourself, there is a "law in our members which wars against the law that is in our mind," so that, in fact, we love ourselves more than our neighbor.

The grace of God which is revealed in Christ is regarded by Christian faith as, on the one hand, an actual "power of righteousness" which heals the contradiction within our hearts. In that sense Christ defines the actual possibilities of human existence. On the other hand, this grace is conceived as "justification," as pardon rather than power, as the forgiveness of God, which is vouchsafed to man despite the fact that he never achieves the full measure of Christ. In that sense Christ is the "impossible possibility." Loyalty to him means realization in intention, but does not actually mean the full realization of the measure of Christ. In this doctrine of forgiveness and justification, Christianity measures the full seriousness of sin as a permanent factor in human history. Naturally, the doctrine has no meaning for modern secular civilization, nor for the secularized and moralistic versions of Christianity. They cannot understand the doctrine precisely because they believe there is some fairly simple way out of the sinfulness of human history.

It is rather remarkable that so many modern Christians should believe that Christianity is primarily a "challenge" to man to obey the law of Christ; whereas it is, as a matter of fact, a religion which deals realistically with the problem presented by the violation of this law. Far from believing that the ills of the world could be set right "if

only" men obeyed the law of Christ, it has always regarded the problem of achieving justice in a sinful world as a very difficult task. In
the profounder versions of the Christian faith the very utopian illusions, which are currently equated with Christianity, have been rig-
orously disavowed.

Nevertheless, it is not possible to regard pacifism simply as a
heresy. In one of its aspects modern Christian pacifism is simply a
version of Christian perfectionism. It expresses a genuine impulse in
the heart of Christianity, the impulse to take the law of Christ seriously and not to allow the political strategies, which the sinful character of man makes necessary, to become final norms. In its profounder forms this Christian perfectionism did not proceed from a
simple faith that the "law of love" could be regarded as an alternative
to the political strategies by which the world achieves a precarious
justice. These strategies invariably involve the balancing of power
with power; and they never completely escape the peril of tyranny
on the one hand, and the peril of anarchy and warfare on the other.

In medieval ascetic perfectionism and in Protestant sectarian
perfectionism (of the type of Meno Simons, for instance) the effort
to achieve a standard of perfect love in individual life was not presented as a political alternative. On the contrary, the political problem
and task were specifically disavowed. This perfectionism did not
give itself to the illusion that it had discovered a method for eliminat-
ing the element of conflict from political strategies. On the contrary,
it regarded the mystery of evil as beyond its power of solution. It was
content to set up the most perfect and unselfish individual life as
a symbol of the Kingdom of God. It knew that this could only be
done by disavowing the political task and by freeing the individual
of all responsibility for social justice.

It is this kind of pacifism which is not a heresy. It is rather a
valuable asset for the Christian faith. It is a reminder to the Christian
community that the relative norms of social justice, which justify
both coercion and resistance to coercion, are not final norms, and
that Christians are in constant peril of forgetting their relative and
tentative character and of making them too completely normative.

There is thus a Christian pacifism which is not a heresy. Yet
most modern forms of Christian pacifism are heretical. Presumably
inspired by the Christian gospel, they have really absorbed the Renaissance faith in the goodness of man, have rejected the Christian doctrine of original sin as an outmoded bit of pessimism, have reinter-

preted the Cross so that it is made to stand for the absurd idea that perfect love is guaranteed a simple victory over the world, and have rejected all other profound elements of the Christian gospel as "Pauline" accretions which must be stripped from the "simple gospel of Jesus." This form of pacifism is not only heretical when judged by the standards of the total gospel. It is equally heretical when judged by the facts of human existence. There are no historical realities which remotely conform to it. It is important to recognize this lack of conformity to the facts of experience as a criterion of heresy.

All forms of religious faith are principles of interpretation which we use to organize our experience. Some religions may be adequate principles of interpretation at certain levels of experience, but they break down at deeper levels. No religious faith can maintain itself in defiance of the experience which it supposedly interprets. A religious faith which substitutes faith in man for faith in God cannot finally validate itself in experience. If we believe that the only reason men do not love each other perfectly is because the law of love has not been preached persuasively enough, we believe something to which experience does not conform. If we believe that if Britain had only been fortunate enough to have produced 30 per cent instead of 2 per cent of conscientious objectors to military service, Hitler's heart would have been softened and he would not have dared to attack Poland, we hold a faith which no historic reality justifies.

Such a belief has no more justification in the facts of experience than the communist belief that the sole cause of man's sin is the class organization of society and the corollary faith that a "classless" society will be essentially free of human sinfulness. All of these beliefs are pathetic alternatives to the Christian faith. They all come finally to the same thing. They do not believe that man remains a tragic creature who needs the divine mercy as much at the end as at the beginning of his moral endeavors. They believe rather that there is some fairly easy way out of the human situation of "self-alienation." In this connection it is significant that Christian pacifists, rationalists like Bertrand Russell, and mystics like Aldous Huxley, believe essentially the same thing. The Christians make Christ into the symbol of their faith in man. But their faith is really identical with that of Russell or Huxley.

The common element in these various expressions of faith in man is the belief that man is essentially good at some level of his being. They believe that if you can abstract the rational-universal man from what is finite and contingent in human nature, or if you can only cultivate some mystic-universal element in the deeper levels of man's consciousness, you will be able to eliminate human selfishness and the consequent conflict of life with life. These rational or mystical views of man conform neither to the New Testament's view of human nature nor yet to the complex facts of human experience.

In order to elaborate the thesis more fully, that the refusal of the Christian Church to espouse pacifism is not apostasy and that most modern forms of pacifism are heretical, it is necessary first of all to consider the character of the absolute and unqualified demands which Christ makes and to understand the relation of these demands to the gospel.

## II

It is very foolish to deny that the ethic of Jesus is an absolute and uncompromising ethic. It is, in the phrase of Ernst Troeltsch, an ethic of "love universalism and love perfectionism." The injunctions "resist not evil," "love your enemies," "if ye love them that love you what thanks have you?" "be not anxious for your life," and "be ye therefore perfect even as your father in heaven is perfect," are all of one piece, and they are all uncompromising and absolute. Nothing is more futile and pathetic than the effort of some Christian theologians who find it necessary to become involved in the relativities of politics, in resistance to tyranny or in social conflict, to justify themselves by seeking to prove that Christ was also involved in some of these relativities, that he used whips to drive the money-changers out of the Temple, or that he came "not to bring peace but a sword," or that he asked the disciples to sell a cloak and buy a sword. What could be more futile than to build a whole ethical structure upon the exegetical issue whether Jesus accepted the sword with the words: "It is enough," or whether he really meant: "Enough of this" (Luke 22:36)?

Those of us who regard the ethic of Jesus as finally and ultimately normative, but as not immediately applicable to the task of securing justice in a sinful world, are very foolish if we try to reduce the ethic so that it will cover and justify our prudential and relative standards and strategies. To do this is to reduce the ethic to a new legalism. The significance of the law of love is precisely that it is not just another law, but a law which transcends all law. Every law and every standard which falls short of the law of love embodies contingent factors and makes concessions to the fact that sinful man must achieve tentative harmonies of life with life which are less than the best. It is dangerous and confusing to give these tentative and relative standards final and absolute religious sanction.

Curiously enough the pacifists are just as guilty as their less absolutist brethren of diluting the ethic of Jesus for the purpose of justifying their position. They are forced to recognize that an ethic of pure non-resistance can have no immediate relevance to any political situation; for in every political situation it is necessary to achieve justice by resisting pride and power. They therefore declare that the ethic of Jesus is not an ethic of non-resistance, but one of non-violent resistance; that it allows one to resist evil provided the resistance does not involve the destruction of life or property.

There is not the slightest support in Scripture for this doctrine of non-violence. Nothing could be plainer than that the ethic uncompromisingly enjoins non-resistance and not non-violent resistance. Furthermore, it is obvious that the distinction between violent and non-violent resistance is not an absolute distinction. If it is made absolute, we arrive at the morally absurd position of giving moral preference to the non-violent power which Doctor Goebbels wields over the type of power wielded by a general. This absurdity is really derived from the modern (and yet probably very ancient and very Platonic) heresy of regarding the "physical" as evil and the "spiritual" as good. The *reductio ad absurdum* of this position is achieved in a book which has become something of a textbook for modern pacifists, Richard Gregg's *The Power of Non-Violence*. In this book non-violent resistance is commended as the best method of defeating your foe, particularly as the best method of breaking his morale. It is suggested that Christ ended his life on the Cross because he had not completely mastered the technique of non-violence, and must for this reason be regarded as a guide who is inferior to Gandhi, but whose significance lies in initiating a movement which culminates in Gandhi.

One may well concede that a wise and decent statesmanship will seek not only to avoid conflict, but to avoid violence in conflict. Parliamentary political controversy is one method of sublimating political struggles in such a way as to avoid violent collisions of interest. But this pragmatic distinction has nothing to do with the more basic distinction between the ethic of the "Kingdom of God," in which no concession is made to human sin, and all relative political strategies which, assuming human sinfulness, seek to secure the highest measure of peace and justice among selfish and sinful men. . . .

We have, in other words, reinterpreted the Christian gospel in terms of the Renaissance faith in man. Modern pacifism is merely a final fruit of this Renaissance spirit, which has pervaded the whole of modern Protestantism. We have interpreted world history as a gradual ascent to the Kingdom of God which waits for final triumph only upon the willingness of Christians to "take Christ seriously." There is nothing in Christ's own teachings, except dubious interpretations of the parable of the leaven and the mustard seed, to justify this interpretation of world history. In the whole of the New Testament, Gospels and Epistles alike, there is only one interpretation of world history. That pictures history as moving toward a climax in which both Christ and anti-Christ are revealed.

The New Testament does not, in other words, envisage a simple triumph of good over evil in history. It sees human history involved in the contradictions of sin to the end. That is why it sees no simple resolution of the problem of history. It believes that the Kingdom of God will finally resolve the contradictions of history; but for it the Kingdom of God is no simple historical possibility. The grace of God for man and the Kingdom of God for history are both divine realities and not human possibilities.

The Christian faith believes that the Atonement reveals God's mercy as an ultimate resource by which God alone overcomes the judgment which sin deserves. If this final truth of the Christian religion has no meaning to modern men, including modern Christians, that is because even the tragic character of contemporary history has not yet persuaded them to take the fact of human sinfulness seriously.

v

The contradiction between the law of love and the sinfulness of man raises not only the ultimate religious problem how men are to have peace if they do not overcome the contradiction, and how history will culminate if the contradiction remains on every level of historic achievement; it also raises the immediate problem how men are to achieve a tolerable harmony of life with life, if human pride and selfishness prevent the realization of the law of love.

The pacifists are quite right in one emphasis. They are right in asserting that love is really the law of life. It is not some ultimate possibility which has nothing to do with human history. The freedom of man, his transcendence over the limitations of nature and over all historic and traditional social situations, makes any form of human community which falls short of the law of love less than the best. Only by a voluntary giving of life to life and a free interpenetration of personalities could man do justice both to the freedom of other personalities and the necessity of community between personalities. The law of love therefore remains a principle of criticism over all forms of community in which elements of coercion and conflict destroy the highest type of fellowship.

To look at human communities from the perspective of the Kingdom of God is to know that there is a sinful element in all the expedients which the political order uses to establish justice. That is why even the seemingly most stable justice degenerates periodically into either tyranny or anarchy. But it must also be recognized that it is not possible to eliminate the sinful element in the political expedients. They are, in the words of St. Augustine, both the consequence of, and the remedy for, sin. If they are the remedy for sin, the ideal of love is not merely a principle of indiscriminate criticism upon all approximations of justice. It is also a principle of discriminate criticism between forms of justice.

As a principle of indiscriminate criticism upon all forms of justice, the law of love reminds us that the injustice and tyranny against which we contend in the foe is partially the consequence of our own injustice, that the pathology of modern Germans is partially a consequence of the vindictiveness of the peace of Versailles, and that the ambition of a tyrannical imperialism is different only in degree and not in kind from the imperial impulse which characterizes all of human life.

The Christian faith ought to persuade us that political controversies are always conflicts between sinners and not between righteous men and sinners. It ought to mitigate the self-righteousness which is an inevitable concomitant of all human conflict. The spirit of contrition is an important ingredient in the sense of justice. If it is powerful enough it may be able to restrain the impulse of vengeance sufficiently to allow a decent justice to emerge. This is an important issue facing Europe in anticipation of the conclusion of the present war. It cannot be denied that the Christian conscience failed terribly in restraining vengeance after the last war. It is also quite obvious that the natural inclination to self-righteousness was the primary force of this vengeance (expressed particularly in the war guilt clause of the peace treaty). The pacifists draw the conclusion from the fact that justice is never free from vindictiveness, that we ought not for this reason ever to contend against a foe. This argument leaves out of account that capitulation to the foe might well subject us to a worse vindictiveness. It is as foolish to imagine that the foe is free of the sin which we deplore in ourselves as it is to regard ourselves as free of the sin which we deplore in the foe.

The fact that our own sin is always partly the cause of the sins against which we must contend is regarded by simple moral purists as proof that we have no right to contend against the foe. They regard the injunction "Let him who is without sin cast the first stone" as a simple alternative to the schemes of justice which society has devised and whereby it prevents the worst forms of anti-social conduct. This injunction of Christ ought to remind every judge and every juridical tribunal that the crime of the criminal is partly the consequence of the sins of society. But if pacifists are to be consistent they ought to advocate the abolition of the whole judicial process in society. It is perfectly true that national societies have more impartial instruments of justice than international society possesses to date. Nevertheless, no impartial court is as impartial as it pretends to be, and there is no judicial process which is completely free of vindictiveness. Yet we cannot dispense with it; and we will have to continue to put criminals into jail. There is a point where the final cause of the criminal's anti-social conduct becomes a fairly irrelevant thing in comparison with the task of preventing his conduct from injuring innocent fellows.

The ultimate principles of the Kingdom of God are never irrelevant to any problem of justice, and they hover over every social situation as an ideal possibility; but that does not mean that they can be made into simple alternatives for the present schemes of relative justice. The thesis that the so-called democratic nations have no right to resist overt forms of tyranny, because their own history betrays imperialistic motives, would have meaning only if it were possible to achieve a perfect form of justice in any nation and to free national life completely of the imperialistic motive. This is impossible; for imperialism is the collective expression of the sinful will-to-power which characterizes all human existence. The pacifist argument on this issue betrays how completely pacifism gives itself to illusions about the stuff with which it is dealing in human nature. These illusions deserve particular censure, because no one who knows his own heart very well ought to be given to such illusions.

The recognition of the law of love as an indiscriminate principle of criticism over all attempts at social and international justice is actually a resource of justice, for it prevents the pride, self-righteousness and vindictiveness of men from corrupting their efforts at justice. But it must be recognized that love is also a principle of discriminate criticism between various forms of community and various attempts at justice. The closest approximation to a love in which life supports life in voluntary community is a justice in which life is prevented from destroying life and the interests of the one are guarded against unjust claims by the other. Such justice is achieved when impartial tribunals of society prevent men "from being judges in their own cases," in the words of John Locke. But the tribunals of justice merely codify certain equilibria of power. Justice is basically dependent upon a balance of power. Whenever an individual or a group or a nation possesses undue power, and whenever this power is not checked by the possibility of criticizing and resisting it, it grows inordinate. The equilibrium of power upon which every structure of justice rests would degenerate into anarchy but for the organizing center which controls it. One reason why the balances of power, which prevent injustice in international relations, periodically degenerate into overt anarchy is because no way has yet been found to establish an adequate organizing center, a stable international judicatory, for this balance of power.

A balance of power is something different from, and inferior to, the harmony of love. It is a basic condition of justice, given the sinfulness of man. Such a balance of power does not exclude love. In fact, without love the frictions and tensions of a balance of power would become intolerable. But without the balance of power even the most loving relations may degenerate into unjust relations, and love may become the screen which hides the injustice. Family relations are instructive at this point. Women did not gain justice from men, despite the intimacy of family relations, until they secured sufficient economic power to challenge male autocracy. There are Christian "idealists" today who speak sentimentally of love as the only way to justice, whose family life might benefit from a more delicate "balance of power."

Naturally the tensions of such a balance may become overt; and overt tensions may degenerate into conflict. The center of power, which has the function of preventing this anarchy of conflict, may also degenerate into tyranny. There is no perfectly adequate method of preventing either anarchy or tyranny. But obviously the justice established in the so-called democratic nations represents a high degree of achievement; and the achievement becomes the more impressive when it is compared with the tyranny into which alternative forms of society have fallen. The obvious evils of tyranny, however, will not inevitably persuade the victims of economic anarchy in democratic society to eschew tyranny. When men suffer from anarchy they may foolishly regard the evils of tyranny as the lesser evils. Yet the evils of tyranny in fascist and communist nations are so patent, that we may dare to hope that what is still left of democratic civilizations will not lightly sacrifice the virtues of democracy for the sake of escaping its defects.

We have a very vivid and conclusive evidence about the probable consequences of a tyrannical unification of Europe. The nature of the German rule in the conquered nations of Europe gives us the evidence. There are too many contingent factors in various national and international schemes of justice to justify any unqualified endorsement of even the most democratic structure of justice as "Christian." Yet it must be obvious that any social structure in which power has been made responsible, and in which anarchy has been overcome by methods of mutual accommodation, is preferable to either anarchy or tyranny. If it is not possible to express a moral preference for the justice achieved in democratic societies, in comparison with tyrannical societies, no historical preference has any meaning. This kind of justice approximates the harmony of love more than either anarchy or tyranny.

If we do not make discriminate judgments between social systems we weaken the resolution to defend and extend civilization. Pacifism either tempts us to make no judgments at all, or to give an undue preference to tyranny in comparison with the momentary anarchy which is necessary to overcome tyranny. It must be admitted that the anarchy of war which results from resistance to tyranny is not always creative; that, at given periods of history, civilization may lack the resource to fashion a new and higher form of unity out of momentary anarchy. The defeat of Germany and the frustration of the Nazi effort to unify Europe in tyrannical terms is a negative task. It does not guarantee the emergence of a new Europe with a higher level of international cohesion and new organs of international justice.

But it is a negative task which cannot be avoided. All schemes for avoiding this negative task rest upon illusions about human nature. Specifically, these illusions express themselves in the failure to understand the stubbornness and persistence of the tyrannical will, once it is fully conceived. It would not require great argumentative skill to prove that Nazi tyranny never could have reached such proportions as to be able to place the whole of Europe under its ban, if sentimental illusions about the character of the evil which Europe was facing had not been combined with less noble motives for tolerating Nazi aggression.

A simple Christian moralism is senseless and confusing. It is senseless when, as in the World War, it seeks uncritically to identify the cause of Christ with the cause of democracy without a religious reservation. It is just as senseless when it seeks to purge itself of this error by an uncritical refusal to make any distinctions between relative values in history. The fact is that we might as well dispense with the Christian faith entirely if it is our conviction that we can act in history only if we are guiltless. This means that we must either prove our guiltlessness in order to be able to act; or refuse to act because we cannot achieve guiltlessness. Self-righteousness or inaction are the alternatives of secular moralism. If they are also the only alternatives of Christian moralism, one rightly suspects that Christian faith has become diluted with secular perspectives.

In its profoundest insights the Christian faith sees the whole of human history as involved in guilt, and finds no release from guilt except in the grace of God. The Christian is freed by that grace to act in history; to give his devotion to the highest values he knows; to defend those citadels of civilization of which necessity and historic destiny have made him the defender; and he is persuaded by that grace to remember the ambiguity of even his best actions. If the providence of God does not enter the affairs of men to bring good out of evil, the evil in our good may easily destroy our most ambitious efforts and frustrate our highest hopes.

## VI

Despite our conviction that most modern pacifism is too filled with secular and moralistic illusions to be of the highest value to the Christian community, we may be grateful for the fact that the Christian Church has learned, since the last war, to protect its pacifists and to appreciate their testimony. Even when this testimony is marred by self-righteousness, because it does not proceed from a sufficiently profound understanding of the tragedy of human history, it has its values.

It is a terrible thing to take human life. The conflict between man and man and nation and nation is tragic. If there are men who declare that, no matter what the consequences, they cannot bring themselves to participate in this slaughter, the Church ought to be able to say to the general community: We quite understand this scruple and we respect it. It proceeds from the conviction that the true end of man is brotherhood, and that love is the law of life. We who allow ourselves to become engaged in war need this testimony of the absolutist against us, lest we accept the warfare of the world as normative, lest we become callous to the horror of war, and lest we forget the ambiguity of our own actions and motives and the risk we run of achieving no permanent good from this momentary anarchy in which we are involved. . . .

# VII. OLD OPTIONS AND NEW DIRECTIONS

Since the just war theory condemns unlimited war, twentieth century weapons of mass destruction and new policies of total warfare create new problems for Christian ethics. Moralists and church bodies, therefore, both Catholic and Protestant, condemn all but unavoidable, defensive war by limited means; they criticize obliteration bombing and nuclear weapons; they uphold the immunity of non-combatants; they debate the morality of guerrilla warfare, retaliatory strikes, and deterrent stockpiling. Some, like Robert Drinan, conclude that the just war theory is outdated and that we must opt for prudential pacifism with a policy of non-violent resistance in international affairs; others, like Paul Ramsey, argue that modern weaponry must be restricted so as to make possible the legitimate defense and limited war that is a tragic necessity in a violently divided world.

For further reading:

Bennett, J. C., ed. *Nuclear Weapons and the Conflict of Conscience.* Scribner, 1962.
———. *Foreign Policy in Christian Perspective.* Scribner, 1966.
Finn, J., ed. *A Conflict of Loyalties.* Pegasus, 1968.
Flannery, H. W., ed. *Pattern for Peace—Catholic Statements on International Order.* Newman Press, 1962.
Merton, Thomas, ed. *Breakthrough to Peace.* New Directions, 1962.
Nagle, W. J., ed. *Morality and Modern Warfare.* Helicon Press, 1960.
O'Brien, William V. *War and/or Survival.* Doubleday, 1969.
———. *Nuclear War, Deterrence and Morality.* Newman Press, 1967.
Ramsey, Paul. *The Just War—Force and Political Responsibility.* Scribner, 1968.
Tucker, Robert. *The Just War, A Study in Contemporary American Doctrine.* Johns Hopkins Press, 1960.
Wasserstrom, Richard., ed. *War and Morality.* Wadsworth, 1970.
Zahn, Gordon C. *War, Conscience and Dissent.* Hawthorne Books, 1967.

## 1. ROBERT DRINAN (1920–    )

Until recently, Roman Catholics have by and large adopted a just war theory. A Jesuit scholar who is former dean of Boston College Law School and was elected to Congress in 1970, Drinan represents the new variety of Catholic pacifism that arose first in response to the threat of a nuclear holocaust and then in opposition to the Vietnam war. His position resembles that of many Protestants, but he stands out by virtue of such constructive new proposals as appear in the following selection.

## IS PACIFISM THE ONLY OPTION LEFT FOR CHRISTIANS?

From *Vietnam and Armageddon* (1970), chap. 14.

The term "pacifist" has never had a very positive connotation among most Christians and perhaps particularly not among Catholics. If one advocates pacifism or even expresses sympathy with the idea, almost immediately virtually every Christian will ask if the speaker believes that each individual has a moral right to protect himself in the ·event that his life is threatened. It is somehow assumed that the pacifist must be an absolutist in that he is opposed to all use of force or violence to protect any objective. Every dictionary definition of "pacifist," however, stresses that the term has always been restricted to the use of "military" force. Despite this widely accepted definition of pacifism, there is nonetheless a rather universal resistance to the concept on the grounds that it is naive and unrealistic.

In a definitive book, *Pacifism in the United States, from the Colonial Era to the First World War,* Peter Brock treats all facets of pacifism. He concedes that, throughout most of the period he surveys, pacifists at their best constituted a small elite and at worst, an exclusive clique. At the same time Professor Brock indicates by his massive documentation that the pacifism of the Quakers, Mennonites, and other similar religious groups had an enormous impact on American society—an influence which may possibly be witnessing its flowering in the outcries from every social class and every age group which have made the war in Vietnam the most detested in American history.

Many theological strands entered into the formulation of American pacifism. The Anabaptists and the Mennonites denounce war basically because of their theological conceptions against what they conceive to be the tyranny of the state. In the 19th century and thereafter, pacifism in America tended to be essentially an optimistic creed which placed its faith in the eventual perfectibility of man.

The few Protestant theologians who have argued vigorously and consistently on behalf of pacifism are today more persuasive than most Christians would imagine. It may be that the chilling fear of the atomic mushroom, and our anguished nightmares about the horrors of Vietnam, precondition us to accept any line of argument which would ease our anxiety and guilt about the fundamental irrationality of the foreign policy which the United States has pursued for almost twenty-five years.

The theological sorites for pacifism is much more sophisticated than even well-informed Catholics might surmise. The theological defenders of pacifism do not rely upon any literalist or oversimplified version of Scripture to support their argument. Inevitably they rely upon Scripture, both the Old and the New Testaments, but they orchestrate this with quotations from the early Christian Fathers and from theologians in almost every age of Christianity.

One's viewpoint on pacifism depends upon one's priorities concerning the ultimate objectives of organized society. In the inevitable disorder and violence which characterize all societies, if one starts with the premise that society's foremost objective is to minimize the number of deaths caused by social and political unrest and violence, it would appear to follow—especially since the advent of modern or total war—that almost any social or political calamity should be accepted; otherwise, any contrary policy would be inconsistent with the objective of minimizing the number of deaths at the hands of those who would overthrow or occupy a particular nation.

If on the other hand one starts with the premise that the preservation of the fundamental rights of peoples is on certain occasions an objective for which even the lives of men may be sacrificed, then pacifism is hardly a viable option. An appealing case can be made for the exaltation of the basic rights of human beings in the instance of genocide. The searing book, *While Six Million Died*, by Arthur D. Morse, is a powerful document which indicts the United States, particular the State Department, for appalling apathy and carelessness in the face of Nazi genocide.

If a person feels that the preservation of national borders or the protection of the social, political, or religious freedom of a nation-state justifies at least a defensive war, there is hardly any place at all in such a scheme of things for pacifism. . . .

Even though scholars and Christians will continue to debate about the existence and validity of pacifism in the New Testament and in early Christianity, the fact is that the Christians of the first three centuries constitute, by their lives and by their achievements, the greatest proof in all history that a nonviolent "war" of love is infinitely more powerful than the sword and is incapable of being destroyed by any armed conflict. They gave witness to the irreducible conflict between the nonviolent Christian and the tyranny of state absolutism. It is a form of pacifism which produced a long line of martyrs who submitted to the sword. And it was pacifism which, in the ultimate analysis, caused Constantine to recognize that Christianity could not be exterminated. He surrendered, not necessarily because of any genuine conversion or because Christians had become a majority (in the year 313 A.D. they were still a very small minority), but simply because he recognized that no amount of armed force could effectively deny to the Christian revolutionaries the right to exist in the Roman Empire.

This example of the early Christians, contrasted with the Cold War between the Soviet Union and the United States, forces the mind to the crucial question: Can or must a Catholic be a pacifist in the present situation? A Catholic *may*, of course, be a pacifist if he judges that the evidence of Christian history makes pacifism a live option for himself; a Christian *must* be a complete pacifist if his intellect has persuaded his conscience that this is the *only* option available to him since, in the ultimate analysis, the voice of conscience—as Martin Luther King and Cardinal Newman would agree—is the voice of God.

It may not be necessary, however, for most Christians to reach this absolute decision and to condemn all war under any conditions as immoral. The immorality of atomic warfare has been unequivocally condemned by Vatican II, and all conventional wars which might be waged in the modern world can hardly pass muster under the various requirements of the theory of the just war.

Even if one is a pacifist, however, either on the principle of the immorality of all wars or because one thinks that all possible modern wars are unjustifiable, such a position does not resolve all of the problems concerning the extent to which a Christian can cooperate in a society in which he is compelled by countless laws to contribute to the massive military preparations of his nation. About the only specific relief which the Second Vatican Council and the American bishops have given to persons opposed to modern war is the recommendation that the state give immunity, not merely to the pure pacifist but to the selective conscientious objector. Such immunity is still not available in the United States where there is compulsory peacetime military conscription—an institution which all popes during the past century have inveighed.

The Christian in America who is opposed to all modern wars is required to pay federal taxes of which approximately 60 percent goes for some type of military preparedness. This is one reason why the actions by which some strike out at various manifestations of the military empire in America are understandable. The destruction of draft files by the Catonsville Nine, and similar actions by Christians in Milwaukee and elsewhere, may be a dramatic "homily" against the evils of militarism; and the sincerity and heroism of those who participate in such activities is beyond dispute. But for persons not inspired to engage in this type of prophetic witness, what is the most logical and effective way to be heard? What can be done to change the course of a nation, so blinded by the alleged evils of communism and its purported threat to the security of the nation, that it has become persuaded that it is a duty of patriotism to continue to support the national commitment to provide military solutions to social and economic problems around the globe?

I would suggest that the time has come for Christians, and particularly Catholics, to stop theorizing about the "possibility" of a just war, to take a realistic view that bilateral disarmament of the Soviet Union and the United States is highly improbable, and to start advocating a policy of passive resistance or militant nonviolence toward any nation which would seek to conquer America, seize our assets, and control our minds.

Following such an option would undoubtedly require unilateral risk and would, concededly, leave the American people open to a certain defenselessness against the new instrument of total destruction. It is appropriate to recall, however, that unilateral disarmament on the part of the United States would by no means necessarily result in a larger number of dead than would result if one or more of the other atomic powers, by accident or by design, launched a nuclear war on a fully armed America. Scientific leaders such as Dr. Edward Teller have estimated that in a nuclear war probably no more than 10 percent of the American population would be wiped out. Assuming, then, that some twenty million Americans would be killed in a "first strike" war launched by one of the nuclear nations, does it follow that such an attack becomes more probable if the United States tells the world that it has abandoned its policy of "massive retaliation" and that it has surrendered its policy of atomic "sufficiency" because it has realized that this is a policy of incitement as much as it is a policy of deterrence?

This suggested policy of nonviolence should not, however, be construed or dismissed as a passive surrender or a defeatist compliance with a foreign power thought to be a possible aggressor. The proposed alternative would openly confront the fact that the mutual terror which now exists between America and the Soviet Union is so hideous that no different arrangement could be worse.

The disarmament would be accompanied by a warning to the entire world that the American people will not be governed by any foreign power. If conquered by superior military force, they will become a totally ungovernable people who will drive out the aggressor by highly sophisticated techniques of nonviolence developed, if need be, with all of the fantastic resources which America now puts in the hands of its military complex. All these techniques of civil disobedience and noncooperation, which were used in Gandhi's movement, would be developed by the application of the discoveries which the behavioral sciences have unlocked with regard to motivation and the dynamics of morale.

The very thought of even partial unilateral disarmament is without doubt unthinkable to many, if not most people, in the United States. But on the assumption that the Russians and other potential "enemies" of America retain their sanity, there is literally no chance at all that any political authority would consciously choose to start a nuclear war. . . .

Even the best-informed and most devout Christians dismiss

unilateral disarmament as a virtual invitation to the Russians to destroy the nation. One of the very few Catholics to delve into the strategy of a "war by love," conducted by nonviolence or passive resistance, is Gordon Zahn, a former professor at Loyola University in Chicago and now a professor at the University of Massachusetts. Professor Zahn, the author of the challenging book, *German Catholics and Hitler's War*, argues eloquently in an excellent brochure, *An Alternative to War*, and in *War, Conscience and Dissent*, that the only way for Christians to act in the present nuclear stalemate is to resort to the techniques of nonviolence. Professor Zahn summarizes his argument as follows:

> Since the quest for national security through violence has worked us into a corner where a resort to the means of violence now available to us would most likely provoke our own destruction and, with it, the destruction of a significant part of the world's population, the techniques of nonviolence being proposed as an alternative would present—assuming, of course, they were given the benefit of a degree of acceptance and official support comparable to that lavished upon the techniques of violence—the only reasonable hope for escape from that dilemma.[1]

Professor Zahn quite rightly insists that "we are dealing with something far more profound than a mere difference in policy options." He puts it this way:

> Our question ultimately concerns our basic conceptions of man. Is man, after all is said and done, a creature whose behavior is finally controlled through promises of physically satisfying rewards and threats of violently induced pain; or is he something greater, the deepest wellsprings of whose behavior contain forces responsive only to the power of love and recognition of common identity?[2]

Professor Zahn realistically concedes that the "mounting of a well-conceived and disciplined campaign of civil disobedience and noncooperation against an opponent using the means of violence might end with total victory for the latter." But he suggests that since the destruction of millions of lives by America is the only possible

1. *An Alternative to War* (New York: Council on Religion and International Affairs, 1963), pp. 22-23.
2. Ibid., p. 31.

alternative, then "it is better to perish as the victim of the inhumanity of others than to save oneself (or one's nation) by making others the victims of our own inhuman acts."

The essence of Professor Zahn's difference with those Christians who feel that the United States should continue to have not a superiority, but a "sufficiency" of deterrent power, rests in Zahn's conception of human nature. It is his conviction that "even the totalitarian automaton will have to react as a man at some point," and consequently the "advocate of nonviolence is an optimist in that, trusting in the spiritual nature and destiny of man, he is confident that the capacity to love and to bear whatever sacrifices such love may entail is greater than the human capacity for evil. . . ."

In *War, Conscience and Dissent* Zahn argues brilliantly that the longer the Free World subscribes to the philosophy of deterrence the "greater will grow the likelihood (one might almost say the certainty!) that one side or the other will strike the fatal spark and bring about the world-destroying exchange we are trying so hard to convince ourselves is impossible."

Can anyone fathom the profound reasons why so very few Catholics in America follow the guidelines set forth so powerfully by the Catholic pacifist Gordon Zahn? Zahn himself furnishes one reason when he expresses his disappointment in the "frank unwillingness on the part of Church leaders to impose what may be regarded as too great a burden or impossible demands upon their faithful lest such excessive expectations cause a drop in active membership. . . ."[3] Mr. Zahn goes on to affirm that the Church "must itself be reconverted—or at least, rewakened—as to those value affirmations at least which, in its time of origin and its time of greatest glory, have always made it an institution for the transformation of society. . . ."

As I myself have read and reread Gordon Zahn's writings, I find my mind resisting his conclusions because, if I accept them, I must also believe that countless human beings and millions of Catholics have succumbed to nationalism and have compromised their faith to the point where they are willing to allow and even to participate in the massive violation of God's commandment, "Thou shalt not kill." In order to embrace Gordon Zahn's directives I must accept the proposition that the leaders and the faithful in the Catholic Church in America have been blinded over the past twenty-five years by the policies of public figures who have built a military empire ostensibly

3. Ibid., p. 27.

to preserve the safety of the American people, but which actually constitutes a system that requires American Christians each day to participate in the moral evil of threatening to inflict harm; this, when everyone knows that the infliction of such harm is inherently immoral.

At least one other American Catholic, James W. Douglass, sees the dilemma of the modern Christian as clearly as Gordon Zahn. He presents it in these words:

> One must either revolt against the disorder of the present system, for the sake of each man's right to the means of a human life, or cease being human oneself. The process of inhumanity and slow murder has already gone too far to allow an intermediate choice.[4]

Mr. Douglass' volume illustrates in a theological and mystical way the hideousness of the predicament in which America now finds itself. He points out, for example, that the total expenditure of the Peace Corps for an entire year is equal to the cost of thirty-two hours of the Vietnam war.

Mr. Douglass' treatment of the legal-moral issues of the nuclear age is arresting, but not always entirely clear or specific. He interweaves theology with the chronicle of contemporary events in such a manner that, though the language and the vision are intriguing, one is not entirely certain that a resolution of any problem is worked out at any particular level. He has, however, some magnificent statements on the problem of war such as the following:

> The roots of violence in man go far deeper than the just war doctrine and baptized nationalism characteristic of the Constantinian phase of Church history. In the history of man, the Church's involvement in violence has been merely a religious justification and extension of a prior human reality, the pervasive violence in mankind as a whole and its raging presence in each human heart.[5]

The "raging instinct in each human heart" towards violence has been described by Freud as the "death instinct." In Freud's famous public reply in 1933 to Albert Einstein's question to him, "Why does mankind wage war?" Freud stated that the underlying reason for

4. *The Non-Violent Cross: A Theology of Revolution and Peace* (New York: The Macmillan Company, 1968), p. 8.
5. Ibid., p. 218.

war was the profound instinct in all human beings impelling them towards aggression and destruction. Freud consequently felt that there is no way to suppress the destructive tendencies of the death instinct within man, which has led mankind in almost every generation to the carnage of war, except by diverting these aggressive tendencies into channels other than that of warfare. Christian theologians would be inclined to state that man's instinct towards aggression and destruction is traceable to the sinfulness, and even inhumanity, which came to man after his fall from grace. Any explanation of war, however, or even of violence, must be articulated in more sophisticated and existential terms than the simple declaration that man, although redeemed, is still prone to violence because he is neither angel nor animal. The fact is that many acts of violence—and perhaps almost all wars—have been justified and rationalized throughout human history by eloquent if confused expressions of higher values, and even of the supreme value of love.

Is there than any middle ground between those who, like Gordon Zahn and James Douglass, opt for pacifism as the only Christian answer to the present arms race, and those who desire somehow to disarm gradually on a mutually agreeable basis and thus restore some semblance of rationality to the highly industrialized nations of the earth?

As much as I personally would like to claim that there is hope in working for disarmament, and all the other steps which would reverse the hysteria and irrationality which have dominated the twenty-five years of the nuclear age, I cannot see any significant promising signs or discover any probative evidence that such a reasonable solution is being worked out, or even can be worked out.

At the same time I and countless other millions have to be realistic and recognize that the mere suggestion of any unilateral weakening of the American defense posture is almost always greeted by the vast majority of Americans with scorn and ridicule. It may be that a significant number of young persons would be much more receptive to proposals that the United States take the initiative by some bold, daring, and even dangerous steps by which the arms race escalation could be reversed.

If one accepts the stark fact that the United States can contribute to peace only by some courageous, unilateral method of slowing the arms race then it follows that Catholics in America are involved in a collective silence which makes the silence of German Catholics in the decade of Hitler's atrocities almost insignificant by contrast. If, in other words, one comes to the conclusion that the situation is as desperate as Gordon Zahn and James Douglass relate, then one must accept the corollary that the one-fourth of the American nation who claim allegiance to the Catholic Church have acquiesced in nationalism or, even worse, in American capitalism, in a way which is a basis compromise with the unalterable principles of their religion.

Regardless, however, of one's own ultmate conviction with regard to the possible irreversibility of America's policy, everyone must work in some way to shock the mind and heart of America, which some twenty years ago adopted a policy of militaristic anticommunism that has now made it the most formidable bastion and fortress in the history of mankind. It is almost a great triumph even to raise a doubt in the average American's mind about the existing foreign policy of his country. To persuade him that his country made a tragic mistake, or committed a serious evil or sin twenty years ago, is almost impossible in most cases. Attempting to change the mind of any American adult who has subscribed to his nation's bipartisan foreign policy since the Truman Doctrine of 1948 is comparable to attempting to change the attitudes of a Southern segregationist towards integrated schools or of a white Northern racist toward interracial neighborhoods.

Theoretically it should be easier to alter the views of Catholics with respect to this question because of the rich Catholic tradition favoring the family of nations and urging the solidarity of all men throughout the world. The melancholy fact is, however, that it is probably more difficult to disabuse Catholics of their "hawkishness" against communism than it is other Americans. This phenomenon may be attributable to the rising socioeconomic status of Catholics; or to the almost paranoid fear of communism which entered into the psyche of Catholics as a result of the atrocities against the Catholic Church imputed to communism in the Mexican and Spanish revolutions, and in the Soviet take-over of Eastern Europe after the Second World War.

Without withdrawing my endorsement of the presentation of the starkness of America's moral dilemma as outlined by Gordon Zahn and James Douglass, I would like to suggest several intermediate or long-range proposals which, at the very least, may soften the abrasiveness in the Soviet-United States relationship. These proposals may, on the other hand, create some thawing of the feeling between the two armed camps that would lead to the withering away of their

angry confrontation which has characterized the nuclear age.
Proposals aimed at this objective would include the following:

## 1. Reeducation of Young Americans

Clearly the reeducation of the young in America, with respect to the
world they enter as adults, is imperative. It is almost self-evident that
elementary and secondary education does not today prepare its students for the "One World" in which we now live. Edwin O. Reischauer, former U.S. ambassador to Japan, states this well in these
words:

> Our elementary and secondary education, backed up by a lot of
> home conditioning, tends to convey a very misleading impression
> of the history of mankind, confirming false assumptions that the
> West is and has been superior to the other civilizations of man-
> kind; and that its 19th century position of dominance over the
> rest of the world is natural and will continue indefinitely into the
> future. These are dangerous misconceptions for Americans to
> harbor in the second half of the 20th century.[6]

Reischauer insists that he would not tolerate the existence of a
19th century education in the natural sciences in contemporary American schools. He therefore maintains that we "should not tolerate
in it the equally important field of the study of human civilization and
the relations between nations." He urges that all young American
children be taught about the world as it is, describing it as follows:

> This is no longer a purely Western or even Western-dominated
> world. China and India are by far the most populous countries
> on the globe. Japan is a major economic and cultural force, show-
> ing promise of soon becoming the third most powerful nation in
> the world. It, as well as Pakistan, Indonesia, and Brazil over-
> shadow in population the traditional great powers of Western
> Europe. The problems and wars that might blight our future are
> more likely to emerge from the unstable non-Western world than
> from the Occident.[7]

Is it visionary to think and to hope that Catholic schools in

6. *Beyond Vietnam: The United States and Asia* (New York: Random
House, Inc., 1967), p. 235.
7. Ibid., p. 242.

America might possess the tradition and the propensities for developing an imaginative and bold curriculum along the lines suggested by Professor Reischauer? Within the Catholic theological and philosophical tradition, as nowhere in Protestant or Jewish religious thought, there exists a body of truths and principles regarding the necessity, indispensability, and urgency of an international community made up of all nations linked together in the family of man and joined by the overarching principle of human equality and human solidarity.

Can the richness of this tradition be explored and exploited to the point where American Catholic elementary and secondary schools would be known as institutions in which students learn of the possibility and urgent necessity for an entirely new international order based on justice and motivated by brotherly love? At this particular time, when Catholic schools are seeking a new justification or raison d'etre, could they find this purpose in the pressing need in America for schools which will make their students fully aware of the problems and prospects of the peoples of Asia, Africa, and the Third World?

Difficulties involved in such a task are formidable. It is questionable how many of the present personnel and pupil population of Catholic schools would have even a remote interest in changing the European-Christian orientation of their schools to a worldwide or global focus. Furthermore, public reaction to any school with a global orientation is likely to be adverse, and the opposition would come not merely from forces on the Right, but from the educational bureaucracy of the country. Such a shift in their focus would also seriously jeopardize any chances which Catholic schools might have at this time for further federal and state financial assistance for the secular aspects of their educational programs.

Catholic secondary schools could offer courses in Russian and Chinese, seminars in Buddhism, and offerings on all aspects of the probems of the Third World. Their freedom from the rigidities of the public school hierarchy would allow them to experiment in very significant ways with programs which could help a new generation of Americans to escape that myopia, excessive patriotism, and indifference to non-European cultures—all of which have combined to create and to perpetuate America's foreign policy of the last twenty years. This policy, in effect, has created a new Chinese wall—this time by nuclear warheads—in order to keep the "barbarians" far from our shores. Such a policy is likely to continue until the schools of America persuade a new generation that the West must understand the rich and diverse cultures and religions of the non-Western peoples, who outnumber Occidentals by close to 3 to 1.

It is difficult to think of a challenge to Catholic schools in America that is more important or pressing than the need to develop a curriculum which would begin to prepare them to live as citizens and as Christians in a world whose under-developed nations will not long tolerate the squandering of mankind's resources to their detriment and deprivation in the Soviet-American impasse.

## 2. Reduction in the International Sales of American Weapons

A second area for promising reform is existing American policy with regard to the furnishing of arms to foreign powers. In 1968 the United States spent $79.3 billion for military purposes while the Soviet Union spent $35.8 billion. For the United States this meant some 10 percent of its national income in that year.

During 1968 the United States was the largest supplier of weapons to the nations of the world. The total came to nearly $719 million including sales, grants, and training. Both the Soviet Union and the United States gave military aid to the Middle East before and during 1968. The Middle East showed the sharpest rise in military spending, increasing by nearly 20 percent annually over the last three years. Arms spending by developing nations has also been rising, usually at the annual rate of about 7.5 percent, although national production of nonmilitary items has been increasing in those countries by about 5 percent and often a good deal less.

The commercial motivation and the industrial empires behind the distribution by the United States of all types of military weapons to all types of nations around the globe has been exposed in such books as *The War Business: The International Trade in Armaments* by George Thayer. As never before, Mr. Thayer has demonstrated that the United States is ultimately responsible for allowing the introduction of unneeded and unmanageable sophisticated weapon systems, such as jet fighters, tanks, and submarines, into relatively tranquil locales in Latin America. Thus America has permitted the creation of mini-arms races between poverty-stricken nations which have little or no basis for conflict.

On a related problem, John Kenneth Galbraith, in his volume, *How to Control the Military,* revealed that nearly seven hundred retired generals, admirals, and navy captains are employed by the ten largest defense contractors, thus intensifying the complex linkage between the manufacturers of arms and the Pentagon itself. Equally chilling is the revelation of Richard J. Barnet in his volume, *The Economy of Death*. In a Kafka-like story the author shows how the public has been consistently shortchanged by irrational and wasteful decisions, as, for example, the expenditure of more than $23 billion worth of missiles that were never deployed.

Is there any way by which the facts revealed in these volumes can somehow become operative in American public policy? The ordinary person, even if he never questions the need for some kind of defence system, feels voiceless and powerless in confrontation with the public policy—indeed, a private-public conspiracy—by which the United States continues to merchandise the weapons of war to the entire world, and thereby makes war more probable. Papal statements have been frequent and eloquent in condemning the introduction of armaments into nations which very often can ill-afford to spend their limited resources on this type of product. American commentators of every sort have frequently pointed out that the United States, in allowing corporations to create and then satisfy the desire for weapons in foreign nations, is in effect promoting a military solution to complex social problems.

Is there any way by which the highly organized units of the Catholic Church in America can initiate and coordinate a national campaign to turn American policy around, at least insofar as the merchandising of arms to other nations is concerned? The monthly *Catholic Worker*, the *Catholic Peace Fellowship*, and similar groups certainly advocate the diminution of the sale of American weapons to foreign nations; but these peace groups have never been near the mainstream of American Catholic activity. On the question of the severe control of such sales, however, could there not be a Catholic consensus which would make its voice heard, much like the crusade mounted by Congressman Richard D. McCarthy on chemical-biological warfare, which led, in November 1969, to President Nixon banning those forms of warfare, at least in a defensive war?

One wonders whether it is possible to arouse the indignation of American Catholics concerning any one of the outrages which now go on in the name of America's foreign policy. Over the past generation they have been united and emboldened to speak out on issues related to discrimination against Catholics running for public office, practices denying aid to Catholic schools, and laws designed to ease abortion statutes. If it is possible at all to have any area of consensus among Catholics on the overall issue of peace and war, it would appear that such a consensus might and could happen with regard to the dismaying fact that American munition makers are the merchants of death throughout the world.

### 3. Unilateral Disarmament

For all Christians who are unable or unwilling to accept the proposals of the pure pacifists, the third fruitful area for exploration is bilateral disarmament. The record, to be sure, is not encouraging. Starting in 1946 with the meetings of the United Nations Atomic Energy Commission, which spent several months considering the Baruch version of the Acheson-Lilienthal proposal for the control of atomic energy, there has been a long series of meetings between the delegates of the Eastern and Western powers in various attempts to arrest the arms race. In 1952 the United Nations Disarmament Commission initiated a series of meetings which proved to be almost fruitless. In 1954 and 1955 the same commission held a series of somewhat more productive meetings in London. The record of such meetings, including the Geneva conferences, have produced libraries of books and learned articles but few results in the diminution of the actual amount of military hardware in the possession of the major powers.

The case for unilateral disarmament has been made effectively by Erich Fromm in the volume *Arms Control, Disarmament and National Security*. In reading his essay, in conjunction with the twenty-two essays in this volume, one is struck by the fact that there appear to be so many psychological inhibitions towards any disarmament on the part of both the Soviet Union and the United States that, ultimately, if the nuclear stalemate is ever to be broken, it may have to be through some form of limited unilateral disarmament by either country. Fromm, a professor of psychoanalysis at Michigan State University, compares the American dogma that "the Russians cannot be trusted" to a paranoiac's unshakable conviction in the validity of a delusion simply because the delusion is logically possible. Americans have come to think, in other words, that since a Russian attack is possible, it is therefore certain, unless we resist it at every moment. Fromm points out that, without indulging in irresponsible antimilitarism, America as a nation must learn that the only sane and realistic way of conducting the affairs of individual, as well as national life, is to deal with probabilities and not mere possibilities.

Those who find Erich Fromm's position unconvincing should at least give the most serious consideration to a more limited concept of unilateral disarmament, such as the position which has been called by Charles Osgood "graduated unilateral action or disengagement." In his well-known article on this subject,[8] Mr. Osgood suggests that an act of unilateral disarmament should be clearly disadvantageous to the side making it and should be able to be so perceived by the enemy, who recognizes that the external threat to his existence has been reduced. Furthermore, the unilateral act of disarmament should, according to Osgood, be of such a nature that reciprocal action by the enemy may be tactfully taken, since the initiator's act has been made in full view of the entire world in a way which cannot be construed as a mere trick.

Actions consistent with Mr. Osgood's position would, for example, be decisions to share scientific information, to reduce the number of troops outside the continental United States, to evacuate one or more military bases, and to admit Red China to the United Nations.

Despite the clear desirability of having some type of disarmament, however acquired, the gloomy fact remains that disarmament, even for the diplomats professionally involved in it, is an unending series of difficult and seemingly unanswerable questions. Outside observers to the disarmament conferences conducted over the past several years face the further difficulty of seeking needles of serious discussion in haystacks of propaganda. In September 1959, for example, Soviet Premier Khrushchev appeared before the United Nations General Assembly and proposed "general and complete disarmament." Although the West regarded this proposal as a hypocritical travesty on history and logic, Western diplomats, not desiring to be maneuvered into a position of seeming bellicosity before world opinion, turned up with their own disarmament plan. Discussions, which were mostly denunciations, lingered on in a maze of unrealism until June 27, 1960, when all negotiations were terminated.

The frustrations felt by both parties to this conference, so often duplicated in similar conferences during the twenty-five years of the nuclear age, resulted in large part from the constant fear of both the Soviet Union and the United States of being assaulted and pulverized

8. *Bulletin of Atomic Scientists* (1960).

by the opponent. This mutual fear is perceptively described by Herman Kahn who, as a strategic analyst and military planner with the Rand Corporation, is not a proponent of unilateral disarmament. Kahn writes that

> Aside from the ideological differences and the problem of security itself, there does not seem to be any objective quarrel between the United States and Russia that justifies the risks and costs that we subject each other to. The big thing that the Soviet Union and the United States have to fear from each other is fear itself.[9]

This fear is widely articulated in the United States to mean that the Soviet Union is out to conquer the world for communism and that, if the United States disarmed even in a limited way, Russia would be all the more eager to accomplish her desire for world domination. Although those most learned in Soviet intentions, and in the theory and application of Marxism, state that the alleged desire of Russia for world domination is an erroneous interpretation of the nature of the present-day Soviet Union, it would seem to be almost impossible to convince any significant number of individuals in America that the Russian revolution, as designed by Lenin and Trotsky, is no longer operative. Hardly anyone in America, aside from the specialists, recognizes that the victory of Stalin and the annihilation of almost all the old Bolsheviks brought about a radical change in the nature of Soviet communism. The system which Stalin built was neither socialist nor revolutionary but, rather, a form of state capitalism based upon authoritarian methods of planning and economic centralization.

Once again very few Americans realize that Khrushchev did not change the basic character of Soviet society. He did not make it a revolutionary or even a socialist regime but one of the more conservative and even class-ridden regimes in the Western world. It is therefore a pernicious oversimplification to try to explain Khrushchev by quoting Marx, Lenin, or Trotsky, and thereby deducing that the dominant ambition of the Soviet Union is to conquer all capitalist and under-developed nations as soon as feasible. Such a notion, so widely held in the United States, demonstrates not only a total failure to understand the historical development which has taken place in Russia, but also an inability or incapacity to appreciate the enormous difference between facts and ideologies.

9. *Stanford Research Institute Journal* (1959).

American fears and phobias regarding the intentions imputed to Communists over the past generation have made every public official, appointed or elected, at every level of government, avoid any view which might earn him the description of being "soft" on communism. Since this charge would be made against the proponent of even the most insignificant unilateral steps towards disarmament, we must realistically admit that any advocacy of new alternatives in this area cannot reasonably be expected to come from governmental authority; therefore the burden and the pressing duty to shatter the idol of anticommunism in America must come from Christians and others who are persuaded that the only possible way of ending the risk of horrifying war rests in a form of unilateral action by the United States. It may be that such action, by rejecting the hatred of communism so dominant over the last generation, will affirm the great spiritual values of democracy in such a way that the Communists, and all peoples of the earth, will experience an abatement of that fear of extinction which has so shriveled the consciences of Americans and all others involved in the nuclear stalemate of the Cold War.

There is some indication that the American mind is ambivalent or divided with respect to the advisability of continuing the bipartisan foreign policy of the past generation. It is significant, as Eugene V. Rostow notes in his book, *Law, Power and the Pursuit of Peace*, that "President Truman and President Johnson were destroyed politically by Korea and Vietnam." Hopefully there is a slowly rising tide of opinion in the United States that would openly concede that the Soviet Union and America are like scorpions in a bottle which cannot move without inflicting massive damage on each other. At the same time there is a persistently held view that the best thing that the United States can now achieve is some type of stabilization of the balance of terror. What is clearly needed is a determination on the part of the American public and the United States government to achieve major reductions in nuclear forces and ultimately to secure their elimination under a system of effective international control. Since the first deliberations on the Baruch Plan almost twenty-five years ago, the terrible contest in superfluous strategic weapons between Russia and the United States has taken on the aura of an international game in which the stakes are beyond human imagination. But the very concept of a "game" promotes the further concept that a gain for one side is inevitably a loss for the other. The game is senseless, however, because both sides lose by "winning," and neither side can win except by stopping the "game."

For Christians and humanists who believe in the inviolability and sanctity of every human life, the imperious call to disarmament is a summons to subdue those fears that have made prisoners and cowards of the millions of people who are victims of the illusions and delusions of the nuclear era.

### 4. Creation of New Political Directions

Those who are not entirely persuaded that unilateral disarmament is the one way to bring peace may work towards the prevention of war by the creation of a new political party in America or by the "capture" of an existing national political party. Any suggestion that Christians—and especially Catholics—who are interested in peace should form a new political party immediately brings united and hostile reactions, accompanied by adverse reports about the history and activities of Church-affiliated political parties in Europe.

The emergence of a political party devoted to peace is, however, inevitable in the United States. Therefore the only question is the extent to which Christians will fashion and formulate the positions and the platform of the political party that will be born of America's revulsion at the foreign policy which has brought about a nuclear nightmare, genocide in Asia, and a scandalous situation in which the richest nation on earth becomes richer while hunger and illiteracy grow among more than one-half of humanity.

One of the most serious obstacles to the formation of a political movement seeking a radical change in America's foreign policy is the hope or illusion that somehow things will work out so that a new party will not be necessary. Indeed, amidst the agonies of protest against the Vietnam war, few if any of the militants look to the larger issues of America's stance in the world after the Vietnam holocaust.

In the emergence of a movement for an entirely new foreign policy, a second serious difficulty is the real impossibility for most American citizens to acquire accurate knowledge about the actual implementation of America's foreign policy. A series of events related by Henry A. Kissinger in his book, *American Foreign Policy: Three Essays*,[10] illustrate the point. Mr. Kissinger, prior to his becoming a close adviser to President Nixon on foreign policy, wrote the following:

The sequence of events that led to negotiations [in Vietnam]

10. (New York: W. W. Norton & Company, Inc., 1969), p. 101.

probably started with General Westmoreland's visit to Washington in November 1967. On that occasion, General Westmoreland told a joint session of Congress that the war was being militarily won. He outlined "indicators" of progress and stated that a limited withdrawal of United States combat forces might be undertaken beginning late in 1968. On January 17, 1968, President Johnson, in his State of the Union address, emphasized that the pacification program—the extension of the control of Saigon into the countryside—was progressing satisfactorily. Sixty-seven percent of the population of Vietnam lived in relatively secure areas; the figure was expected to rise. A week later, the Tet offensive overthrew the assumptions of American strategy." [11]

This incident is a dramatic illustration of the serious loss of credibility which the United States government has now sustained with its people. Almost countless other incidents in which the United States has misstated the facts about its operations in a foreign country could be cited. One, that affected me and the other seven members of the U. S. Study Team on Political and Religious Freedom in South Vietnam, occurred in the White House itself in May 1969. On that occasion a highly placed official of the National Security Council assured some members of the Study Team that the number of political prisoners in South Vietnam had certainly gone down and that the number of such individuals was no longer a problem. The embassy in Saigon, however, conceded after rigorous cross-examination that the number of political prisoners in South Vietnam had in fact gone up over the past several months—due in large part to the activities of the U. S. Pacification Program!

Americans who are determined to take appropriate political action to bring about a radical change in the foreign policy of their nation face an almost insurmountable obstacle in the impossibility of acquiring accurate information from their own government with regard to what this nation's personnel are doing in foreign lands. The clandestine political activities of the CIA constitute a further barrier to the people having real knowledge of how its government functions in the world. As Edwin O. Reischauer says in *Beyond Vietnam*, the covert activities of the CIA "are a net loss to us abroad, and running counter as they do to our own concepts of morality, they probably do even more serious internal injury to us at home." [12]

11. Ibid., p. 101.
12. Reischauer, *op. cit.*, p. 221.

American Christians who aspire to mount an offensive against a government that has sought to keep the truth from its people, and even, on occasion, to deceive them, face a task of immense difficulty. As Christians they must follow the piercing insights in a volume entitled *The Politics of the Gospel* by Jean Marie Paupert. This French lay theologian shows that Christianity is an utterly incarnational religion and, consequently, politics must be coextensive with life. For Paupert—and perhaps for all totally convinced Christians—the teaching of the Gospel must in some sense be both entirely religious and entirely political. Although Paupert has succeeded in elucidating an explicit political teaching from his exegesis of the scriptural text, he does not elaborate on the application of these principles to the reformation of a government which has become militaristic.

The difficulties facing those who would try to work out a new foreign policy for America by political means will almost certainly increase rather than decrease. Militarism on the one hand moves forward with a vigorous self-pollination, utilizing the appeals of communism, national defense, and patriotism, all put together in an amalgam somewhat like a religion, as the basis on which the defense establishment can justify its existence and its expansion. On the other hand the world after Vietnam will almost inevitably bring about some form of neoisolationism in America. If the Viet Cong succeed in taking over South Vietnam, the voices of anticommunism will plead that now the Communists are a thousand miles nearer to the United States than before and that consequently we must rearm even more extensively. Those Americans who desire a completely new foreign policy will conclude from the Vietnam experience that any intervention in a guerrilla war in an underdeveloped nation does not make sense for America and that as a result the United States should retreat to a position of relative isolationism in the world.

Once again, Catholics, by reason of their fruitful theological and philosophical tradition, should theoretically be in a better position to develop the mystique and ideology for a political movement which would be based on the concept that America has a role to make possible the good life for all of humanity. The Catholic tradition has rejected views such as those of Hobbes and Locke. The Catholic viewpoint of the state has refused to accept the individualistic social contract theory, which seeks to restrict the role of a state to the minimal function of preventing the more violent acts of men who are deemed to be essentially asocial. The political ideal accepted by Catholic tradition goes back to the Greeks, and teaches that the purpose of society is to fulfill man's nature within a community, to make possible for him the good life, and to assist him to realize his highest intellectual and spiritual potentialities.

American political theory has generally embraced an unsettled combination of both these competing moral and political philosophies. An uneasy alliance of these two objectives runs, for example, throughout the ideologies present in the American public school. Within the next few years America must make some decision as to which of these contending philosophies it will choose with regard to its role in the world. All but the most fervid nationalists must admit that the rich nations of the earth, like America, have an obligation to the poor nations, just as the wealthy states of the United States have an obligation to the poorer ones. The crucial question will be the extent to which the American social contract contains more than the Hobbes-Lockean imperatives of the minimal protection of life, liberty, and property. Those who feel that America cannot limit itself to this lowest attainable goal must come to some agreement as to the content and extent of America's commitment to a common enterprise, whose aim is a better life both for the citizens of the United States and for all mankind.

Americans who reject the notion that the United States can protect itself and other nations in the Free World by a policy of massive militarism must determine the extent to which this country can be or should be "messianic." In the formation of this nation, America certainly spoke in "messianic" terms. The nation stated in the Declaration of Independence that *all* men are created equal and endowed with certain rights. During the early days of American history there was the constant proclamation that the era of kings was over and that American independence was the first blow in a world revolution for freedom and prosperity.

For those who desire a radically new foreign policy, the ultimate question is whether the basic social contract which binds Americans together has always had implicit within it a world mission as one of its components. This world mission, or idealism, is apparent in Woodrow Wilson's Fourteen Points and in Franklin Roosevelt's Four Freedoms. A century ago it was adumbrated by Abraham Lincoln in these words:

I have often inquired of myself, what great principle or idea it was that kept this Confederacy so long together. It was not the mere matter of the separation of the colonies from the motherland; but something in that Declaration giving liberty, not alone of the people of this country, but hope to the world for all future time. It was that which gave promise that in due time the weight should be lifted from the shoulders of all men, and that all should have an equal chance. This is the sentiment embodied in that Declaration of Independence. . . .

In the world after the Vietnam war, the 6 percent of humanity who live in the United States will, as never before, be scrutinized by the 94 percent of humanity, or more than three billion people, whose lives and destinies will be affected in countless ways by the policies which the United States adopts. Catholics constitute about one-fourth of that 6 percent living in the nation whose public decisions within the next few years can produce or prevent political anarchy and economic collapse around the globe.

It seems self-evident, then, that American Catholics have before them an opportunity of surpassing importance and urgency—perhaps the most significant opportunity which they have ever had in the history of the United States. If Catholics, aided by many others, can define and refine the wealth of their theological and political traditions, and articulate and act upon them in sociopolitical ways, they may be able to persuade the nation that it has a moral commitment to mankind which it should observe, not only because it is useful to America, but—more importantly—because it is right.

## 2. PAUL RAMSEY (1913–    )

Perhaps the best known Protestant ethicist on the subject of war is Princeton University's Paul Ramsey. His prolific writings appraise historical and contemporary work on the subject while interpreting and upholding a Christian form of the just war theory which he traces to Augustine. Christianity fuses love with justice and natural law. Ramsey's ethic is therefore based as much on the agape principle as it is on deontological principles, but he stands in plain opposition to any attempt to reduce morality to prudence or to make moral judgments on purely utilitarian grounds.

The following selection appeals both to the agape principle and to natural law in taking stock of recent discussions on nuclear weapons.

## THE JUST WAR AND NUCLEAR DETERRENCE

From *War and the Christian Conscience* (1961), chap. 7.

We have examined the thought of a number of men who, from differing points of view and at diverse places in their analysis, find their Christian consciences buckling under the weight of the problem of existing weapons and the probable conduct of war by such means. Responsibility for directing defense to justifiable ends and choosing justifiable means, held together in the traditional theory, break apart in the face of the nature of warfare today and in the future. This leads to what has been misnamed "nuclear pacifism" or "relative Christian pacifism." This is not the name for it, since the correct conclusion on this matter can be arrived at only from an earnest attempt to apply the principles of the just war. That always entailed that some war, and some of the use of means, should be declared unjustifiable; and Christian support and participation be withheld at that point. Some today think about this problem largely in terms of the amount of devastation involved in modern war, and they deliver their verdict against specific weapons as such. There can be "no greater evil" than war with A-bombs, but war with conventional weapons may still be a lesser evil than the evil resisted; or war with smaller A-bombs but not the largest may still be justified; or war with A-bombs but not with H-bombs; or, finally, some specified and limited

341

use of megaton weapons may still be licit, but not "all out" nuclear warfare. It is better, it should be said, to begin with some principle that runs right through the various weapons that might be used, determining licit and illicit actions in the military use of all weapons, even if finally this in effect compels the conclusion that some weapon in and of itself is immoral. It is better, in short, to begin with the traditional immunity from direct killing surrounding noncombatants in the just-war theory, than with only the limitation of proportionate grave reason or lesser evil. The verdict about a single weapon may be the same from these two approaches; but the Christian in his conscience will know better where he is and why he is there in coming to a decision not willingly to engage in such a war, or such use of a weapon in a war where, in his view, just means are also used.

The second approach will also make clear that the Christian still operates from the sound premise that all moral means may be mounted against an attack, no matter how greatly increased the force may have to be. This position is radically different from what deserves the name of "nuclear pacifism" today—a pacifism which, so to speak, is again on the offensive in response to the nuclear crisis, and which secretly may hope to win some theological battles at the same time, against recent theological "realism" and on behalf of a, now proved, coincidence of a "pure" Gospel ethic of non-violent resistance with political prudence. "There is now no conflict," writes A. J. Muste, "between ethical sensitivity or Gospel obedience, on the one hand, and prudence on the other." This statement is supported by citing "a prominent American theologian" who now agrees that unilateral scrapping of nuclear weapons would be "better policy *in terms of prudence*"; and this is said to "wipe out" the distinction between pacifists and non-pacifist Christians who feel they must be "politically responsible." The present writer cannot take responsibility for the fact that the theologian in question may have stated his position only in terms of "prudence," i.e., "lesser evil" or the balancing of evil and good effects, and not also in terms of the other clear and more primary principles of the just-war theory. Perhaps pacifism and prudential nonpacifism are now forced to say much the same thing upon the particular matter in question, but the spirit and rationale behind each are greatly different. That theologian should, and probably did, have in mind an analysis of the just war which, when he concludes from this that the main weapon today should be abandoned and never used, at one and the same time upholds the probable necessity of other warfare and therefore the *positive* moral obligation to make it morally possible.

Unfortunately, it may be true that apologists for the just-war doctrine today, especially in Protestant circles, have formulated their position too exclusively in terms of prudence. This is all that stands or falls by the argument advanced in a book that is still one of the best of Christian responses to the atomic crisis.[1] Professor Long distinguishes between a secular ethic, which is "calculative morality" or a "problem-solving ethic," and a religious-vocational ethic, which is an ethic of "obedience." He grants that in the past, and in principle whenever the situation permits this, a religious ethic of obedience contains an element of calculation; but there is this difference in *how* it is contained. "In a secular ethic calculation is a *reliance;* it is a means of 'saving the situation.' In a religious ethic calculation is *a service;* it is used to find the best means of implementing the demands of faith" and of obedience. "The Christian finds that he must again balance claims; and calculation is now affirmed, not as a reliance, but as a means of service," when he faces the task of relating the ultimate demand of *agape* to the concrete needs of everyday experience.

What has happened since the atom bomb burst upon the world is that "a religious ethic must rediscover obedience in a situation in which calculation becomes less and less possible." Neither pacifism nor bellicism can afford any longer to be concerned primarily with historical success; neither can derive its choices backward from prudential consideration of what will work or save the situation. "Neither pacifism nor nonpacifism, if either is suggested as a workable technique, is adequate to handle the situation created by weapons of great power." The real import of the bomb is not that pacifism is proved to be workable, nor even that nonpacifism is proved unworkable, but that any "horizontal and calculative approach to the problem of force" is now wholly inadequate. "An ethic that would rely solely upon analysis of the given factors of a situation in deciding its course of action, and depend solely upon historical accomplishment for its vindication, does not make sense in an atomic age."

What does this position demonstrate, on the assumption (which we are not concerned to question here) that its analysis is correct? It demonstrates that perhaps a largely prudential nonpacifism is today

---

1. Edward Leroy Long, Jr.: *The Christian Response to the Atomic Crisis.* Copyright, 1950, by W. L. Jenkins, The Westminster Press.

inadequate. It shows that the case for choosing war as the lesser evil has become exceedingly difficult to make. But actually the just-war theory never attempted that alone, not until the final point when proportionate grave reason in the several effects of military action were weighed as in a balance. Such counting of the cost was never very certain, nor was a nation believed to be in the position of guaranteeing the actual outcome simply by making these calculations, without which, of course, it could not proceed. Prudence might declare a war to be unjustified; but by itself it was never supposed to be able to justify it. Calculations that come up with no measure of good over evil results predicted cannot, of course, lead to "a service"; but this should control our deliberations only after we know what has to be served, and how morally this service may be undertaken (on the assumption for the moment that it may be effective).

At bottom, in the just-war theory there was demanded "an ethical choice that is based finally upon the intrinsic nature of the act as judged by an ultimate frame of reference, rather than upon the overt effect of the act upon the immediate situation." These, significantly, are the words with which Professor Long describes his own nonprudential pacifism to which he judges Christian prudential nonpacifists will be driven in the atomic era. If instead they are driven to a restoration of the just-war theory, this will be so not because of miscalculation but precisely because of an ethic of obedience, in which calculation is only, but is required as, a service. The just-war theory will be restored because Christian love shapes itself for enactment in terms of certain principles of right or proper conduct, before ever calculating the consequences to see whether one effect justifies another. And if in doing this men are driven also to draw the line at the use of certain weapons, or at certain uses of all weapons, the reason will not be simply that the prudential ground on which they formerly depended has now been cut from under them by the force of modern weapons. Their views will in no sense be a "nuclear pacifism" or nuclear disarmament; but rather "rational nuclear armament," or at least "rational armament."

Professor Long, of course, is not alone accountable for how he opposes the doctrine of war he opposes. The fact is that in Protestant circles in recent years this is all we have clearly known and effectively said on the question. Since in one lump "killing" and the number killed was believed to be the thing to reconcile with Christian conscience and with the love-commandment, in case a total economic blockade of a nation was believed to be most effective, when in short this proposed action passed the test of prudence as a lesser evil, that was asserted to be the way to bring an enemy to heel and keep him there. Hit him in the belly, i.e., the civilian population as a whole, and shorten the war, i.e., the killing of combatants! . . . In other words, lacking any very firm moral distinction between killing "unjust aggressors" or the fighters and killing non-fighters, lacking the impulse to determine and control the means we intend to use for any end, and being fittingly modest about claiming justice to be wholly (or even, on balance, more) on one side, we have justified warfare largely in terms of assertedly "nice" but precarious predictions of good and evil consequences. What we are witnessing now is not, it is to be hoped, the substitution of one prudential judgment (pacifism) for another (non-pacifism), or the isolation or elevation of obedient action from any consideration of the service to be done, but a return to a proper location of the work of prudence, i.e., after a determination of the right military action, or if not *after,* then clearly *along with* judgment as to the intrinsic nature of the act proposed and its conformity or non-conformity with the nature of limited or justified warfare. This surely is the highest limit to be placed on war, not first in terms of weaponry but by keeping war subordinate to the ends-means of civil life. A symptom of what we have to recover from is the widespread opinion that rules for the immunity of noncombatants is only a detail added incidentally to the theory in the Middle Ages, a dispensable relic of the age of chivalry or of the pageantry wars of the eighteenth century; and that prudence will be sufficient to guide us in the conduct of war or the limitation of war. (To this, pacifists now seem to add that prudence added to obedience would be sufficient to eliminate war altogether, were it not for those people who want to make war morally possible again just when it has become impossible). . . .

The moralist, however, should take care how he advises, if he presumes to advise, statesmen and military leaders upon questions of application that involve matters of fact which, as moralist, he has no expert knowledge of nor responsibility for determining. After all, diplomats and commanders do not preach our sermons on Sunday morning; nor do we have charge of the defense of this nation over any weekend. Therefore, I say simply that any weapon whose every use must be for the purpose of directly killing noncombatants as a means of attaining some supposed good and incidentally hitting some military target is a weapon whose every use would be wholly immoral. I will also add that the manufacture and possession of a weapon whose every use is that just described, and the political employment of it for the sake of deterrence, is likewise immoral. Seriously threatening to kill an innocent man for some good end, say, in order to compel him to take a Salk vaccination or to negotiate is, as means, the same as threatening to kill him for some evil end, say, to get him to hand over his pocketbook. At this point, the reader should be reminded of what was said earlier in this book about politics as an arena of "deferred repentance," along with the need for the clear enunciation of principles, such as those just stated. This, the moralist can only say, is the moral context of policy decision.

Findings of fact, however, may not be so clear. This difficulty was taken into account by the distinction, made by the Provisional Study Document of the W. C. C., between "all out" nuclear warfare and a possible use of such weapons in a more limited fashion (subject to the further limitation that even this should not be initiated first). I confess I find it difficult to imagine a limited use of hydrogen weapons, especially if smaller, even fractional kiloton atomic weapons would be just as destructive of legitimate military targets and less indirectly destructive of civil life. I think, therefore, that we have to say that megaton weapons would always destroy military objectives only incidental to the destruction of a whole area; and that in the very weapon itself, its use, its possession, or the threat to use it, warfare has passed beyond all reasonable or justifiable limits. But this is a question of weapon facts and of the military attack that has been mounted, or may be concentrated in a certain place. There may be politically prudent reasons for the unilateral or negotiated abandonment of this weapon anyway; but the *Grenzmorality* of its merely military possession and use depends on whether in fact, now or in the future, there are any conceivable circumstances in which it would have importance against military targets against which less powerful weapons would not serve as well. In the fluidity of historical events and changes in the concentration of political and military power perhaps this cannot be entirely ruled out as a possibility.

The Provisional Study Document does not rule it out, in its statement about a discipline that is able to possess yet not use nuclear power. This has been misunderstood by A. J. Muste as clinging to the belief that it is moral to possess weapons for their deterrent value, which, however it would be immoral ever to use. Instead, the use that should unequivocally be renounced, in the opinion of this Commission, is "all out" use. If it had not held open the question whether there might not be a legitimate use (though not *first* use) of these weapons, in limited fashion, I do not see how their possession as such could be justified. I agree with Muste that there is intolerable contradiction between prohibiting any use and allowing possession (for deterrence or any other reason), but not between prohibiting all-out use or first use and allowing possession. "To have but not to use" was not the dilemma of the Christians on this Commission, as Muste supposes; but "to have and not to use all out." The latter is only an enormously difficult policy, that of limited war, even "for the time being"; while the former, if every use of the weapon is bound to be immoral, would be morally repulsive. The commission did not say this. What it said was that, allowing that not every possible use of megaton weapons would be necessarily immoral, a nation or group of nations need not announce in advance the precise point at which it will understand all-out use to begin and to be prohibited to itself. In other words, the Commission counts on a deterrent effect *in addition* to the use of force that may be intended or justifiable, i.e., from a quantity of force resolutely not intended to be used, or intended to be not used, or from uncertainty as to where the point is beyond which a disciplined nation will not go. It seems to me that this may be questioned, on grounds both of morality and security; and it was so questioned, as we have seen, by members of the Commission itself.

But what this means is that it is difficult if not impossible to determine the exact nature of the force that is intended to be used and that intended to be not used; for a nation itself to know this, and not just for it to decide whether to announce the point or not. Not to announce would be deceit; and worse, for it is surely immoral even to leave standing an assumption that one may use immoral means. But not to know in advance is another matter. There is therefore everything to be gained from repeated announcement that it is the power of the military attack that we intend to destroy or force to withdraw, by every legitimate means and with the limitation, running through the use of all weapons we possess, that a whole people are not the object to be indiscriminately and violently repressed. If this means in fact that it is *certain* that specific weapons have to be expressly renounced, or particular uses unilaterally proscribed, then, it seems to me, a clear statement of this is also desirable. From an immoral, wholly irrational deterrent no deterrence worth having can come, for the simple reason that the "just" are more deterred from using such weapons, or from making such use of them, than the "unjust" are deterred from employing lesser, but still powerful, means to gain their ends by the practically non-existent danger that "we" will use them. What is the use of now devoting our energy to changing the balance of terror, or of defense against this open-ended terror and violence, in our favor, when we were rightly unwilling to use the monopoly we once had in atomic weapons—not only unwilling to use these weapons in actual fact but *therefore* unable to translate the sole possession of them into usable political power to attain limited goals in the cold war? Is it not the case that once the monumental bluff of the massive deterrent is called, the West, if it lacks sufficient conventional and small atomic weapons, would have no sane alternative but to accept a settlement on the enemy's terms? The Great Deterrent leaves us without a link between force and purpose. We needed then and need now some substitute for the kind of warfare that can in no sense be an extension of national policy; and this can only mean the creation of the possibility of limited applications of power. The more this is understood, the better. If this requires the designation of open cities, by agreement or unilaterally, and publication of specific policies as to the limited use of weapons, or the means we are willing to use in certain areas of the world to preserve stated interests, that is well; for an enemy cannot know what he really has to fear unless he also knows what he has not to fear, and (what is more important) we cannot translate power into policy without letting him know. He will probe anyway, and find out. In politics, there is perhaps some usefulness in bluffing about the weapons we may or may not possess, but very little usefulness in bluffing about what we intend or are willing to do with the weapons we are known to have. The risks involved in this are the risks of walking the earth as men who do not deny that they know the difference between murder and war, or between warfare that is justified and that which exceeds all limits. The risks are the risks of seeing to it that war, if it comes, will have some minimal national purpose connected with it. Nevertheless, the moralist as such cannot decide the whole question that must rest with the leaders of government, as to whether in fact it may sometimes be necessary to use a given weapon in circumstances which the moralist may not envision and which might then be brought under the tradition of civilized warfare of which the moralist has the duty to speak. Perhaps, then, the Commission of the World Council of Churches was wise in leaving rather open the conclusions they were able to reach. (I say this against my own "better judgment" in the matter of megaton weapons as such, or for that matter the upper ranges of kiloton weapons.)

There is one final question. Against a nation known to possess the H-bomb, and believed to be willing to use it all-out, would we be justified in mounting every reasonable and moral defense by limited means? By discrediting the all-out use of the ultimate weapons available today, have we not destroyed the moral basis for a nation's making any defense at all? While limited war may have been justifiable in the past, against an enemy who, whatever his intentions, had only limited means, has not the possession by even one side and his potential threat to make all-out use of megaton weapons rendered all defense immoral, on the grounds that it would be utterly useless? Since the preservation of desirable peace and order is the only justifying reason for the use of violence, would not self-defense by means of lesser weapons be *morally unjustifiable because impracticable?* Does it not follow that the only right thing to do in these circumstances is to sue for peace on the enemy's terms?

It seems to me that an answer to this question is to be found in the fact that megaton weapons are no longer weapons *of war,* and that their all-out use would not be *war.* We have to find out whether the enemy wants to make *war* or not. We have to determine, upon a breakdown of negotiation and of attempts to compromise a conflict in which two nations both find themselves too vitally challenged to give in, and when there is to be resort to a trial of strength, whether this is to be the arbitrament of *arms* or not, in the course of which the will of one nation upon the issue in question may be broken or both be compelled to accede to a settlement they were unwilling to accept before making trial for a better advantage. We have to find out whether the appeal is to be to the *ultima ratio* of war or the *ultima irratio* of immoral mutual devastation. In the past, it was, of course, immoral for a nation to mount a defense which it itself knew in advance to be useless. That meant, in advance, to know that the national purpose had to be altered and a settlement sought. When it is complete devastation, however, that is threatened, and not war, a nation still has the right and the duty to make it clear that it is ready for war, and mighty powerful war, if that is the weapon the enemy chooses. In its quest for a connection between force and national purpose, a nation need not face an imagined state of affairs when it will have no national purpose as the reason for now giving up every embodiment of national purpose. In fact, no nation *can* do this. It is right that the enemy be made to realize that he will have to exceed the limits of warfare to gain his ends, that he will have to destroy utterly where he thought to conquer and to bend. Then only will he be deterred from using a weapon that is not a weapon of war. The enemy's political power depends mainly on his possession and use of weapons *of war*, not on his possession of weapons that exceed the purposes of war; and clearly, our possession of the same non-military weapons of destruction deters mainly ourselves from positive action. To renounce this, and at the same time to mount the greatest force that may morally be used, would require the enemy to ask himself the searching question whether there is any point in gaining what can only be gained by power greater than war. To our surprise this may be a world in which security and the power of making a moral defense are joined together by a cord not lightly broken; and one in which there is such a reality as the natural law of warfare which nations cannot fall below *or* exceed in the power they mount without ceasing to be nations with purpose.

The fact of the matter is that, eschewing pre-emptive war and conceding the first strike, the supposed deterrent effect of our great weapons lies in our second-strike capability alone, or in such capability as will remain after the first strike. Since this is known well enough to any potential enemy, and since our capability to deliver unacceptable damage to him after receiving the first strike is dubious indeed, wherein now lies the deterrence? Such deterrence may not actually be feasible, or rather it may work only because he too may deter mainly himself from the use of his own morally unshootable, because politically purposeless, weapons. In any case, nothing in the present world situation can provide sufficient reason for altering radically the very meaning of *ratio* even in a nation's appeal to *ultima ratio* of war, least of all for Christians who have come to an understanding of what is reasonable and just in the conduct of war only from a love-transformed justice and a faith illuminated reason. To this they would tempt us whose moral premises are so thin as to lead logically to the verdict which justifies most of all that act of war which will be the most immoral, because the most stupid and politically purposeless, in the whole history of warfare, namely, the unleashing of counter-nuclear retaliation by means of push-buttons. This—the end result of replacing the just war by the aggressor-defender war—is certainly a *dictamen irrationis* now passed off as military necessity. To press the button in counter-retaliation will also be the most unloving deed in the history of mankind, only exceeded by those who, for the sake of some concern of theirs, cause the little ones to stumble and fall into hell. I had rather be a pagan suckled in a creed outworn, terrified at the sight of hands made impure by any shedding of blood, than a skilful artisan of technical reason devising plans to carry out such a deed. I also doubt if any man not wholly dispossessed of humanity can actually purpose and will to do any such thing. Here is exposed to view the natural connection between power and purpose in political action which is at all human. Technology and reflex action may, however, "do" it anyway (if that can still be called "doing").

# A FINAL WORD

But in the last days it shall come to pass, that the mountain of the house of the Lord shall be established in the top of the mountains, and it shall be exalted above the hills; and people shall flow unto it. And many nations shall come, and say, Come, and let us go up to the mountain of the Lord, and to the house of the God of Jacob; and he will teach us of his ways, and we will walk in his paths: for the law shall go forth of Zion, and the word of the Lord from Jerusalem. And he shall judge among many people, and rebuke strong nations afar off; and they shall beat their swords into plowshares, and their spears into pruninghooks: nation shall not lift up a sword against nation, neither shall they learn war any more. But they shall sit every man under his vine and under his fig tree: and none shall make them afraid: for the mouth of the Lord of hosts hath spoken it. For all people will walk every one in the name of his god, and we will walk in the named of the Lord our God for ever and ever. [Micah 4:1-5]

# INDEX

Arbitration, 5, 88, 154, 274-83, 288, 292-300

Authority to make war, 5, 92, 107-8, 114, 118-19, 135, 139-40, 145-46, 157-59, 202-4, 208-9, 220, 223

Benefits of war, 13-22, 279-81, 284-90, 296-97

Cause, just, 1, 3, 4, 22, 25, 29, 49, 64-65, 71, 92, 104, 107, 118, 134-35, 142-43, 149-53, 168, 179, 201-2, 205-16, 223, 226, 236-37, 245-47, 252-53, 265, 267, 285, 294, 317, 349

Christian realism, 3, 6, 7, 301-13, 342

Civil war, 18-22, 69, 71, 82, 262-63

Conquest, 3, 5, 17, 20, 27, 29, 118-19, 197, 219-20, 252-62, 274, 286

Declaration of war, 5, 25, 29, 107-8, 118, 203-4, 219, 294

Deterrence, 321-24, 341-51

Disarmament, 295-96, 321-27, 329-35, 346, 353

Double effect, principle of, 5, 92, 222, 345

Glory of war, 16, 17, 30, 89-90, 161, 182, 291, 296

Government
    Christians and, 2, 7, 35, 39-43, 48-50, 55-60, 156, 173-76, 185-89, 303
    purposes of, 2, 5, 20-23, 26-27, 35, 39, 51-54, 61, 68-71, 78, 80-81, 107, 143, 149, 152, 172, 206-14, 229, 250-52, 263, 268, 284-90, 338, 349

Guerrilla warfare, 5, 317, 338

Holy war, 1, 3, 87-91

Human rights, 3, 118-36, 180, 193, 234, 239-49, 254, 259-61, 266, 269, 274, 284, 319, 338-39

Intention, just, 5, 19, 22, 23, 28, 30, 55, 62-63, 65-67, 71-72, 92, 100, 108-9, 113, 135-36, 140-48, 158-61, 179, 183, 187, 208, 302

International law, 3, 8, 131-36, 193-98, 220-21, 226, 232-37, 252-62, 273-83, 287-90, 294-300

Love, law of, 3-9, 35-36, 42, 51-54, 61-63, 77-78, 81-82, 118, 143, 160, 165, 195, 240, 291, 297-300, 301-8, 341, 344, 350

Means, just, 5, 6, 7, 18, 31, 55-60, 92, 104, 111-12, 118-19, 135, 140, 153, 202, 206, 219-23, 226, 237, 243, 294, 317, 341-51

Military service, 2, 4, 35, 39, 43-47, 48-50, 61-64, 109-11, 140-46, 156-64, 199-200, 216-18

Natural law, 3, 8, 9, 24-31, 36, 39, 44, 51-54, 61, 63, 65, 67-68, 73-83, 87, 92-101, 123, 127, 129-33, 140, 165, 168, 171, 193-98, 201, 203, 208-14, 221, 226-37, 239-52, 257-61, 275-77, 284, 301, 328, 338, 341, 350

Negotiation, 29, 87, 104, 134, 150, 154, 169, 349

Non-combatant immunity, 5, 19, 29-30, 87, 104-5, 118, 219-22, 254-57, 261, 289, 294, 297, 317, 341-42, 345

Non-violence, 37-39, 42, 48, 51-54, 107, 110-11, 113-14, 145, 185-89, 292-94, 306, 317, 320-27, 342

Nuclear war, 4, 5, 317, 319-21, 329, 335, 341-51

Objectives, limited, 5, 13, 28, 29-30, 118, 135, 219, 297, 306, 317, 341

Old Testament wars, 6, 7, 57-58, 61, 64, 67-68, 144, 151, 166, 174, 182, 199, 262

Pacifism
  prudential, 3, 139, 179, 236, 317-27, 341-45
  Social-Gospel, 3-8, 273, 291-300, 301-13
  vocational, 2-8, 35, 92, 106-11, 139, 185-89, 199-200, 301-13, 319-21, 341-42

Pagans, equal rights of, 3, 13, 17, 18, 87-91, 118-36, 212-14

Peace
  love of, 5, 6, 22-23, 29, 45, 63, 70-83, 118, 142, 178, 185-89, 276
  nature of, 74-77, 351

Preventive war, 5, 135-36, 201-2, 350

Prisoners of war, 5, 15, 17-19, 29-31, 63, 289, 295, 297

Rebellion, 3, 5, 42-43, 48, 69, 114-17, 147-49, 155, 165, 167, 174-75, 185-89, 193, 223-25, 239, 260-69

Reparations, 25, 119, 204, 207-9, 219-21, 237, 241-42, 256-57, 261

Rule of laws, 3, 4, 5, 9, 22, 24-26, 92-101, 169, 226-37, 250-52, 263-65, 273-84, 291-300

Selective conscientious objection, 4, 118, 140, 159-60, 193, 214-18, 321

Self-defense, 4, 25, 35, 37, 48, 91, 92, 101, 108, 113, 122, 134-36, 149-52, 157, 168, 200-2, 205-14, 241-47, 266, 269, 286, 293, 317, 320, 349-51

Sixth commandment, 6, 7, 324

Social Gospel, on war and peace, 3, 6, 7, 273, 291-300, 301-5, 319

Spoils of war, 17-18, 20, 220, 254

Two vocations, doctrine of, 2, 7, 35, 49-50, 92, 110-11, 146, 185-89, 303